ECONOMIC ISSUES, PROBLEMS AND PERSPECTIVES

FOREIGN DIRECT INVESTMENT (FDI)

POLICIES, ECONOMIC IMPACTS AND GLOBAL PERSPECTIVES

ECONOMIC ISSUES, PROBLEMS AND PERSPECTIVES

Additional books in this series can be found on Nova's website under the Series tab.

Additional e-books in this series can be found on Nova's website under the e-book tab.

GLOBAL ECONOMIC STUDIES

Additional books in this series can be found on Nova's website under the Series tab.

Additional e-books in this series can be found on Nova's website under the e-book tab.

ECONOMIC ISSUES, PROBLEMS AND PERSPECTIVES

FOREIGN DIRECT INVESTMENT (FDI)

POLICIES, ECONOMIC IMPACTS AND GLOBAL PERSPECTIVES

ENZO GUILLON
AND
LUCAS CHAUVET
EDITORS

New York

Copyright © 2013 by Nova Science Publishers, Inc.

All rights reserved. No part of this book may be reproduced, stored in a retrieval system or transmitted in any form or by any means: electronic, electrostatic, magnetic, tape, mechanical photocopying, recording or otherwise without the written permission of the Publisher.

For permission to use material from this book please contact us:
Telephone 631-231-7269; Fax 631-231-8175
Web Site: http://www.novapublishers.com

NOTICE TO THE READER

The Publisher has taken reasonable care in the preparation of this book, but makes no expressed or implied warranty of any kind and assumes no responsibility for any errors or omissions. No liability is assumed for incidental or consequential damages in connection with or arising out of information contained in this book. The Publisher shall not be liable for any special, consequential, or exemplary damages resulting, in whole or in part, from the readers' use of, or reliance upon, this material. Any parts of this book based on government reports are so indicated and copyright is claimed for those parts to the extent applicable to compilations of such works.

Independent verification should be sought for any data, advice or recommendations contained in this book. In addition, no responsibility is assumed by the publisher for any injury and/or damage to persons or property arising from any methods, products, instructions, ideas or otherwise contained in this publication.

This publication is designed to provide accurate and authoritative information with regard to the subject matter covered herein. It is sold with the clear understanding that the Publisher is not engaged in rendering legal or any other professional services. If legal or any other expert assistance is required, the services of a competent person should be sought. FROM A DECLARATION OF PARTICIPANTS JOINTLY ADOPTED BY A COMMITTEE OF THE AMERICAN BAR ASSOCIATION AND A COMMITTEE OF PUBLISHERS.

Additional color graphics may be available in the e-book version of this book.

Library of Congress Cataloging-in-Publication Data

ISBN 978-1-62808-403-0

Published by Nova Science Publishers, Inc. † New York

CONTENTS

Preface		vii
Chapter 1	Chinese and Indian Investment in Africa's Extractive Industries: Implications for Local Industrial Development *Judith Fessehaie*	1
Chapter 2	What Determines Productivity Spillovers from Foreign Direct Investment? A Case Study of Mexico *Jacob A. Jordaan*	43
Chapter 3	FDI and Economic Growth: Evidence from the EU at the Regional Level *Adolfo Maza, José Villaverde, María Gutiérrez-Portilla and Paula Gutiérrez-Portilla*	73
Chapter 4	Outward FDI to China and the Parent Firm's Ability to Create Value Added per Worker *Shu-Chin Huang and Chang-Ching Lin*	103
Chapter 5	Foreign Direct Investment on ASEAN's Income Inequality Revisited: A Spatial Panel Data Model Approach *Nathapornpan Piyaareekul Uttama*	127
Chapter 6	Global Trends in R and D-Intensive FDI: Opportunities and Challenges for Developing Countries *José Guimón*	155
Chapter 7	The Impact of Corruption on the Timing and Mode of Entry by U.S. Firms in China *Rossitza B. Wooster and Jacob Billings*	175
Chapter 8	The Proliferation of Free Trade Agreements and their Impact on Foreign Direct Investment: An Empirical Analysis on Panel Data *Bassem Kahouli and Samir Maktouf*	195
Chapter 9	Union Structure and Inward FDI *Minas Vlassis and Stefanos Mamakis*	213

Chapter 10	Inward FDI Performance and Determinants of FDI Regional Disparity in China *Lucy Zheng*	**229**
Chapter 11	Trade, FDI, Exchange Rate, and the Effect of Corporate Tax Reduction Policy *Hiroyuki Nishiyama*	**241**
Chapter 12	Foreign Direct Investment and Productivity Spillovers: Evidence from Plant-Level Data *Jayjit Roy and Mahmut Yasar*	**255**
Chapter 13	Regional FDI Spillovers in the Swiss Service/Construction Industry: The Role of Spillover Mechanisms and Local Technological Characteristics *Lamia Ben Hamida*	**265**
Index		**287**

PREFACE

In this book, the authors present topical research in the study of the policies, economic impacts and global perspectives of Foreign Direct Investment (FDI). Topics discussed include Chinese and Indian investment in Africa's extractive industries; a case study in Mexico of productivity spillovers from Foreign Direct Investment; evidence from the EU at the regional level of FDI and economic growth; outward FDI to China and the parent firm's ability to create value added per worker; Foreign Direct Investment on ASEAN's income inequality revisited; global trends in R&D-intensive FDI; the impact of corruption on the timing and mode of entry by U.S. firms in China; the proliferation of Free Trade Agreements and their impact on FDI; Union structure and inward FDI; inward FDI performance and determinants of FDI regional disparity in China; trade, FDI, exchange rate, and the effect of corporate tax reduction policy; evidence from plant-level data of FDI and productivity spillovers; and regional FDI spillovers in the Swiss service/construction industry.

Chapter 1 - Following the commodity price boom and a surge of inward FDI, African resource-rich countries are increasingly focusing on developing backward and forward linkages to their extractive industries in order to promote industrial development. Simultaneously, China and India are emerging as key strategic sources of FDI into Africa's extractive industries. This article therefore investigates whether Chinese and Indian FDI are likely to have a distinctive impact on a linkage development-based industrialisation strategy.

This research is framed within the Global Value Chains (GVCs) approach and it draws on findings from the International Business Literature on China and India OFDI to argue that firm ownership, in terms of country of origin, of the mining firms shapes the governance of extractive industries GVCs, which, in turn, affects the opportunities for local linkage development.

The case study focuses on backward linkages to Zambia's copper value chain. The research is based on primary data collected in Zambia in 2009. A total of 78 interviews with mining companies, supply firms and private and public sector representatives were conducted. The primary data was supplemented by secondary and archival material.

The key findings corroborate the hypothesis that new investors have a distinctive impact on local value chain dynamics. After comparing Chinese, Indian and Northern and South African driven value chains, significant variations in value chain governance with regard to outsourcing strategies, selection of suppliers, performance requirements and buyer-supplier cooperation were found. These variations are determined by differential access to capital markets and the state, different experiences with FDI in extractive industries, and business cultures. As a result of these findings, this paper argues that these governance patterns have significant implications for Zambia's backward linkage development strategy.

Chapter 2 - There is a growing acceptance of the idea that spillovers constitute a central component of the impact that FDI firms create in a variety of developed and developing host economies. These non-market effects occur when foreign-owned firms act as source of new knowledge and technologies, resulting in positive efficiency or productivity effects among domestic firms. The actual evidence on these productivity effects is characterized by a considerable degree of heterogeneity, however. Overall, it appears that evidence of positive spillovers that occur between industries is more robust than findings on intra-industry spillovers. In particular, suppliers of FDI firms in host economies may benefit from positive productivity effects.

In response to the large degree of heterogeneity of the evidence on the overall prevalence of FDI spillovers, recent research is focusing on identifying factors that influence these externalities. In particular, several studies look at the role of inter-firm linkages as channel of FDI spillovers, the level of technological differences between FDI and domestic firms and the location pattern of economic activity within host economies.

In this chapter, the author critically examines research on these potential determinants. The author does this in the following way. First, the author conducts a selective survey of research on these factors, focusing on limitations and inconsistencies in the research approaches and available evidence. Findings on the importance of inter-firm linkages as channel of FDI spillovers are of a mixed nature. Econometric evidence on the importance of these inter-firm linkages is indirect of nature and does not clarify how spillovers are transmitted. Findings from more qualitative research are more informative on this, but suffer from the feature that it is not clear whether FDI firms are different from comparable domestic firms regarding the degree to which they share technologies with their suppliers. Also, the actual impact on the suppliers is usually omitted from the analysis. Research on the effect of the technology gap between FDI and domestic firms is hindered by the feature that different studies report positive effects of either a small or large technology gap. Findings of a positive effect of a large technology gap on spillovers are in strong contrast to the standard interpretation of the technology gap as direct inverse indicator of the level of absorptive capacity of domestic firms. As for research on the effect of location patterns of economic activity in host economies, there is a strong prediction that agglomeration enhances FDI spillovers. However, there are only a small number of studies that look at this direct relation.

Second, the author conducts a selective review of studies on FDI spillovers in Mexico and the author conducts new multivariate analysis using data that the author collected among foreign-owned and Mexican producer firms and local suppliers in the North East of Mexico. In contrast to most host economies that have been the subject of one or a small number of FDI spillovers studies, there is a multitude of evidence on the spillover impact of foreign-owned firms in the Mexican economy. Importantly, several recent studies on Mexico specifically address the importance of inter-firm linkages, the technology gap and agglomeration as potential determinants of FDI spillovers. The multivariate analysis that the author conducts is focused on obtaining further evidence on whether FDI firms differ from Mexican producer firms in terms of the level and nature of technology transfers that they provide their suppliers with. Also, the analysis investigates whether and how the level of technological differences between producer firms and their local suppliers influences positive impacts that the suppliers may experience as a result of their business linkages with their client firms.

The main findings from the survey of research on FDI spillovers in Mexico can be summarized as follows. First, most studies present evidence that indicates that Mexican firms are subject to FDI spillovers. Studies that only look at intra-industry effects tend to find positive productivity effects among Mexican firms. Studies that distinguish between intra-industry and inter-industry effects find that positive effects are particularly pronounced among suppliers of FDI firms. Second, the technology gap enhances FDI spillovers. The estimated positive effect of the technology gap contradicts the traditional interpretation of this gap as inverse indicator of absorptive capacity of domestic firms. Instead, a large technology gap captures the large scope for domestic firms to improve, offering incentives to these firms to try and absorb new technologies. Third, agglomeration and geographical proximity between firms enhance FDI spillovers. At the same time, spillovers do also materialize between Mexican regions. Finally, the analysis of the survey data from the North East of Mexico strongly supports the notion that FDI firms create positive spillovers among their suppliers and that the technology gap enhances this impact. FDI firms are significantly more involved in several types of technology transfers than comparable Mexican producer firms. This applies in particular to technology transfers that have a direct impact on the production processes of suppliers. Findings from the multivariate analysis show that suppliers of FDI firms are more likely to experience large positive impacts, even after controlling for the levels of support that they receive from their client firms. The positive effect of the technology gap is also confirmed, as the likelihood that suppliers experience large positive impacts from their business dealings with their client firms is enhanced by a large technology gap between the two types of firms.

Chapter 3 - Over the last decades, Foreign Direct Investment (FDI) has become one of the main drivers of economic growth, both at national and regional levels. Economic theory suggests that international capital flows should improve the allocation of resources and consequently should promote growth. In fact, FDI is an essential instrument to spread technology from the most to the least developed countries because it causes positive externalities and spillover effects. It also helps to increase human capital formation and productivity among firms as well as to foster integration through international trade. All these changes enhance economic growth.

The European Union (EU) has been one of the main recipients of FDI in the current era of globalization, which has given rise to a vast literature about the issue. Within this branch of the literature there are, however, just a few studies devoted to the study of FDI at regional level. For this reason, the main purpose of this manuscript is to investigate the link between FDI and economic growth across European regions (NUTS2) over the period 2000-2007. This topic, always important, is even more relevant at the current time. The EU is now immersed in an economic and financial crisis, which has reduced significantly both FDI inflows and intra-EU flows. Even though it seems unlikely to recover the FDI highest level reached in 2007, a suitable atmosphere for foreign investment could contribute to mitigate its negative consequences for European regional development. This is the reason why host countries should have a proper environment for investment as well as an institutional framework to implement policies focused on attracting capital flows.

The main results of the manuscript can be summarized as follows: firstly, FDI is quite concentrated at regional level; secondly, FDI has contributed to enhance economic growth in European regions and finally, FDI has not led to the process of convergence during the sample period.

Chapter 4 - The force of globalization has forced Taiwanese Information and Electronics suppliers to invest in mainland China. Traditionally, increases in a company's value added per worker were commonly associated with changes in physical capital, human capital and production technologies. However, changes in value added can also be the result of outward FDI because of capital leakage, export substitution, import penetration, technology transfer, and higher earnings from the subsidiary than the parent company, which further encourages firms to lower domestic production. This paper estimates the impact of outward FDI in mainland China on parent firms' abilities to create domestic value added per worker in the Information and Electronics sector in Taiwan using samples from 1991 to 2006. The results show that outward FDI in China lowers parent firms' value added per worker in Taiwan during this period. It implies that the government should develop strategies to increase domestic productivity while opening cross-strait investment.

Chapter 5 - The Association of Southeast Asian Nations (ASEAN) is recognized as one of the most attractive regions to foreign investors, according to the declaration to create ASEAN Economic Community in 2003. It was commonly believed that the investment liberalization will help to foster economic growth and development and income inequality reduction in ASEAN member countries.

However, from World Bank database, the income inequalities are raising in most of the ASEAN member countries; this phenomenon exhibits serious concerns for policymakers in this region.

This chapter revisits the impact of foreign direct investment (FDI) on income inequalities for selected Asian countries (Indonesia, Malaysia, Philippines, Singapore, Thailand and Vietnam) during the period 1985-2011. A FDI-led inequality model is developed by incorporating trade, economic integration, financial development and spatial effect as proxy for economic geography in the model specification and a spatial fixed effect model is used to estimate the model.

The estimated results reveal that income inequality is negatively affected by an increase in bilateral trade and financial development, whereas bilateral FDI and economic integration stimulate income inequality in ASEAN. The results also indicate that third-country (spatial) effects of income inequality, trade and financial development have positive relationships with income inequality in such ASEAN countries, whereas spatial effects of FDI and economic integration are important determinants to reduce the inequality gap in ASEAN.

Thus, the ASEAN economic agreements and policies should be tailored, integrated and harmonized in order to achieve the desired outcome of becoming ASEAN Economic Community and to foster the sustainable and equitable economic development in ASEAN.

Chapter 6 - The available evidence shows that the geography of corporate research and development (R and D) is becoming more multi-polar, which brings along new opportunities for some developing countries. However, global competition to attract FDI in R and D has become very intense, and developing countries that fail to raise their technological capabilities in line with the needs of multinational companies will remain marginalized from global innovation networks. Building on a critical review of the existing literature and on a variety of country-specific examples, the aim of this chapter is to unveil the policy options available for developing countries to attract R and D-intensive FDI.

Chapter 7 - This chapter investigates the factors that determine U.S. firms' expansion strategies with respect to the timing and resource commitment in China between 1980 and 2005. The authors collect a new firm-level, cross-industry sample to document when and how firms invest. The authors find that earlier entry is undertaken by firms with larger advertising expendituresand ones that are more labor intensive. Additionally, investments by firms with high RandD expenditures occur in the later years. The authors analyze the role of corruption using three popular indexes: The World Bank's Worldwide Governance Indicators Project (1996-2005), Transparency International's corruption perceptions index (1980-2005), and Political Risk Services Group's quality of government index (1984-2005). The authors find evidence to support the hypothesis that higher corruption levels delay firms' entry and discourage high-equity commitment.

Chapter 8 - In recent decades, there have been an unprecedented number of regional agreements about the crucial characteristics of the international economic relations. Many countries have begun to explore and participate in the RIA. The rise and development of capital movements and FDI are considered the primary objectives of these agreements. This article focuses on the study of the influence of regional integration, foreign direct investment in several groups over the period 1970-2009. It introduces several variables related to regional integration (trade integration index, index of financial integration and dummy variables) to test their effects on the FDI in these countries. This study examines a panel of 35 countries. The results found show the existence of a strong relationship between the factors of economic integration and the FDI in these countries.

Chapter 9 - In a union-duopoly strategic context the authors explore the endogenous determination and the effects of the unionization structure in a market facing the possibility of inward foreign direct investments (FDI). The authors' findings suggest that, if the foreign firm's unit cost under exports-x is lower than its unit cost under FDI-c, then the domestic unionization structure is irrelevant with FDI decisions. If on the other hand c is lower than x, yet high enough, inward FDI will be − optimally in terms of social welfare − deterred in the equilibrium, so long as the domestic labour market is left to auto-regulate to a centralized union structure, hence, to a centralized wage bargaining regime. If however c is low enough, then a benevolent social planner will have to enforce decentralized union structure and wage bargaining − optimally inducing or accommodating inward FDI − in contrast to the domestic union's best interest which would have otherwise − sub-optimally led to a centralized union structure/wage bargaining regime.

Chapter 10 - This study investigates China's inward FDI performance and determinants of FDI regional disparities among the three macro-regions of China. A panel dataset at provincial level and the GLS statistics model are used to identify the factors of FDI regional disparities by considering provincial and regional characteristics. The empirical results indicate that variations in economic openness and industrial and economic development are the prime causes of the unbalance regional distribution of China's inward FDI. The study further discusses the impact of FDI regional disparities on China's economy and finally, the policy implications are provided to reduce the degree of FDI regional disparity.

Chapter 11 - This chapter investigates the policy effect of decreasing the corporate tax rate on the economy and welfare of a home country and a foreign country using a two-country model with international trade, foreign direct investment (FDI), and an exchange rate. Decreasing the corporate tax rate leads to an appreciation of the domestic currency and increases the FDI inflows. If the corporate tax rate in the home country is higher than that in the foreign country (Case 1), the tax reduction policy increases the real national income and improves welfare in the home country via a decrease in home prices, but it can either increase or decrease the income and welfare in the foreign country, because the effect of this policy on foreign prices is ambiguous. That is, in Case 1, this policy can be either a prosper-thy-neighbor or a beggar-thy-neighbor policy, depending on conditions. On the other hand, if the corporate tax rate in the home country is lower than that in the foreign country (Case 2), the policy can either increase or decrease the home country's income and welfare, but it certainly decreases the foreign country's income and welfare. Therefore, this policy can be either a beggar-thyself or a beggar-thy-neighbor policy in Case 2. The basic cause of the ambiguity of the policy effects on the foreign (the home) income and welfare in Case 1 (Case 2) depends on the production relocation according to FDI by multinational enterprises responding to the policy change. In conclusion, contrary to the conventional wisdom, in an era of globalization, it's not always true that the corporate tax reduction policy leads an economic expansion and a welfare improvement. This analytical result can be a theoretical rationale for reviewing the current trend of corporate tax reduction in the world.

Chapter 12 - Foreign direct investment (FDI) is often advocated as one of the main sources of international technology diffusion and productivity enhancement in developing (host) countries. Given the policy implications, in this study, the authors explore whether foreign ownership is associated with spillover effects by using plant-level data from Indonesian manufacturing industries over the period 2001-2007. The authors' results indicate that positive spillovers to domestic firms are plausible; an increment in the foreign equity share in an industry in a province is associated with significantly higher productivity of plants. These effects, however, are more pronounced for plants with greater foreign equity share.

Chapter 13 - This chapter analyzes regional spillover effects from Switzerland. It covers firms in services/construction, whereas most existing studies deal with manufacturing. The author highlights the role of spillover mechanisms and the absorptive capacity of local firms in assessing regional benefits. The author hypothesizes that the size and the extent of regional spillovers depend largely upon the interaction between their channels and the existing technological capacities of local firms. Moreover, only local firms which have largely invested in the absorption of foreign technologies benefit from regional spillovers. The results confirm to a great extent my hypotheses.

In: Foreign Direct Investment (FDI)
Editors: Enzo Guillon and Lucas Chauvet

ISBN: 978-1-62808-403-0
© 2013 Nova Science Publishers, Inc.

Chapter 1

CHINESE AND INDIAN INVESTMENT IN AFRICA'S EXTRACTIVE INDUSTRIES: IMPLICATIONS FOR LOCAL INDUSTRIAL DEVELOPMENT

Judith Fessehaie[*]

Research Associate, PRISM, University of Cape Town
Industrial Development Expert, TradeMark Southern Africa

ABSTRACT

Following the commodity price boom and a surge of inward FDI, African resource-rich countries are increasingly focusing on developing backward and forward linkages to their extractive industries in order to promote industrial development. Simultaneously, China and India are emerging as key strategic sources of FDI into Africa's extractive industries. This article therefore investigates whether Chinese and Indian FDI are likely to have a distinctive impact on a linkage development-based industrialisation strategy.

This research is framed within the Global Value Chains (GVCs) approach and it draws on findings from the International Business Literature on China and India OFDI to argue that firm ownership, in terms of country of origin, of the mining firms shapes the governance of extractive industries GVCs, which, in turn, affects the opportunities for local linkage development.

The case study focuses on backward linkages to Zambia's copper value chain. The research is based on primary data collected in Zambia in 2009. A total of 78 interviews with mining companies, supply firms and private and public sector representatives were conducted. The primary data was supplemented by secondary and archival material.

The key findings corroborate the hypothesis that new investors have a distinctive impact on local value chain dynamics. After comparing Chinese, Indian and Northern and South African driven value chains, significant variations in value chain governance with regard to outsourcing strategies, selection of suppliers, performance requirements and buyer-supplier cooperation were found. These variations are determined by differential access to capital markets and the state, different experiences with FDI in extractive industries, and business cultures. As a result of these findings, this paper argues that these

---

[*] Email: judith.fessehaie@uct.ac.za; jfessehaie@trademarksa.org

governance patterns have significant implications for Zambia's backward linkage development strategy.

INTRODUCTION

Africa's extractive industries are attracting increasing levels of investment originating from emerging economies, in particular China and India. As the contribution of these industries to Africa's GDP growth and its treasuries grow, African governments are devising strategies to move away from continued dependence on exports of unprocessed commodities to promote industrialisation. There is a growing consensus that one way to do that is by developing upstream and downstream linkages to the extractive industry sector [African Union and UNECA, 2013; Morris, Kaplinsky, and Kaplan, 2012]. This has been reflected in a number of policy documents adopted at the continental level, such as the African Mining Vision, 2009, and the Action Plan for the Accelerated Industrial Development of Africa, 2008; and at a regional level, such as the Southern Africa Development Community (SADC) Industrial Development Policy Framework, 2012, and the East Africa Community (EAC) Industrialisation Strategy, 2012 - 2032.

A critical question that has remained largely unexplored in the academic literature concerns the implications for linkage development in Africa in response to China and India's entry as major producers in the global value chains of extractive industries. Until now, research on China and India's impact on Africa has focused on the indirect and direct trade effects, rather than local industrialization [Broadman, 2007; Jenkins and Edwards, 2006; Kaplinsky and Morris, 2009]. However, the role of China and India in supporting or curtailing the development of linkage opportunities in producer countries deserves more attention as African governments devise strategies to develop downstream and upstream linkages. This chapter therefore investigates the implications of Foreign Direct Investment (FDI) from China and India on the development of upstream industries in Zambia's copper value chain.

The first section presents the dynamics of the global copper value chain, in terms of price, demand, supply and factors underpinning the competitiveness of mining firms. This is followed by an analysis of the key drivers of Chinese and Indian FDI, with a particular focus on the engagement with Africa, and the possible implications on opportunities for local industrialisation. The third section provides a background of Zambia's copper value chain, including an overview of investments by Chinese and Indian firms into copper production, and the historical trajectory of the local supply industry. The fourth section discusses the distinctive governance of Chinese and Indian-driven value chains by comparing them to value chains driven by Northern and South African mining firms. Governance is analysed in terms of barriers of entry, the selection of local suppliers; market requirements (Critical Success Factors); and buyer-supplier relationships. The impact of value chain governance on local supplier upgrading is discussed in the fifth section. The last section concludes.

GLOBAL DYNAMICS IN THE COPPER MARKET

Since 2003, the world copper market has experienced a price boom due to rising Asian demand and slow supply response from producing countries (see Figure 1). Annual prices in the 1980s averaged 1,839 US$/t, while in the 1990s they reached an average of 2,223 US$/t. Between 2003 and 2007, copper prices increased by 300 per cent and reached an annual average of 7,131 US$/t in 2007. Following the recent global economic downturn, prices however declined and fell drastically to the low-level of 3,105 US$/t in December 2008 but they promptly recovered to an average of 6,263 US$/t in the second semester of 2009. In 2010, demand from the advanced economies and from China increased again, causing prices to overtake the pre-crisis level, with an average of 7,538 US$/t in 2010, 8,823 US$/t in 2011, and 7,958 US$/t in 2012.

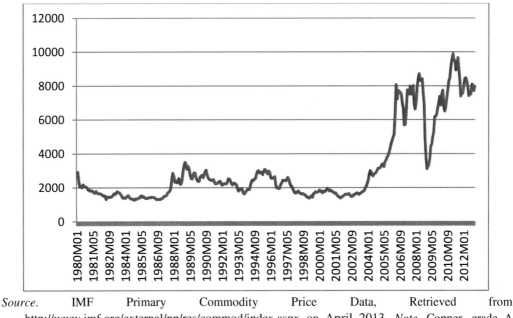

Source. IMF Primary Commodity Price Data, Retrieved from http://www.imf.org/external/np/res/commod/index.aspx on April 2013. *Note.* Copper, grade A cathode, CIF European ports

Figure 1. Copper LME spot price (January 1980- December 2012, US$/mt).

The copper price boom has been largely driven by China's demand for infrastructure and housing development and its consumer goods market [Farooki and Kaplinsky, 2011; GFMS, 2011]. Whilst industrialised nations underwent a process of dematerialisation, where the resource intensity of their economic activities decreased [Radetzki, 2008], copper demand from China, India and other emerging economies has been increasingly substantially, as these countries embarked on the resource-intensive stage of economic development.

Looking at the sectoral consumption of copper by major consuming countries and regions in 2009, China accounted for 27 per cent of global copper usage in construction, 49 per cent in electrical and electronic equipment, 35 per cent in transportation, 42 per cent in consumer and general products, and 19 per cent in industrial machineries [GFMS, 2011]. China dwarfed the other countries and regions in every sector, with the exception of industrial machinery, where Europe maintained its global competitiveness.

Between 1990 and 2010, China's copper consumption grew on average by 14.2 per cent per year, compared to -1.3 per cent in North America and -0.1 in the EU [GFMS, 2011]. Only India's copper consumption showed a similarly aggressively high growth rate, which averaged at 8 per cent per year. Despite this high growth rate, India's copper consumption, which was mainly used for manufacturing goods for domestic and export markets, was, in value terms, more than ten times smaller than China's [GFMS, 2011].

In an effort to meet its growing demand, China increased copper ore production and scrap collection, becoming, together with Zambia, the main source of copper output growth in the past years. China also increased its reliance on imports, becoming the world's leading copper importer. In 2011, China imported 28.9 per cent of all traded copper ore, as well as 28.9 per cent of all traded refined copper [Trademap data, Retrieved on 13/04/2013 from http://www.trademap.org/]. Furthermore, between 2007 and 2011, China's copper ore imports had grown by 15 per cent in value and refined copper imports had grown by 22 per cent during the same period. During this period China also became a large source of investment in the copper mining sectors of developed and developing countries through highly strategic investment project. These projects were very linked to the state, which allowed China to introduce a model that combined aid, infrastructure development, and natural resource extraction. This model was first implemented in Angola and later in the Democratic Republic of Congo (DRC), it was also replicated by India in Nigeria [Pal, 2008; Wang, 2007]. India's investments into Africa's extractive industries have also been remarkable. For example, these investments include an acquisition of Zambia's largest copper mining assets. Furthermore, in 2011, China and India ranked third and fourth amongst the largest sources of FDI flows to Africa, and sixth and seventh in terms of FDI stock [UNCTAD, 2013].

China and India's investment in Africa's mineral sector was facilitated by the privatisation process of mining assets that took place in many developing countries as part of their structural adjustment programmes [Humphreys, 2009; Radetzki, 2008]. Mining companies from developed countries that were investing in mining assets in Africa were increasingly scrutinised and under pressure from global networks of civil society groups to meet environmental and social sustainability standards [World Bank and IFC, 2003]. This resulted in initiatives such as the Extractive Industry Transparency Initiative aimed at increasing financial transparency from corporate and host countries; and the International Council on Mining and Metals aimed at addressing human rights and environmental concerns. Chinese and Indian investors were largely unaffected by these pressures, which fed concerns by civil society groups and researchers because an increasing share of mineral production, including copper, was owned and controlled by MNEs from China and India. Indeed, by 2009, half of the top 30 mining companies originated from emerging economies [Humphreys, 2009].[1] Eight of these fifteen companies produced copper.

From the 2000s onwards, the copper industry witnessed a process of market consolidation fuelled by frenzy M&A activities. Copper has a high value per unit weight, which allows its tradability on the global market. With 77 per cent of the value-added

---

[1] This list included SOEs and companies listed in London which maintained management in the countries of establishment. Emergent economies include Brazil, Russia, Chile, Mexico, South Africa, Poland, India, Indonesia, and Kazakhstan.

accruing at mining stage, mining is a highly profitable business [UNCTAD, 2007], especially after the copper price boom. To increase copper production and maximise shareholder-value, Multinational Enterprises (MNEs) increasingly focused on acquiring smaller mining companies, as a faster avenue to expand capacity in comparison to greenfield investment projects [Farooki and Kaplinsky, 2012]. Greenfield investment projects involve long gestation periods. This was one of the factors underlying the rise in copper price, together with a number of other supply-side constraining factors, such as: falling ore grades in developed areas (US, Chile), exchange rate risks, political instability and labour disputes in producing countries, and increasing costs of exploring and mining new areas [ICSG, 2010; UNCTAD, 2007].[2] Production costs, in particular, had risen following the higher cost of consumables, raw materials and fuel, which alone accounted for around 10 per cent of mining costs, depending on the mining method [GFMS, 2011].

The value of M&A activities in metal and oil sectors jumped from US$ 9.6 billion in 2005, to US$ 43.2 billion in 2006. Peak levels were reached in 2008, with US$ 87 billion worth of acquisitions, which then slowed down to US$ 47 billion in 2009, and US$ 68 billion in 2010 [UNCTAD, 2011, Annex I.5]. The number of M&A deals jumped from 227 in 2005 to 530 in 2010 [UNCTAD, 2011, Annex I.6].

The capacity to conclude high value M&A and start greenfield mining projects started to define the competitive advantage of mining companies. Technological innovation on the contrary was not a significant source of economic rents because the copper mining industry only witnessed two major technological breakthroughs in the past 100 years. The first breakthrough was the introduction of new concentrating techniques based on flotation rather than gravity, and the second was the introduction of the electro-winning process [Bartos, 2007].

In order to undertake brownfield or greenfield investments, two areas became critical for firm competitiveness: organisational capabilities, and access to capital. Over the past decades, mining companies borrowed managerial practices and techniques usually associated with other industries (such as automobile and electronics industries) and adapted them to the mining sector [Culverwell, 2000]. Just-in-time, total quality management and total cost management quickly became some of the cost-saving managerial practices used in purchasing and supply chain management. Developing organisational capabilities to manage complex financial and production networks became even more important in light of the increased internationalisation of companies. Despite Chinese companies being disadvantaged in terms of world-class management and knowledge of foreign markets [He and Lyles, 2008], they had a strong competitive advantage in terms of access to capital. Given the high risks, long gestation periods and capital required by mining investment, Chinese resource companies were best placed to drive investment in new mining projects. This was facilitated by state-owned banks, direct state funding, and access to high levels of retained earnings not disbursed to share-holders [Moss and Rose, 2006; Morck, Yeung, and Zhao, 2008; Wang, 2007].

---

[2] Future production from large greenfield investment in Latin America and Asia was expected to relax supply constraints [GFMS, 2011].

THE EMERGENCE OF CHINA AND INDIA IN MINERALS-BASED GLOBAL VALUE CHAINS

The rise of China and India in the minerals-based global value chain has followed very different paths, which was state-driven in China and private sector-led in India.

Pattern of Chinese Foreign Direct Investment

Chinese FDI started from very low levels, but grew fast in the past 20 years [Broadman, 2007; Wang, 2007]. According to UNCTAD data, average annual FDI flows amounted to US$ 453 million in the 1980s, they increased to US$ 2.3 billion in the 1990s, and reached US$ 18.3 billion in the 2000s.[3] In 2011, China's FDI flows amounted to US$ 65 billion, and its FDI stock to US$ 366 billion.[4]

At the turn of the century, developing countries overtook developed countries as the largest recipient of Chinese FDI [Buckley et al., 2008]. The growth of Chinese engagement in Africa was remarkable. In absolute terms, Chinese FDI flows to Africa showed a 73-fold increase in the 2003-2008 period, compared to a 34-fold increase to non-OECD countries and 8-fold to OECD countries [Hurst, 2011, using approved data]. Removing FDI to Hong Kong, the Cayman, and the British Virgin Islands,[5] and with more up-to-date data, Gelb [2010] calculated that in 2008, Africa was the top destination of China's FDI flows and the second largest destination of FDI stock after Asia.

By the end of 2012, more than 2000 Chinese firms had invested in 50 African countries [Business Daily, 31.3.2013] and Chinese FDI stock in Africa stood at US$16 billion by the end of 2011 [UNCTAD, 2013]. South Africa was the leading recipient of Chinese FDI in the continent, followed by Sudan, Nigeria, Zambia and Algeria. Chinese firms that invested in Africa made investments in the manufacturing, services, resource extraction, and agriculture [UNCTAD, 2013].

The growth of Chinese outward investment activity was heavily influenced by government policy. Reforms to encourage outward FDI started as early as 1979, when the 'open door' policy was launched, and continued cautiously until the 1990s. China embarked on a decisive reform path with the 'going global' policy, launched in 1999 and formally adopted in 2001 [Brautigam, 2009; Cheung and Qian, 2009]. Such reforms targeted highly strategic investment projects, such as: securing scarce natural resources, acquiring R&D, technological capabilities, and global competences; creating goods and services export opportunities; and strengthening economic ties with partner countries [UNCTAD and UNDP, 2007; Zhan, 1995].

In recent years, international business scholars have become increasingly interested in the determinants of China's FDI. These scholars have tested Dunning's eclectic paradigm, or OLI

---

[3] Annual FDI flows data for the 1980s cover the period 1982-1989.

[4] Caution is required when analysing Chinese FDI data. Balance of payment-based data does not cater for "round tripping", that is capital invested abroad and re-invested back in order to benefit from tax exemptions [Buckley et al., 2008; Cheng and Ma, 2008; OECD, 2008].

[5] The three destinations accounted for around 80 per cent of total China OFDI in the 2003-2008 period. The final destination of these investment was difficult to ascertain [Cheng and Ma, 2010; Gelb, 2010].

(ownership advantages, location endowments, internalisation) [Dunning, 1977, 1981], on Chinese FDI data. It was found that firms were markedly guided by natural resources and market seeking motives [Buckley et al., 2007; Cheng and Ma, 2010; Cheung and Qian, 2009]. Moreover, investment was strongly associated with institutional variables, such as the 'going global' policy and the need to externalise international reserves [Cheng and Ma, 2010; Cheung and Qian, 2009; Yao, Sutherland, and Chen, 2010]. Buckley et al. [2007] found that Chinese FDI was positively correlated to political risks and higher market returns in the host countries. According to the authors, capital market imperfections granted Chinese investors soft budget constraints, reducing their aversion to risks of investment project failures.

State support in China took the form of subsidies, tax incentives, and market intelligence both at home and through investment promotion centres abroad. Fiscal incentives privileged investment projects were linked to the export of Chinese machinery, plants, and equipment [Sauvant, 2004]. Concessional loans, export credits and international guarantees as well as direct capital contribution and subsidies associated with official aid programmes were channelled mainly, but not exclusively, through the policy banks [Moss and Rose, 2006]. In 1995, in a major reform of its Africa aid programme, China set up a concessional loan fund through China Export-Import Bank (Exim Bank) [Brautigam, 2009]. By doing so, China encouraged joint venture investments in manufacturing and agriculture. China also encouraged the establishment of assembly factories, and exploration and investment in forestry and mineral resources. These were, from China's point of view, win-win projects: Africa received much needed investment capital; Chinese firms were assisted in entering new markets, creating demand for Chinese equipment and machinery, and speeding up the relocation of sunset industries outside China. Under FOCAC 2006, China committed US$ 5 million in preferential loans and export credit through China's Exim Bank [Moss and Rose, 2006; OECD, 2008; Wang, 2007].[6] Moreover, China's Development Bank allocated US$ 5 billion to a development fund that supports Chinese FDI in Africa.

Since the early 2000s, China's presence abroad became more heterogeneous, in size, motivations, behaviour [Gill and Reilly, 2007]. Nevertheless, China's outward investment remained dominated and driven by SOEs, which are a critical factor in explaining China's FDI patterns [Buckley et al., 2008; Cheung and Qian, 2009; Morck, Yeung, and Zhao, 2008]. According to estimates by Cheng and Ma [2010], in 2006, 86.4 per cent of OFDI flows and 82.1 per cent of OFDI stock was concentrated in few Central Government SOEs.[7] In the natural resource sector the dominance of SOEs was particularly significant [Gelb, 2010; OECD, 2008].

The dominance of SOEs in China's OFDI had implications for the strategies underlying such investments. This is because Chinese SOEs were not driven exclusively by profit-maximisation motives, but also had to fulfill broad political objectives [Cheung and Qian, 2009; Gill and Reilly, 2007; Hurst, 2011]. Given the level and quality of support received by

---

[6] The government also established special funds to provide direct subsidies and discounted loans to Chinese OFDI enterprises establishing plants and/or R&D centres abroad or conducted various forms of economic and technical co-operation in agriculture [OECD, 2008]. Moreover, SINOSURE, established in 2001 to provide investment insurance, was increasingly targeting FDI in Africa.

[7] The remaining shares of FDI flows and stocks were owned by provincial SOEs (Beijing, Shanghai, and Guangdong) and by collectively- and privately- owned non-SOEs [Cheng and Ma, 2010]. Private firms represented a miniscule share, accounting for 1 per cent of total FDI stock in 2006.

the state, they could do so and focus on national strategic objectives mentioned earlier, such as, securing scarce natural resources, and strengthening economic ties with partner countries.

The reform process of SOEs received a decisive push in the mid-1990s, when an emboldened political leadership, eager to tackle more strongly the decreasing profitability of SOEs and the piling up of non-performing loans, embarked on the *zhuada fangxiao* strategy ("grasping the big and letting go of the small"). As small firms were mostly sold to employees and privates or let go bankrupt, large SOEs were restructured by diversifying the ownership structure. More than 20,000 companies were turned into joint stock companies, their shares sold to employees or, for around 1,400 firms, allowed to float on the stock exchange [Li and Putterman, 2008]. To supervise and improve the governance of almost 200 SOEs, in 2003, the State-owned Assets Supervision and Administration Commission of the State Council (SASAC) was established [Sharma, 2009]. SASAC put in place measures to ensure that non-performing SOEs would exit the market, whilst the others, the *dragon heads* (or "national champions"), reached international competitiveness [Brautigam, 2009].

Whilst ambitious, the reform process did not fundamentally alter the role played by the state. Through public listing, Beijing aimed at increasing private sector participation and improving corporate governance, with positive effects on SOEs performance. Nevertheless, around two thirds of the shares were not tradable, and were state-owned (directly and indirectly, through legal persons) [Li and Putterman, 2008, Morck, Yeung, and Zhao, 2008]. Moreover, state investment funds also held tradable shares, and cross-shareholding by SOEs was common [Morck, Yeung, and Zhao, 2008]. Stock markets signalled limited information to investors due accounting practices that were not standard and limited transparency. Also, most large SOEs were not listed. Overall, government and security regulatory authorities enjoyed substantial decision-making power.

State-ownership ensured that the state had controlling voting power in SOEs, and appointed corporate managers [Morck, Yeung, and Zhao, 2008; Sharma, 2009]. The company Party Committee yielded substantial decision-making power, either directly by chairing the board, or indirectly through the influence of the Central Party. In the largest SOEs, the Party Committee appointed top executives based on orders from the Communist Party's Organisational Department, it also monitored their performance and determined their prospects for career advancement. Top executives were often promoted in the Party and State bureaucracy, and vice versa.

Whilst output and productivity grew as a result of the reform process, they were still low by international standards [Naughton, 1994; Zhang, Zhang, and Zao, 2001], especially in terms of world-class management, technology, know-how, and knowledge of foreign markets [Soares de Oliveira, 2008; He and Lyles, 2008]. This was particularly true in the extractive industries sector [Kuo, 2007].

Compared to the private sector, SOEs enjoyed favourable treatment in terms of subsidies and taxes, exclusive market access to a wide range of sectors, and preferential access to soft and hard infrastructure as well as bank lending [Sharma, 2009]. China's capital markets were instrumental in supporting SOEs and the national industrialisation efforts. Even after major regulatory reforms of the banking sector, lending by the three state-owned policy banks, namely China Development Bank, Export-Import Bank of China and China Agricultural Development Bank, was biased in favour of SOEs with a high risk profile, and offering lower marginal returns to capital [Dollar and Wei, 2007, Sharma, 2009]. The banks moral-hazard behaviour was induced by the expectation that government implicitly guaranteed these loans [Dollar and Wei, 2007].

In summary, Chinese FDI was distinctive in at least the following three respects: an unusual level of highly strategic investment, for a developing country; a lack of aversion to political risks; and the strong influence of policy factors. These observations called for a redefinition or expansion of traditional investment and comparative advantage theories to incorporate institutional factors, namely the role of the state [Aggarwal and Agmon, 1990].

Pattern of Indian Foreign Direct Investment

Until the 1980s, between two thirds and the totality of annual Indian OFDI flows targeted developing countries [Pradhan, 2007]. For three decades, Indian outward FDI was largely regional in scope and market-seeking [Kumar, 2007; Pradhan, 2007]. Import-substitution policies in developing host countries created markets for Indian firms, which had experience in protected domestic markets with similar factor and market conditions to the host countries. They operated small-scale firms, with adapted technologies at the end of the product cycle. With liberalisation taking place across the developing world, these investments were no longer profitable, as Indian firms had to compete globally, rather than domestically or regionally.

Unlike China, India's economic reforms were hastily introduced as a response to the balance of payment crisis in 1991 [Sharma, 2009]. The 1991 New Economic Policy (NEP) consisted of wide-ranging trade and investment liberalisation measures and sectoral and macro-economic reforms that turned the page on a long history of strong government intervention. As far as the industrial sector was concerned, the NEP removed burdensome licensing requirements for establishing or expanding industrial units. Market entry restrictions under the Monopolies and Restrictive Trade Practices Act (1970) were also eased. In the past, under the Act, larger private enterprises were allowed only in selected sectors, whilst heavy industries, mining, telecommunications, and other sectors were reserved for the State outright. According to Pradhan [2008], it was these sectoral and firm size restrictions that spurred the pre-1990 wave of OFDI by few private companies. Birla, Tata, Thapar and the like, constrained in their domestic market, pursued their strategy of scale and sectoral expansion overseas. With time, these private investors developed significant experience and knowledge on managing cross-border alliances, more so than their Chinese counterparts [Hattari and Rajan, 2010].

Liberalisation led to a consolidation of the industrial and services sectors, with surviving Indian firms emerging "leaner and meaner" [Nayyar, 2008, p. 126]. Rather than being assisted by the government, Indian firms had to find the resources to overcome the weakness of the government. This process however was highly selective and only few MNEs, particularly in the steel and software industries, grew to operate at the technological frontier and developed internationally competitive marketing and brands.

Following the NEP and its liberalisation of the outward FDI regime, levels, destination, and drivers of Indian FDI changed significantly [Hattari and Rajan, 2010; Kumar, 2007; Pradhan, 2007; Sauvant, 2004]. In value terms, India's outward FDI became significant only by the turn of the century. FDI flows, which stood at a meager annual average of US$ 4.4 million in the 1980s and US$ 70 million in the 1990s, jumped to annual averages of US$ 8 billion in the 2000s. In 2011, FDI flows amounted to US$ 14.8 billion, and FDI stocks reached US$ 111.3 billion.

From 2000 onwards, developed countries absorbed most Indian OFDI activity. Much of this FDI were strategic asset- and efficiency- seeking flows aimed at acquiring technological and R&D capabilities (energy, telecom), controlling marketing and distribution networks (automotive, information technology), and branding (consumer goods, pharmaceuticals).[8] To this end, Indian MNEs moved into full or majority ownership, privileged M&A and broadened the sectoral distribution of their FDI [Hattari and Rajan, 2010; Kumar, 2007; Nayyar, 2008; Tolentino, 2008].

By the end of 2011, India's total FDI stock in Africa stood at about US$14 billion [UNCTAD, 2013]. Indian FDI flows to Africa targeted manufacturing (chemicals, rubber and plastic products, transport equipment), and services (software development, financial and insurance, and transportation). For example, in 2011, 80 per cent of Indian investments in eight East African countries were in the services sector [UNCTAD, 2013]. Natural resources attracted a small share of India's total FDI flows, mainly constituted of three deals in the oil and gas sector in Sudan and Libya, which were led by state-owned ONGC Videsh Ltd [Pal, 2008; Pradhan, 2008].

With regard to the capital market, under the NEP, prudential and supervisory regulations were strengthened and implemented in conformance with international standards, interest rates were also deregulated and credit controls eliminated. The Indian banking sector worked relatively well in financial intermediation and allocating credit to the private sector. This was reflected in India's outward investment activities as follows, international M&A by Indian enterprises were undertaken by privately-owned firms with relatively easy access to the stock market [Gupta, 2005; Kumar, 2007; Nayyar, 2008; Pal, 2008; Sauvant, 2004]. Overall, Indian MNEs were experienced with corporate governance standards required from the stock exchange, had healthy balance sheets, and enjoyed robust credit ratings

Whist ridden with inefficiencies and incomplete reforms at home, Indian enterprises were profit-driven and operated in a context of market-based institutions. Indian OFDI firms relied on existing ownership advantages, accrued from technological and managerial competence, financial strength, and overseas expertise, which lay behind the global competitiveness of large, but also small and medium-sized Indian investors [Hattari and Rajan, 2010; Pradhan, 2004; Sauvant, 2004]. The 1990s reforms allowed firms to pursue their growth and internationalisation strategies, but did they not drive this process. In other words, the reforms "enabled Indian firms to move across borders; but it did not drive Indian firms to move across borders" [Nayyar, 2008, p. 126]. Critically for our discussion on outward FDI, the interaction of state ownership and capital market imperfections found in China, was not found in India and did not affect the level, nature and direction of outward FDI investment. With the exception of some state oil companies, Indian FDI was largely driven by private enterprises, with little coordination with the government. Indeed, before 1991, when directed at promoting South-South trade, Indian OFDI were more policy-driven than they would ever be after this date [Hattari and Rajan, 2010; Pradhan, 2008].

---

[8] High-profile Indian M&A included Tata acquisition of Jaguar and Ford, Tata Tea acquisition of Tetley, Asian Paints acquisition of Berger International, and software companies' investing in the US in order to acquire the domain knowledge of clients and new business opportunities.

Comparing China and India FDI

While both China and India pursued market-, efficiency- and strategic asset- seeking in developed countries, for India these were the bulk of its OFDI. Conversely, most Chinese investment targeted market- and natural resource- seeking investments in developing countries. Sun et al. [2012] compared 1,526 M&A transactions by Chinese and Indian MNEs in the period between 2000-2008, during which Chinese and Indian firms completed M&A for a total value of US$ 130 and 60.5 billion respectively. The top ten cross-border overseas participants, in value terms, were mostly SOEs for China, and all privately-owned for India. Indian investment was smaller-sized and targeted forward integration to tap into the European (58.4 per cent of M&A value) and US markets (22.9 per cent). China M&A activities had a significant regional reach, with Hong Kong capturing 40.5 per cent of total M&A value.[9] Natural resources accounted for the bulk of total M&A value in both China and India, although Indian M&A were significant also in knowledge-intensive and manufacturing sectors (26.3 and 16.6 per cent of total deals, respectively).

Differential access to capital markets underlined China and India's response to the global economic crisis. In 2008, total FDI flows declined by 16 per cent. In 2009, FDI outflows declined by a further 43 per cent. China's outward FDI into the non-financial sector (mainly extractive industries) grew unabatedly [Davies, 2009; Yao, Sutherland, and Chen, 2010]. On the contrary, being governed by market parameters and affected by the credit crunch and declining sales and profits growth, Indian OFDI declined drastically, especially in the manufacturing sector [Pradhan, 2009]. Comparing the first half of 2009 with the same period in 2008, Indian overseas acquisition fell by 64.7 per cent in value (from US$ 8 billion to US$ 2.8 billion) and 80 per cent in number of deals (from 140 to 28). In the primary sector, only the oil and gas sector was not affected due to a large-scale acquisition by state-owned OVL in Siberia, but in the mineral sector, investment slowed down. Major energy MNEs disinvested in some countries.

Lastly, China and India differed in terms of sourcing strategies. Unlike India, China's outward investment was explicitly geared towards the promotion of Chinese exports, as envisaged by the going global policy and Exim Bank guidelines. Broadman [2007] found this sourcing pattern in his survey of Chinese investors in Africa. There was however evidence that Chinese corporations followed practices which differed from Beijing guidelines [Gill and Reilly, 2007; Li, 2010]. This was more likely if they invested retained earnings rather than Exim Bank funds. Overall, though, comprehensive empirical research on Chinese investors' sourcing patterns was scarce. Whether Chinese investors on the ground were more influenced in their sourcing decision by Beijing-defined export promotion objectives or by profit-maximisation was a critical determining factor for domestic upstream industries in the host countries. This research question was nevertheless, largely ignored in the international business literature with the impact of China and India's outward FDI on local industrialisation patterns in the host countries falling largely outside the research agenda of international business scholars.

---

[9] This should be interpreted with caution in view of the discussion on data reliability. Other important deals were closed in the UK (16.4 per cent, 12 deals) and the US (8.6 per cent, 77 deals). Canada, South Africa, Australia and Singapore were also important destinations [Sun et al., 2012].

ASIAN-DRIVEN GLOBAL VALUE CHAINS AND AFRICA'S INDUSTRIALISATION

Issues of local industrialisation and upstream linkage development are at the core of the Global Value Chain (GVC) research agenda, which focuses on the nature of linkages, how they are governed, the opportunities they offer for growth and upgrading to firms and countries [Gereffi1994, 1999; Kaplinsky and Morris, 2001]. This agenda, developed in the 1990s, was widely adopted by scholars to interpret global changes in the organisation of production. A large body of GVC empirical studies, inductively, led to the development of key theoretical concepts, in particular those of upgrading and governance.

Upgrading referred to a country or region firms' capabilities to improve their position in global value chains. Researchers adopted a four-fold definition for such capabilities [Humphrey and Schmitz, 2002]. Upgrading consisted of improvements in the production process, for example through re-organisation of the production systems or new technologies (process upgrading); moving into higher more sophisticated product lines (product upgrading); moving into higher-skills content functions (functional upgrading), and moving into new production activities (inter-sectoral or chain upgrading).

A critical proposition of the GVC literature was that opportunities for developing countries' firms to upgrade, as well as their access to markets and economic returns, were critically determined by the way GVCs were governed, i.e. by the content and quality of buyer-supplier relationships [Humphrey and Schmitz, 2000; Kaplinsky and Morris, 2001]. Unpacking the governance concept, a wide range of functions were identified: deciding what was to be produced, selecting of participants in the value chain and determining of their roles, determining how to handle the flow of products and services along the chain, setting key performance standards, monitoring and, in case of failure, sanctioning or assisting suppliers.

Critically, by controlling the production process, lead firms appropriated and distributed value created along the GVCs. Lead firm strategies in terms of value chain cooperation also determined the opportunities for developing countries firms to upgrade. Lall [1980] identified this value chain cooperation as "direct relationships established by firms in complementary activities which are external to 'pure' market transactions" [p. 204]. These consisted of, among others, direct assistance to suppliers to establish their businesses or to locate in close proximity to the buyers, information sharing to facilitate production and investment planning and technical cooperation.[10] By analysing the relational components of global production networks, GVC research argued that the determinants of the competitiveness of a firm did not rest exclusively within the firm, but also in the nature of its relationship with suppliers/buyers.

According to Humphrey and Schmitz [2002], lead firms moved away from market-based relationships and adopted tighter forms of governance in response to various pressures. Weak suppliers' capabilities in developing countries often required buyers' cooperation. Increased competition in the retail sector emphasised product differentiation and innovation, which in turn, required customized, complex suppliers' relationships. Moreover, buyers had to exercise

---

[10] In Lall's analysis [1980], assistance to suppliers was defined as *linkages*. Other linkages included financial assistance, raw material procurement to ensure quality and availability of supplies, managerial training, setting up a negotiation procedure to determine prices, allocating inventory and product development costs, sharing of replacement markets, etc.

greater control over labour, safety and environmental processes, while lean production systems intensified coordination requirements with suppliers. In sectors characterised by non-price competition, risks were more accentuated and thus tighter forms of governance had to be expected [Humphrey and Schmitz, 2001]. Gereffi, Humphrey, and Sturgeon [2005] proposed that governance was determined not only by suppliers' capabilities but also by the complexity of knowledge embedded in a transaction (in terms of product and process specification), and the extent to which this knowledge could be codified.

Whilst GVC literature provided the analytical framework to explore the process of linkage development, the emerging role of China and India as home countries of lead firms driving mineral GVCs, remained largely unexplored. Kaplinsky, Terheggen and Tijaja [2010] were an exception by looking at the impact of exporting to Chinese buyers rather than European ones. They found that the depth of local conversion of tropical products by Asian and African producing countries was reduced, with processing activities relocated to the Chinese food processing and furniture industries.

There was a paucity of GVC research also in terms of extractive industries, [Bridge, 2008; Morris, Kaplinsky, and Kaplan, 2012]. The question of linkage development opportunities however assumed growing importance as natural-resource seeking investments from Asia into Africa increased.

This chapter investigates the opportunities for local upstream linkage development in Chinese- and Indian-driven copper value chains operating in Africa. In particular, it is hypothesised that Chinese-driven value chains will operate differently from Northern-driven value chains because of the role of the state and the capital market imperfections underlying China's investment in African extractive industries. The literature suggests that Chinese-driven copper value chains should operate as enclaves, since one of the strategic objectives of China's OFDI projects is to increase sourcing of machinery and equipment from China. It is expected that Chinese-driven mining firms lack a corporate policy to increase local sourcing because economic efficiency and civil society pressure are not key drivers of their corporate decisions. However, reports of discrepancy between policies set in Beijing and the practice of Chinese corporations on the ground [Gill and Reilly, 2007; Li, 2010], open the door to the possibility that Chinese mining firms do not behave as enclaves. Moreover, given capital market imperfections in the home country, the Chinese-driven copper value chain is expected to be relatively insulated from the 2008/2009 economic crisis.

Indian-driven copper value chains are hypothesised as behaving similarly to Northern-driven value chains since they are privately owned and profit driven. This implies that economic efficiency, rather than broader, state-level strategic objectives, should inform the sourcing strategies of Indian firms operating in Africa. However, unlike Northern-driven value chains, it is expected that Indian mining firms are relatively unaffected by civil society pressures to increase economic opportunities for local suppliers.

Zambia offers a suitable case study to investigate these questions for several reasons. Firstly, it enjoyed a relatively peaceful history after decolonisation in 1964, and had a long history of copper mining, which implies that upstream linkages are somehow developed. It is thus possible to analyse changes across firms and time. These questions are important for Zambia's development trajectory as copper is the leading export sector and recipient of inward FDI. Lastly, the ownership structure of Zambia's copper industry is heterogeneous with Chinese, Indian, South African, Canadian, Australian and European investors. Copper is also an interesting mineral since it showed the lowest price volatility amongst hard commodities, experienced one of the highest price surges and attracted exploration activities on a global scale.

This chapter draws on primary data, mainly of a qualitative nature, collected through a cross-sectional survey conducted in the Copperbelt, North-Western and Lusaka Provinces, Zambia, in 2009. Interviews were based on a questionnaire that included both open-ended and closed-ended questions. Two parallel samples, comprising buyers (the mining companies) and suppliers, were instrumental in exploring their relationship along the value chain. According to the 2009 data, the sample of buyers covered 77 per cent of total copper production volume. The sample included mining companies from developed countries, South Africa and China. The total population of suppliers in 2009 is estimated to lie in a range of 150 to 200 firms based on private sector organisations' directories and data shared by the mining companies. The survey population was composed of 95 firms, which were mainly based in the supply clusters of Kitwe and Ndola, of which 50 firms were sampled (see Table 1). Moreover, key respondents from 16 public and private sector institutions provided qualitative data to shed light onto the policy dimension. Additional data was collected from the Zambia Consolidated Copper Mines (ZCCM) National Archive in Ndola. The archive hosts a valuable collection of documents concerning the copper sector during the pre-privatisation period.

Two important limitations of the data collected were was the lack of quantitative data and the difficult access to mining companies, as some were geographically remote or experiencing difficulties due to labour unrest. The political controversy surrounding the mining tax regime at the time of fieldwork made the mining companies' reluctant to share financial reports and procurement figures.

Table 1. Firms' sample characteristics, 2009

	Zambian owned	**Foreign owned**	**Joint Ventures**	**Sub-Total**
Manufacturers	8	14	1	23
Services	10	11	6	27
Sub-Total	18	25	7	50

Source. Author's fieldwork data

BACKGROUND ON ZAMBIA'S COPPER SECTOR: PAST AND PRESENT

Profile of Zambia's Copper Sector

Copper mining in Zambia dates back to the early twentieth century. The newly-independent Zambia nationalised the copper mines in 1969 and these were later consolidated into the Zambia Consolidated Copper Mines (ZCCM), which were majority-owned by the Zambian government (60.3 per cent), with a minority share owned by Anglo-American Corporation (27.3 per cent) [Lungu, 2008]. Nationalisation took place on the back of high copper prices and an ambitious policy agenda to anchor broad-based social and economic development to the copper sector. After the mid-1970s, Zambia's copper sector came under increasing pressure from, on the one hand, plummeting world copper prices, and on the other hand, as a result of limited re-investment by the government-owned producer in exploration, mine development, and crucially, in mines re-capitalisation. Copper output fell and revenues were largely used to subsidise social sectors [Lungu, 2008]. Falling production and revenues from the mining sector forced the government to increase dependence on foreign borrowings.

In the 1990s, Zambia undertook a Structural Adjustment Programme in which the privatisation of the copper sector was a core requirement for external donors. ZCCM was dismantled and, between 1997 and 2001, all the mines but one were sold to foreign investors. Transactions over Konkola Copper Mines (KCM), the largest mine at the time, were concluded in 2004. Thus, in a relatively short period, the ownership structure of Zambia's copper mines changed radically. Not only did ownership shift to private multinational companies, but also for the first time, Asian investors entered the sector as major players (Table 2). In 2009, the largest sources of FDI stock were Canada and India, which held 19.17 per cent and 17.10 per cent respectively of total inward FDI stock. Australia and Switzerland ranked third and fourth, holding around 11 per cent each of total FDI. China was the fifth largest investor.[11]

By 2011, additional large FDI flows targeting the mining sector originated from Australia (US$ 2.2 billion, Zambia's largest source of FDI stock), Canada (US$ 600 million), and China (US$ 250 million, the 4th largest source of FDI stock) [Bank of Zambia, 2012].

Table 2. Zambia's inward FDI stock (2009, US$ million and percentage)

			By component		
			Equity	Reinvested Earnings	Other capital
	US$ million	%	US$ million	US$ million	US$ million
Canada	1,433.00	19.17	98	1,335.00	0
India	1,277.90	17.10	564	172.2	541.7
Australia	810.4	10.84	751	58.1	1.3
Switzerland	805.4	10.78	37.9	46	721.5
China (incl. HK)	597.4	7.99	196.1	72.7	328.6
Netherlands	524.2	7.01	234.1	67.4	222.8
South Africa	510	6.82	61.1	137.3	311.6
UK	465.7	6.23	114.6	106.2	244.9
Africa (excl. ZA)	270.6	3.62	146.9	21.7	101.8
ROW	778.7	3.89	96.5	74.8	119.4
Total world	7,473.50	100.00	2,316.70	2,271.30	2,885.60

Source: Bank of Zambia, 2010

Table 3 shows the ownership structure of Zambia's copper sector. As in other African countries, Zambia's mineral sector had been traditionally dominated by American, European and South African corporations [UNCTAD, 2007]. In 2000, developed countries still held 78 per cent of Zambia's total inward FDI stock, while India and China together accounted for

---

[11] These are based on actual investment (Bank of Zambia) rather than pledged investment data (collected by the Zambia Development Agency).

only 4.6 per cent [UNCTAD, 2008]. By 2009, the aggregate share of FDI stock sourced from China and India however rose to 25 per cent as FDI flows increased.

China's entry into Zambia's mining sector has been gradual. With funding from China ExIm Bank, the state-owned China Non-Ferrous Metals Corporation (CNMC) acquired a small mine, NFC Mining Co (NFCA), in 1998. China's 2001 *going global* policy targeted strategic outward FDI projects in mineral resources which received comprehensive financial and political support [Morck, Yeung, and Zhao, 2008; Moss and Rose, 2006; Sauvant, 2004]. CNMC was one of China's largest state-owned enterprises, under direct supervision of the State-owned Assets Supervision and Administration Commission of the State Council (SASAC). CNMC corporate objectives were set out in central five-year plans, SASAC guidelines and with national policies to promote Chinese investment along the entire mining value chain [CNMC, 2010]. In the 2000s, CNMC's presence in Zambia's copper sector expanded with the acquisition of additional mines and a $800 million investment into the Chambishi Zambia-China Economic and Trade Cooperation Zone (ZCCZ). The key investments into this zone consisted of the Chambishi Copper Smelter, acid plants, and a copper semi-fabricates manufacturing plant.[12]

India is the most recent entrant into Zambia's mining sector. In 2004, London-based Vedanta Resources acquired KCM assets, with a commitment to develop the Konkola Deep Mining Project. This project was of key strategic importance targeting a three-fold increase in Konkola mines' output. Unlike the Chinese company, Vedanta was a listed company, which was similar to other large mining companies owned by Australian, European, North American, and South African interests.[13]

In 2010, Zambia was the largest copper producer in Africa and the seventh largest in the world. Copper exports jumped from $474 million in 2000 to almost $4 billion in 2008, falling to $3.17 billion in 2009 due to a drop in copper price, which was partially offset by increased production volumes. By 2011, copper exports reached US$ 6.8 billion, thanks to a combination of price recovery and new production, which brought total volumes to over 600,000 tonnes. In the 2007-2011 period, copper exports contributed around four fifths of total foreign exchange earnings, 10 per cent of formal employment, and 10 per cent of GDP. The positive performance of the copper sector in Zambia was the result of exceptionally favourable world copper prices, as well as the injection of new investment capital after privatisation. Investments by the new owners of the mines went into plant rehabilitation, expansions and new projects [Chamber of Mines, 2005].

Local Upstream Industries

The local supply chain in Zambia's mining sector was populated by a heterogeneous group of firms (Figure 2). The privatisation process that took place in the 1990s was a key event that shaped the composition of the Zambian mining sector's local supply chain [Fessehaie, 2012b]. Backward linkage development was a key component of Zambia's

---

[12] China was also investing in a US$ 500 million ZCCZ sub-zone in Lusaka for light manufacturing and services.

[13] In 2012 China Non-Ferrous Metals Corporation, which already owned two listed companies in China, announced plans to float its Zambian assets on the Hong Kong Stock Exchange [http://www.chinamining.org]. Chinese state-owned enterprises have access to significant internal resources because the state retains control of the majority of the shares and companies do not have to distribute dividends [Morck, Yeung, and Zhao, 2008].

industrialisation strategy during the period that mines were nationalised. Linkage development was pursued through a combination of direct state ownership of part of the supply industry, preferential sourcing, import substitution industrialisation and value chain cooperation between ZCCM, its suppliers and public research and training institutions [World Bank, 1992]. The local supply chain was characterised by significant manufacturing activity, undertaken by SOEs and family-run businesses established by European and Asian migrants.

In the 1980s however a combination of declining copper price, poor management of ZCCM and a fall in revenues resulted in critical problems for the supply chain [World Bank, 1992]. Economy-wide foreign exchange shortages and ZCCM liquidity constraints curtailed the supply firms' capacity to import parts and inputs, and ZCCM capacity to pay suppliers regularly and on time [ZCCM, 1994; World Bank, 1992]. Moreover, inefficient supply chain management by ZCCM implied weak capability to monitor suppliers and, if necessary, exclude them from the supply chain. Low levels of competition and weak R&D capabilities, among other factors, caused local manufacturers to fall behind international standards of quality and price performance [ZCCM, 1994; 1997]. Yet local manufacturers were not excluded from the supply chain because ZCCM was mandated to procure locally and lacked the foreign exchange to import. Moreover, procurement departments were often corrupt which created incentives for local suppliers to invest in personal networks in order to remain in the supply chain.

The privatisation process had a lasting impact on the extent and depth of Zambia's backward linkages to copper mining [Fessehaie, 2012b]. Respondents from the privatised mining companies explained that they focused on their core business, abandoning the previous strategy that saw ZCCM involved in a diversified range of non-mining related activities, such as tourism. The new mine owners introduced higher standards and applied supply chain management techniques developed in their global mining operations. Manufacturing activities declined, with few firms able to compete with imported goods, especially from South Africa. The services sector became predominant. Respondents from all the private sector organisations and government reported that, although some regional conglomerates invested in plants in Lusaka and Kitwe, most foreign and domestic investment moved into the service sector, which was less exposed to competition from imports. OEM suppliers relocated their manufacturing activities in low-cost production countries, whilst they established a direct presence in the Copperbelt, through subsidiaries focusing on distribution and after-sale services. By focusing on after-sale services and imposing warranty agreements, OEMs protected the profitable spare parts, repair, and maintenance supply links from competition. This strategy diminished the value-added content of their local activities and eroded the skill base in manufacturing activities, whilst it contributed to local skills creation in servicing and repair activities.

Only a few local service providers responded to the new market requirements by specialising into value-added, capital- and skills- intensive service activities, such as engineering services and specialised transport. By contrast, most service providers were positioned in the low value-added segments of the supply chain, characterised by low entry and exit barriers. The rise in number of low-value added suppliers was reported consistently by all respondents as the key feature of the Copperbelt supply industry in the 2000s, and was identified by supply chain managers in the mining companies as the most pressing constraint on supply chain development. These supply firms were import agents, generally operating on an ad hoc basis, without formal, established premises. Rather than developing technical competencies or specialising, these "briefcase businessmen" lobbied government and developed social networks within the mining companies to secure orders. With low overhead costs, their transactions were highly profitable and displaced established suppliers. Estimates of the number of these briefcase businessmen during this early post-privatisation period vary widely, between a few hundreds and 5,000. However, by 2009, most briefcase businessmen were no longer active. Following the copper price collapse in 2008, the mining companies focused intensively on cost-reduction and as a result excluded briefcase businessmen from the supply chain given that they were seen as inefficient and unreliable suppliers.

During the privatisation process, the Zambian government moved away from interventionist policies. This left firms to adjust without the support of skills, technological and industrial policies and with difficult and expensive access to investment and working capital.[14] From the mid-2000s, Zambia's National Development Plan and other industrial policy and strategy documents put more emphasis on private sector development, but focusing on export-oriented activities and copper mining beneficiation (2006 Fifth National Development Plan, 2008 Commercial, Trade and Industrial Policy; 2006 Zambia Development Agency Act). Moreover, the bilateral development agreements with the mining firms (signed under the provisions of the 1995 Mines and Minerals Act), included non-binding, best endeavor provisions of the development of local supply firms.

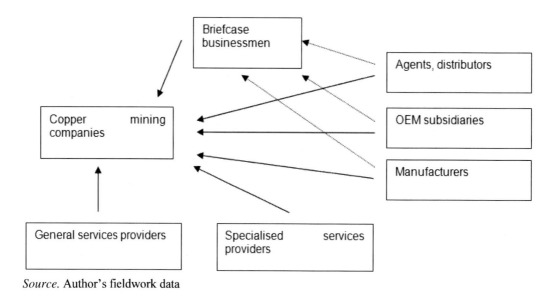

Source. Author's fieldwork data

Figure 2. Firms populating local upstream linkages to Zambia's copper mining sector.

---

[14] Zambia's ratio of private sector credit to GDP was lower than the average for low-income SSA [IMF, 2008]. Moreover, access to bank credit was extremely expensive, with one of the highest interest rates in the region. Bank loan rates ranged from 30-40 per cent for local currency in nominal terms (though in real terms, interest rates were 10.2 per cent in 2009), and 10-15 per cent on US dollar borrowing [IFC, 2005; World Development Indicators database, 2012; Interviews, 2009].

Table 3. Ownership structure of Zambia's copper sector, 2009

Mines	Investor	Year of acquisition	Corporate structure [a]	Mining assets	2008 Refined copper output
Kansanshi Copper-Gold Mines Plc	First Quantum Minerals Ltd, Canada (79,4%), ZCCM (20,6%)	2001	Listed on LSE, TSX	Kansanshi	215, 300 mt
Konkola Copper Mines Plc (KCM)	Vedanta Resources, India (79,4%), ZCCM (20,6%)	2004	Listed on LSE	Nchanga, Konkola, Chingola, Nampundwe, Chililabombwe	131, 700 mt
Mopani Copper Mines Plc	Glencore International AG, Switzerland (73,1%), First Quantum Minerals Ltd, Canada (16,9%), ZCCM (10%)	2000	Private equity	Nkana, Mufulira	113, 400 mt
Luanshya Mines	CNMC (85%), ZCCM IH (15%)	2009	SOE	Luanshya, Mulyashi	44, 500 mt
Chambishi Mines NFC Africa Mining Co	CNMC Corp (90%), ZCCM IH (10%)	1998	SOE	Chambishi	30, 700 mt
Chambishi Metals	CNMC (85%), ZCCM IH (15%)	2009	SOE	Chambishi smelter, slag dumps	21, 100 mt
Lumwana Copper Project	Equinox Minerals Ltd, Canada/Australia (95,6%), ZCCM HI (4,4%)	1999	Listed on ASX TSX	Lumwana	7, 200 mt (just started operations)
Bwana Mkubwa	First Quantum Minerals Ltd, Canada (79,4%), ZCCM (20,6%)	1997	Listed on LSE, TSX	SX-EW plants	5, 900 mt (but capacity of plus 30.000 mt)
Chibuluma	Metorex Limited, South Africa (85%), ZCCM IH (15%)	1997	Listed on the JSE	Kalulushi	5, 200 mt (Usually production averages 15, 000 mt)

Source. Fessehaie [2012a]

DISTINCTIVENESS OF CHINESE AND INDIAN DRIVEN COPPER VALUE CHAINS IN ZAMBIA

Three categories of mining firms were identified (see Table 4) in order to operationalise the concept of ownership. North American, European, and South African mining firms were categorised as *Traditional buyers or mining firms*. These types of buyers were characterised by Western corporate structures and incentive systems. They also had significant experience in the extractive sector. South African FDI closely matched FDI from the Western countries, in terms of size, sectors, and preference for formal governance structures [Henley et al., 2008]. In fact, the corporate behavior of South African and Western mining companies in Zambia were found to be largely similar.

The Indian mining firm entered Zambia's copper value chain through a large-scale brownfield investment, acquiring large copper mining assets as well as downstream processing units. It inherited old equipment and plants, which required significant re-capitalisation as well as investment to develop deep-mining projects. In contrast, the Chinese mining firm entered with a relatively small brownfield investment in copper production, and progressively expanded capacity in mining output and downstream processing.[1] The analysis of the Indian value chain was subject to a major limitation as the Indian buyer was not included in the buyers' sample. The analysis of the Indian value chain therefore was based on data sourced from the suppliers' sample and from the sample of key institutions. Both groups of respondents were remarkably consistent in the responses they provided.[2]

Table 4. Buyers' sample characteristics

Category	Case-studies	Key features
Traditional buyers	Kansanshi Mines Bwana Mkubwa Mopani Copper Mines Chibuluma	Home countries: Canada, Switzerland, South Africa; all but one were listed companies
Chinese buyers	NFCA just acquired Luanshya Copper Mines and Chambishi Smelter	Chinese ownership SOE Not listed
Indian buyers	KCM	Indian ownership Privately owned Listed

Source. Author's compilation from various sources

---

[1] The establishment year and type of investment could impact on local supply chain development. A time lag may occur before buyers become familiar with the local supply cluster and develop supply relationships. Moreover, greenfield investors may require long time to develop local supply relationships because they do not inherit existing procurement systems. Establishment year and type of investment cut across ownership: the sample characteristics of these buyers ensured that Chinese and Indian mining firms were no different from Traditional buyers in this respect.

[2] KCM was reluctant to grant an interview, probably because it was under intense scrutiny and criticism over its failure to pay suppliers during the economic crisis. Furthermore, an uprising in Chingola over miner wages made it not possible to attempt further contact.

In this section three aspects of value chain governance by Traditional, Chinese and Indian mining firms are discussed, which are: entry and selection of suppliers; market parameters set in the supply chain; and the upgrading of local supplier capabilities.[3] Each of these aspects of governance impact on the opportunities for local supplier firms to enter the mining value chain and to upgrade.

Entry and Selection of Suppliers

Entry barriers for local suppliers were critically determined by the extent and nature of outsourcing by mining companies. In other words, what mattered for the entry of local firms was the 'make or buy' decision of mining companies and the extent to which goods and services were purchased locally rather overseas.[4]

Traditional mining firms tended to outsource activities outside their core business [Chamber of Mines, 2005]. They preferred a localised supply chain whenever possible because dealing with overseas suppliers increased transaction costs, for example US suppliers who were unfamiliar with Zambia required upfront payment.

Traditional buyers selected suppliers on the basis of well-established procurement procedures based on selective tenders. Traditional buyers relied heavily on past relationships as a selection criterion when they registered preferred suppliers. The effectiveness of this selection criterion was reinforced by the tendency of Traditional buyers to employ their procurement staff from a small labour pool, which often consisted of expatriates. These employees had worked in many Traditional mining firm procurement departments and had developed trusting relationships with preferred suppliers, which they carried with them when they moved between mining firms. The trust content of these relationships was high because the Traditional mining firms were socially embedded in a small business community. Selection based on past relationships ensured that suppliers were reliable and knew the operating requirements of the mines, but it excluded new, potentially competitive entrants. Traditional buyers also had a high level of brand loyalty for critical supply links, such as capital equipment and components. This made it easy for OEM subsidiaries and distributors of established brands from Europe, Australia, North America and South Africa to maintain their market positions. In contrast, distributors of new brands were at a disadvantage.

Traditional buyers did grant some market access for non-critical supplies to well-connected briefcase businessmen as a result of political pressure. Traditional buyers re-organised their supply chains as prices collapsed in 2008, tightening the screening process, reducing the presence of briefcase businessmen and focusing on developing relationships with selected, capable suppliers. Buyers conducted direct auditing of the premises of all registered and potential suppliers. The auditing process nevertheless became selective and

---

[3] The overwhelming majority of supply firms agreed that ownership mattered in shaping their relationships with buyers. In general, the categorisation proposed is consistent with the views of the respondents. They referred to "Indians" and "Chinese" as two very distinct types of buyers, and treated Traditional buyers as a homogenous group.

[4] It was not possible to compare quantitative data on local procurement across mining firms because of they referred to different years, some included fuel and electricity costs, some contracted labour, and generally the mining firms were reticent in sharing detailed financial records with researchers.

entry barriers remained high for many potential suppliers because resources allocated to the buyer procurement departments were insufficient.

In comparison, the Chinese mining firm was more vertically integrated. The Chinese buyer had considerable room for manoeuvre to set up its organisation when it acquired Chambishi Mine, as it did not inherit supply contracts or capital equipment. From the early stages, the Chinese mining company invested in in-house engineering services (electrical, mechanical) and a foundry in order to minimise the risk of relying on local suppliers that did not meet its expectations in terms of volume and price. Exploration and drilling services were also vertically integrated. The Chinese buyer's strategy curtailed opportunities for local suppliers in these sub-sectors.

Whilst the Chinese buyer was more vertically integrated than its Traditional counterparts, it nevertheless procured a wide range of goods and services locally and regionally, including: capital equipment and spares, explosives, steel plates, oil, rubber products, cement, lubricants, tyres, components, and personal protective equipment. This finding is further corroborated by the analysis of import flows of mining supplies presented in Figure 3. South Africa was the key supply hub for the Zambian mining sector, accounting for more than half of total imports in the 1998-2009 period. China became a significant supplier only from 2005 onwards, supplying 9 per cent of total imports between 2005 and 2009. Interviews with mining managers confirmed that efficiency and price were driving procurement decisions. This suggested a misalignment between the Chinese mining firm's outsourcing strategy and the formal corporate objectives of the parent company, which targeted expansion both upstream and downstream in the metal mining value chain.

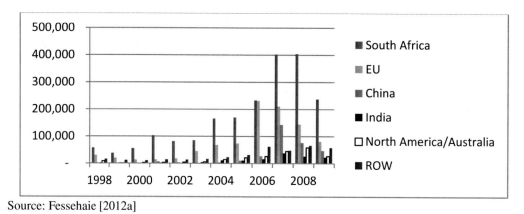

Source: Fessehaie [2012a]

Figure 3. Imports of mining-related capital equipment, 1998-2009 (US, '000).

Entry barriers to the Chinese supply chain were low. Chinese buyers were willing to try new products, new suppliers and they had low brand loyalty. Poor knowledge of local suppliers and cultural and language barriers opened the supply chain to a large number of briefcase businessmen during the early stages of the investment. The Chinese buyer acquired a closed mine, unlike other companies, inheriting only 112 employees who had been retained for care and maintenance. The Chinese expatriate staff was relatively segregated from local communities, living and socialising in different physical spaces. This curtailed the buyer's opportunity to absorb pre-existing organisational practices, and meant it had to set up new systems [Haglund, 2010]. The Chinese buyer re-organised its supply chain over time so as to exercise stronger governance over the selection of participants. The Chinese buyer invested and relied on extensive auditing since it lacked the social embeddedness with historical suppliers which characterised the Traditional buyers. Many suppliers reported being visited by the Chinese buyer immediately after bidding for a tender, when they had to to wait a long time before Traditional buyers would agree to visit their premises.

The Indian mining firm was more vertically integrated than Traditional buyers, similar to the Chinese buyer, for example the firm built an in-house equipment maintenance unit. The Indian buyer did not appear to pursue backward integration with suppliers in its home country. Imports of mining capital supplies from India ranged between 3 and 5 per cent (see Figure 3) from the time of the acquisition of KCM in 2004 until 2009.

Entry barriers to the Indian supply chain were low, particularly for non-critical supply links. The Indian supply chain was markedly price-driven also as a result of the 2008/2009 economic crisis, when the mining firm experienced liquidity problems that delayed payments to local suppliers by several months. The Indian buyer switched to new suppliers and new brands during this period in order to avoid disruptions in the supply of goods and services. This was relatively easy to do for non-critical supply links, which were characterised by low quality and reliability entry requirements and intense competition between local firms, including briefcase businessmen. By maintaining low entry barriers, Indian buyers were also able to negotiate lower prices with new suppliers who were eager to enter the market, as well as with regular suppliers who were willing to make sacrifices to remain in the supply chain.

Critical Success Factors

The market parameters set by the buyers are referred to as critical success factors (CSFs). CSFs are *'order qualifying'* (that is, firms need to achieve these in order to participate in these markets), or *'order winning'* (that is, the critical factors which lead particular firms to succeed, perhaps by selling at a price premium). In the past, these CSFs largely consisted of price and reliability, but they are increasingly determined by other factors (quality, lead times, standards) and differentiated by value chain, market, and sector [Kaplinsky and Morris, 2001].

In this section, we focus on CSFs such as price competitiveness, product quality, lead times, trust, reliable delivery, and the capacity to learn and keep up with innovation. CSFs vary depending on whether they concerned critical or non-critical supply links. 'Critical supply' was defined as 'supplies which, if not available, could cause production to stop'. The financial implications of a failure in a supply link, therefore, defined how 'critical' a supply was. Criticality was affected by scarcity which is determined by the degree of competition along a specific supply link and the level of competences of local suppliers. Such supplies included, among others, equipment and maintenance services of valves, pumps, hydraulics, lime, etc. This correlates with the view of Humphrey and Schmitz [2001] that the determinants of governance are not the intrinsic characteristics of the product, such as its closeness to the technological frontier, but rather the risks faced by the buyers. This risk is defined by uncertainties on the suppliers' competences and by losses incurred if the suppliers fail to perform.

Table 5. Critical Success Factors in Traditional, Chinese and Indian value chains

CSF	Traditional value chain	Chinese value chain	Indian value chain
Quality	Order-qualifying CSF for all supplies	Order-qualifying CSF for critical supplies	Not important
Trust	Order-qualifying CSF for all supplies	Order-winning CSF for all supplies	Not important
Lead times	Order-winning CSF for all supplies	Order-winning CSF for all supplies	Order-winning CSF for all supplies
Learning and innovation capabilities	Order-winning CSF for all supplies	Not important	Not important
Price	Order-qualifying CSF for all supplies	Order-qualifying CSF for non-critical supplies	Order-winning CSF for all supplies

Source. Author's fieldwork data

Table 5 summarises variations in CSFs by buyer ownership. Quality was an order-qualifying CSF in both the Chinese and Traditional value chains. Mining is a long-term investment, in which buyers tend to focus on total cost of supply, which takes into account the cost of spares and components, maintenance requirements and product performance during the entire life-span of the product. The supply of high quality products was cost-effective in the long period. Moreover, there were critical supplies for which high quality reduced the risk of a breakdown, which could result in potentially negative consequences for operations. For example, poor quality pumping systems increased the risk of flooding and the consequent suspension of ore extraction activities. Quality-based parameters were the result of a learning process in the Chinese value chain. Cost-cutting strategies resulted in defective equipment and long lead times during the early phases. Total costs of supply increased with time, as sub-standard products broke down and required replacement or repairs. The Chinese buyer hence became increasingly quality-conscious for critical supply links, such as capital equipment and components.

In the Indian value chain, in contrast, quality was markedly less important. Procurement managers were placing small orders to be supplied at low cost and with short lead times as price became the paramount CSF and short-term cost-cutting measures became prevalent. Competing exclusively on price was difficult for Zambian suppliers operating in a high cost environment. This emphasis on price-only competitiveness meant that the Indian buyer was also unwilling to enter into after-sale agreements, which were critical to support the upgrading of service providers into stock-holding functions, and maintenance and repair functions.

Trust was intended both in terms of competence trust (firm's competence to provide products and services at high professional standards) and contractual trust (suppliers would fulfil their contractual obligations). In the Traditional supply chain, trust was an order-qualifying CSF, and it was built through long term relationships and high social embeddedness. In the Chinese supply chain, building trust took more time and resources because of language and cultural barriers. Suppliers who took the initiative to build a relationship with the buyer had to invest resources to earn trust. Low initial levels of trust caused inefficient outcomes, as buyers failed to devise technical and operational solutions jointly with the suppliers. By sharing the costs of these failed projects, suppliers invested in reputational assets and long-term relationships (see Box 1). In this sense, trust became an order-winning CSF.

Box 1. Building trust-based relationships in the Chinese driven value chain

Two critical, high-performing suppliers explained the long process required to build relationships in the Chinese supply chain. One supplier was promptly audited by the Chinese buyer, but its small physical premises did not convince the buyer of the firm's capabilities. The firm was given the opportunity to enter the Chinese buyer's supply chain only after more than one year. When the buyer requested assistance with a technical problem with the pumping equipment, the firm conducted underground work several times without compensation. The firm invested in the relationship by working closely with Chinese operations personnel, providing advice, solving technical problems and explaining the characteristics of their products. Low trust levels and language barriers proved to be the main challenges. The firm eventually gained the trust of the buyer's procurement, engineering and production departments. Building trust enabled the firm to establish a solid business relationship with the buyer. The manager reported that "it's difficult to get them to trust you, but once they do, the business relationship is good".

Another large, well-known supplier incurred significant sunk costs to enter the Chinese supply chain. The Chinese buyer provided the wrong specifications for a large construction project, ignoring the supplier's advice, and the project failed. The supplier was paid, but decided to re-do the project at its own expenses. The manager explained, "we wanted to prove [to] the Chinese that you can work with us, we are not just there to make money…I want to build a relationship for the long-term and I want to preserve my reputation". He continued, "we'll provide good technical advice and would rather extend the payment terms in order to do a proper job rather than take shortcuts and get paid immediately". The Chinese buyer then re-contracted the supplier for a long-term project. The Chinese ZCCZ Vice Deputy Manager confirmed that this was an example of a good partnership (Interviews, 2009). The supplier was able to expand its capacity and diversify into new products in order to meet the demand of ZCCZ.

Source: Interviews, 2009

In the Indian value chain, reciprocal trust was low due to poor information flows and widespread corruption. Suppliers identified price negotiations as the main content of their relationship. In fact, the Indian buyer engaged in multiple price negotiations for the same transaction. These negotiations were unbalanced given the suppliers' high transactional dependency on the Indian buyer (the largest mining company in 2009). Profit margins for most local suppliers squeezed as a result, but their threat to exit their supply chain was not credible because competition was stiff. Only OEMs and other critical suppliers could exert a credible threat to exit the supply chain, because they supplied critical equipment and services and because competition was limited. For this reason, they were the only group of suppliers not affected by delayed payment schedules.

Lead times were an order-winning CSF in Chinese, Indian and Traditional value chains. In particular suppliers highlighted that the Chinese buyer expected the goods to be delivered "on-the-spot" and preferred multiple, ad hoc purchases rather than large batches that required maintaining large stocks. In general, short lead times enabled buyers to outsource stock-holding of spares, materials and components. Poor access to capital by local suppliers nevertheless constrained investment in the stock-holding which was critical to reducing lead times.

Learning and innovation capabilities were important for Traditional buyers. This was an order-winning CSF irrespective of the technological intensity of the supply links. Traditional buyers created incentives for suppliers to innovate and upgrade by placing emphasis on innovation, as these efforts would be rewarded in the market place. The Chinese and Indian buyers attached less weight to learning and innovation capabilities compared to Traditional buyers. These buyers failed to recognise the benefits of such dynamics capabilities because they found it difficult to develop a trust-based relationship and to engage in problem solving jointly with suppliers. This reduced incentives for suppliers to upgrade and innovate.

Buyers differed substantially on the role of price. The Indian value chain was markedly price-driven. Price was similarly one of the most important CSFs for Traditional buyers. Price became an order-qualifying CSF for them, within the context of quality and trust. The Chinese buyer by contrast rated price significantly less than quality, lead times, trust and reliability. This reflected a shift for the Chinese buyer from a predominantly price-driven supply chain to a quality-driven one. The Chinese buyer nevertheless further qualified this requirement. The supply chain for non-critical supply links was markedly more price-driven and the buyer was willing to compromise on quality.

The variance in the rating of price as a CSF can be attributed to underlying differences in corporate response to the 2008/2009 economic crisis. All the non-Chinese mining firms were listed companies with the exception of one, and thus faced shareholder value responsibilities and transparency requirements. The mining industry generally resorted to production cuts, cost cutting measures and halting new investment projects when faced with falling copper prices and a credit crunch [ICSG, 2009]. Table 6, drawn from company reports for 2009, illustrates responses by non-Chinese mining companies in Zambia. All of the mines focused on cutting production costs. The Indian mining firms in particular cut costs by a sharp 52 per cent, which squeezed local suppliers' margins and delayed payments by as much as six months. Only critical suppliers (OEMs, fuel companies) managed to be paid, by coordinating efforts and threatening to suspend supplies. Low profit margins and payment delays meant that suppliers who relied heavily on supplying the Indian buyers struggled to remain in business, and did not invest in upgrading.

The Chinese mining firm in contrast had a counter-cyclical expansion, with the acquisition and re-capitalisation of a new mine and continued investment in the China-Zambia Chambishi Economic Zone. The Chinese buyer did not cut production or development projects, and neither retrenched workers. The Chinese buyer instead focused on selecting suppliers on the basis of efficiency, quality and reliability. Price was weighted much less in its rating of CSFs for this reason.

Table 6. Anti-crisis corporate strategies by selected mining companies, 2009

Company	Response to the crisis	Production costs
Chibuluma	Cash flow improvement Increased production volumes Lower capital expenditures (largest capital investment were undertaken in previous years)	Cash costs increased from US$ 2663/t in 2008 to US$ 2793/t in 2009
Kansanshi, Bwana Mkubwa	Cost saving programme, lower input costs Increased production volumes	Production costs in 2009 at US$ 0.99/pound, 15% lower than in 2008
Konkola Copper Mines Plc (KCM)	Cost curtailment; Renegotiate all contracts for supplies, commodities and logistics Increase recoveries Shut down of high-cost Nkana smelter Reduced manpower by 2000 workers Continuation of construction of new smelter and Konkola Deep Mining Project	Production costs decreased from 292.8 centr/lb in 2008 to 140 cents/lb in March 2009
Lumwana Copper Project	Improving suppliers' after-sale services for capital equipment	US$ 1.49/pound (1st year of production)

Source. Fessehaie [2012a]

Relationship with Suppliers

Buyers were generally dissatisfied with the performance of the local supply chain. Their response to weak local supplier capabilities, in terms of cooperation to upgrade local suppliers, varied considerably along ownership patterns (Table 7).

Table 7. Nature of buyers-suppliers relationships

Traditional buyers	Chinese buyers	Indian buyers
Long-term relationship Formalised, selective Direct and indirect cooperation for supply chain upgrading	For critical supply links: trust-based, informal agreements For non-critical supply links: arm's length relationships No cooperation	Arm's length relationship Arms' length relationships No cooperation Late payments, low trust

Source. Author's fieldwork data

Traditional mining firms were aligning their supply practices to global practices that were becoming predominant also in the global mining sector [Walker and Minnitt, 2006]. These required buyers to focus on core competence, reduce the size of supply networks to fewer, bigger suppliers, set highly detailed and demanding standards for core suppliers, and intensively monitor supplier performance. The key implication of a more selective and supportive approach to supply chain management was that value-addition had to increase in the local supply chain. For example, as a response to the economic crisis, Traditional buyers focused on outsourcing stock-holding functions, because they increased inventory and warehousing costs, tied up working capital, and were not part of the buyer's core business. In order to outsource this function, buyers focused on developing long-term relationships with a selective number of suppliers with which they concluded forward purchasing agreements (FPAs). Whist this process was highly selective (Box 2), it was also more conducive to foster upgrading processes as suppliers could plan investment in stock levels, improve inventory management processes on the basis of agreed prices and volumes, and had the collateral to access working capital from the bank.

Box 2. Forward Purchasing Agreements: exclusion and upgrading

Long-term contracts helped suppliers plan in advance and invest in upgrading. Building selective, long-term relationships, nevertheless, implied that other suppliers exited from that particular supply link.

A Traditional buyer re-organised its supply chain for personal protective equipment (PPE) in 2001-02 by outsourcing procurement functions for all equipment to an intermediary firm. The intermediary firm purchased from local manufacturers and from overseas. One of the suppliers interviewed was sub-contracted by this intermediary firm. The supplier was able to increase its profit margins by charging the standard price with no discounts, and was able to plan production and investment in advance.

In 2004 another company was contracted by the mining firm to coordinate PPE supplies. This new company shifted to another local manufacturer, also included in our sample. The latter was able to expand its market and undertake process and product upgrading. The first supplier, on the other hand, found it very difficult to re-enter the supply link. In sum, there was a trade-off between the number of participants in the supply chain and the opportunity to upgrade.

Source: Interviews (2009)

Traditional buyers cooperated with their suppliers directly or indirectly to achieve upgrading, with two out of three buyers doing both. The type and frequency of cooperation are shown in Table 8. Indirect cooperation took place through the International Finance Corporation Suppliers Development Programme. In terms of direct cooperation, buyers engaged consistently in intense information exchange flows and negotiations. They also provided advance payment to improve delivery reliability, and assisted suppliers with transport to reduce lead times. By transporting products domestically and from South Africa, buyers reduced lead times and transport costs because they consolidated different batches of supplies and dealt with freight, customs etc. Less frequently, the buyers would assist suppliers with product quality improvement, jointly running quality tests and providing quality feedbacks. There was a preference for longer-term contractual relationships, as discussed previously.

Traditional buyers rarely engaged in deeper forms of cooperation, such as joint product development, staff training, technical upgrading and development of quality assurance systems. There was however one exception, with one of the three buyers assisting suppliers to develop internal quality assurance systems by sending qualified personnel to audit supplier structures and processes and provide technical recommendations.

Table 8. Type and intensity of Traditional buyers' cooperation with their suppliers (frequency)

	Not at all	Sometimes	Consistently
Information exchange		1	2
Negotiation of payment and delivery conditions		2	1
Joint product development	2	1	
Cooperation for product quality improvement		3	
Actions to improve delivery time		1	2
Actions to improve delivery reliability	1		2
Actions for adapting production to smaller / larger batches	2	1	
Change suppliers less than before		2	1
Cooperation in technical upgrading	2	1	
Cooperation in staff training	3		
Cooperation in developing quality assurance system	2	1	

Source. Author's fieldwork data. *Note.* n=3

The Chinese buyer displayed distinctively different characteristics in respect of assistance to firms within its supply chain. Its relationship with suppliers was fundamentally market-based. Chinese buyers were consistently reported by suppliers as "very good customers" and "result-oriented". They paid on-time and reduced red tape to the minimum. Opening up entry opportunities to suppliers however did not translate into strategies facilitating or supporting upgrading. The Chinese buyer did not provide any direct or indirect assistance to suppliers. Indeed, the buyer engaged consistently only in negotiations regarding payment and delivery times, and did not engage in any other forms of cooperation indicated in the questionnaire.

The exception to the Chinese mining firm's primarily market-based supply chain relationships was in respect of critical products and services, with the Chinese firm being willing to move to longer term relationships in critical supply links. Price negotiations ceased once the trust relationship was built to be the only determinant of the relationship, with tacit agreements that good performance be rewarded with more orders.

The Indian buyer relied on arm's length market transactions: low trust, no brand or supplier loyalty, high propensity to switch suppliers and no cooperation.[5] Suppliers reported that the Indian buyer did not provide suppliers with an opportunity to discuss problems, but rather rescinded contractual relationships immediately. The underlying reason, according to few suppliers, was that the Indian buyer lacked the solid technical experience of other mining houses. They pursued a short-term, profit-maximising perspective which left no room for investment in an efficiency- and quality- driven supply chain.

---

[5] Only one firm inserted in the Indian value chain reported cooperating with the buyer in sourcing raw materials.

A recurrent theme emerging from the interviews was the contrast with supply chain management by the previous owner, Anglo-American Corporation (AAC), which ran KCM mining assets from 2000 to 2002. AAC developed trust-based relationships with suppliers, including practices such as cooperation on quality management, open book accounting, open door policy, joint product development and promotion of linkages between South African manufacturers and local firms. AAC also set up the first supplier development programme in the Copperbelt. The Indian mining firm inherited it and completed it, but this was not followed up by orders to the suppliers as envisaged by the programme. Neither was supply chain development included in its Corporate Social Responsibility (CSR) Policy. The buyer failed to internalise supply chain development in its own long-term strategy similar to the Chinese lead firm. The Indian buyer did not provide direct or indirect assistance, and its supply chain management negatively impacted supplier incentives and resources to upgrade.

A different level of internalisation of supply chain development underlined the variance in governance types between Traditional, Chinese and Indian buyers. The Chinese mining company relied heavily on government-to-government intermediation [Buckley et al., 2008; Haglund, 2010]. Zambia and China concluded five cooperation agreements spanning the multi-facility economic zones, cooperation in the mining sector, infrastructural projects, and cultural exchanges. The Chinese mining firm did not see local supply chain development as part of its corporate strategy and did not invest in embedding itself into the local cluster. It was not registered in the Chamber of Mines or active in the Kitwe Chamber of Commerce and Industry, and did not participate in the IFC Suppliers Development Programme. In its view, localisation of upstream linkages was the responsibility of the Zambian government and was to be catalysed by investment in the China-Zambia Chambishi Economic Zone. The Indian mining firm could not rely on government-to-government intermediation. Such a relationship with the local business community was inherited by AAC whilst it was formally a member of the Chamber of Commerce and Industry as well as the Chamber of Mines.[6] This made little substantial difference when compared to the Chinese buyer. These institutional mechanisms were only marginally successful in facilitating negotiations with suppliers when the Indian buyer suspended payments to local suppliers during the economic crisis.

Mining firms from developed countries and from South Africa in contrast saw local supply chain development as part of their CSR activity, including the need for their suppliers to meet health, safety and environmental standards (Company Reports for 2009). Two out of three Traditional buyers indeed indicated that whilst the supply chain was driven by efficiency and profit-maximisation, there was an element of CSR behind the decision to favour local suppliers in some non-critical areas, such as civil construction of local schools. No such policy existed in the Chinese or Indian value chains. Moreover, Traditional buyers were also the only group of buyers to engage in forms of horizontal cooperation. While the content and effectiveness of such cooperation were still weak, buyers were supporting an institutionalised form of cooperation - the Zambia Institute of Purchasing and Supply – which aimed at building local supply chain management and development expertise.

---

[6] Anglo-American Corporation, now called Anglo-American, acquired KCM assets thanks to a provision in the nationalisation measures of 1969 that granted AAC the right to buy back KCM if the mines were to be privatised. After agreeing to acquire KCM by the government in 2000, AAC reversed its decision two years later, assessing KCM as not profitable.

LOCAL SUPPLY CHAIN TRAJECTORIES

This section now turns to a firm-level analysis of supply chain performance based on survey data for 50 suppliers. Firm-performance is assessed in relation to sales growth in the five years preceding the industry downturn in 2008, in the absence of detailed financial data for responding firms. On this basis, three categories of supply firms are identified: dynamic, static and declining firms.[7] The supplier's upgrading trajectory is also considered in discussing these categories. Upgrading is reflected in terms of the value chain theoretical approach discussed earlier, namely process, product, functional and chain upgrading. Process upgrading was broken down into various actions: improvement of the quality of existing products/services, improvement in production processes through new machineries, enhanced workers' skills, reduction in lead times, introduction and improvement of total quality management systems, and introduction of new organizational and or management techniques. In order to sift out what appeared to be trivial efforts at upgrading, process upgrading was only recognised when two or more changes in manufacturing process were undertaken since most respondents were unable to provide quantitative estimates of expenditure on process upgrading. Product upgrading was defined as introduction of new products, functional upgrading as undertaking new functions, for example design or servicing, and chain upgrading as the movement into a different value chain.

Dynamic Firms

24 firms, or 48 per cent of the total sample, were positioned on a trajectory of growing sales to the mining sector, and upgrading. All of these firms were inserted into the Traditional buyers-driven value chain. One third of the firms supplied Traditional buyers only, either out of an explicit corporate strategy or as the only opportunity to enter the mining supply chain under the IFC Suppliers' Development Programme. The remaining two thirds of this group also supplied Chinese and Indian buyers. These firms supplied a variety of products: mining capital equipment, spares and components, engineering services, specialised transport services, consumables.

Linkages to Traditional buyers were important to support the dynamic firms' upgrading processes. Only Traditional buyers supported suppliers' upgrading efforts according to respondents from the supply firms. Table 9 shows the type and frequency of assistance received by supply firms. Information flows and negotiations were intensive. Between 41.7 and 50 per cent of suppliers cooperated with their Traditional buyers on an ad hoc basis or, to a less extent, consistently on the following: joint product development, actions to improve quality of specific products, lead times, and delivery reliability. More than half of the growing firms moved towards longer-term relationships with their buyers. Cooperation nevertheless did not tackle areas such as the establishment of quality assurance systems, technical upgrading and staff training. Traditional buyers' supply chain development efforts focused on suppliers characterised by the following: critical suppliers, medium or low capability, strong

---

[7] Sales growth in the ensuing discussion refers to sales to the mining sector. A number of supplier firms also sold into non-mining sectors.

locational advantages. Traditional buyers also cooperated with non-critical suppliers indirectly, through the IFC Suppliers Development Programme.

Table 9. Dynamic suppliers' trajectory: Type and intensity of vertical cooperation with buyers (frequency and percentage)

Type of cooperation	Not at all	Sometimes	Consistently	NA
Information exchange	5 (20.8)	10 (41.7)	9 (37.5)	
Negotiation of payment and delivery conditions	3 (12.5)	8 (33.3)	13 (54.2)	
Joint product development	14 (58.3)	10 (41.7)		
Cooperation for product quality improvement	12 (50.0)	10 (41.7)	2 (8.3)	
Actions to improve delivery time	12 (50.0)	11 (45.8)	1 (4.2)	
Actions to improve delivery reliability	14 (58.3)	8 (33.3)	2 (8.3)	
Actions for adapting production to smaller / larger batches	18 (75.0)	3 (12.5)		3 (12.5)
Change suppliers less than before	10 (41.7)	9 (37.5)	4 (16.7)	1 (4.2)
Cooperation in technical upgrading	23 (95.8)	1 (4.2)		
Cooperation in staff training	22 (91.7)	1 (4.2)	1 (4.2)	
Cooperation in developing quality assurance system	21 (87.5)	3 (12.5)		

Source. Author's fieldwork data. *Note.* n=24

For one important sub-group, engineering firms, market expansion opportunities were curtailed by two factors. Firstly, they were locked out of a valuable market as the Chinese buyer vertically integrated engineering services whilst the Indian buyer internalised some maintenance services. Secondly, their competitive advantage was progressively eroded by an ageing workforce. Such workforce was difficult to replace due to the poor public technical education system and market failures which made internal training costly. Skills scarcity constrained upgrading into high-tech repairing services and expansion into larger volumes of business.

Another important source of cooperation was backward linkages to parent companies abroad, which characterised 71 per cent of the suppliers inserted in a dynamic trajectory. Local supply firms inserted in such value chains consisted of mining OEM subsidiaries, distributing mining equipment and spares, and providing after-sale services; manufacturers owned by international or regional corporations; and sole distributors of OEMs and manufacturers based in South Africa, US, Europe, and Australia. The parent companies and technology suppliers provided incentives and resources (capital, knowledge, know how) to pursue product and process upgrading. All the firms with these types of backward linkages operated on global standards.[8]

---

[8] Neither the nationality of ownership nor the sub-sector of activity emerged as important factors in the upgrading efforts of suppliers. Almost one third of this group of supplier firms was Zambian-owned, and 42 per cent of

Many firms in the dynamic trajectory pursued 'deep' forms of upgrading (that is, upgrading on a number of fronts) (Figure 4). In total, process upgrading was undertaken by 83 per cent of the firms. More than half of the firms (54 per cent) focused exclusively on process upgrading, mainly in terms of improvement of production processes. They did so by investing in capital equipment, upskilling their workforce and introducing or improving their quality management systems. A third of this group invested in a combination of product, process or functional upgrading. Lastly, three firms undertook functional and chain upgrading, moving into more demanding value chains, which was an exception in the total sample of suppliers.

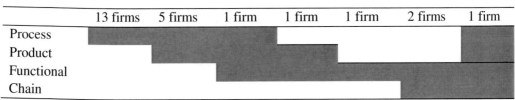

Source. Author's fieldwork data. Note. n=24

Figure 4. Dynamic suppliers' trajectory: type of upgrading processes (frequency).

Static Firms

Static suppliers comprised a group of seven smaller firms with largely unchanged sales (in real terms, taking account of inflation). They were established after privatisation, and most of them relied on the expertise of the owner, who also managed every aspect of the firm. Whilst individual expertise was sufficient for them to remain in business, these small-scale firms failed to grow into more complex managerial and organisational structures that could accommodate upgrading processes. Moreover, they supplied non-critical products characterised by high levels of competition and low entry barriers. Whilst most static suppliers also supplied Traditional buyers, they received no assistance from their buyers because their links were marginal in the mining companies' supply chain management strategy (for example pharmaceutical products, cars, civil engineering).

Declining Firms

There were 19 firms positioned in a declining trajectory, of which seven fared particularly badly in terms both of sales growth and upgrading.[9] The distinctive feature of this group was their exclusion from tightly governed value chains. In terms of forward linkages, these firms operated in supply links characterised by low locational advantages and low knowledge and capital entry barriers, which implied that no buyer had interest in assisting them. Some of these firms however benefitted from the IFC Suppliers Development

---

the group were manufacturing firms, producing inputs such as plastic and steel products, office furniture, paints, consumables and personal protective equipment.

[9] Declining firms were losing orders from buyers and were characterised by shrinking profit margins and sales. However they had not exited from the mining supply chain yet.

Programme. Table 11 shows the type and intensity of assistance received by declining firms. Information exchange and negotiations were intensive, with 74 and 85 per cent of firms respectively reporting ad hoc or continuous engagement. Another 42 per cent of firms cooperated occasionally or consistently on product quality and delivery reliability, whilst 54 per cent of firms benefitted from the collective transport arrangements set up by Traditional buyers. In terms of joint product development and longer contractual relationships however only 26 and 32 per cent of firms, respectively, received any assistance, compared with 42 and 54 per cent of dynamic firms. Moreover, between 84 and 95 per cent of firms received no assistance in improving production processes, establishing quality assurance systems, and in technical upgrading, or workers training.

Table 10. Declining suppliers' trajectory: type and intensity of vertical cooperation with buyers (frequency and percentage)

Type of cooperation	Not at all	Sometimes	Consistently
Information exchange	5 (26.3)	6 (31.6)	8 (42.1)
Negotiation of payment and delivery conditions	3 (15.8)	10 (52.6)	6 (31.6)
Joint product development	14 (73.7)	4 (21.1)	1 (5.3)
Cooperation for product quality improvement	11 (57.9)	6 (31.6)	2 (10.5)
Actions to improve delivery time	9 (47.4)	6 (31.6)	4 (21.1)
Actions to improve delivery reliability	11 (57.9)	7 (36.8)	1 (5.3)
Actions for adapting production to smaller / larger batches	16 (84.2)	2 (10.5)	1 (5.3)
Change suppliers less than before	13 (68.4)	4 (21.5)	2 (10.5)
Cooperation in technical upgrading	17 (89.5)	2 (10.5)	0
Cooperation in staff training	18 (94.7)	1 (5.3)	0
Cooperation in developing quality assurance system	16 (84.2)	3 (15.8)	0

Source. Author's fieldwork data. *Note.* n=19

This group was largely composed of manufacturing firms (13 out of 19) that were established and flourished during the period of import-substitution industrialisation. As such, they lacked backward linkages to MNEs, unlike the OEM subsidiaries or domestic suppliers of foreign technology. Manufacturers lost market shares because they had been excluded from the supply links for spares and components, controlled by the OEMs and their subsidiaries. Furthermore, they could not compete with the R&D, global production networks and economies of scale of OEMs. For services providers, exclusion from GVCs prevented access to external knowledge and resources, in particular capital. Profit margins were very low and often squeezed further when transacting through briefcase businessmen, since they operated in price-driven supply links.[10]

---

[10] OEM subsidiaries would charge briefcase businessmen the same price they would charge the mine, sometimes more. As they were the exclusive distributors, briefcase businessmen had no choice but to accept their price. Local manufacturers, on the other hand, were competing with each other to receive orders from well-connected briefcase businessmen.

Figure 5 shows the type of response undertaken by these firms. For seven firms, there was no capability to arrest their exit from the mining value chain, as they undertook no upgrading effort. What set apart 12 other firms was their efforts to upgrade in the face of declining sales to the mining sector. Process and product upgrading was undertaken by firms out of their own resources, but often with the objective of diversifying into the following non-mining sectors: generic consumer goods and components for the transport industry. Other firms upgraded within the IFC Suppliers' Development Programme. The programme's impact was however limited due to low absorption capacity and poor access to capital in the context of high real interest rates. Other firms changed their functions in the chain but a closer look suggests that *downgrading* was more frequent than upgrading, as the new functions were less technologically demanding.

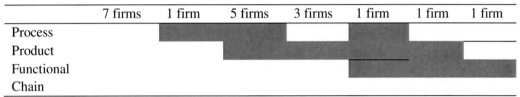

Source. Author's fieldwork data. *Note.* n=19

Figure 5. Declining suppliers' trajectory: type of upgrading processes (frequency).

Conclusion

Booming commodity prices and investment flows in Africa's extractive industries open important opportunities for local upstream industries development. This chapter investigated the impact of China and India's FDI in Zambia's copper sector on the trajectory of local supply firms. Some of these firms had a long history of supplying the mining sector because during the mines nationalisation period, upstream linkages development was seen as key to the country's industrialisation strategy. Zambia's local supply chain together with these older firms was populated by firms established after the mines privatisation, which were mostly service providers. Indeed the fast-paced dismantlement of interventionist policies by the Zambian government had a profound impact on the level of value added taking place in the local supply chain. As manufacturing value added shrank, more firms entered the mining supply chain in links characterised by very low levels of value added content, such as basic trading operations.

Opportunities for local supply firms to remain competitive and upgrade were largely determined by internal dynamics to the mining value chains as the Zambian government substantially withdrew from policies to support local suppliers, not only by removing protectionist measures, but also by reducing support for, among others, skills development, technological upgrading and access to capital. This chapter found that such dynamics were significantly shaped by buyers' ownership patterns. Three distinctive value chains in particular were identified: one driven by Northern and South African mining firms, one driven by the Chinese mining firm, and one driven by the Indian mining firm.

Whilst the literature suggests that the Chinese mining firm would operate as enclave, sourcing goods and services from the home country, this chapter found that local suppliers had important market access opportunities to the Chinese value chain. Some supply links were curtailed because they had been vertically integrated by the Chinese buyer, but overall, a broad range of supplies were outsourced locally, and especially from South Africa, the regional hub for mining supplies. Moreover, for critically important supplies, it was observed that market requirements of the Chinese buyer were converging with those of Northern and South African buyers. Procurement decisions were based on quality, reliability and lead times considerations. This was the result of a learning curve in which the Chinese buyer focused on total cost management and privileged established, reputable suppliers to briefcase businessmen. Supplier selection was conducted on the basis of a broad-based auditing process, because the buyer could not rely on high level of social embeddedness in the local business community. This, in turn, guaranteed new entrants and new brands an opportunity to enter the supply chain.

As expected, the Chinese value chain was largely insulated by the 2008/2009 economic crisis, which allowed the mining firm to expand investment in Zambia's copper sector with positive effects on local suppliers. Such countercyclical investment was underlined by the state-owned mining firm privileged access to state resources and its pursuance of long term strategic objectives related to access to copper resources. Whilst entry opportunities for local suppliers were significant, the Chinese value chain did not offer any form of cooperation to upgrade local supplier capabilities. This failure to internalise supplier development functions can be ascribed to its reliance on state-to-state relations, and a lack of pressures to adopt corporate social responsibility policies.

The Indian value chain showed problematic aspects in terms of local upstream industries development. Unlike the Chinese one, the Indian mining firm was severely and negatively affected by the economic crisis. As a result, cost-cutting measures were put in place which consisted of maintaining very low entry barriers, delaying payment to existing suppliers, and emphasising price and lead times in the firm procurement decisions. Due to the local suppliers' dependence on its supply chain, it was possible for the Indian buyer to sustain this strategy during and after the crisis, and, in effect, to shift its investment risks on local suppliers. This strategy undermined the opportunity for local suppliers not only to upgrade, for which no assistance was put in place, but also to remain in the mining supply chain. In fact, many suppliers went out of business because delayed payments implied they could not honour their debts with local commercial banks. The lack of a CRS policy was noticeable in this, as well as in the Chinese, value chain.

If buyer-supplier cooperation could not be found in the Chinese and Indian value chains, only other forms of linkages, namely backward linkages in the form of equity (local subsidiaries) and non-equity (sole distributorship agreements) relationships allowed some local suppliers to participate of their value chains and perform well in terms of sales, and product and process upgrading. If firms lacked these backward linkages, success in the mining supply chain required them to participate in the value chain driven by Northern and South African mining companies. Entry barriers were high in these value chains, because buyers had high levels of social embeddedness and relied on historical suppliers, but for selected suppliers who did participate, there were formal and informal mechanism of cooperation which facilitated local upgrading processes. Whilst these buyer-supplier relationships were instrumental in promoting local upgrading process, it is important to underline the limitations of such cooperation. It did not extend to the areas of skills, technological upgrading, product design, and quality management systems.

For Zambia, this has multiple implications. Firstly, in order to seize the opportunity to develop local upstream industries linked to the booming copper mining sector, Zambia has to engage with the mining companies and encourage them to engage in formal and informal buyer-supplier cooperation. In doing this, a strategy has to be devised which takes into account the variance in value chain governance amongst different owners, as the issues that need to be dealt with differ in the Chinese, Indian, Northern and South African value chains. This strategy should not be cast in stone, because the distinctive characteristics of Chinese and Indian value chains may change. As the Chinese private sector becomes increasingly involved in outward investment projects, in future, there could be a convergence with FDI from Northern countries. Listed, privately-owned Chinese companies might differ a little from their Northern counterparts. On the other hand, as few Indian SOEs invest in Africa's extractive industries, they could resemble Chinese SOEs in some aspects, for example on the countercyclical nature of their investment patterns.

Secondly, Zambia needs to develop an industrial strategy to assist local manufacturing firms and services providers with skills, technology, access to capital and management capabilities. Whilst this is true for other manufacturing and services sectors, local upstream industries are characterised by some attractive features from a policy perspective in that they are composed of a significant number of firms, relative to the Zambian context, and the demand for mining supplies is destined to grow as Northern and emerging economies invest in Zambia and its neighbouring country, the Democratic Republic of Congo, where the copper mining sector is expanding considerably.

ACKNOWLEDGMENTS

I am grateful for the generous assistance of Raphael Kaplinsky and Mike Morris under the Making the Most of Commodities research programme (http://commodities.open.ac.uk/mmcp), as well as the comments of an anonymous external reviewer.

REFERENCES

African Union. (2009). *African mining vision 2050*. Addis Ababa, Ethiopia.
African Union. (2008). *Action Plan for the Accelerated Industrial Development of Africa*. 10th Ordinary Session of the African Union Assembly of Heads of State and Government held in Addis Ababa, Ethiopia, in January 2008.
African Union, & UNECA. (2013). *Making the most of Africa's commodities: Industrialising for growth, jobs, and economic transformation.* (Economic report on Africa 2013). Addis Ababa, Ethiopia: Economic Commission for Africa.
Aggarwal, R. & Agmon, T. (1990). The International Success of Developing Country Firms: Role of Government-Directed Comparative Advantage. *Management International Review* 30 (2), 163-180.

Bank of Zambia. (2012). Foreign Private Investment and investor perceptions in Zambia – 2012. Lusaka, Zambia. Retrieved on 15/04/2013 from http://www.boz.zm/

Bank of Zambia. (2010). Foreign Private Investment and investor perceptions in Zambia – 2010. Lusaka, Zambia. Retrieved on 15/04/2011 from http://www.boz.zm/

Bartos, P. J. (2007). Is mining a high-tech industry? Investigations into innovation and productivity advance. *Resources Policy, 32*(4), 149-158.

Brautigam, D. (2009). *The dragon's gift: The real role of China in Africa.* Oxford, UK and New York, NY: Oxford University Press.

Bridge, G. (2008). Global production networks and the extractive sector: Governing resource-based development. *Journal of Economic Geography, 8*(3), 389-419.

Broadman, H. (2007). *Africa's silk road: China and India's new economic frontier.* Washington, DC: The World Bank.

Buckley, P. J., Cross, A. R., Tan, H., Xin, L., & Voss, H. (2008). Historic and emergent trends in Chinese outward direct investment. *Management International Review, 48*(6), 715-748.

Buckley, P., A. Cross, H. Tan, Xin, L., & Voss, H. (2007). The determinants of Chinese outward foreign direct investment. *Journal of International Business Studies* 38, 499–518.

Business Daily. (2013). *Africa should strive for more benefits from ties with China.* (31.3.2013). Retrieved from http://www.businessdailyafrica.com/Opinion-and-Analysis/Africa-should-strive-for-more--benefits-from-ties-with-China/-/539548/1735384/-/6j2pcfz/-/index.html

Chamber of Mines of Zambia. (2005). *Survey of the Zambian mining industry 1995 to 2004.* Ndola, Zambia: Mission Press.

Cheng, L. K., & Ma, Z. (2010). China's outward foreign direct investment. In R. C. Feenstra, & S. J. Wei (Eds.), *China's growing role in world trade* (pp. 545-578). Chicago, IL: University of Chicago Press.

Cheung, Y-W & Qian, X. (2009). Empirics of China's outward foreign direct investment. *Pacific Economic Review* 14, 312–41.

China Non-Ferrous Metals Corporation (2010). *Company profile.* Retrieved from http://www.cnmc.com.cn

Culverwell, M. (2000). *The mining cluster in Antofagasta: Integrating small and medium suppliers into the productive chain.* Unpublished manuscript.

Davies, K. (2009). While global FDI falls, China's outward FDI doubles. *Columbia FDI Perspectives, 5*, 1-3.

Dollar, D., & Wei, S. J. (2007). *Das (wasted) kapital: Firm ownership and investment efficiency in China.* (Report No. 13103). Cambridge, MA: National Bureau of Economic Research.

Dunning, J. H. (1977). Trade, location and economic activity and the multinational enterprise: A search for an eclectic approach. In B. G. Ohlin, P. O. Hesselborn & P. M. Wijkman (Eds.), *The international allocation of economic activity* (pp. 395-418). London, UK: Macmillan.

Dunning, J. H. (1981). *International production and the multinational enterprise.* London, UK: Allen & Unwin.

Farooki, M., & Kaplinsky, R. (2012).*The impact of China on global commodity prices: The global reshaping of the resource sector.* London, UK: Routledge.

Fessehaie, J. (2012a). *The dynamics of Zambia's copper value chain*. (Unpublished PhD Thesis). University of Cape Town, South Africa.

Fessehaie, J. (2012b). What determines the breadth and depth of Zambia's backward linkages to copper mining? The role of public policy and value chain dynamics. *Resources Policy* 37, p. 443 – 451.

Gelb, S. (2010). *Foreign direct investment links between South Africa and China*. (Paper prepared for African Economic Research Consortium project on China-Africa Economic Relations). Johannesburg, South Africa: The EDGE Institute.

Gereffi, G. (1994). The organization of buyer-driven global commodity chains: How United States retailers shape overseas production networks. In G. Gereffi & M. Korzeniewicz (Eds), *Commodity Chains and Global Capitalism*. (pp. 95-122). Westport, CT: Praeger.

Gereffi, G. (1999). International trade and industrial upgrading in the apparel commodity chain. *Journal of International Economics 48*(1), 37-70.

Gereffi, G., Humphrey, J., & Sturgeon, T. (2005). The governance of global value chains. *Review of International Political Economy, 12*(1), 78-104.

GFMS. (2011). *Copper survey 2011*. London, UK: GFMS Ltd.

Gill, B. & Reilly, J. (2007). The tenuous hold of China Inc. in Africa. *Washington Quarterly 30*(3), 37-52.

Gupta, N. (2005). Partial privatization and firm performance. *The Journal of Finance, 60*(2), 987-1015.

Haglund, D. (2010). *Policy evolution and organisational learning in Zambia's mining sector*. (Unpublished PhD Thesis). University of Bath, UK.

Hattari, R., & Rajan, R. S. (2010). India as a source of outward foreign direct investment. *Oxford Development Studies, 38*(4), 497-518.

He, W., & Lyles, M. A. (2008). China's outward foreign direct investment. *Business Horizons, 51*(6), 485-491.

Henley, J., Kratzsch, S., Külür, M., & Tandogan, T. (2008). *Foreign direct investment from China, India and South Africa in sub-Saharan Africa: A new or old phenomenon?* (Research Paper No. 2008/24). Helsinki, Finland: UNU- World Institute for Development Economics Research.

Humphrey, J. & Schmitz, H. (2001). Governance in global value chains. *IDS Bulletin* 32 (3), Brighton: Institute of Development Studies.

Humphrey, J., & Schmitz, H. (2002). How does insertion in global value chains affect upgrading in industrial clusters? *Regional Studies, 36*(9), 1017-1027.

Humphrey, J., & Schmitz, H. (2001). Governance in global value chains. *IDS Bulletin, 32*(3), 19-29.

Humphrey, J., & Schmitz, H. (2000). *Governance and upgrading: Linking industrial cluster and global value chain research*. (IDS Working Paper No. 120). Brighton, UK: University of Sussex.

Humphreys, D. (2009). *Emerging players in global mining*. (Extractive Industries for Development series Report No. 5). Washington, DC: World Bank.

Hurst, L. (2011). Comparative analysis of the determinants of China's State-owned outward direct investment in OECD and non-OECD countries. *China & World Economy, 19*(4), 74-91.

International Copper Study Group (ICSG). (2010). World copper factbook 2010, Lisbon: ICSG.

International Copper Study Group (ICSG). (2009). Impact of lower copper prices and world economic downturn on copper supply and demand, *ICSG Insight 5*. Lisbon: ICSG.

Jenkins, R., & Edwards, C. (2006). The economic impacts of China and India on sub-Saharan Africa: Trends and prospects. *Journal of Asian Economics, 17*(2), 207-225.

Kaplinsky, R. & Morris, M. (2009). Chinese FDI in Sub-Saharan Africa: Engaging with large dragons. *European Journal of Development Research* 21(4), 551–59.

Kaplinsky, R. & Morris, M. (2001). A Handbook for value chain research', Institute of Development Studies, University of Sussex, www.globalvaluechains.org

Kaplinsky, R., Terheggen, A., & Tijaja, J. P. (2010). *What happens when the market shifts to China? The Thai cassava and Gabon timber value chains.* (World Bank Policy Research Working Paper No. 5206). Washington, DC: World Bank.

Kumar, N. (2007). Emerging TNCs: Trends, patterns and determinants of outward FDI by Indian enterprises. *Transnational Corporations, 16*(1).

Kuo, C. C. (2007). The productivity efficiency of state-owned enterprises. In S. Lin, & S. Song (Eds.), *The revival of private enterprise in China* (pp. 257-269). Aldershot, UK: Ashgate.

Lall, S. (1980). Vertical inter-firm linkages in LDCs: An empirical study. *Oxford Bulletin of Economics and Statistics, 42*(3), 203-226.

Li, W., & Putterman, L. (2008). Reforming China's SOEs: An overview. *Comparative Economic Studies, 50*(3), 353-380.

Lungu, J. (2008). Copper mining agreements in Zambia: Renegotiation or law reform? *Review of African Political Economy, 35*(117), 403-415.

Mikesell, R. F. (1971). The contribution of petroleum and mineral resources to economic development. In R. F. Mikesell (Ed.), *Foreign investment in the petroleum and mineral industries: Case studies of investor-host country relations* (pp. 3-28). Baltimore, MD: Johns Hopkins Press.

Morck, R., Yeung, B., & Zhao, M. (2008). Perspectives on China's outward foreign direct investment. *Journal of International Business Studies, 39*(3), 337-350.

Morris, M., Kaplinsky, R., & Kaplan, D. (2012). One thing leads to another: Promoting industrialisation by making the most of the commodity boom in sub-Saharan Africa. Raleigh: North Carolina, Lulu.com.

Moss, T. & Rose, S. (2006). China ExIm Bank and Africa: New lending, new challenges. *CGD Notes*. Washington: Centre for Global Development.

Naughton, B. (1994). What is distinctive about China's economic transition? State enterprise reform and overall system transformation. *Journal of Comparative Economics, 18*(3), 470-490.

Nayyar, D. (2008). The internationalization of firms from India: Investment, mergers and acquisitions. *Oxford Development Studies, 36*(1), 111-131.

OECD. (2008). *Investment policy reviews - China 2008: Encouraging responsible business conduct.* Paris, France: Organisation for Economic Co-operation and Development.

Pal, P. (2008). *Surge in Indian outbound FDI to Africa: An emerging pattern in globalization?* Mimeo.

Pradhan, J. P. (2009). *The global economic crisis: Impact on Indian outward investment.* (Paper No. 16579). Munich, Germany: Munich University.

Pradhan, J. P. (2008). *Indian direct investment in developing countries: Emerging trends and development impacts.* (Paper No. 12323). Munich, Germany: Munich University.

Pradhan, J. P. (2007). *Growth of Indian multinationals in the world economy: Implications for development.* (Paper No. 2007/04). Munich, Germany: Munich University.

Pradhan, J. P. (2004). The determinants of outward foreign direct investment: A firm-level analysis of Indian manufacturing. *Oxford Development Studies, 32*(4).

Radetzki, M. (2008). *A handbook of primary commodities in the global economy.* New York, NY: Cambridge University Press.

Sauvant, K. P. (2004). New sources of FDI: The BRICs. Outward FDI from Brazil, Russia, India and China. *The Journal of World Investment & Trade, 6*(5), 639-709.

Sharma, S. D. (2009). *China and India in the age of globalization.* New York, NY: Cambridge University Press.

Soares de Oliveira, R. (2008). Making sense of Chinese oil investment in Africa. In C. Alden, D. Large & R. Soares de Oliveira (Eds.), *China returns to Africa: A rising power and a continent embrace* (2nd ed., pp. 83-109). London, UK: Hurst.

Southern Africa Development Community (2012). SADC Industrial Development Policy Framework, 2012.

Sun, S. L., Peng, M. W., Ren, B., & Yan, D. (2012). A comparative ownership advantage framework for cross-border M&As: The rise of Chinese and Indian MNEs. *Journal of World Business, 47*(1), 4-16.

Tolentino, P. E. (2008). *The determinants of the outward foreign direct investment of China and India: Whither the home country?* (Working Paper 2008-049). Helsinki, Finland: UNU-World Institute for Development Economics Research.

UNCTAD (2013). *Global Investment Trends Monitor.* Special Edition 25 March 2013. Retrieved from http://www.safpi.org/sites/default/files/publications/webdiaeia2013d6_en.pdf

UNCTAD. (2011). World Investment Report 2011: Non-equity modes of international production and development. New York: United Nations.

UNCTAD. (2008). Africa Investment Directory, Volume X, New York and Geneva: UNCTAD.

UNCTAD. (2007). World Investment Report 2007: Transnational corporations, extractive industries and development. New York: United Nations.

UNCTAD, & UNDP. (2007). *Asian foreign direct investment in Africa: Towards a new era of cooperation among developing countries.* New York, NY and Geneva, Switzerland: United Nations.

Walker, M. I., & Minnitt, R. C. A. (2006). Understanding the dynamics and competitiveness of the South African minerals inputs cluster. *Resources Policy, 31*(1), 12-26.

Wang, J. Y. (2007). *What drives China's growing role in Africa?* (WP/07/211). Washington, DC: International Monetary Fund.

World Bank, & IFC. (2003). *Mining reform and the World Bank: Providing a policy framework for development.* Washington, DC: IFC.

World Bank. (1992). *Program performance audit reports: Export rehabilitation and diversification project (loan 2391-ZA).* ZCCM National Archives (File 2.5.4i), Ndola, Zambia.

Yao, S., Sutherland, D., & Chen, J. (2010). China's outward FDI and resource seeking strategy: A case study on Chinalco and Rio Tinto. *Asia-Pacific Journal of Accounting & Economics, 17*(3), 313-326.

Zambia Consolidated Copper Mines Ltd. (1997, February 15). *Evaluation and monitoring team review of procurement procedures and practices.* ZCCM National Archives (File 24.7.8b), Ndola, Zambia.

Zambia Consolidated Copper Mines Ltd. (1994, April 28). [Letter from Techpro Procurement]. ZCCM National Archives (File 8.1.5c, Shelf 9.5.94), Ndola, Zambia.

Zambia Consolidated Copper Mines Ltd. (1992). *Contract placement procedures manual for working cost expenditures routine and minor projects (G2/92).* ZCCM National Archives (File n/a), Ndola, Zambia.

Zhan, J.X. (1995). Transnationalization and outward Investment: The case of Chinese firms. *Transnational Corporations* 4 (3), 67–100

Zhang, A., Zhang, Y., & Zhao, R. (2001). Impact of ownership and competition on the productivity of Chinese enterprises. *Journal of Comparative Economics,* 29(2), 327-346.

In: Foreign Direct Investment (FDI)
Editors: Enzo Guillon and Lucas Chauvet

ISBN: 978-1-62808-403-0
© 2013 Nova Science Publishers, Inc.

Chapter 2

WHAT DETERMINES PRODUCTIVITY SPILLOVERS FROM FOREIGN DIRECT INVESTMENT? A CASE STUDY OF MEXICO

Jacob A. Jordaan[*]
Department of Economics and Business Administration, VU University, Amsterdam, the Netherlands

ABSTRACT

There is a growing acceptance of the idea that spillovers constitute a central component of the impact that FDI firms create in a variety of developed and developing host economies. These non-market effects occur when foreign-owned firms act as source of new knowledge and technologies, resulting in positive efficiency or productivity effects among domestic firms. The actual evidence on these productivity effects is characterized by a considerable degree of heterogeneity, however. Overall, it appears that evidence of positive spillovers that occur between industries is more robust than findings on intra-industry spillovers. In particular, suppliers of FDI firms in host economies may benefit from positive productivity effects.

In response to the large degree of heterogeneity of the evidence on the overall prevalence of FDI spillovers, recent research is focusing on identifying factors that influence these externalities. In particular, several studies look at the role of inter-firm linkages as channel of FDI spillovers, the level of technological differences between FDI and domestic firms and the location pattern of economic activity within host economies.

In this chapter, I critically examine research on these potential determinants. I do this in the following way. First, I conduct a selective survey of research on these factors, focusing on limitations and inconsistencies in the research approaches and available evidence. Findings on the importance of inter-firm linkages as channel of FDI spillovers are of a mixed nature. Econometric evidence on the importance of these inter-firm linkages is indirect of nature and does not clarify how spillovers are transmitted. Findings from more qualitative research are more informative on this, but suffer from the feature that it is not clear whether FDI firms are different from comparable domestic firms

---
[*] Email: j.a.jordaan@vu.nl

regarding the degree to which they share technologies with their suppliers. Also, the actual impact on the suppliers is usually omitted from the analysis. Research on the effect of the technology gap between FDI and domestic firms is hindered by the feature that different studies report positive effects of either a small or large technology gap. Findings of a positive effect of a large technology gap on spillovers are in strong contrast to the standard interpretation of the technology gap as direct inverse indicator of the level of absorptive capacity of domestic firms. As for research on the effect of location patterns of economic activity in host economies, there is a strong prediction that agglomeration enhances FDI spillovers. However, there are only a small number of studies that look at this direct relation.

Second, I conduct a selective review of studies on FDI spillovers in Mexico and I conduct new multivariate analysis using data that I collected among foreign-owned and Mexican producer firms and local suppliers in the North East of Mexico. In contrast to most host economies that have been the subject of one or a small number of FDI spillovers studies, there is a multitude of evidence on the spillover impact of foreign-owned firms in the Mexican economy. Importantly, several recent studies on Mexico specifically address the importance of inter-firm linkages, the technology gap and agglomeration as potential determinants of FDI spillovers. The multivariate analysis that I conduct is focused on obtaining further evidence on whether FDI firms differ from Mexican producer firms in terms of the level and nature of technology transfers that they provide their suppliers with. Also, the analysis investigates whether and how the level of technological differences between producer firms and their local suppliers influences positive impacts that the suppliers may experience as a result of their business linkages with their client firms.

The main findings from the survey of research on FDI spillovers in Mexico can be summarized as follows. First, most studies present evidence that indicates that Mexican firms are subject to FDI spillovers. Studies that only look at intra-industry effects tend to find positive productivity effects among Mexican firms. Studies that distinguish between intra-industry and inter-industry effects find that positive effects are particularly pronounced among suppliers of FDI firms. Second, the technology gap enhances FDI spillovers. The estimated positive effect of the technology gap contradicts the traditional interpretation of this gap as inverse indicator of absorptive capacity of domestic firms. Instead, a large technology gap captures the large scope for domestic firms to improve, offering incentives to these firms to try and absorb new technologies. Third, agglomeration and geographical proximity between firms enhance FDI spillovers. At the same time, spillovers do also materialize between Mexican regions. Finally, the analysis of the survey data from the North East of Mexico strongly supports the notion that FDI firms create positive spillovers among their suppliers and that the technology gap enhances this impact. FDI firms are significantly more involved in several types of technology transfers than comparable Mexican producer firms. This applies in particular to technology transfers that have a direct impact on the production processes of suppliers. Findings from the multivariate analysis show that suppliers of FDI firms are more likely to experience large positive impacts, even after controlling for the levels of support that they receive from their client firms. The positive effect of the technology gap is also confirmed, as the likelihood that suppliers experience large positive impacts from their business dealings with their client firms is enhanced by a large technology gap between the two types of firms.

1. INTRODUCTION

Recent decades have seen a rapid growth of empirical research on spillovers from Foreign Direct Investment (FDI). Productivity spillovers arise when the presence and operations of foreign-owned firms influence the performance of domestic firms through non-market effects. In particular, FDI firms may act as source of new technologies, resulting in improved efficiency or productivity among domestic firms. In line with the growing emphasis on the importance of externalities in processes of economic growth and development, there is an increasing belief that FDI spillovers constitute a central component of the impact that FDI firms generate in the world economy (Venables and Barba-Navaretti, 2005; Caves, 2007). In fact, for many developing economies, FDI firms may represent the only or at least the main source of new technologies (UNCTAD, 2005; Dunning and Lundan, 2008).

The actual empirical evidence on positive FDI spillovers is mixed, however. This applies in particular to evidence on the occurrence of intra-industry spillovers, productivity effects among domestic firms that operate in the same industries as the foreign-owned firms. Following initial findings that suggest that domestic firms benefit from positive intra-industry spillovers, more recent studies present a variety of findings ranging from significant positive to insignificant to significant negative externalities (Görg and Greenaway, 2004; Lipsey and Sjöholm, 2005). Findings on FDI spillovers that arise between industries appear somewhat more robust. In particular, several studies present findings that suggest that suppliers of FDI firms in host economies benefit from positive externalities (e.g. Blalock and Gertler, 2008; Smarzynska, 2004). Having said this, other studies fail to identify such positive effects, further questioning the overall prevalence of positive spillovers that can be linked to FDI firms (Jordaan, 2009; 2012a).

In response to this high level of heterogeneity of the body of evidence, recent research is attempting to improve the empirical identification of FDI spillovers by looking at factors that may influence these externalities. Although there is a variety of such factors that may be important (see Blomström and Kokko, 2003), the literature reflects that three factors are investigated most frequently. These factors are inter-firm linkages as channel of FDI spillovers, the technology gap between FDI and domestic firms and the location pattern of economic activity within host economies. However, the evidence of the effects of these determinants also appears to be characterized by a considerable degree of heterogeneity, caused by inconsistencies in the interpretation of the determinants or degrees of incompleteness of the empirical analysis of their effects.

For instance, findings from econometric studies that identify positive FDI spillovers between industries are taken as evidence that inter-firm linkages facilitate these externalities. However, such findings only constitute indirect evidence that inter-firm linkages do indeed play such a role. It also remains unclear how and why spillovers may be transmitted via these inter-firm linkages. As for the effect of the technology gap, there is conflicting evidence that a small or a large technology gap can promote positive spillovers. Furthermore, the standard interpretation of the technology gap as direct inverse indicator of the level of absorptive capacity of domestic firms appears to be inconsistent with underlying theoretical considerations (Jordaan, 2012a; 2013). Finally, the importance of the location pattern of economic activity in a host economy relates to the notion that agglomerations of activity can influence FDI spillovers. Although there are strong indications to expect that agglomeration or geographical proximity between firms can have a direct impact on FDI spillovers (see Jordaan, 2009; 2008b), the majority of research does not look at this direct effect. Instead, several studies try to assess whether FDI spillovers occur across geographical space within host economies (see e.g. Driffield, 2006). Although evidence of such spatial spillovers is clearly important, it does not fully clarify whether and how agglomeration or geographical proximity between firms influences productivity spillovers from FDI firms.

The purpose of this chapter is to analyse research that tries to assess whether and how inter-firm linkages, the technology gap and agglomeration or geographical proximity are important for FDI spillovers. I do this by conducting a selective survey of empirical research on FDI spillovers in Mexico. Many host economies have been subject to one or a small number of FDI spillover studies. In contrast, the impact of FDI firms in Mexico has been the subject of empirical research for several decades, offering a richness of evidence that is not available for other host economies. Importantly, inter-firm linkages, the technology gap and agglomeration feature in several recent studies on FDI spillovers in the Mexican economy, offering a good opportunity to analyses the role of these determinants. In extension of surveying existing evidence, I also present new evidence on the importance of FDI firms and the technology gap for the creation of spillovers by analyzing data from firm-level surveys that I conducted among FDI and Mexican producer firms and local suppliers in the North East of Mexico.

The chapter is constructed as follows. In section two I provide a selective review of evidence and the limitations of current research on the effects of inter-firm linkages, the technology gap and agglomeration on FDI spillovers. In section three I review key studies on FDI spillovers in Mexico, focusing on evidence that relates to these determinants. A majority of studies on the impact of FDI in Mexico identify externality effects. Most of the studies that look only at intra-industry spillovers present findings that suggest that Mexican firms benefit from positive externality effects. However, findings from studies that distinguish between intra- and inter-industry effects suggest that positive spillovers occur mainly among suppliers of FDI firms. As for the effect of the technology gap, most studies find that a large gap fosters positive spillovers, in direct contrast to the interpretation of the technology gap as inverse indicator of the level of absorptive capacity of domestic firms. Instead, the estimated positive effect of the technology gap suggests that this gap captures the scope for domestic firms to improve. Findings on the spatial dimensions indicate that agglomeration clearly enhances FDI spillovers. At the same time, there is also evidence that FDI spillovers materialize between regions within Mexico.

In section four I conduct multivariate regression analysis using data that I obtained from surveying FDI and Mexican producer firms and local suppliers in the North East of Mexico. In this analysis, I focus on obtaining more detailed evidence on whether FDI firms are creating positive spillovers among local suppliers and whether and how the technology gap influences these effects. The findings are in strong support of the notions that type of ownership and the technology gap both influence spillovers. Findings from the survey among producer firms indicate that these firms are involved in a variety of types of technology transfers, trying to improve the performance of the local suppliers. FDI firms are significantly more involved in creating these technology transfers than Mexican firms when it comes to trying to improve actual production processes of the suppliers. Looking at the suppliers, Mexican firms that operate as supplier to FDI firms are significantly more likely to experience positive impacts from their business dealings with these firms. This positive effect is robust to controlling for the level of support that the suppliers receive from their client firms. Furthermore, suppliers are also significantly more likely to experience large positive impacts when the level of technological differences with their client firms is large, in line with the notion that a large technology gap fosters rather than hinders the occurrence of positive spillovers.

Finally, section five summarizes and concludes.

2. DETERMINANTS OF FDI SPILLOVERS: A SELECTIVE LITERATURE REVIEW

2.1. Introduction

Multinational enterprises (MNEs) play a central role in the world economy. Via engaging in FDI in a large number of host economies, MNEs are one of the key channels via which new technologies are disseminated internationally (Venables and Barba-Navaretti, 2005; Caves, 2007; Dunning and Lundan, 2008). Countries benefit from inward FDI as it enhances the overall level of technology in their economies. Furthermore, in addition to this direct technology effect, host economies may benefit from important indirect effects when efficiency or productivity of domestic firms is influenced by the presence and operations of foreign-owned firms. For instance, domestic firms may learn about new technologies that are used by FDI firms. If domestic firms are able to absorb these new technologies into their production processes, any resulting efficiency or productivity effects constitute positive externalities, as there is no market capturing these technology flows (Blomström and Kokko, 1998). In addition to such demonstration effects, productivity spillovers may also occur via processes of labor turnover, when domestic firms benefit from hiring workers that gained special skills when previously working for FDI firms (Lipsey and Sjöholm 2005). Inter-firm linkages constitute another channel of spillovers, when FDI firms act as source of new technologies to domestic supplier firms in host economies. Finally, domestic firms may also be forced to become more productive via the occurrence of a competition effect, as the entry of FDI firms enhances the level of competition on the host economy market. If domestic firms are unable to respond to the increase in competitive pressure and see their market share decrease considerably, they may experience negative externalities as a result of a decrease in scale economies in their production (see Aitken and Harrison, 1999).

There is a growing acceptance that FDI spillovers constitute a central component of the impact that FDI firms may generate in host economies. However, the empirical evidence is far less consistent. Early studies present findings of a positive association between productivity of domestic firms or industries and the industry presence of FDI, which is interpreted as evidence of positive intra-industry FDI spillovers (Görg and Greenaway, 2004). However, findings from more recent studies challenge the notion that positive FDI spillovers are prevalent. For instance, Barrios and Strobl (2002) and Girma et al. (2001) find no substantial evidence of positive FDI spillovers. Furthermore, Aitken and Harrison (1999) and Djankov and Hoekman (2000) present evidence of a negative association between the industry presence of FDI firms and productivity of domestic firms, suggesting that FDI firms may create negative externalities.

Findings on inter-industry externalities appear more robust in suggesting that FDI firms generate positive spillovers among domestic firms. In particular, several studies present evidence that FDI firms create positive spillovers among suppliers in host economies. A good example is Blalock and Gertler (2008), who conduct an econometric study of FDI spillovers in Indonesia. Whereas they fail to find any significant intra-industry spillovers, their findings indicate that the presence of FDI in a given industry is positively associated with productivity of domestic firms in industries that supply inputs to the industry. Similar evidence of positive spillovers among suppliers is provided by Girma and Wakelin (2007) and Driffield (2004) for the UK, Javorcik and Spatareanu (2011) for Romania, Monastiriotis and Jordaan (2011) for Greece and Liu (2008) for China. Having said this, the evidence is again characterized by a certain degree of heterogeneity, as other studies fail to identify any positive inter-industry spillovers (e.g. Crespo et al. 2007; Blyde et al, 2004).

2.2 FDI Spillovers via Inter-Firm Linkages

Overall, the econometric evidence on FDI spillovers appears to suggest that positive productivity spillovers are more likely to arise between industries. In particular, suppliers of FDI firms are likely to experience positive effects when foreign-owned firms act as source of new technologies to these domestic firms. Whereas FDI firms may try to prevent technology leakage to competitors operating in similar industries, they may be less concerned about technologies being shared with domestic firms in other industries (Kugler, 2006; Moran, 2005). Also, input-output markets are usually characterized by frequent contacts between limited numbers of buyers and sellers, creating scope for the non-market sharing of information and technologies (Giroud and Scott-Kennel, 2009). Furthermore, FDI firms may be more willing to share technologies when they want to improve the performance of their suppliers[1].

Findings of positive FDI spillovers among domestic firms in input-supplying industries constitute important evidence that input-output linkages are conducive to transmitting technologies. Yet, it is important to recognize the limitations of this type of evidence. The vast majority of evidence is based on linking the FDI presence in a given industry to other industries in a host economy using input-output tables (see e.g. Smarzynska, 2004). Doing this captures the intensity with which various industries are linked, but the resulting evidence on inter-industry FDI spillovers only constitutes indirect evidence that inter-firm linkages are the main channel via which spillovers materialize. It remains unclear to what degree other channels such as demonstration effects or processes of labor turnover also play a role. Furthermore, the econometric evidence does not clarify why and how FDI firms transmit new technologies. To find answers to such questions, related research that is more qualitative of nature is more suited.

---

[1] Of course, FDI firms benefit from sharing technologies with their suppliers in the form of more cost-effective or better quality inputs. However, as it is very difficult in practice for foreign-owned firms to obtain full compensation for the support that they offer, the common assumption is that supportive linkages established by FDI firms result in positive spillovers (Blomström and Kokko, 1998). This is especially the case when the support offered by a FDI firm can be used by the suppliers to improve their performance for other client firms (see Jordaan, 2011c).

Case studies and small scale surveys try to obtain detailed information on how FDI firms engage in technology sharing activities and what types of technologies are provided to help improve suppliers in host economies. A good example of this research approach is Potter, Moore and Spires (2002, 2003), who present detailed findings from a survey among FDI firms in the UK economy. Their findings indicate that the informal sharing of views and ideas and visits by staff of FDI firms to inspect production processes constitute important ways via which technologies and knowledge are shared with suppliers. Looking at the types of support that the foreign-owned firms provide, assistance with quality control systems, production development and cost control processes are offered most frequently. Crone and Roper (2001) conduct a survey among FDI firms in Northern Ireland and find that FDI firms are often involved in providing direct assistance with improving production processes of their suppliers. Javorcik and Spatareanu (2005; see also Javorcik, 2008) present evidence from the Czech Republic that FDI firms frequently provide financial support and training programs to their suppliers[2].

Findings from this more qualitative approach provide rich information on how linkages with suppliers may generate positive spillovers. However, the drawback of case studies and small scale surveys is that it is very difficult to generalize their findings. Furthermore, two important questions usually remain unaddressed. The first of these is the central question that underlies all research on FDI effects, whether FDI firms actually differ from domestic firms in their operations. Qualitative studies usually only include FDI firms in their samples, making it impossible to ascertain whether technology transfers by FDI firms differ from technology transfers that domestic firms create. Second, suppliers are usually also not included in the samples. By excluding those firms from the analysis, it becomes very difficult to identify and understand the actual effects on the recipients of the support.

Overall, the empirical evidence on the importance of inter-firm linkages as facilitator of FDI spillovers among suppliers in host economies is of a varied nature. Several econometric studies find positive associations between FDI and productivity of domestic firms in input-supplying industries, suggesting that suppliers are subject to positive spillovers. This evidence is indirect however, and does not clarify whether and how inter-firm linkages actually facilitate these spillover effects. More qualitative research is more informative in this respect, showing that FDI firms are often involved in a variety of activities that involve the transfer of technologies to their suppliers. Given the characteristics of this research approach and the feature that research samples usually only consist of FDI firms, it is difficult to generalize findings from individual studies. Also, it is difficult to ascertain whether FDI firms create more technology transfers than comparable domestic firms in host economies or to assess the actual impact of these transfers on their suppliers.

2.3. FDI Spillovers and the Technology Gap

The level of technological differences between FDI and domestic firms is often seen as an important factor influencing the occurrence of FDI spillovers (Jordaan, 2011b; 2012a). The standard interpretation of the technology gap is that it can be taken as a direct inverse

---

[2] For a survey of older findings from case studies and surveys on supportive linkages that FDI firms may establish, see UNCTAD (2001).

indicator of the level of absorptive capacity of domestic firms. Following this interpretation, positive FDI spillovers are less likely to occur when the technology gap is large, as domestic firms are less likely to be able to absorb spillovers from technologically sophisticated FDI firms. An example of an early study that presents findings in line with this interpretation is Kokko (1994). Using a dataset with unpublished census data from 1970 of a sample of Mexican manufacturing industries, Kokko finds that positive spillovers do not materialize in those industries that are characterized by a high presence of FDI firms and a large technology gap between FDI and Mexican firms. Other studies that present findings of a similar effect of the technology gap include Haddad and Harrison (1993) for Morocco and Girma (2005) for the UK.

In contrast to these findings, other studies present findings that are not in line with the standard interpretation of the technology gap as direct inverse indicator of absorptive capacity. For instance, Sjöholm (1999) conducts an empirical analysis of drivers of firm level productivity growth in Indonesia and finds that dynamic positive FDI spillovers only materialize in industries that are characterized by a large technology gap. Other studies present findings that identify a positive effect of the technology gap in those industries with a high FDI presence. For example, Haskel et al. (2007) estimate FDI spillovers for the UK and find a positive effect of an interaction variable between the technology gap and FDI industry presence. Similar findings for other countries are presented by Zukowska-Gagelmann (2000) for Poland and Castellani and Zanfei (2003) for Spain, Italy and France.

The contrasting evidence on the effect of the technology gap on FDI spillovers calls for a closer examination of the interpretation of the technology gap. This closer examination suggests that the standard interpretation of the technology gap can be challenged (Jordaan, 2012a; Jordaan, 2013). The link that is made between the technology gap and the level of absorptive capacity of domestic firms harks back to the concept of catch-up, originally devised to understand how international flows of technology between advanced and lagging countries can foster processes of convergence (Keller, 1996; Gershenkron, 1962; Nelson, 1968). A sufficient level of absorptive capacity is important, as it allows lagging countries to absorb new technologies. However, the second key component in the catch-up process is the level of technological differences between the two groups of countries. When the technology gap is large, there is ample scope for lagging countries to learn and improve, speeding up the process of economic and technological convergence. Applying this idea to the materialization of FDI spillovers suggest that, all else equal, a large technology gap may foster rather than hinder these externalities (Blomström and Wang, 1992; Findlay, 1978). Of course, domestic firms must have a sufficient level of absorptive capacity to adopt new technologies, but this requirement is different from simply interpreting the technology gap as a direct inverse indicator of absorptive capacity of domestic firms. In addition to this, there is the argument that the materialization of spillovers is partly conditional on the active participation by firms that may benefit from them (Rodrik, 1992; see also Goh, 2005). Domestic firms are more likely to try to absorb new technologies when the technology gap is large, as the size of the gap indicates that there is a large scope to improve and benefit from new technologies.

In summary, it is clear that the technology gap between FDI and domestic firms can influence positive FDI spillovers. The evidence is conflicting, as different studies find that a small or a large gap may foster positive externalities. A closer examination of what the concept of the technology gap entails and captures suggests that a positive relation between a large technology gap and positive FDI spillovers is more in line with underlying theories. The size of the gap reflects the scope for domestic firms to learn and improve, also offering incentives to these firms to try and absorb new technologies that FDI firms may disseminate.

2.4. FDI Spillovers and Agglomeration

The level of agglomeration of economic activity is increasingly seen as another potentially important determinant of FDI spillovers. Recent contributions in the fields of regional economics and new economic geography emphasize the externality-creating features of agglomerations of economic activity within countries. Agglomerations of economic activity are characterized by thick labor markets, dense inter-firm linkages and are conducive to the creation and dissemination of knowledge spillovers, all generating positive externalities or agglomeration economies (Rosenthal and Strange, 2004; Duranton and Puga, 2004). It is very likely that FDI spillovers are facilitated by agglomeration, given the strong similarity between the channels of FDI spillovers and the mechanisms that create agglomeration economies (see Jordaan, 2009). As discussed earlier, inter-firm linkages are an important channel via which FDI firms transfer technologies to their suppliers. As such linkages are facilitated by agglomeration, it is likely that FDI firms that operate in an agglomeration in a host economy create more inter-firm linkages, fostering positive productivity effects. Another example is the facilitation of knowledge spillovers in an agglomeration, which is very likely to have a positive effect on FDI spillovers that occur via demonstration effects.

The most direct hypothesis that follows from the large degree of similarity between the channels that transmit FDI spillovers and the mechanisms that create agglomeration economies is that FDI spillovers are directly affected by the level of agglomeration of economic activity in a host economy. Looking at the available evidence, there is only a small number of studies that address this direct effect[3]. The general finding of these studies is that agglomeration does have a direct impact on FDI spillovers. For instance, Driffield and Munday (2001) and De Propris and Driffield (2006) find for the UK that positive FDI spillovers only materialize in agglomerated industries. Barrios et al. (2006) report similar findings for Ireland. Monastiriotis and Jordaan (2011) present findings for Greece that indicate that geographical proximity is important, as positive FDI spillovers only occur at small regional scales. Menghinello et al. (2010) identify interaction effects between FDI spillovers and agglomeration economies in Italy, further confirming the notion that agglomeration can directly influence FDI productivity effects.

Instead of analyzing the direct impact of agglomeration, a number of studies look at other geographical dimensions of FDI spillovers. Several studies estimate for the presence of regional FDI spillovers. For instance, Blalock and Gertler (2008) present evidence suggesting that positive externalities among suppliers occur at the regional level in Indonesia. Sjöholm (1998) also looks at the regional dimension of FDI spillovers in this host economy and finds evidence of positive regional inter-industry and negative regional intra-industry spillovers. In extension of this, several other studies try to assess whether FDI spillovers occur between regions within host economies. In line with the general body of evidence on FDI spillovers,

---

[3] The importance of addressing the relation between agglomeration and FDI spillovers is underlined by findings from studies of FDI location factors that find that FDI firms are attracted to agglomerations of economic activity within host economies (see e.g. Head et al. 1995, for the US and Disdier and Mayer 2004 for the European Union).

the evidence is heterogeneous but does suggest that spatial dimensions may play a role (Jordaan, 2009). For the UK for instance, Driffield (2004) finds evidence of positive inter-regional inter-industry FDI spillovers. Similar evidence for Hungary is presented by Halpern et al. (2007).

Overall, research on the role of agglomeration or geographical proximity as factor influencing FDI spillovers is in clear support of the notion that geographical space matters for FDI externalities. The large similarity between the channels of FDI spillovers and mechanisms underlying agglomeration economies suggest a direct impact of agglomeration on these FDI effects. The small number of studies that look at this direct effect confirm that agglomeration does enhance positive FDI spillovers. In addition to this, findings from other studies show that geographical proximity may be important, as FDI spillovers may occur particularly at sub-national levels within host economies. However, other findings indicate that FDI spillovers may also materialize between regions.

3. FDI Spillovers in the Mexican Economy

3.1. Inward FDI in Mexico

Mexico belongs to a small group of developing countries that have received substantial levels of international investment for several decades (UNCTAD, 2005). Importantly, in response to the economic crises that plagued the Mexican economy in the 1970s and 1980s, the government drastically changed its main development strategy. The policy of import substitution was abandoned and replaced by a stringent policy of economic liberalization and trade promotion. State-owned enterprises were sold off at a rapid rate, import restrictions were largely abolished and exporting activities started to receive structural support (ten Kate, 1992). As part of this new development strategy, laws restricting foreign investment were loosened on several occasions to promote inward FDI into the economy (Ramirez, 2003; Pacheco-Lopez, 2005). More and more industries have been opened up to international investment and restrictions concerning levels of foreign ownership of firms have been abandoned rapidly (Jordaan, 2009). As a result, Mexico now belongs to a group of countries in the world economy with the least restrictive policies towards inward FDI (OECD, 2007).

Figure 1 shows the development of inward FDI into Mexico for the period 1981-2009. Following the change in development strategy at the end of the 1980s, the level of inward FDI flows has increased substantially. This increase received a further impulse following the creation of the North American Free Trade Agreement (NAFTA) in 1994 and further relaxations of the laws governing foreign-owned firms in the Mexican economy (Love and

Hidalgo, 2000). The effect of the NAFTA agreement appears to have been substantial. For instance, Cuevas et al. (2005) estimate that the creation of NAFTA generated FDI flows into Mexico some 60% more than would have been the case in the absence of this trade agreement. As a result of the large increase in FDI flows, the relative importance of FDI in the Mexican economy has increased sharply. As figure 1 indicates, the total stock of FDI as share of total Mexican GDP has increased from a little over 5 % before the introduction of economic liberalization and trade promotion to about 15% at the end of the 1990s, reaching more than 30% in 2009.

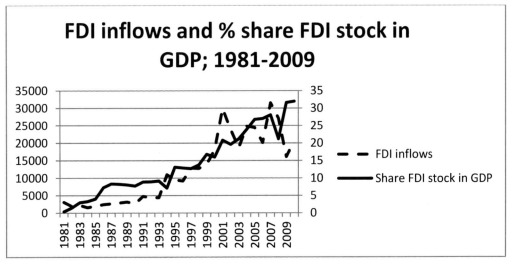

Source: UNCTAD, at www.unctad.org

Figure 1. FDI flows measured in millions of US dollars.

3.2. FDI Spillovers in Mexico: A First Look at the Evidence

In line with the growing importance of foreign-owned activity in the Mexican economy, there has been considerable interest in identifying FDI productivity effects. For instance, Ramirez (2000, 2006) conducts time series analysis to identify the effect of FDI on aggregate productivity. Based on the analysis of a dataset for the period 1960-1995, the findings indicate a positive association between changes in the stock of FDI and aggregate labor productivity, which Ramirez (2000, 2006) interprets as evidence of the presence of positive FDI spillovers.

The majority of research on FDI spillovers consists of the analysis of industry or plant level data for different time periods. Evidence based on the analysis of 1970s manufacturing industry data suggests that domestic firms are benefitting from positive FDI spillovers. Blomström and Persson (1983) report a positive effect of the industry level of FDI on labor productivity of Mexican-owned industry shares. In a related study, Blomström (1986) finds that a high industry level of FDI lowers industry deviation from best practice productivity. Kokko (1994, 1996) uses the same dataset and largely confirms the presence of positive spillovers. For the period 1970-1975, Blomström and Wolff (1994) identify a positive intra-industry FDI effect on both industry productivity growth and productivity convergence between domestic and foreign-owned firms.

Findings based on the analysis of a plant level dataset for the second part of the 1980s are somewhat more diverse. Aitken et al. (1996) find that the industry level of FDI is positively associated with industry wages. However, this effect largely disappears when omitting FDI firms from the analysis, suggesting that it is mainly foreign-owned firms that benefit from FDI spillovers. Using the same dataset, Aitken et al. (1997) focus on another type of externalities in the form of positive market access spillovers. This type of spillovers occurs when domestic firms benefit from knowledge and experience incorporated into FDI firms that are active on international markets. Their findings show a significant positive effect of industry FDI on the likelihood that Mexican firms are engaged in exporting activities, suggesting that these positive market access spillovers do materialize.

Grether (1999) and Kosteas (2008) use the dataset to identify FDI productivity spillovers. Grether (1999) finds a negative association between the industry level of FDI and relative efficiency of Mexican plants, suggesting that industries with a high level of FDI participation are characterized by large differences between the productivity of Mexican plants and best practice plants. Although this is not necessarily evidence of negative spillovers, it does suggest that a large presence of FDI may lower the diffusion of new technologies. Kosteas (2008) finds that the industry presence of FDI firms is positively associated with productivity of Mexican firms, indicating the presence of positive productivity spillovers.

Finally, Jordaan (2005, 2008b, 2008c, 2011a) presents evidence for the 1990s that suggests that FDI firms are creating productivity spillovers both of an intra- and inter-industry nature. Jordaan (2005; 2011a) uses unpublished national level manufacturing industry data derived from the 1994 economic census and finds a positive effect of intra-industry FDI on labor productivity of Mexican firms. Jordaan (2008b) uses unpublished manufacturing industry data from the same source, focusing on national level industries and industries in Mexico City and the border states, as these regions incorporate a majority share of FDI activity. The findings from this study are more diverse. When distinguishing between the intra-industry presence of FDI and FDI spillovers that may occur among suppliers of FDI firms, the findings indicate the presence of negative intra-industry spillovers and positive productivity effects among suppliers. Using less disaggregated regional industry data for all 32 Mexican states for the same period, Jordaan (2008c) finds similar effects: FDI firms appear to be generating negative externalities at the intra-industry level, whereas suppliers of foreign-owned firms experience positive productivity effects.

3.3. FDI Spillovers in Mexico: The Technology Gap and Agglomeration

Overall, there is substantial evidence that FDI firms are creating productivity spillovers in the Mexican economy. On balance, it appears that positive spillovers are more prevalent than negative externalities. Having said this, the most recent evidence that is based on estimations that distinguish between intra-industry spillovers and spillovers among suppliers of FDI firms appear to suggest that in particular Mexican firms that supply inputs to FDI firms are benefitting from positive spillovers.

Technology Gap

Several studies address the question whether the technology gap influences the occurrence of FDI spillovers. As mentioned earlier in section 2.3, Kokko (1994) finds that positive spillovers do not materialize in manufacturing industries that are characterized by a high presence of FDI and a large technology gap with Mexican firms. Kokko labels these industries as "enclave" industries, where large technological differences prevent domestic firms from absorbing new technologies. In contrast to this, Blomström and Wolff (1994) find the opposite effect for the period 1970-1975. Their findings indicate that the initial level of technological differences between foreign-owned and Mexican firms has a positive effect on the level of productivity growth of Mexican firms. Also, it favors the speed of productivity convergence between the two types of firm.

Jordaan (2005, 2008b, 2008c) presents evidence of the effect of the technology gap for a more recent time period. Jordaan (2005, 2008b) presents evidence in strong contrast to Kokko's (1994) findings. Using both national level industry data and data for states with a majority share of FDI, the findings indicate a positive effect of an interaction variable between industry FDI and the technology gap. This suggests that industries that are characterized by a large presence of FDI and large technological differences between foreign-owned and domestic firms are benefitting more from positive spillovers than industries in general. Also, Jordaan (2005) compares the spillover effect from FDI between industries that are characterized by either a small or a large technology gap and finds that positive spillovers are most pronounced in industries with a large technology gap.

The analysis of all Mexican states presented in Jordaan (2008c) finds a general positive effect of the technology gap on productivity of Mexican firms, in line with the findings reported by Blomström and Wolff (1994). Importantly, the study by Jordaan (2008b) also finds that the technology gap may enhance positive spillovers among suppliers of FDI firms. Also, the findings from this study identify a certain degree of regional heterogeneity in the impact of the technology gap on FDI spillovers, as some of the border states appear to benefit more from the positive effect of the technology gap than Mexican regions on average.

All these findings are in line with the alternative interpretation of the technology gap as discussed in section 2.3. The majority of the findings on the effect of the technology gap in Mexico cannot be explained by interpreting the technology gap as inverse indicator of the level of absorptive capacity of Mexican firms. Instead, they suggest the appropriateness of the alternative interpretation that the size of the technology gap reflects the scope for potential improvements that domestic firms may experience. When the technology gap is large, domestic firms have a large scope to learn and absorb new technologies, resulting in larger positive spillovers. This process is likely to be further facilitated by the feature that domestic firms have more incentives to try and absorb new technologies, as a large technology gap indicates that the potential gains from doing so are large. The feature of the findings by Jordaan (2008b) that the positive effect of the technology gap can vary between regions suggests that considerations of absorptive capacity remain important. The rejection of the interpretation of the technology gap as direct inverse indicator of absorptive capacity does not mean that absorptive capacity is unimportant. Instead, it suggests that the level of absorptive capacity facilitates the creation of positive spillovers, spillovers that are more likely to occur when the technology gap is large. The regional heterogeneity in the positive impact of the technology gap on positive spillovers suggests that Mexican firms in some states are better able to absorb new technologies than firms in other states.

Agglomeration

Several studies on the effects from FDI in Mexico address in some shape or form the relations that may exist between agglomeration or geographical proximity and FDI spillovers. Two recent studies that confirm that these relations are import to address are Jordaan (2008a; 2012b). Jordaan (2008a) analyses regional FDI flows to the 32 Mexican states during the period 1986-2006 to identify regional characteristics that influence the location decision of FDI firms. The findings indicate that regions that contain agglomerations of economic activity are characterized by higher levels of FDI inflows, after controlling for the effects of regional demand, wage level, schooling and infrastructure. Jordaan (2012b) uses a large set of plant level location decisions for the period 1994-1999, when Mexico experienced a large rise in inward FDI following the creation of NAFTA. Based on the estimation of conditional logit location models, the findings confirm that FDI firms gravitate towards those Mexican states that incorporate agglomerations of economic activity.

Jordaan and Rodriguez-Oreggia (2012) present an empirical analysis of drivers of regional growth in Mexico for the period 1989-2004. In this analysis, they include several indicators of agglomeration economies and regional FDI. The findings indicate that both regional FDI and agglomeration economies have played an important role as key drivers of regional growth during this period. Depending on how regional FDI is defined, the growth effect from the regional presence of FDI activity is negative or positive, suggesting that both negative and positive spillovers may be important.

Aitken et al. (1997) present findings that suggest that geographical proximity between FDI and domestic firms is important for spillovers to materialize. The positive effect of exporting FDI firms on the likelihood that Mexican firms engage in exports is only identified at the regional (state) level, suggesting that geographical proximity between FDI and domestic firms is important for knowledge spillovers to arise. Having said this, findings by Jordaan and Rodriguez-Oreggia (2012) and Jordaan (2008c) indicate that FDI spillovers are not necessarily confined at the regional level. Jordaan and Rodriguez-Oreggia (2012) find that regional FDI affects growth both at the intra- and inter-regional level, indicating that FDI spillovers materialize across geographical space. Jordaan (2008c), using more detailed regional manufacturing industry data presents further evidence of such spatial effects. As is the case with intra-regional effects, FDI firms appear to create negative spatial intra-industry spillovers and positive spatial productivity effects among suppliers of Mexican firms. The findings also indicate that geographical space is important in the sense that spatial spillovers decrease with inter-regional distance. Interestingly, this study also presents additional findings that confirm the positive effect of the technology gap, as positive inter-regional spillovers are enhanced when the level of technological differences between the spillover sending and receiving regions is high.

Finally, Jordaan (2005, 2008b) presents findings that address the direct effect of agglomeration on FDI spillovers. Jordaan (2005) separates manufacturing industries into industries with a high or a low level of agglomeration. Comparing the estimated spillover effect of intra-industry FDI for the two groups of industries shows that positive spillovers only occur in industries with a high agglomeration score. Findings from adding interaction variables to the regression model also suggest that agglomeration enhances positive spillovers, with the caveat that this only appears to be the case for those highly agglomerated industries that are also characterized by a large technology gap. The positive effect of an interaction variable between the industry level of agglomeration and industry FDI is confirmed by Jordaan (2008b) when estimating determinants of labor productivity for Mexico City and the border states.

4. FDI SPILLOVERS AMONG LOCAL SUPPLIERS: EVIDENCE FROM NUEVO LEÓN, MEXICO

4.1. Introduction

The previous section has found that positive spillovers are most pronounced among Mexican suppliers of FDI firms. Also, several studies find that the technology gap and agglomeration are both important factors influencing FDI spillovers. In this section, I conduct multivariate analysis to obtain further evidence on whether and how FDI and the technology gap may affect spillovers among suppliers. For this, I use data that I obtained from firm level surveys that I carried out in Nuevo León, Mexico during 2000-2001. This state, located in the North East of Mexico, offers a particularly good setting to study the operations and effects of FDI firms. After Mexico City, Nuevo León contains the second most important agglomeration of manufacturing activity in the country and the region has a long history of manufacturing production, both by Mexican and foreign-owned firms.

One of the advantages of the data is that the survey was conducted among both Mexican and foreign-owned manufacturing firms. As discussed earlier in section 2.2, small scale surveys that analyses FDI linkages with suppliers are usually based on samples that consist only of foreign-owned firms. This makes it impossible to address the central underlying question whether FDI firms are different from domestic firms. The firm level survey among producer firms in Nuevo León was carried out specifically among a set of comparable large Mexican and foreign-owned manufacturing firms, allowing for a robust comparison between the two types of firms. The second advantage of the data is that I applied a second survey among a random sample of suppliers to Mexican or FDI firms in the regional economy. The information from this survey makes it possible to identify determinants of the actual impact that materializes from input-output linkages between the producer firms and their suppliers[4].

Technology Transfers from Producer Firms

To get a detailed impression of the types of technology transfers that FDI firms engage in, I use data from the producer survey. The main findings on technology transfers are presented in the first half of table 1 (see also Jordaan, 2009; Jordaan, 2011c; 2013). Following UNCTAD (2001), I distinguish between technology transfers that can be classified as technological support and technology transfers that can be classified as organizational support. The main difference between the two types of support is that technological support concerns types of technology transfers that have a direct impact on the production processes of the suppliers. Organizational support has a positive effect on the overall performance of the suppliers besides their actual production processes.

The findings in table 1 indicate that producer firms are actively engaged in a variety of technology transfers. Assistance with technical production and quality control issues occurs most frequently, followed by the provision of product designs and specifications. Other types of support that occur relatively often include assistance to new suppliers, the provision of special tools and training programs for staff of suppliers. Importantly, FDI firms are significantly more supportive to their suppliers. For several types of support, the percentage

---

[4] For further information on the research design and firm level surveys, see Jordaan (2009; 2013).

of firms among FDI firms that provides support frequently is significantly larger than the percentage among Mexican firms. The difference between the two types of producer firm applies mainly to support that has a direct impact on the production processes of suppliers, suggesting that FDI firms are a particularly good source of new technologies to their suppliers.

Table 1. Technology Transfers to Local Suppliers

Findings from Producer Survey		
Technology Transfers between producer firms and local suppliers	FDI producer firms	Mexican producer firms
Technological Support		
Product designs and specifications	71.8 (a)	14.8
Machinery	25.6 (a)	3.7
Special tools	59 (a)	11.1
Technical production and quality control	84.5 (b)	66.7
Training programs	59 (a)	22.2
Organizational Support		
Assistance to new suppliers	61.5	59.3
General business and organization development	35.9	25.9
Grant/loans/accelerated payments	33.3 (a)	11.1
Assistance with sourcing	48.7	33.3
Cooperation in developing new inputs	56.4	63.6
Findings from Supplier Survey		
Importance of Technology Transfers	Suppliers of FDI firms	Suppliers of Mexican firms
Level of support is very satisfactory	53.7 (a)	11.4
Technology transfers received from one client firm can be used to improve performance for other client firms	90.7 (a)	60.0
Technological support is very important to be efficient supplier to client firms	53.7	40
Organizational support is very important to be efficient supplier to client firms	33.3	26.7

Source: producer survey and supplier survey.
a and b indicate significance levels of 1 and 5%; based on Chi-square test.
The first part of the table reports % of FDI and Mexican firms that offer technology transfers frequently.
The second part of the table reports % of suppliers of FDI and Mexican firms that agree with the statements.

The second part of table 1 contains some findings from the supplier survey, conducted among suppliers of FDI or Mexican producer firms. Overall, suppliers of FDI firms appear to experience more technology transfers, as the percentage of firms among these suppliers that indicates the level of support to be very satisfactory is significantly higher than the percentage of firms among suppliers of Mexican firms. Another important finding is that a significantly larger share of firms among suppliers of FDI firms indicates to be able to use the support received from one client firm to improve their performance for other firms. As discussed earlier in section 2.2, this wider reach of the impact of supportive linkages enhances the likelihood that technology transfers provided by producer firms result in positive spillovers. The last two statements in table 1 show that there is no difference in the importance of support that the two types of supplier firm receive. It could have been the case that FDI firms select suppliers that need more support, for instance because they have less information about suitable suppliers in the regional economy than Mexican firms have. If so, this could be a partial explanation for their higher level of supportiveness. This does not seem to be the case, as there is no difference in the importance of the support that suppliers of FDI and Mexican producer firms receive.

Importantly, Jordaan (2011d) presents corroborating evidence from analyzing additional data from the survey among local suppliers. In line with the findings from the producer survey, a comparison of the responses of suppliers of FDI firms or Mexican firms indicates that suppliers of foreign-owned firms are more frequently experiencing a variety of types of technology transfers. Again, this appears to be the case especially for types of technology transfer that aim to directly improve production processes of the suppliers. At the same time, the survey also shows that suppliers of FDI firms find it harder to work as supplier to these firms. For example, suppliers of foreign-owned firms experience more problems in the areas of technological differences with their client firms, stricter quality specifications for their inputs and stronger price demands. In combination, these findings suggest that FDI firms put stronger pressure on their suppliers to improve, whilst at the same time offering more support to help the suppliers to achieve these improvements.

4.2. Econometric Model

To obtain more evidence on whether FDI firms create positive spillovers among their suppliers and how the technology gap may influence this impact, I use data from the supplier survey. The dichotomous dependent variable takes the value of 1 when a supplier firm indicates to have experienced a large overall improvement as a result of its dealings with its main client firms and 0 otherwise. The nature of the dependent variable makes the logit regression model appropriate, relating to the odds that a supplier firm has experienced a large positive impact. These odds can be defined as the ratio of the probability that a supplier has experienced such an impact (π) over the probability that the supplier has not experienced a large positive impact ($1-\pi$). Taking the log of this ratio gives the logit, which can be used in a logit regression model to be estimated with maximum likelihood techniques. The regression model is specified as follows:

$$\ln\left(\frac{\pi}{1-\pi}\right) = \beta 0 + \beta Size + \beta Experience + \beta\, Dependence + \beta Production \\ + \beta Contract + \beta TechSupport + \beta OrgSupport + \beta FDISupplier \\ + \beta TechGap + \varepsilon$$

The model controls for a number of supplier characteristics that may influence the likelihood that suppliers experience a large positive impact. The variable SIZE is measured as the number of employees and tests the hypothesis that large suppliers have more resources to devote to absorbing new technologies. The variable EXPERIENCE is measured as the number of years that a firm has been active in the regional economy as supplier. The expected effect of this variable is positive, under the assumption that an experienced supplier has developed more experience and skills to absorb new technologies. The variable DEPENDENCE captures the extent to which a supplier is reliant on a small number of client firms in the region. This variable takes the value of 1 when a majority of a supplier's sales are linked to 2 or 3 client firms and 0 otherwise. The variable PRODUCTION captures the degree to which a supplier's production process is specialized. The variable is measured on a Likert scale, where a higher score indicates a higher level of specialization. The expected effect of this variable is negative, as a higher level of specialization may make it more difficult for client firms to offer suitable support. The variable CONTRACT captures the type of business linkages that a supplier has with its main client firms. This dichotomous variable takes the value of 1 for market transactions "at arms' length" and 0 for business linkages that are characterized by more frequent inter-firm contacts, usually of an informal nature. The expected effect of this variable is negative, under the assumption that some level of informal contacts between buying and selling parties is necessary for the sharing and transmission of new technologies. The variables ORGSUPPORT and TECHSUPPORT capture the levels of organizational and technological support that a supplier firm receives from its main client firms. I include these two variables to control for the feature that FDI firms offer significantly more support, as shown in table 1.

The variables FDISUPPLIER and TECHGAP are the two main variables of interest. The variable FDISUPPLIER takes the value of 1 when a supplier has only or mainly FDI firms in the region as client firms and 0 otherwise. An estimated positive effect of this variable can be taken as strong evidence that type of ownership does matter for the creation of positive spillovers. The variable TECHGAP captures the level of technological differences between a supplier and its main client firms. Suppliers were asked to indicate on a Likert scale the level of technological differences between them and their main client firms, where a high score reflects a large technology gap. Following the findings from the econometric studies on FDI spillovers in Mexico as discussed in section three, the expected effect of this variable is positive.

4.3. FDI, Technology Gap and Impact on Local Suppliers

The main findings from estimating the regression model are presented in table 2. The first column with findings contains the estimated effects of the control variables on the likelihood that a supplier firm has experienced a large overall positive impact as a result of its business linkages with its main client firms in the region. The estimated effects are reported in the form of marginal effects at the means. Each of the reported effects indicate the change in the dependent variable from a 1-unit change in one of the independent variables, calculated when the other control variables are set to their mean values.

Most of the control variables have a significant effect on the probability that a supplier has experienced a large positive impact. The positive effect of the variable controlling for the size of a supplier suggests that larger supplier firms have more resources to devote to absorb new technologies. The positive effect of the level of experience suggests that firms that have a lot of experience working as supplier to producer firms in the region are better in absorbing new technologies. The level of specialized production has a negative effect, suggesting that suppliers that are very specialized in their production are less likely to experience a large positive impact. This may be explained by the feature that technologies that may be transmitted from the producer firms are too generic for these suppliers, lowering the positive impact that these transfers may create. The estimated effect of the type of contract is also negative, indicating that technology transfers are less likely to materialize between producer firms and suppliers when their business relationships are characterized by arms' length market transactions.

Table 2. Determinants of Positive Impacts among Suppliers: FDI and the Technology Gap

	Large positive impact	Large Technological Impact	Large Organizational Impact
Size	0.03 (a)	-0.09 (a)	-0.05
Experience	0.12 (a)	-0.16 (a)	0.15 (a)
Dependence	-0.06	-0.38 (a)	-0.006
Production	-0.16 (a)	-0.27 (a)	0.03 (a)
Contract	-0.19 (a)	-0.21 (a)	-0.04
TechSupport	0.008	0.78 (a)	0.04 (a)
OrgSupport	0.04 (a)	0.006	0.29 (a)
FDISupplier	0.32 (a)	0.39 (a)	-0.13
TechGap	0.17 (a)	0.23 (a)	0.03
R2	0.22	0.69	0.38
Log Likelihood	-46.34	-20.63	-38.16
Chi Square	25.89 (a)	92.39 (a)	46.70 (a)
% nr. Cases predicted correctly	76.3	90.7	82.5
Number of firms	100	100	100

Source: Supplier Survey; a indicates significance level of 1%.
Reported effects are marginal effects at the means. Estimations include industry dummies for car, electronics and chemical industries.

For the overall impact, it appears that technology transfers that can be classified as organizational support are the most important types of support. As for the effect of having foreign-owned firms as clients firms, the findings indicate that type of ownership clearly matters. When controlling for the variety of factors that may influence the probability that a supplier experiences a large positive impact, having FDI client firms significantly improves the probability that this impact occurs. Importantly, the findings also confirm that the technology gap enhances the probability that a large positive impact occurs. This positive effect of the technology gap can be explained by the alternative interpretation of the technology gap as discussed in section 2.3. When the level of technological differences between producer firms and suppliers is large, there is a large scope for the suppliers to improve. This is likely to stimulate the suppliers to try and absorb new technologies from their client firms.

The next two columns present the findings when the dependent variable is either a large positive impact of a technological or an organizational nature. For the technological impact, the level of technological support is very important, in line with expectations. Both the size and experience variables now carry negative coefficients. This suggests that a large technological impact is concentrated among relative young supplier firms in the region that are relatively of smaller size. For the organizational impact, regional experience does enhance the likelihood that a large impact occurs. For this type of impact, it is organizational support that matters, as expected.

Looking at the effects of type of ownership of client firms and the technology gap, there are important differences between the two sets of findings. Having foreign-owned firms as client firms increases the probability that a supplier experiences a large technological impact. Type of ownership does not matter for the materialization of a large impact of an organizational nature. Similarly, the effect of the technology gap differs between the two types of impact. A large technology gap favors the materialization of a large technological impact, whereas technological differences between suppliers and their client firms do not affect a large organizational impact. This suggests that technological differences between producer firms and their suppliers reflect in particular the scope of supplier firms to achieve large improvements of a technological nature, improvements that are directly related to their production processes.

The econometric findings indicate that the size of the technology gap enhances the probability that a supplier experiences a large overall positive impact and a large technological impact. To obtain a better understanding of how the technology gap is related to these impacts, I explore the effect of type of ownership of client firms on the probability of suppliers experiencing these large impacts, under different levels of the technology gap. The main findings are presented in figure 2.

Figure 2 shows the predictive margins for suppliers of FDI firms and suppliers of Mexican firms experiencing large positive impacts, at increasing levels of the technology gap. The figure shows two important features. First, there is a clear and largely consistent difference between the probability that suppliers of Mexican or foreign-owned firms experience large positive impacts, indicated by the strong persistence of the difference between the solid and dotted lines. This applies to both the overall impact and the impact of a technological nature. The difference between the two types of supplier becomes somewhat smaller with an increase in the size of the technology gap when looking at the overall impact, but this only occurs at high values of the technology gap.

Second, the likelihood that suppliers experience a large overall impact and a large technological impact increases with larger values of the technology gap. The results reported in table 2 identify the general positive effect of the technology gap. Figure 2 shows that the predicted probability of suppliers experiencing positive impacts increases with increasing levels of the technology gap. This suggests that a growing technology gap reflects an increasing scope for suppliers to improve, creating more incentives for the suppliers to actively try to absorb new technologies from their client firms. Importantly, this positive relation between the technology gap and the probability that large positive impacts are experienced by the supplier firms applies more or less equally to suppliers of Mexican firms and suppliers of FDI firms. There is a difference between the two types of supplier in terms of the predicted probability of experiencing large positive impacts, but this difference does not change much with increasing values of the technology gap. Only when the technology gap is relatively very large does the difference in predicted probability of experiencing a large overall positive impact decrease somewhat between the two types of supplier. Overall, this indicates that the positive effect of the technology gap applies to all suppliers, irrespective of the type of ownership of their client firms. This finding underlines the importance of the technology gap as independent factor influencing productivity spillovers

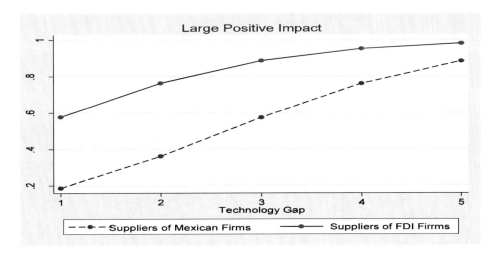

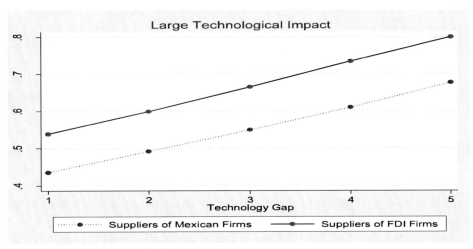

Average predicted margins, at 95% CIs.

Figure 2 Predictive Margins Large Positive Impact and Large Technological Impact; Suppliers of Mexican Firms and Suppliers of FDI Firms; Increasing Size of Technology Gap.

Summing up, the empirical analysis in this section provides corroborating evidence for the notion that type of ownership of client firms matters for the degree and nature of spillovers that local suppliers experience and that the technology gap has a positive effect on these spillovers. The comparison between FDI firms and Mexican producer firms indicates that foreign-owned firms are significantly more involved in various technology transfers that have a direct impact on the production processes of their suppliers. The findings from the econometric analysis indicate that suppliers of FDI firms are more likely to experience a large overall positive impact and a large impact of a technological nature. The feature that this finding is robust to controlling for the level of support that the suppliers receive from their client firms strongly supports the notion that foreign-owned firms create larger positive spillovers among their suppliers. As for the technology gap, the estimations identify a positive effect on the likelihood that suppliers experience a large overall positive impact and a large technological impact. This positive effect of the technology gap applies to both suppliers of FDI firms and domestic producer firms, confirming the independent positive effect of the technology gap on the materialization of positive spillovers via inter-firm linkages.

SUMMARY AND CONCLUSIONS

There is a growing acceptance of the notion that spillovers constitute a central component of the impact that FDI firms can create. When FDI firms act as source of new technologies in host economies, domestic firms experience important efficiency or productivity improvements. However, the empirical evidence on the occurrence of these effects is far less consistent. Especially for productivity spillovers that may occur in the same industries in which FDI firms operate, there is strong conflicting evidence suggesting that foreign-owned firms may create positive or negative externalities or do not create any significant productivity effects among domestic firms. Evidence on inter-industry spillovers is somewhat more robust; in particular, several studies find that domestic firms that operate in industries that provide inputs to industries with a large FDI presence appear to be subject to positive productivity spillovers.

In response to the heterogeneity of the evidence on the overall prevalence of FDI spillovers, recent research is focusing on identifying factors that influence these externalities. Three factors are investigated most frequently: input-output linkages between FDI firms and suppliers, the level of technological differences between FDI and domestic firms and the location pattern of economic activity within host economies. However, the evidence on the effects of these factors is characterized by certain limitations which I discuss in this chapter. Econometric evidence on positive inter-industry spillovers does not clarify how positive spillovers occur between FDI firms and suppliers. Evidence from more qualitative studies is more informative, presenting detailed information on the degrees and types of technology transfers that FDI firms may create. The drawback of this approach is that findings are often specific to individual studies, making it difficult to generalize the evidence. Also, the question whether technology transfers by FDI are different from technology transfers created by comparable domestic firms in host economies is usually not addressed. Firms that receive the technology transfers are also usually omitted from the analysis, making it difficult to assess the actual impact that technology transfers may create.

The standard interpretation of the technology gap is that it can be taken as a direct inverse indicator of the level of absorptive capacity of domestic firms. This suggests that a small technology gap favors positive spillovers. However, most of the evidence suggests that a large instead of a small gap favors such positive effects. This positive effect can be explained by interpreting the technology gap as capturing the scope for domestic firms to improve. Provided that domestic firms have a sufficient capacity to absorb new technologies, a large technology gap indicates that the firms can achieve substantial improvements. In addition to this, a large gap is also likely to act as a positive incentive towards domestic firms to try and absorb new technologies, as the gains from doing so will be large.

The location pattern of economic activity is likely to influence FDI spillovers as agglomerations foster the creation of channels that transmit externalities. The limited number of studies that look at the direct relation between agglomeration and FDI externalities find that agglomeration can directly enhance these spillovers. In addition to this, several other studies find that FDI spillovers may be particularly confined at subnational levels within host economies. At the same time, these spillovers may also be transmitted between regions.

To obtain a better understanding of how these three factors may influence FDI spillovers, I conduct a selective review of empirical evidence on the impact of foreign-owned firms in the Mexican economy. Mexico constitutes a particularly good economy on which to conduct such a review, as the impact of FDI firms has been the subject of a large number of studies covering several decades. This offers a richness of findings that is not available for most other host economies. Also, the role of inter-firm linkages, the technology gap and agglomeration feature prominently in several recent studies on this host economy. In extension of this review, I also present new empirical findings on the nature, degree and impact of technology transfers between FDI firms and Mexican suppliers from surveys that I carried out in the state of Nuevo León.

The main findings of the survey on Mexico can be summarized as follows. First, on balance the evidence clearly indicates that Mexican firms experience productivity spillovers from the presence and operations of FDI firms. Most studies that look only at the presence of intra-industry spillovers find evidence of positive externalities. However, findings from studies that distinguish between intra-industry and inter-industry effects indicate that positive spillovers materialize in particular among Mexican firms that supply inputs to FDI firms. Second, the evidence indicates that both the technology gap and agglomeration play significant roles. Importantly, most of the evidence on the effect of the technology gap suggests that large technological differences between FDI and domestic firms foster the occurrence of positive spillovers. As such, the findings for Mexico are in line with the alternative interpretation of what the technology gap captures. As for the effects of agglomeration, the evidence indicates that agglomeration has a direct positive effect on the occurrence of spillovers. Also, there is evidence that FDI spillovers are more pronounced at the regional level. Having said this, related findings indicate that these spillover effects may also occur between regions, be it that these effects decrease with increasing inter-regional distance.

The new empirical evidence that I present in this chapter on technology transfers between producer firms and suppliers shows that FDI firms are engaged in a variety of transfers of technologies to their local suppliers. Importantly, a comparison between FDI and Mexican producer firms shows that foreign-owned firms are significantly more supportive. This applies in particular to various types of technology transfers that have a direct impact on the production processes of the local suppliers, suggesting that FDI firms are a particularly good source of new technologies to domestic firms. Furthermore, findings from the multivariate analysis of factors that influence positive impacts that local suppliers experience from business dealings with their client firms show that type of ownership clearly matters. Suppliers of FDI firms are significantly more likely to experience large overall and technological impacts, even when the estimations control for the levels of technological and organizational support that the suppliers receive from their client firms. The findings also confirm that the technology gap matters for positive impacts that suppliers experience. The estimated effect of the technology gap is positive, in line with the alternative interpretation of what the technology gap captures. Furthermore, the estimated positive effect of the technology gap applies to both suppliers of foreign-owned and Mexican firms. This indicates that the technology gap has an independent effect on the occurrence of productivity spillovers among local suppliers, irrespective of the type of client firm.

Given the high degree of heterogeneity of the evidence on the overall prevalence of FDI spillovers, future research will need to continue to address the role of determinants of these externalities. This chapter identifies limitations of research on several of these determinants that need to be addressed, limitations that are strongly related to policy making. The contrasting findings on the effect of the technology gap are a good example of this. The standard interpretation of the technology gap suggests that host economy governments that want to promote FDI spillovers should attract foreign-owned firms that are technologically not too advanced from domestic firms. Most of the evidence of the effect of the technology gap in Mexico and the alternative interpretation of what this gap captures suggests however that positive spillovers are better promoted by attracting FDI firms that are technologically substantially more advanced than domestic firms. The caveat to this policy implication is that host economy governments also need to try to enhance the capacity of domestic firms to absorb new technologies in order to let the positive effect of a large technology gap materialize.

Given that FDI firms tend to locate in agglomerations of economic activity within host economies, research on the spatial dimensions of FDI spillovers needs to provide more evidence on the direct effects of agglomeration on these externalities. In particular, more evidence and a better understanding are required on how agglomeration facilitates the creation and functioning of channels that transmit FDI spillovers. At the same time, related evidence indicates that FDI spillovers may also materialize across geographical space. This also has clear policy implications, as policies to attract new FDI firms into a given region in a host economy may result in the materialization of externality effects in other regions.

Finally, considering the evidence on FDI spillovers that may arise via inter-firm linkages, there is a clear need to extend and develop quantitative research that uses types of data that is usually obtained via more qualitative studies. Policies that try to influence the occurrence of FDI externalities are much more likely to be successful when they are based on the types of detailed information that is provided by qualitative studies. However, in order to be able to use such information, more careful research designs are required to ensure that findings from individual studies can be generalized. Also, future research must try to address the central underlying question whether FDI firms are actually different from comparable domestic firms. Governments often face difficult questions whether to promote domestic firms or to attract more foreign-owned firms into their economies. Clear evidence on whether and how foreign-owned firms may create larger beneficial impacts among domestic firms than comparable domestic producer firms will help substantially in addressing these questions. Furthermore, future research must also start to explicitly include suppliers into the research samples. By omitting suppliers from the studies, it remains unclear what the actual impacts may be from the technology transfers that FDI firms (and domestic firms) may be creating. More detailed evidence on whether and how technology transfers may benefit local suppliers will help host economy governments to design effective policies that can help these firms absorb and benefit from new technologies that are transmitted by FDI firms.

REFERENCES

Aitken, B., Harrison, A. and Lipsey, R.E. (1996) Wages and foreign ownership: A comparative study of Mexico, Venezuela and the United States. *Journal of International Economics*, vol. 40(3-4), p. 345-371.

Aitken,B., Hanson, G. and Harrison, A.E. (1997) Spillovers, foreign investment and export behavior. *Journal of International Economics*, vol. 43(1-2), p. 103-132.

Aitken, B.J. and Harrison, A.E. (1999) Do domestic firms benefit from direct foreign investment? Evidence from Venezuela. *The American Economic Review*, vol. 89(3), p. 605-618.

Barrios, S. and Strobl, E. (2002) Foreign direct investment and productivity spillovers: Evidence from the Spanish experience. *Review of World Economics*, vol. 138(3), p. 459-481.

Barrios, S. Bertinelli, L. and Strobl, E. (2006) Co-agglomeration and spillovers. *Regional Science and Urban Economics*, vol. 36(4), p. 467-481.

Blalock, G. and Gertler, P.J. (2008) Welfare gains from foreign direct investment through technology transfer to local suppliers. *Journal of International Economics*, vol. 74(2), p. 402-421.

Blomström, M. (1986) Foreign investment and productivity efficiency: The case of Mexico. *Journal of Industrial Economics*, vol. 35(1), p. 97-110.

Blomström, M. and Persson, H. (1983) Foreign investment and spillover efficiency in an underdeveloped economy: Evidence from the Mexican manufacturing industry. *World Development*, vol. 11(6), p. 493-501.

Blomström, M. and Kokko, A. (1997) Regional integration and foreign direct investment. *NBER Working Paper Series*, paper nr. 6019. Cambridge, MA: National Bureau of Economic Research.

Blomström, M. and Kokko, A. (1998) "Multinational Corporations and Spillovers". *Journal of Economic Surveys*, vol. 12(3), p. 1-31.

Blomström, M. and Wang, J-Y. (1992) Foreign investment and technology transfer: A simple model. *European Economic Review*, vol. 36(1), p. 137-155.

Blomström, M. and Wolff, E. (1994) Multinational corporations and productivity convergence in Mexico. In Baumol, W., Nelson, R. and Wolff, E. (eds.) *Convergence of productivity: Cross-national studies and historical evidence*. Oxford: Oxford University Press.

Blyde, J., Kugler, M. and Stein, E. (2004) Exporting versus outsourcing by MNC subsidiaries: What determines FDI spillovers? *Discussion Papers in Economics and Econometrics*. Southampton: University of Southampton.

Castellani, D. and Zanfei, A. (2003) Productivity gaps, inward investment and productivity of European firms. *Economics of Innovation and New Technology*, vol. 12, p. 450-468.

Caves, R. E. (2007) *Multinational enterprises and economic analysis*. Cambridge: Cambridge University Press.

Crespo, N., Proenca, I., and Fontoura, M.P. (2007) FDI spillovers at the regional level: Evidence from Portugal. *School of Economics and Management Working Paper Series*, Paper nr. 28. Lisbon: Technical University of Lisbon.

Crone, M. and Roper, S. (2001) Local learning from multinational plants: Knowledge transfers in the supply chain. *Regional Studies*, vol. 35(6), p. 535-548.

Cuevas, A., Messmacher, M. and Werner, A. (2005) Foreign direct investment in Mexico since the approval of NAFTA. *World Bank Economic Review*, vol. 19(3), p. 473-488.

De Propris, L., and Driffield, N. (2006) The importance of clusters for spillovers from foreign direct investment and technology sourcing. *Cambridge Journal of Economics*, vol. 30(2), p. 277-291.

Disdier, A. C. and Mayer, T. (2004) How different is Eastern Europe? Structure and determinants of location choices by French firms in Eastern and Western Europe. *Journal of Comparative Economics*, vol. 32, p. 280-296.

Djankov, S. and Hoekman, B. (2000) Foreign ownership and productivity growth in Czech enterprises. *World Bank Economic Review*, vol. 14(1), p. 49-64

Driffield, N. (2004) Regional policy and spillovers from FDI in the UK. *Annals of Regional Science*, vol. 38(4), p. 579-594.

Driffield, N. (2006) On the search for spillovers from FDI with spatial dependency. *Regional Studies*, vol. 40(1), p. 107-119.

Driffield, N. and Munday, M. (2001) Foreign manufacturing, regional agglomeration and technical efficiency in UK manufacturing industries: A stochastic production frontier approach. *Regional Studies*, vol. 35(5), p. 391-399.

Dunning, J.H. and Lundan, S.M. (2008) *Multinational enterprises and the global economy*. Cheltenham: Edward Elgar.

Duranton, G. and Puga, D. (2004) Micro-foundations of urban agglomeration economies. In: Henderson, V.J. and Thisse, J.F. (eds.) *Handbook of urban and regional economics*, vol. 4. Amsterdam: North Holland.

Findlay. R. (1978) Relative backwardness, direct foreign investment and the transfer of technology: A simple dynamic model. *The Quarterly Journal of Economics*, vol. 92(1), p. 371-393.

Gershenkron, A. (1962) *Economic backwardness in historical perspective*. Cambridge, MA: Belknap Press of Harvard University Press.

Girma, S. (2005) Absorptive capacity and productivity spillovers from FDI: A threshold regression analysis. *Oxford Bulletin of Economics and Statistics*, vol. 67(3), p. 281-306.

Girma, S. and Wakelin, K. (2007) Local productivity spillovers from foreign direct investment in the UK electronics industry. *Regional Science and Urban Economics*, vol. 37(3), p. 399-412.

Girma, S., Greenaway, D. and Wakelin, K. (2001) Who benefits from foreign direct investment in the UK? *Scottish Journal of Political Economy*, vol. 48(2), p. 239-248.

Giroud, A. and Scott-Kennel, J. (2009) Multinationals' linkages in international business: A framework for analysis. *International Business Review*, vol. 18(6), p. 1-34.

Goh, A-T. (2005) Knowledge diffusion, input suppliers' technological effort and technology transfer via vertical relationships. *Journal of International Economics*, vol. 66(2), p. 527-540.

Gorg, H. and Greenaway, D. (2004) Much ado about nothing? Do domestic firms really benefit from foreign direct investment? *World Bank Research Observer*, vol. 19(2), p. 171-197.

Grether, J.M. (1999) Determinants of technology diffusion in Mexican manufacturing: A plant-level analysis. *World Development*, vol. 27(7), p. 1287-1298.

Haddad, M. and Harrison, A. (1993) Are there positive spillovers from direct foreign investment? Evidence from panel data for Morocco. *Journal of Development Economics*, vol. 42(1), p. 651-74.

Halpern, L. and Murakozy, B. (2007) Does distance matter in spillover? *Economics of Transition*, vol. 15, p. 781-805.

Haskel, J.E., Pereira, S.C. and Slaughter, M.J. (2007) Does inward Foreign Direct Investment boost the productivity of domestic firms? *The Review of Economics and Statistics*, vol. 89)3), p. 482-496.

Head, K.C., Ries, J.C. and Swenson, D.L. (1995) Agglomeration benefits and location choice: Evidence from Japanese manufacturing investments in the United States. *Journal of International Economics*, vol. 38, p. 223-247

Javorcik, B.S. (2008) Can survey evidence shed light on spillovers from Foreign Direct Investment? *World Bank Research Observer*, vol. 23(2), p. 139-159.

Javorcik, B.S. and Spatareanu, M. (2005) Disentangling FDI spillover effects: What do firm perceptions tell us? P.45-72. In: Moran, T.H., Graham, E.M. and Blomström, M. (eds.) *Does foreign direct investment promote development*? Washington, DC: Institute for International Economics.

Javorcik, B.S. and Spatareanu, M. (2011) Does it matter where you come from? Vertical spillovers fom foreign direct investment and the origin of investors. *Journal of Development Economics*, vol. 96(1), p. 126-138.

Jordaan, J.A. (2005) Determinants of FDI-induced externalities: New empirical evidence for Mexican manufacturing industries. *World Development*, vol. 33(12), p. 2103-2118.

Jordaan, J.A. (2008)a State characteristics and the locational choice of foreign direct investment: Evidence from regional FDI in Mexico 1989-2006. *Growth and Change*, vol. 39(3), p. 389-413.

Jordaan, J.A. (2008)b Intra- and inter-industry externalities from foreign direct investment in the Mexican manufacturing sector: New evidence from Mexican regions. *World Development*, vol. 36(12), p. 2838-2854.

Jordaan, J.A. (2008)c Regional foreign participation and externalities: New empirical evidence from Mexico. *Environment and Planning A*, vol. 40(12), p. 2948-2969.

Jordaan, J.A. (2009) *Foreign Direct Investment, Agglomeration and Externalities*. Farnham: Ashgate Publishing Limited.

Jordaan, J.A. (2011)a Cross-sectional estimation of FDI spillovers when FDI is endogenous: OLS and IV estimates for Mexican manufacturing industries. *Applied Economics*, vol. 43(19), p. 2451-2463.

Jordaan, J.A. (2011)b Technology gap, agglomeration and FDI spillovers: A survey of the literature. In: DeSare, T. and Caprioglio, D. (eds.) *Foreign investment: Types. Methods and impacts*. Haupage, NY: Nova Science Publishers.

Jordaan, J.A. (2011)c FDI, local sourcing and supportive linkages with domestic suppliers: The case of Monterrey, Mexico. *World Development*, vol. 39(4), p. 620-632.

Jordaan, J.A. (2011)d Local sourcing and technology spillovers to Mexican suppliers: How important are FDI and supplier characteristics? *Growth and Change*, vol. 42(3), p. 287-319.

Jordaan, J.A. (2012)a Empirical estimations of FDI spillovers: A critical survey. In: Mendez, S.A. and Vega, A.M. (eds.) *Econometrics: New research*. Haupage, NY: Nova Science Publishers.

Jordaan, J.A. (2012)b Agglomeration and the location choice of foreign direct investment: New evidence from manufacturing FDI in Mexico. *Estudios Económicos*, vol. 27(1), p. 61-97.

Jordaan, J.A. (2013) Firm heterogeneity and technology transfers to local suppliers: Disentangling the effects of foreign ownership, technology gap and absorptive capacity. *The Journal of International Trade and Economic Development*, vol. 22(1), p. 71-93.

Jordaan, J.A. and Rodriguez-Oreggia, E. (2012) Regional growth in Mexico under trade liberalization: How important are agglomeration and FDI? *The Annals of Regional Science*, vol. 48(1), p. 179-202.

Keller, M. (1996) Absorptive capacity: On the creation of and acquisition of technology in development. *Journal of Development Economics*, vol. 49(1), p. 199-227.

Kugler, M. (2006) Spillovers from foreign direct investment: within or between industries? *Journal of Development Economics*, vol. 80(2), p. 444-477.

Kokko, A. (1994) Technology, market characteristics and spillovers. *Journal of Development Economics*, vol. 43(2), p. 279-293.

Kokko, A. (1996) Productivity spillovers from competition between local firms and foreign affiliates. *Journal of International Development*, vol. 8(4), p. 517-530.

Kosteas, V.D. (2008) Foreign direct investment and productivity spillovers: A quantile analysis. *International Economic Journal*, vol. 22(1), p. 25-41.

Lipsey, R.E. and Sjoholm, F. (2005) The impact of FDI on host countries: Why such different answers? P.23-44. In: Moran, T.H., Graham, E.M. and Blomström, M. (eds.) *Does foreign direct investment promote development?* Washington, DC: Institute for International Economics.

Liu, Z. (2008) Foreign direct investment and technology spillovers. *Journal of Development Economics*, vol. 85(1-2), p. 176-193.

Love, J.H. and Hidalgo-Lage, F. (2000) Analyzing the determinants of US direct investment in Mexico. *Applied Economics*, vol. 32(10), p. 1259-1267.

Menghinello, S., De Propris, L. and Driffield, N. (2010) Industrial districts, inward foreign investment and regional development. *Journal of Economic Geography*, vol. 10(4), p. 539-558.

Monastiriotis, V. and Jordaan, J.A. (2011) Does FDI promote regional development? Evidence from local and regional productivity spillovers in Greece. *Eastern Journal of European Studies*, vol. 1(2), p. 139-164

Moran, T.H. (2005) How does FDI affect host country development? Using industry case studies to make reliable generalizations, p. 281-314. In: Moran, T.H., Graham, E.M. and Blomström, M. (eds.) *Does foreign direct investment promote development?* Washington, DC: Institute for International Economics.

Nelson, R.R. (1968) A diffusion model of international productivity differences. *The American Economic Review*, LVIII, p. 1219-1248.

OECD (2007) *Economic Survey of Mexico 2007: Maximizing the gains from integration in the world economy*. Paris: Organisation for Economic Cooperation and Development.

Pacheco-Lopez, P. (2005) Foreign direct investment, exports and imports in Mexico. *World Economy*, vol. 28(8), p. 1157-1172.

Potter, J., Moore, B. and Spires, R. (2002) The wider effects of inward Foreign Direct Investment in manufacturing on UK industry. *Journal of Economic Geography*, vol. 2, p. 279-310.

Potter, J., Moore, B. and Spires, R. (2003) Foreign manufacturing investment in the United Kingdom and the upgrading of supplier practices. *Regional Studies*, vol. 37(1), p. 41-60.

Ramirez, M.D. (2000) Foreign direct investment in Mexico: A cointegration analysis. *The Journal of Development Studies*, vol. 37(1), p. 138-162.

Ramirez, M.D. (2003) Mexico under NAFTA: A critical assessment. *The Quarterly Journal of Economics*, vol. and Finance, vol. 43(5), p. 863-892.

Ramirez, M.D. (2006) Is foreign direct investment beneficial for Mexico? An empirical analysis. *World Development*, vol. 34(5), p. 802-817.

Rodrik, D. (1992) Closing the productivity gap: Does trade liberalization really help? P.155-175, In: Helleiner, G. (ed.) *Trade policy, industrialization and development: New perspectives*. Oxford: Clarendon.

Rosenthal, S. and Strange, W. (2004) Evidence of the nature and sources of agglomeration economies. In: Henderson, V.J. and Thisse, J.F. (eds.) *Handbook of urban and regional economics*, vol. 4. Amsterdam: North Holland.

Sjöholm, F. (1998) Productivity growth in Indonesia: The role of regional characteristics and foreign investment. *Economic Development and Cultural Change*, vol. 47(3), p. 559-584.

Sjöholm, F. (1999) Technology gap, competition and spillovers from direct foreign investment: Evidence from establishment data. *The Journal of Development Studies*, vol. 36(1), p. 53-73.

Smarzynska, B.K. (2004) Does foreign direct investment increase the productivity of domestic firms? In search of spillovers through backward linkages. *The American Economic Review*, vol. 94(3), p. 605-627.

ten Kate, A. (1992) Trade liberalization and economic stabilization in Mexico: Lessons of experience. *World Development*, vol. 20(5), p. 659-672.

UNCTAD (2001) *World Investment Report 2001: Promoting Linkages*. Geneva: United Nations Conference on Trade and Development.

UNCTAD (2005) *World Investment Report 2005: Transnational Corporations and the internationalization of R&D*. Geneva: United Nations Conference on Trade and Development.

Venables, A.J. and Barba Navaretti, G. (2005) *Multinational Firms in the World Economy*. Oxfordshire: Princeton University Press.

Zukowska-Gagelmann, K. (2000) Productivity spillovers from foreign direct investment in Poland. *Economic Systems*, vol. 24(3), p. 232-256.

In: Foreign Direct Investment (FDI)
Editors: Enzo Guillon and Lucas Chauvet

ISBN: 978-1-62808-403-0
© 2013 Nova Science Publishers, Inc.

Chapter 3

FDI AND ECONOMIC GROWTH: EVIDENCE FROM THE EU AT THE REGIONAL LEVEL

Adolfo Maza[*], *José Villaverde, María Gutiérrez-Portilla and Paula Gutiérrez-Portilla*
Department of Economics, University of Cantabria
Avda. de los Castros, Santander, Spain

ABSTRACT

Over the last decades, Foreign Direct Investment (FDI) has become one of the main drivers of economic growth, both at national and regional levels. Economic theory suggests that international capital flows should improve the allocation of resources and consequently should promote growth. In fact, FDI is an essential instrument to spread technology from the most to the least developed countries because it causes positive externalities and spillover effects. It also helps to increase human capital formation and productivity among firms as well as to foster integration through international trade. All these changes enhance economic growth.

The European Union (EU) has been one of the main recipients of FDI in the current era of globalization, which has given rise to a vast literature about the issue. Within this branch of the literature there are, however, just a few studies devoted to the study of FDI at regional level. For this reason, the main purpose of this manuscript is to investigate the link between FDI and economic growth across European regions (NUTS2) over the period 2000-2007. This topic, always important, is even more relevant at the current time. The EU is now immersed in an economic and financial crisis, which has reduced significantly both FDI inflows and intra-EU flows. Even though it seems unlikely to recover the FDI highest level reached in 2007, a suitable atmosphere for foreign investment could contribute to mitigate its negative consequences for European regional development. This is the reason why host countries should have a proper environment for investment as well as an institutional framework to implement policies focused on attracting capital flows.

---

[*] E-mails: mazaaj@unican.es; villavej@unican.es; maria.gutierrezp@alumnos.unican.es; paula.gutierrezpo@alumnos.unican.es.

The main results of the manuscript can be summarized as follows: firstly, FDI is quite concentrated at regional level; secondly, FDI has contributed to enhance economic growth in European regions and finally, FDI has not led to the process of convergence during the sample period.

Keywords: Foreign direct investment; economic growth; European regions

INTRODUCTION

One of the most striking developments of the last few decades is the tremendous growth of Foreign Direct Investment (FDI) in the global economy. This growth has been even more spectacular since mid-nineties,[1] therefore making FDI a vital component of the economic strategies put forward by most developed and developing countries. Europe, and more specifically the European Union (EU), has traditionally been one of the main recipients of FDI, particularly since the launching of the single market program, the introduction of the euro and the last two enlargements.[2] Therefore, the study of FDI is of paramount interest, especially from a policy-oriented point of view.

Accordingly, there are numerous studies analyzing topics related to FDI for the European case, topics such as the determinants for the location of FDI, its spatial distribution, the role played by FDI as an engine of economic growth, etc. Most of these studies, however, have been carried out at national level, paying none or scant attention to the regional level (for a review, see, among others, Barba and Venables, 2004).

Although this focus on the national level could seem quite surprising as such type of analysis involves serious problems of aggregation (the European countries are of widely differing sizes and encompass different number of regions), there is a clear reason behind it: the lack of FDI homogeneous statistical information for the EU regions. This being so, different authors and institutions have tried to circumvent this difficulty, producing various outcomes among which stand out the so-called FDIRegio database and the Elios[3] database, both of which offer directly observed regional data. These databases are, without any doubt, very interesting, but they suffer, in our opinion, from a critical drawback: they just offer regional information about the number of foreign firms establishing affiliates in some EU countries but not on the amounts invested by these companies.[4] Considering this, the present chapter makes use of a different FDI database built by Polasek and Sellner to analyze regional

---

[1] FDI inflows in the world increased nearly fivefold between 1996 and 2007, from $386.1 billion in 1996 to $1833.3 billion in 2007.

[2] We are specifically referring to the EU27. According to the EU foreign direct investment yearbook (EUROSTAT, 2008), the share of EU FDI inflows (excluding intra-EU flows) in world FDI flows was around 20% in 2006 while the United States, for example, presented a share of 18%. If FDI flows between EU countries were computed, the share would be more than double.

[3] Elios stands for European Linkages and Ownership Structure.

[4] FDIRegio is a database obtained from Amadeus database compiled by the Bureau Van Dijk. For each company, this database provides, among other things, information about the year of incorporation, the country/region of origin and destination, the ownership structure and the sector of activity of the company.

Elios database was built at the University of Urbino (Italy) and collects information from Dun & Brasdstreet's Who owns whom. The information, collected for the five largest European countries, refers, for each firm, to the name and country of the ultimate owner, the sector of activity, location and year of establishment.

globalization.[5] It is true that this database also has some limitations, the main ones being that it does not include any sectoral breakdown or the country of origin, but we consider it is better than FDIRegio and Elios databases as it really offers information about the total amount of FDI in the EU regions that is consistent with the amount of FDI in the EU countries.

Taking advantage of this new database, the aim of this paper is to analyze the impact of FDI on regional economic growth and economic convergence. As it is well known, FDI is generally considered a key factor in fostering economic growth, and this work tries to test if this is true for the European regions. Closely related to this, the paper also tries to assess if FDI has contributed to the process of convergence that, as we will see below, has taken place across European regions. To accomplish this aim, the period 2000-2007 is studied for two main reasons: first, due to data limitations, as FDI series only go to 2006; second because, due to the fact that economic crisis has dramatically changed the economic scenario, it is very risky and definitely not recommended to mix years before and after the crisis outbreak.

Bearing these considerations in mind, this paper is organized as follows. Section 2 briefly reviews the empirical literature devoted to the relationship between FDI and economic growth. Section 3 outlines the pattern of the regional distribution of FDI in the EU trying to unveil which trends and characteristics can be discerned over the sample period. After that, Section 4 assesses the role played by FDI as an engine for economic growth and economic convergence. Finally, Section 5 concludes and offers some policy implications.

I. LITERATURE REVIEW: IMPACT OF FDI ON GROWTH

The role of FDI in the process of economic growth has motivated a vast empirical literature on both developed and developing countries. Different authors have reviewed the recent literature in this field, among which stand out Mello (1997), Ewe-Ghee (2001), Ozturk (2007), Laurenceson and Tang (2007) and Cipollina et al. (2012).

In less developed countries, FDI has long been recognized not only as a way of triggering capital accumulation but also as a major source of technology and know-how transfer that might reinforce future industrialization. In developed countries, FDI allows the introduction of new working practices as well as technology diffusion.

Neoclassical and endogenous growth models provide the framework for most of the empirical studies analyzing the FDI-growth relationship. According to the neoclassical growth theory, growth in a country is stimulated by capital accumulation and this can proceed, among other sources, from FDI. In the neoclassical Solow growth model with diminishing returns to physical capital, FDI has a short-term effect on economic growth just until each country reaches its new steady state (Solow, 1956). The endogenous growth literature points out that FDI may also have a permanent effect on growth because not only does it increase capital accumulation in the receiving country but it also introduces new

---

[5] This database has been built by using the spatial Chow-Lin data interpolation method as described in Polasek and Sellner (2010) and Polasek et al. (2010). As indicated by Polasek and Sellner (2011) "the spatial Chow-Lin procedure uses the relationship between a dependent variable that is only measured at a more aggregate regional level (...) and independent variables that are measured at a more disaggregate regional level (...) to predict the dependent variable at the disaggregate regional level". We gratefully acknowledged these colleagues for offering us this database.

technologies, raises the level of knowledge and skill through labor training (de Mello, 1996a) and enhances competition in the host country by reducing the market power of the existing firms (Barro and Sala-i-Martin, 1995). The scope of externalities and their impact on economic growth in the long run is a key element in endogenous models.

First of all, the relationship between FDI and economic growth could be analyzed adopting a causality approach. In this respect, it is worth mentioning the following group of studies. Using data for 14 EU countries from the period 1970 to 1999, Argiro (2001) performs Granger causality tests finding that the hypothesis of FDI causing growth has been supported in eight cases (Belgium, Denmark, Germany, Greece, France, Netherlands, Austria, Portugal and UK). Just the opposite relation is found for Italy, Finland, Spain and Ireland, whereas there was no causality between FDI and GDP for Sweden. Hansen and Rand (2004) provide a similar causality analysis. For a sample of 31 developing countries covering the period 1970-2000, they conclude that FDI has a significant long-term impact on GDP irrespectively of the level of development. As for the relation of causality between FDI and technology spillovers, Kholdy (1995) analyses the hypothesis that FDI improves the overall efficiency of domestic production, measured in terms of labor productivity, in Mexico, Brazil, Chile, Singapore and Zambia over the period 1970-1990. Using Granger-causality tests, his results do not back up the efficiency spillover hypothesis. However, he proves that FDI is attracted to countries with larger factor endowments, internal markets and more advanced technology. With regard to the direction of causality between outward FDI and exports, Pfaffermayr (1994) assesses it for the Austrian economy in the post-1970 period and discovers a significant causality running in both directions. Likewise, the hypothesis that outward FDI benefits exports is tested for Taiwan and four ASEAN economies (Indonesia, Malaysia, Philippines and Thailand) by Lin (1995). He points out that there is a positive impact of outward FDI on both exports and imports, suggesting that FDI enhances bilateral trade and thereby, economic growth.

Most empirical studies, however, do not pay any attention to the causality issue and assume the existence of a link that goes from FDI to growth, finding that there is a positive impact of the first on the second. Bajo-Rubio and Sosvilla-Rivero (1994) develop an econometric analysis of FDI in Spain during the 1964-1989 period. They state that, when splitting total FDI into manufacturing and non-manufacturing activities, FDI fosters integration into world markets and consequently, promotes faster economic growth. Making use of cointegration techniques, they find a long-term relationship between FDI inflows and some macroeconomic variables such as the level of real GDP, the rate of inflation, the level of trade barriers and the lagged foreign capital stock. Another paper studying the Spanish economy from a regional perspective is the one developed by Bajo-Rubio et al. (2010). These authors assess the effect of FDI on economic growth proving that the Spanish´s entry into the European Union in 1986 has been one of the main drivers of FDI inflows for the following twenty years. Performing a panel data analysis, De Mello (1996b) discovers a positive impact of FDI on output growth in two groups of countries: technological leaders and followers. Mullen and Williams (2005) develop their study for 48 continental US states covering the period 1977-1997. They highlight that inward FDI plays a positive role in regional economic activity. Johnson (2006) shows that FDI inflows enhance economic growth in developing economies but not in developed ones. Dang (2008) states that FDI contributes importantly to Chinese economic development by increasing the total factor productivity and establishing foreign-funded enterprises. Dabla-Norris et al. (2010) find that FDI is linked with growth in low-income countries during the recent globalization period. Additionally, they point out that

FDI outflows to low-income countries depend on economic conditions in advanced countries. Castellani and Pieri (2011) show, for the case of European regions at the NUTS-2 level, that both inward and outward FDI have positive effects on productivity growth, after controlling for a set of regional characteristics such as industry mix or human and technological capital. Elsadig (2012) investigates the effect of foreign investment on Malaysian economy in terms of GDP and other productivity indicators. His results support that FDI improves economic growth during the period 1999-2008. Nevertheless, it may occur that while FDI fosters economic growth, it also leads to an increase in the regional income inequality. This result is demonstrated for the Chinese economy by Tang and Selvanathan (2005). These authors prove that FDI inflows have raised regional income inequality at national, rural and urban levels in China.

Conditional to some factors, other authors also find a positive impact of FDI on economic growth. Borenzstein et al. (1998) show evidence that the effect of FDI on economic growth depends on the level of human capital available in the host economy. These authors, by using data on FDI flows from industrial countries to 69 developing countries over the period 1970-1989, point out that FDI enhances economic growth only when the host economy has sufficient absorptive capability. Alfaro et al. (2004, 2009) carry out their research using data of OECD and non-OECD countries between 1975 and 1995. They state that the level of development of local financial markets is crucial to foster economic growth because only countries with better financial systems can exploit FDI more efficiently. Using cross-section data sample of 46 developing countries characterized by differing trade policy regimes, Balasubramanyam et al. (1996) determine that beneficial effects of FDI, in terms of economic growth, are stronger in export promoting countries than in import substituting ones, that is, the hypothesis put forward by Bhagwati is empirically tested. De Mello (1997) argues that the impact of FDI on economic growth depends on the scope for efficiency spillovers to domestic firms. Developing countries have to reach, therefore, a minimum level of educational, technological and infrastructure development before their being able to benefit from FDI. Borghesi and Giovannetti (2003) point out the importance of institutions for attracting FDI flows. In the same vein, Lee and Mansfield (1996) test the hypothesis that intellectual property protection influences the volume of FDI in the case of outward flows from the US. This finding remains robust to the inclusion of other independent variables such as the degree of openness of the host economy (Wheeler and Mody, 1992). An empirical result supporting the idea that regulation has beneficial effects on host countries by stimulating FDI is the one obtained by Busse and Groizard (2008). However, this does not happen to economies with excessive business and labor regulations. Put it another way, this result indicates that regulations restrict growth through foreign investment inflows only in the most regulated economies. Zhang (2001) analyses 11 economies in East Asia and Latin America and proves that FDI tends to be more likely to promote economic growth in East Asia than Latin America due to the fact that East Asian economies have adopted more liberalized trade regimes, improved human capital, encouraged export-oriented FDI and maintained macroeconomic stability. As can be seen, these authors show that there are factors such as the human capital, financial market regulation, the trade regime, the banking system or the degree of openness in the economy that, especially in developing countries, could play an essential role when examining the FDI impact on the overall economic growth.

Additionally, some empirical studies provide evidence for the existence of a negative relationship between FDI and economic growth. Using heterogeneous panel cointegration, Herzer (2012) examines the effect of FDI on economic growth for 44 developing countries, finding that, on average, there is a negative long-run effect on growth in developing countries, although with large differences across countries. A model-selection approach based on a general-to-specific methodology is adopted to conclude that cross-country heterogeneity in the growth impact of FDI can be explained by cross-country variations in freedom from government intervention, business freedom, FDI volatility, and primary export dependence.

Another strand of literature looks for positive spillovers derived from FDI adopting a microeconomic approach. Such efficiency spillovers are known to emanate from multinationals to domestic firms in the host country through three main channels: movements of highly skilled staff, "demonstration effects" through which foreign affiliates may induce local competitors to adopt superior technologies and techniques, and competition from multinationals that forces domestic firms to update production technologies in order to cope with foreign competition (Blomström and Kokko, 1998). Haskel et al. (2001), employing UK manufacturing plants data, highlight a significantly positive correlation between the domestic plant's total-factor productivity (TFP) and the foreign share of employment in that plant's industry. They also show that spillovers take time to permeate to domestic plants. Barrios and Strobl (2002) claim that only Spanish domestic firms that have the appropriate absorptive capacity are able to take advantage of positive externalities that are often associated with FDI. Barrios et al. (2004) find as well some evidence of positive efficiency spillovers arising from FDI in Ireland and Spain. However, they argue that firms should have the absorptive capacity to capture technological spillovers, and the way they are measured depends on the choice of cut-off point in terms of foreign participation. Allard and Pampillón (2005) emphasize that US FDI has meant an important share of Spanish investment in research and development and has enhanced Spanish productivity. Alfaro and Charlton (2007), using industry-level data for 29 countries over the period 1985-2000, determine that FDI is associated with higher growth in value added. This relation becomes stronger for industries with higher skilled workers and with foreign capital intensity.

More recent studies have focused on the consequences of FDI at sector level. Bode and Nunnenkamp (2011) have analyzed the effect of inward FDI on per capita income and growth of the US states since the mid-1970s. They claim that FDI is associated with less convergence among US states. Both authors add that FDI depends on its qualitative characteristics. In particular, empirical evidence shows that employment-intensity FDI, concentrated on richer states, leads to long-run income growth, while capital-intensity FDI, on poorer states, does not. Cipollina et al. (2012) study a sample of 14 industries for up to 22 developed and developing countries over the period 1992 to 2004 finding a positive impact on FDI of the host countries' growth, stronger in more capital-intensive and technologically advanced sectors.

To conclude, it seems clear that most of the studies analyzed in this section have found a positive relationship between FDI and economic growth. A consensus has been reached on the fact that FDI tends to have a significant and positive effect on economic growth through different channels such as capital formation, technology transfer, efficiency spillover, human capital and skill acquisition, and so on. This is the reason why, in this paper, it is assumed that FDI has a positive effect on growth.

As can be seen, there is a vast literature on the topic of the relationship between FDI and economic growth. Then, to conclude this section with an attempt to offer a snapshot of the current state of knowledge on this issue, Table 1 presents an overview of the empirical studies of FDI and host country economic growth previously mentioned, indicating the approaches and techniques used as well as the most relevant results found in each study.

Table 1. Empirical studies of FDI and economic growth

Study	Type of data	Countries and time period	Empirical approach	Effects of FDI on economic growth
Studies adopting a causality approach				
Argiro (2001)	Panel data	14 European Union Countries 1970-1999	Analysis of causality between inward FDI and economic growth using Granger causality tests and Error Correction Models	FDI causes GDP in 8 cases (Belgium, Denmark, Germany, Greece, France, Netherlands, Austria, Portugal and UK). GDP causes FDI in 4 cases (Italy, Finland, Spain and Ireland). No causality for Sweden.
Hansen and Rand (2004)	Panel data	31 developing countries 1970-2000	Analysis of causality between FDI and GDP using Granger causality tests	Positive. FDI has a significant long run impact on GDP irrespectively of the level of development.
Kholdy (1995)	Panel data	Mexico, Brasil, Chile, Singapore and Zambia 1970-1990	Analysis of causality between FDI and spillover efficiency using Granger causality tests	The efficiency spillover hypothesis is not proved. FDI is attracted to countries with larger factor endowments, internal markets and more advanced technology.
Pfaffermayr (1994)	Time series	Austria Post-1970	Analysis of causality between foreign outward direct investment and exports	Significant causality of foreign outward direct investment and exports in both directions.
Lin (1995)	Panel data	Taiwan and four ASEAN economies (Indonesia, Malaysia, Philippines and Thailand) 1972-1992	OLS regression	Positive. FDI enhances bilateral trade.
Studies finding a positive impact of FDI on economic growth				
Bajo-Rubio and Sosvilla-Rivero (1994)	Time series	Spain 1964-1989	Cointegration techniques	FDI fosters integration into world markets and promotes faster economic growth.

Table 1. (Continued)

Study	Type of data	Countries and time period	Empirical approach	Effects of FDI on economic growth
Bajo-Rubio, Díaz-Mora and Díaz-Roldán (2010)	Panel data	Spanish regions 1987-2000	Regression analysis using GMM	Positive influence of FDI on the evolution of GDP per employee and, consequently, on growth.
Mullen and Williams (2005)	Panel data	48 continental US states 1977-1997	OLS regression	Positive. Inward FDI plays a strong role in regional economic activity.
Johnson (2006)	Cross-section and panel data	90 countries 1980-2002	OLS regression	FDI inflows enhance economic growth in developing economies but not in developed ones.
Dang (2008)	Time series	China 1983-2006	Descriptive analysis	FDI contributes importantly to economic development.
Dabla-Norris, Honda, Lahreche and Verdier (2010)	Panel data	From G7 countries to over 100 developing countries 1985-2007	Regression analysis using GMM	FDI is associated with growth in low-income countries during the recent globalization period. FDI outflows to low-income countries depend on economic conditions in advanced countries.
Castellani and Pieri (2011)	Panel data	European regions at the NUTS 2 level	OLS regression	Both inward and outward FDI have positive effects on productivity growth.
Elsadig (2012)	Time series	Malaysia 1999-2008	OLS regression	Positive. FDI inflows improve Malaysian productivity growth.
Tang and Selvanathan (2005)	Panel data	National, rural and urban level in China 1978-2002	OLS regression	FDI inflows foster economic growth but lead to an increase in regional income inequality.
Borensztein, De Gregorio and Lee (1998)	Panel data	69 developing countries 1970-1989	Seemingly unrelated regressions technique (SUR)	The effect of FDI on economic growth is dependent on the level of human capital available in the host economy.
Alfaro, Chanda, Kalemli-Ozcan and Sayek (2004)	Panel data	OECD and non-OECD countries 1975-1995	OLS regression	Countries with well-developed financial markets gain significantly from FDI in terms of their growth rates.
Alfaro, Chanda, Kalemli-Ozcan and Sayek (2009)		Developed and developing countries	Calibration	An increase in FDI leads to higher growth rates in financially developed countries.
Balasubramanyam, Salisu and Sapsford (1996)	Panel data	46 developing countries 1970-1985	OLS regression	The beneficial effect of FDI, in terms of enhanced economic growth, is stronger in export promoting countries (Bhagwati´s hypothesis).

Study	Type of data	Countries and time period	Empirical approach	Effects of FDI on economic growth
Lee and Mansfield (1996)	Industry level data	100 US firms	OLS regression	Intellectual property protection influences the volume of FDI in the case of outward flows from the US.
Busse and Groizard (2008)	Panel data	84 countries 1994-2003	GMM technique	FDI does not stimulate growth in economies with excessive business and labor regulations.
Zhang (2001)	Cross-country data	11 economies in East Asia and Latin America	Three-step procedure: unit root, cointegration, causality tests	FDI tends to be more likely to promote growth in East Asia than Latin America, as it depends on country-specific characteristics.
Studies finding a negative impact of FDI on economic growth					
Herzer (2012)	Panel data	44 developing countries 1970-2005	Heterogeneous panel cointegration and model-selection approach	FDI has, on average, a negative long-run impact on growth in developing countries, but there are large cross-country differences in the growth effects of FDI.
Studies adopting a microeconomic approach (firm or sector data)					
Haskel, Pereira and Slaughter (2001)	Plant-level panel	UK manufacturing plants 1973-1992	OLS regression	Positive. An increase in foreign presence in UK raises the TFP of industry's domestic plants.
Barrios and Strobl (2002)	Panel data	Spanish manufacturing firms 1990-1998	OLS regression and fixed effects	Positive. Only domestic firms with the appropriate absorptive capacity take advantage of positive externalities from FDI.
Barrios, Dimelis, Louri and Strobl (2004)	Firm-data level	EU periphery: Greece, Ireland and Spain 1992-1997	OLS regression	Positive efficiency spillovers from FDI in Ireland and Spain. Lack of them in Greece.
Allard and Pampillón (2005)	Company-data level	Companies of US and Spanish origin 1993-2005	Description of macro and microeconomic data	US FDI has had positive effects on Spanish productivity.
Alfaro and Charlton (2007)	Industry level data	29 countries 1985-2000	OLS regression	Positive. FDI at the industry level is associated with higher growth in value added.
Bode and Nunnenkamp (2011)	Sector level data	US states since the mid-1970s	Markov chain (distribution dynamics approach)	FDI is associated with less convergence among US states.
Cipollina, Giovannetti, Pietrovito and Pozzolo (2012)	Panel data Sector level data	14 industries for up to 22 developed and developing countries 1992-2004	Regression analysis using GMM	Positive but stronger in capital-intensive sectors and in sectors with higher levels of technological development.

Source: Own elaboration.

Table 2. FDI: levels and growth rates

		FDI		
		Code	Region	Value*
Levels 2000-06	Top 10	FR10	Île de France	35503
		BE10	Bruxelles	11434
		SE11	Stockholm	9504
		BE21	Prov. Antwerpen	8311
		ES30	Comunidad de Madrid	7232
		UKG3	West Midlands	6322
		DK00	DENMARK	6144
		BE24	Prov. Vlaams Brabant	6138
		NL33	Zuid-Holland	5999
		UKI1	Inner London	5902
	Low 10	GR14	Thessalia	7
		ITC2	Valle dAosta/ValléedAoste	6
		GR12	KentrikiMakedonia	5
		GR41	VoreioAigaio	2
		GR42	NotioAigaio	2
		GR21	Ipeiros	1
		GR22	Ionia Nisia	-1
		GR13	DytikiMakedonia	-18
		GR23	DytikiEllada	-19
		GR25	Peloponnisos	-62
	CV			2.1
Growth rates	Top 10	ITF6	Calabria	21494.5
		ITD5	Emilia-Romagna	16463.3
		RO22	Sud-Est	8034.7
		RO41	Sud-Vest Oltenia	7493.3
		RO32	Bucuresti - Ilfov	5880.4
		ITD1	Prov. Aut. Bolzano-Bozen	5709.5
		ITF1	Abruzzo	4805.4
		RO11	Nord-Vest	4695.3
		ITG2	Sardegna	3605.4
		UKJ3	Hampshire and Isle of Wight	3229.4
	Low 10	DE14	Tübingen	-98.2
		DE93	Lüneburg	-112.5
		NL42	Limburg	-113.4
		IE01	Border, Midlands and Western	-115.0
		DE41	Brandenburg - Nordost	-120.2
		NL11	Groningen	-121.9
		ES43	Extremadura	-123.7
		NL41	Noord-Brabant	-126.7
		IE02	Southern and Eastern	-133.1
		NL23	Flevoland	-146.9
	CV			3.9

Note: Levels in 2000m euros; growth rates between sub-periods 2000-02 and 2003-06 in %; CV denotes the Coefficient of Variation.
Source: Own elaboration.

II. INWARD FDI FLOWS IN THE EU AT REGIONAL LEVEL[6]

This section offers an overview of the regional distribution of inward FDI flows in the EU. To do that, we consider a sample of 260 NUTS2 regions (see Appendix 1)[7] between 2000 and 2006. As indicated in the Introduction, we make use of the database provided by Polasek and Sellner, which gives information about the amount of inward FDI at regional level in current million euros. Inward FDI flows have been computed as the difference between consecutive inward FDI stocks, so if the stock for year t is 100 and for year t+1 is 120 (80), this means that FDI flows in year t+1 show an investment (disinvestment) of 20. In the paper, the data have also been transformed from nominal into real terms (considering 2000 as the base year) by means of using national deflators.

Table 2 offers basic information about the average levels of regional FDI as well as the growth rates.[8] For the sake of simplicity, given that the number of regions is too high, we only show the ten highest and ten lowest regions; in any case the information of every region can be found in Appendix 2. As can be seen, the position of Île de France clearly stands out; this region has received each year 35.5 billion euros, well above three times more than the second region in the ranking (Brusells). It is also remarkable that all the regions in the top 10 belong to the EU15. On the contrary, nine out of ten regions with the worst performance are Greek. Regarding growth rates, Irish regions, along with some German and Dutch regions, present the lowest growth rates, while the best performance corresponds to some Italian and Romanian regions. Finally, it is important to point out that regional dispersion is quite high in levels, but even higher in growth rates.

Comments to Table 2 give the impression that FDI is highly concentrated at regional level. To show this in a more precise way, Table 3 reports directly the levels of FDI concentration. As can be seen, just 10 regions concentrate, on average, more than 30% of total FDI during the sample period; additionally, the table indicates that the top 30 regions concentrate 52% of total FDI while the top 50 regions concentrate more than 64%. The difference between these two last percentages indicates that the change in regional concentration due to the regions in the ranking between 30 and 50 is just a bit more than 12 percentage points (less than 1% per region), this meaning that the top 30 regions are those effectively concentrating most of the FDI.

Although informative, these concentration ratios do not offer any relevant clue about the relative performance of the countries. To address this issue, the most common practice is to divide FDI by GDP or population.[9] Regarding this issue, UNCTAD has proposed the use of two indicators: the FDI Performance Index and the FDI Potential Index. The first one is defined as the ratio between FDI and GDP. In the FDI Potential Index, which tries to grasp the country's potential to attract FDI, more scaling variables than just the GDP are used to construct it; more specifically, we have used four variables: per capita GDP, R&D expenditures as percentage of GDP, exports plus imports as percentage of GDP and the percentage of employment in high technology sectors. Anyway, as indicated by UNCTAD "*it*

---

[6] This section has been partially taken from Villaverde and Maza (2012).
[7] We have used NUTS2 definition corresponding to 2003, so Denmark is just one region in our sample.
[8] Because of the large time variability in FDI flows, to compute reliable growth rates we have split our sample period into two sub-periods, namely 2000-2002 and 2003-2006, and calculate the growth rate between them.
[9] The coefficient of correlation between FDI/GDP and FDI/Population ratios is in this case quite high (more than 0.8).

is useful to compare the rankings based on the two indices as a rough guide to whether countries are performing adequately given their (restricted set of) structural assets" (UNCTAD 2002, p. 29). The combination of the two inward FDI indices yields a 2*2 matrix according to which the countries can be considered as either front-runners (high potential and high performance), below-potential (high potential, low performance), above-potential (low-high) and under-performers (low-low).[10] The results are shown in Map 1, from which the following conclusions can be drawn:

Table 3. EU inward FDI concentration at regional level

	Top 10	Top 30	Top 50
2000	33.5	59.9	74.8
2001	37.2	65.7	84.8
2002	163.5	222.8	250.7
2003	33.6	60.5	77.4
2004	57.5	82.8	95.6
2005	43.0	65.4	78.8
2006	32.1	55.0	68.3
2000-06	30.6	52.0	64.3

Source: Own elaboration.

- Most of the front-runner regions (a total of 49) are located in Belgium, Netherlands, Sweden and United Kingdom.
- There is a group of similar size (of 46) of above-potential regions, highlighting the presence of a significant number of Spanish and Polish regions.
- The label of below-potential can be assigned to 64 regions, among which there are 20 German, 6 French and 10 British regions.
- Finally, the rest of regions (a total of 101) can be named under-performers. In this group there are a remarkable number of NMS12 regions, but also regions belonging to Germany (16), Spain (10), France (11), Italy (17) and United Kingdom (11). Most of Greek regions belong to this final group.

Finally, a quick look to the shape of the European FDI/GDP distribution at regional level is performed. To this end, we compute the so-called non-parametric kernel densities. More specifically, we estimate an univariate kernel density function. A density function is a smooth curve which represents the probability distribution of a continuous random variable. The density function is estimated non-parametrically by the kernel method. In formal terms, the kernel density estimate of a series X at a point x is given by the expression:

$$f(x) = \frac{1}{nh} \sum_{i=1}^{n} K\left(\frac{x - X_i}{h}\right) \tag{1}$$

---

[10] The dividing value is always the (population) weighted average of each index.

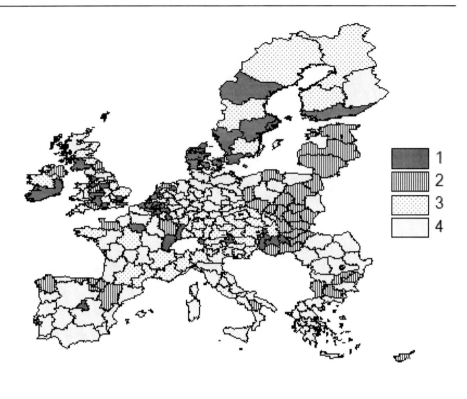

Note: 1. Front-runners; 2. Above-potential; 3. Below-potential; 4. Under-performers

Map 1. Regional classification by FDI performance and potential indices.

where n is the number of observations, whereas K is the kernel function, h the smoothing parameter, X_i the values of the independent variable and x the value of the independent variable for which one seeks an estimate. Intuitively, this method consists of choosing a narrow interval (the so-called smoothing parameter or bandwidth) around the point x and estimating $f(x)$ by the number of observations X_i belonging to the interval. The kernel function is a weighting function giving the weights of the nearby data points in making this estimate.

The results for the regional average values during the whole period, by using a Gaussian kernel function with optimal bandwidth according to Silverman's rule-of-thumb (Silverman, 1986), are shown in Figure 1. As can be seen, the first characteristic of the FDI European distribution is that it is highly concentrated. Anyway, there is a long upper tail representing inward FDI flows towards several regions, such different regions as Bratislavskýkraj, Bruxelles, Gewest, Prov. Vlaams Brabant, Praha, Yugozapaden, Bucuresti – Ilfov and Prov. Antwerpen. On the contrary, there is also a lower tail reflecting, in this case, the performance of Greek regions, as well as some Spanish (Extremadura), Italian (Valle d'Aosta and Sicilia) and Scottish (Highlands and Islands) regions.

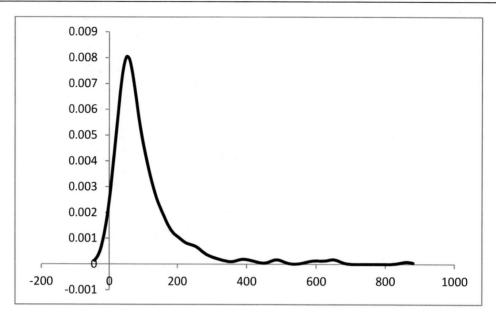

Figure 1. European FDI/GDP distribution at regional level.

III. FDI, GROWTH AND CONVERGENCE

Although in the past governments were somewhat suspicious of inward FDI as, particularly in less-developed countries, they regarded it as a manifestation of "corporate capitalism", potentially jeopardizing national sovereignty and creating social tensions, nowadays things have changed so much that it can be said that governments tend to court (or attract) FDI. This does not mean that, currently, many people are against globalization and, in particular, against the role played by multinational corporations in it. For a survey of pros and cons of FDI, see Lipsey (2002) and Johnson (2006).

Why do governments try to attract FDI? The most direct answer is that inward FDI provides a win situation for the host country: FDI contributes to economic growth and employment and to foster structural change in industrial organization. Although the literature is not conclusive on these points, it is considered that the aforementioned effects come out as a result of multiple direct and spill-over influences, among which those providing long-term financial capital, new technologies and better access to foreign markets (and, therefore, improvements in the trade balance), provoking a crowding-in effect (attracting additional investments), widening the production base, increasing competition, improving the business environment, and raising know-how, managerial expertise and marketing skills are among the most important.

The main aim of this section is to assess if, effectively, FDI has fostered economic growth for the case of European regions. In addition, and making use of the standard convergence approach (Barro and Sala-i-Martin, 1992), we also evaluate whether FDI has also contributed to economic convergence. For this purpose, and taking per capita income as proxy for economic development, this section proceeds in various steps. Firstly, an absolute β-convergence equation, trying to test if poor regions grow faster than richer ones, is estimated; according to this approach, economies converge to the same steady state if the parameter associated to the initial per capita income level is negative and statistically significant. Secondly, an analysis of conditional β-convergence is carried out, in which FDI is included as conditional variable; according to this, it is allowed that European regions have different steady states as they have different flows of FDI. In this way, the effect of FDI on income growth is obtained by means of its own coefficient in the conditional β-convergence equation, while the effect of FDI on economic convergence can be seen by comparing β coefficients in absolute- and conditional β-convergence equations. Thirdly, and for the sake of robustness, additional control variables to explain the structural differences between European regions are considered.

Therefore, an absolute β-convergence equation is estimated and used as a benchmark. Then, the growth rate of per capita income in region i during a period t ($g_{i,t}$) is expressed in terms of per capita income (in logs) during the previous period $t-1$ ($Y_{i,t-1}$) as:

$$g_{i,t} = \alpha + \beta \log(Y_{i,t-1}) + u_{i,t}. \tag{2}$$

The results of this estimation are given in the second column of Table 4, which shows that the coefficient β is negative and statistically significant; this implies that a convergence process did in fact take place between European regions over the period 2000-2007. In addition, this table reports two indicators generally provided in studies of convergence: the speed of convergence[11] and the half-life[12]. The latter represents the number of years necessary to cover half the distance separating European regions from their steady state, assuming that the current convergence speed is maintained. The convergence is apparently very slow: 1.55% per year, implying a half-life of 46.9 years.

Taking this estimation as a point of reference, we can try to assess the effect of FDI flows both on growth and regional disparities. In order to do that, we need to carry out an analysis of conditional β-convergence. We again estimate equation (2), but now including the independent variable $FDI_{i,t-1}$, denoting FDI flows over GDP.

$$g_{i,t} = \alpha + \beta \log(Y_{i,t-1}) + \gamma\, FDI_{i,t-1} + u_{i,t} \tag{3}$$

The results are reported in the third column of Table 4. The coefficient γ associated with FDI is positive and statistically different from zero, this indicating that high FDI flows increase the region's per capita income growth. In other words, our findings confirm the positive relationship between FDI and economic growth. However, the results do not seem to support the idea that FDI plays a role in reducing regional disparities; note that the coefficient linked to initial per capita income remains almost invariant (0.014 versus 0.015, a difference not statistically significant) when this variable is considered; the same occurs, obviously, with the annual speed of convergence (it goes from 1.55 to 1.63%).

In order to check the robustness of the results just discussed, we considered additional control variables to include other factors potentially explaining per capita income growth. The reason is quite simple. There are more variables in addition to initial per capita income that

---

[11] The convergence speed (b) is calculated as $b=-ln(1+T\beta)/T$, where T is the number of years in the sample.
[12] The half-life (τ) is calculated as $\tau = -ln(2)/ln(1+\beta)$.

are behind regional economic growth and, as a result, it is expected that European regions converge to a different steady state. Specifically, we estimate the following equation:

$$g_{i,t} = \alpha + \beta \log(Y_{i,t-1}) + \gamma FDI_{i,t-1} + \delta X_{i,t-1} + d_i + u_{i,t} \qquad (4)$$

Table 4. Absolute and conditional beta convergence

	Absolute β–convergence	Conditional β–convergence	Absolute β–convergence (control variables)	Conditional β–convergence (control variables)
Constant	-0.063*** (0.002)	-0.063*** (0.002)	-0.002 (0.001)	-0.015 (0.001)
$Y_{i,t-1}$	-0.014*** (0.001)	-0.015*** (0.001)	-0.004* (0.002)	-0.005** (0.002)
$FDI_{i,t-1}$		0.005*** (0.001)		0.005** (0.001)
$Inv_{i,t-1}$			0.030** (0.012)	0.024** (0.012)
$HC_{i,t-1}$			0.078*** (0.012)	0.075*** (0.012)
$Wag_{i,t-1}$			0.001 (0.002)	0.001 (0.002)
$Ind_{i,t-1}$			-0.010 (0.008)	-0.011 (0.008)
R² adjusted	0.17	0.19	0.47	0.48
Speed of convergence (%)	1.55	1.63	0.45	0.54
Half-life (years)	46.9	44.7	159.9	131.2

Notes: Standard Error in parenthesis; *** Significant at 99%; ** Significant at 95%;* Significant at 90%. Country dummies have been included in the estimates with control variables.
Source: Own elaboration

where $X_{i,t-1}$ is a vector of control variables that holds constant the steady state of the region i. We have included variables such as the level of investment over GDP ($Inv_{i,t-1}$), human capital ($HC_{i,t-1}$),[13] wages ($Wag_{i,t-1}$) and industry share ($IND_{i,t-1}$). As can be seen, country dummies (d_i) have been incorporated in order to consider the specific characteristics of the regions belonging to each country.

As the next two columns of Table 5 show, the results obtained for the FDI are quite similar. These new findings reinforce that: a) FDI has contributed to economic growth in the European regions; b) FDI has not contributed to the process of convergence. Regarding the speed of convergence, however, the results reveal that it is much lower when we control for structural differences. As for the new variables, our findings unveil the role played by human

---

[13] This is computed as the ratio of the employment at highest level of education (first and second stage of tertiary education) over the total employment. Both data series obtained from Eurostat Database.

capital as an important factor fostering economic growth. For the case of investment, the link with per capita income growth, although it exits, is less significant. Additionally, the coefficients associated to wages and industry share do not result statistically different from zero. With relation to country dummies, these are quite positive and statistically significant for countries such as Latvia, Lithuania, Estonia, Slovakia and Romania, this revealing the existence of some specific characteristics in these countries that are behind their economic growth figures.

CONCLUSION

The EU being one of the main recipients of FDI in the current era of globalization, this paper is devoted to the study of the relationship between FDI and economic growth across the European regions over the period 2000-2007. To accomplish this aim, we firstly carry out a thorough literature review with the conclusion that most of the papers revised point out that FDI tends to have a significant and positive effect on economic growth.

Secondly, the regional distribution of inward FDI flows in the EU is examined, obtaining some interesting results. Regarding levels of regional FDI, the position of Île de France clearly stands out from the sample of 260 European regions as it has received 35.5 billion euros annually, well above the rest. Additionally, it is important to stress that all the regions in the top 10 belong to the EU15 whereas nine out of ten regions with the worst performance are Greek. Considering growth rates, the best performance corresponds to some Italian and Romanian regions while the lowest growth rates belong to some Irish, German and Dutch regions. It seems clear that regional dispersion is quite high in FDI levels, but even higher in growth rates.

Data provide evidence on the fact that FDI is highly concentrated at regional level; namely, just 10 regions make up, on average, 30.6% of total FDI and the top 30 regions concentrate 52% of total FDI during the sample period. In the same vein, the study of the external shape of the distribution (non-parametric kernel densities) backs up the high concentration of European FDI. In order to assess the relative performance of European regions, the FDI Performance Index and the FDI Potential Index are computed. According to these values, regions are classified into four categories: the group named front-runners includes 49 regions, most of which are located in Belgium, Netherlands, Sweden and United Kingdom; the second group (46 regions), labelled as above-potential encompass mostly Spanish and Polish regions; the third one, formed by 64 below-potential regions are situated in their majority in Germany, France and Britain; and the last group called under-performers is heterogeneously constituted by the remaining 101 regions.

With the purpose to evaluate the role played by FDI flows on economic growth and regional disparities, several equations are specified and estimated. To begin with, an absolute ??-convergence equation is estimated as a benchmark, unveiling that a convergence process in per capita GDP has taken place. Next, including FDI flows over GDP as an additional independent variable, an analysis of conditional ??-convergence is carried out, finding that the coefficient associated to this new variable is positive and statistically different from zero, thus implying that FDI has promoted economic growth. However, as the coefficient linked to initial per capita income is roughly the same in both convergence equations, it could not be said that FDI has fostered the convergence process.

For the sake of robustness, a group of control variables, such as the level of investment over GDP, human capital, wages and industry share, are included in the previous model in order to better explain the performance of per capita income growth. Apart from that, country dummies are incorporated as well so as to capture the specific characteristics of each region. As it happens that the coefficients linked to human capital and investment are positive and statistically significant, the results obtained for the FDI support the previous findings: FDI has contributed to economic growth in European regions, but not to the process of convergence.

After having concluded that FDI enhances economic growth, the results of this paper lead to some policy implications. Strategies aiming at promoting human capital and the level of investment together with R&D expenditures, trade openness and employment in high technology sectors should be developed to efficiently attract FDI and consequently foster economic growth, especially in the so-called under-performer regions (those with low FDI Performance and Potential Indices) and, to a lesser extent, in regions showing below-potential and above-potential performance.

APPENDIX 1. LIST OF NUTS2 REGIONS AND ACRONYMS

BELGIUM	
be1 Région de Bruxelles-Capitale	be31 Prov. Brabant Wallon
be21 Prov. Antwerpen	be32 Prov. Hainaut
be22 Prov. Limburg (B)	be33 Prov. Liège
be23 Prov. Oost-Vlaanderen	be34 Prov. Luxembourg (B)
be24 Prov. Vlaams Brabant	be35 Prov. Namur
be25 Prov. West-Vlaanderen	
BULGARIA	
bg31 Severozapaden	bg34 Yugoiztochen
bg32 Severentsentralen	bg41 Yugozapaden
bg33 Severoiztochen	bg42 Yuzhentsentralen
CZEZH REPUBLIC	
cz01 Praha	cz05 Severovýchod
cz02 StredníCechy	cz06 Jihovýchod
cz03 Jihozápad	cz07 Strední Morava
cz04 Severozápad	cz08 Moravskoslezsko
DENMARK	
dk00 Denmark	
GERMANY	
de11 Stuttgart	de91 Braunschweig
de12 Karlsruhe	de92 Hannover
de13 Freiburg	de93 Lüneburg
de14 Tübingen	de94 Weser-Ems
de21 Oberbayern	dea1 Düsseldorf
de22 Niederbayern	dea2 Köln
de23 Oberpfalz	dea3 Münster
de24 Oberfranken	dea4 Detmold
de25 Mittelfranken	dea5 Arnsberg

GERMANY	
de26 Unterfranken	deb1 Koblenz
de27 Schwaben	deb2 Trier
de3 Berlin	deb3 Rheinhessen-Pfalz
de41 Brandenburg - Nordost	dec Saarland
de42 Brandenburg - Südwest	ded1 Chemnitz
de5 Bremen	ded2 Dresden
de6 Hamburg	ded3 Leipzig
de71 Darmstadt	dee Sachsen-Anhalt
de72 Gießen	def Schleswig-Holstein
de73 Kassel	deg Thüringen
de8 Mecklenburg-Vorpommern	

ESTONIA	
EE Estonia	

GREECE	
gr11 AnatolikiMakedonia, Thraki	gr24 StereaEllada
gr12 KentrikiMakedonia	gr25 Peloponnisos
gr13 DytikiMakedonia	gr3 Attiki
gr14 Thessalia	gr41 VoreioAigaio
gr21 Ipeiros	gr42 NotioAigaio
gr22 Ionia Nisia	gr43 Kriti
gr23 DytikiEllada	

SPAIN	
es11 Galicia	es43 Extremadura
es12 Principado de Asturias	es51 Cataluña
es13 Cantabria	es52 ComunidadValenciana
es21 Pais Vasco	es53 IllesBalears
es22 Comunidad Foral de Navarra	es61 Andalucia
es23 La Rioja	es62 Región de Murcia
es24 Aragón	es63 Ciudad Autónoma de Ceuta (ES)
es3 Comunidad de Madrid	es64 Ciudad Autónoma de Melilla (ES)
es41 Castilla y León	es7 Canarias (ES)
es42 Castilla-la Mancha	

FRANCE	
fr1 Île de France	fr51 Pays de la Loire
fr21 Champagne-Ardenne	fr52 Bretagne
fr22 Picardie	fr53 Poitou-Charentes
fr23 Haute-Normandie	fr61 Aquitaine
fr24 Centre	fr62 Midi-Pyrénées
fr25 Basse-Normandie	fr63 Limousin
fr26 Bourgogne	fr71 Rhône-Alpes
fr3 Nord - Pas-de-Calais	fr72 Auvergne
fr41 Lorraine	fr81 Languedoc-Roussillon
fr42 Alsace	fr82 Provence-Alpes-Côte d'Azur
fr43 Franche-Comté	fr83 Corse

IRELAND	
ie01 Border, Midlands and Western	ie02 Southern and Eastern

ITALY	
itc1 Piemonte	ite3 Marche
itc2 Valle d'Aosta	ite4 Lazio
itc3 Liguria	itf1 Abruzzo
itc4 Lombardia	itf2 Molise

(Continued)

ITALY	
itd1 Provincia Autonoma Bolzano-Bozen	itf3 Campania
itd2 ProvinciaAutonoma Trento	itf4 Puglia
itd3 Veneto	itf5 Basilicata
itd4 Friuli-Venezia Giulia	itf6 Calabria
itd5 Emilia-Romagna	itg1 Sicilia
ite1 Toscana	itg2 Sardegna
ite2 Umbria	

CYPRUS
CY Cyprus

LATVIA
LV Latvia

LITHUANIA
LT Lithuania

LUXEMBOURG
LU Luxembourg

HUNGARY	
hu1 Közép-Magyarország	hu31 Észak-Magyarország
hu21 Közép-Dunántúl	hu32 Észak-Alföld
hu22 Nyugat-Dunántúl	hu33 Dél-Alföld
hu23 Dél-Dunántúl	

MALTA
MT Malta

NETHERLANDS	
nl11 Groningen	nl31 Utrecht
nl12 Friesland (NL)	nl32 Noord-Holland
nl13 Drenthe	nl33 Zuid-Holland
nl21 Overijssel	nl34 Zeeland
nl22 Gelderland	nl41 Noord-Brabant
nl23 Flevoland	nl42 Limburg (NL)

AUSTRIA	
at11 Burgenland (A)	at31 Oberösterreich
at12 Niederösterreich	at32 Salzburg
at13 Wien	at33 Tirol
at21 Kärnten	at34 Vorarlberg
at22 Steiermark	

POLAND	
pl11 Lódzkie	pl41 Wielkopolskie
pl12 Mazowieckie	pl42 Zachodniopomorskie
pl21 Malopolskie	pl43 Lubuskie
pl22 Slaskie	pl51 Dolnoslaskie
pl31 Lubelskie	pl52 Opolskie
pl32 Podkarpackie	pl61 Kujawsko-Pomorskie
pl33 Swietokrzyskie	pl62 Warminsko-Mazurskie
pl34 Podlaskie	pl63 Pomorskie

PORTUGAL	
pt11 Norte	pt17 Lisboa
pt15 Algarve	pt18 Alentejo
pt16 Centro (PT)	
ROMANIA	
ro11 Nord-Vest	ro31 Sud - Muntenia
ro12 Centru	ro32 Bucuresti - Ilfov
ro21 Nord-Est	ro41 Sud-Vest Oltenia
ro22 Sud-Est	ro42 Vest
SLOVENIA	
si00 Slovenia	
SLOVAKIA	
sk01 Bratislavskýkraj	sk03 StrednéSlovensko
sk02 ZápadnéSlovensko	sk04 VýchodnéSlovensko
FINLAND	
fi13 Itä-Suomi	fi1a Pohjois-Suomi
fi18 Etelä-Suomi	fi2 Åland
fi19 Länsi-Suomi	
SWEDEN	
se11 Stockholm	se23 Västsverige
se12 ÖstraMellansverige	se31 NorraMellansverige
se21 Småland med öarna	se32 MellerstaNorrland
se22 Sydsverige	se33 ÖvreNorrland
UNITED KINGDOM	
ukc1 Tees Valley and Durham	ukh3 Essex
ukc2 Northumberland, Tyne and Wear	uki1 Inner London
ukd1 Cumbria	uki2 Outer London
ukd2 Cheshire	ukj1 Berkshire, Bucks and Oxfordshire
ukd3 Greater Manchester	ukj2 Surrey, East and West Sussex
ukd4 Lancashire	ukj3 Hampshire and Isle of Wight
ukd5 Merseyside	ukj4 Kent
uke1 East Yorkshire-Northern Lincolnshire	ukk1 Gloucestershire, Wiltshire and Bristol
uke2 North Yorkshire	ukk2 Dorset and Somerset
uke3 South Yorkshire	ukk3 Cornwall and Isles of Scilly
uke4 West Yorkshire	ukk4 Devon
ukf1 Derbyshire and Nottinghamshire	ukl1 West Wales and The Valleys
ukf2 Leicestershire, Rutland and Northants	ukl2 East Wales
ukf3 Lincolnshire	ukm2 Eastern Scotland
ukg1 Herefordshire, Worcestershire, Warks	ukm3 South Western Scotland
ukg2 Shropshire and Staffordshire	ukm5 North Eastern Scotland
ukg3 West Midlands	ukm6 Highlands and Islands
ukh1 East Anglia	ukn Northern Ireland
ukh2 Bedfordshire, Hertfordshire	

Source: Own elaboration.

APPENDIX 2. FDI BY REGIONS: LEVELS AND GROWTH RATES

Acronym	Region	2000	2001	2002	2003	2004	2005	2006	2000-06 Growth rate
BE10	Bruxelles	10190	14489	1650	-4046	18481	24960	14315	11434	53.0
BE21	Prov. Antwerpen	3200	5430	498	7367	8804	17045	15830	8311	303.0
BE22	Prov. Limburg	1374	3593	1176	1669	-422	3182	5464	2291	20.8
BE23	Prov. Oost-Vlaanderen	908	-321	4529	1854	466	5463	4020	2417	73.1
BE24	Prov. Vlaams Brabant	2336	4342	2511	2794	6174	14532	10275	6138	175.7
BE25	Prov. West-Vlaanderen	1097	2384	3260	564	841	7570	3723	2777	41.3
BE31	Prov. Brabant Wallon	339	721	552	-662	974	2276	956	737	64.9
BE32	Prov. Hainaut	251	213	1517	1561	-52	2739	2335	1223	149.2
BE33	Prov. Liège	597	364	985	971	230	4011	2292	1350	189.2
BE34	Prov. Luxembourg	292	-82	-57	-43	164	100	258	90	135.8
BE35	Prov. Namur	102	932	457	830	104	1690	1426	792	103.7
BG31	Severozapaden	-15	21	1	5	20	36	30	14	835.8
BG32	Severentsentralen	-99	122	23	95	112	183	117	79	727.4
BG33	Severoiztochen	-134	178	61	67	216	421	299	158	617.6
BG34	Yugoiztochen	-146	64	7	58	40	140	124	41	457.7
BG41	Yugozapaden	-1077	1776	451	774	1529	2566	2770	1256	398.1
BG42	Yuzhentsentralen	-97	120	-7	99	64	195	241	88	2732.8
CZ01	Praha	5298	1157	3942	517	1148	5648	6441	3450	-0.8
CZ02	StredníCechy	-147	526	-291	-61	580	215	80	129	594.6
CZ03	Jihozápad	43	410	-285	19	253	127	185	107	159.1
CZ04	Severozápad	40	382	-296	101	107	215	76	89	196.2
CZ05	Severovýchod	366	89	141	-298	374	294	129	156	-37.2
CZ06	Jihovýchod	310	53	114	-25	292	341	254	191	35.4
CZ07	Strední Morava	109	522	-223	-398	526	56	280	125	-14.7
CZ08	Moravskoslezko	-1	685	-226	-356	481	193	37	116	-41.9
DK00	DENMARK	27397	4523	-8660	-332	15543	5290	-754	6144	-36.3
DE11	Stuttgart	12102	-491	2932	-526	-1059	680	4813	2636	-79.8
DE12	Karlsruhe	8082	-185	3118	2078	-2987	415	3345	1981	-80.6
DE13	Freiburg	5880	-509	1532	2008	-817	-580	1857	1338	-73.2
DE14	Tübingen	5577	370	1656	-638	-997	64	1758	1113	-98.2
DE21	Oberbayern	17232	-5955	2639	3240	2105	1511	5493	3752	-33.4
DE22	Niederbayern	1993	85	187	-484	306	92	704	412	-79.5
DE23	Oberpfalz	2103	-930	349	215	172	48	587	364	-49.6
DE24	Oberfranken	2025	-284	-90	-477	139	155	722	313	-75.5
DE25	Mittelfranken	5614	-2472	960	210	962	156	1427	980	-49.6
DE26	Unterfranken	2472	-109	518	-291	368	298	1126	626	-60.9
DE27	Schwaben	4625	-1128	1354	638	-431	23	1044	875	-80.3
DE30	Berlin	17639	-7371	-4081	391	1607	3025	4659	2267	17.3
DE41	Brandenburg - Nordost	1303	2083	-881	-805	-306	85	350	261	-120.2
DE42	Brandenburg - Südwest	1368	1047	-392	-116	349	742	489	498	-45.7
DE50	Bremen	3632	214	582	-513	587	-102	1736	876	-71.1
DE60	Hamburg	14940	4778	9323	2598	-4250	1037	8714	5306	-79.1
DE71	Darmstadt	11862	-952	1174	4110	-1980	490	3539	2606	-61.8
DE72	Gießen	2597	-548	194	604	-275	529	607	530	-51.0
DE73	Kassel	1645	-194	557	236	-153	-60	1031	437	-60.6
DE80	Mecklenburg-Vorpommern	1956	-191	-715	213	458	-702	649	238	-55.9
DE91	Braunschweig	2728	-506	-703	547	-1269	309	1376	355	-52.5
DE92	Hannover	4523	-1968	414	1713	-767	-287	1154	683	-54.2
DE93	Lüneburg	2640	-73	349	-236	-434	-764	948	347	-112.5
DE94	Weser-Ems	5357	-266	-227	313	-572	-705	1783	812	-87.4
DEA1	Düsseldorf	10296	-1494	1170	1765	-623	722	2619	2065	-66.3
DEA2	Köln	9920	408	2441	3153	-829	2054	2716	2837	-58.3

Acronym	Region	2000	2001	2002	2003	2004	2005	2006	2000-06	Growth rate
DEA3	Münster	5042	-274	1957	20	-315	-227	1171	1053	-92.8
DEA4	Detmold	4600	690	-1124	-232	726	-114	971	788	-75.7
DEA5	Arnsberg	6517	-684	-442	1961	-1371	-77	1472	1054	-72.4
DEB1	Koblenz	3007	-25	889	65	76	-1039	1052	575	-97.0
DEB2	Trier	996	-185	432	-4	300	-184	64	203	-89.3
DEB3	Rheinhessen-Pfalz	5210	-1162	1887	435	530	-1356	1517	1009	-85.8
DEC0	Saarland	2527	-227	-924	190	853	128	-15	362	-37.0
DED1	Chemnitz	4619	-2509	-838	670	-37	613	842	480	23.2
DED2	Dresden	4803	-1974	541	1148	403	576	709	887	-36.9
DED3	Leipzig	2738	-1707	-468	374	86	231	304	222	32.7
DEE0	Sachsen-Anhalt	6021	-1534	-1112	1302	-673	-83	676	657	-72.8
DEF0	Schleswig-Holstein	3713	-477	-1456	1527	-313	-819	1063	463	-38.5
DEG0	Thüringen	5030	-1267	-588	2156	883	-294	-17	843	-35.5
GR11	AnatolikiMakedonia, Thraki	-49	-57	69	94	27	13	97	28	569.0
GR12	KentrikiMakedonia	-462	36	-128	61	-98	296	331	5	179.8
GR13	DytikiMakedonia	-261	-34	5	42	21	67	32	-18	142.0
GR14	Thessalia	-205	-24	2	-5	56	102	121	7	190.3
GR21	Ipeiros	-97	-92	-14	76	22	13	98	1	177.7
GR22	Ionia Nisia	29	-63	-2	-1	10	8	9	-1	155.3
GR23	DytikiEllada	-183	-124	-30	87	-39	75	84	-19	146.1
GR24	StereaEllada	248	-266	-485	86	378	123	193	40	216.4
GR25	Peloponnisos	-467	-92	-119	18	73	37	113	-62	126.7
GR30	Attiki	1755	149	-153	1843	1167	1594	2548	1272	206.4
GR41	VoreioAigaio	1	-6	3	7	0	3	8	2	856.9
GR42	NotioAigaio	30	-27	4	4	-14	6	10	2	-26.4
GR43	Kriti	39	-17	25	2	-20	30	46	15	-8.1
ES11	Galicia	780	2373	2564	1653	901	2020	1498	1684	-20.3
ES12	Principado de Asturias	212	283	846	54	872	1088	12	481	13.3
ES13	Cantabria	-113	753	30	1123	130	904	435	466	190.1
ES21	Pais Vasco	3951	1652	2637	1537	1387	3127	1850	2306	-28.1
ES22	ComunidadForal de Navarra	800	991	1834	-326	540	894	-14	674	-77.4
ES23	La Rioja	561	301	975	607	240	-57	176	400	-60.6
ES24	Aragón	3142	934	2486	1334	363	1528	1713	1643	-43.6
ES30	Comunidad de Madrid	17281	12127	9785	2384	3586	2500	2959	7232	-78.1
ES41	Castilla y León	1001	1358	1781	1612	53	77	-246	805	-72.9
ES42	Castilla-la Mancha	493	309	327	135	-4	380	77	245	-61.0
ES43	Extremadura	80	-6	55	25	-45	16	-36	13	-123.7
ES51	Cataluña	6413	3719	5787	1814	2052	1379	928	3156	-70.9
ES52	ComunidadValenciana	2045	1884	2463	2463	1892	670	386	1686	-36.5
ES53	IllesBalears	311	151	112	255	-123	235	359	186	-5.3
ES61	Andalucia	1779	1358	2601	1580	-285	1532	823	1341	-52.3
ES62	Región de Murcia	769	383	773	-91	-141	128	313	305	-91.9
ES63	Ciudad Autónoma de Ceuta	3	291	99	226	-119	75	-27	78	-70.6
ES64	Ciudad Autónoma de Melilla	135	168	90	115	20	313	122	138	9.0
ES70	Canarias	1010	399	1303	638	-259	755	-431	488	-80.6
FR10	Île de France	20454	11332	68184	23413	38653	48598	37884	35503	11.4
FR21	Champagne-Ardenne	219	404	-331	612	340	637	585	352	458.4
FR22	Picardie	467	765	-878	833	622	1188	-408	370	371.8
FR23	Haute-Normandie	942	2528	-1562	720	686	1611	1754	954	87.5
FR24	Centre	835	802	-1188	3193	1415	243	2652	1136	1154.1
FR25	Basse-Normandie	726	749	539	641	745	2443	1241	1012	88.7
FR26	Bourgogne	66	1139	-461	1152	575	114	725	473	158.5
FR30	Nord - Pas-de-Calais	241	3081	-1659	3539	2015	2680	2434	1762	381.1
FR41	Lorraine	1222	2617	-1521	2274	1333	3402	2303	1661	201.2

(Continued)

Acronym	Region	2000	2001	2002	2003	2004	2005	2006	2000-06	Growth rate
FR42	Alsace	1165	4206	-4302	7312	4319	3852	3520	2867	1233.9
FR43	Franche-Comté	621	3156	-1545	1612	717	1152	2042	1108	85.6
FR51	Pays de la Loire	1079	5081	-3264	3826	2671	1665	2831	1984	184.6
FR52	Bretagne	1159	3007	-2811	2276	2559	4706	1389	1755	504.8
FR53	Poitou-Charentes	218	1277	-858	1293	1117	743	854	664	372.0
FR61	Aquitaine	390	3197	-1736	1675	2225	2116	1722	1370	213.7
FR62	Midi-Pyrénées	1393	4406	-2368	4234	-2118	2662	4534	1820	103.5
FR63	Limousin	297	546	-100	220	262	529	121	268	14.3
FR71	Rhône-Alpes	1829	5675	-3428	4098	2745	3766	4867	2793	184.8
FR72	Auvergne	179	697	-685	826	410	274	289	284	606.8
FR81	Languedoc-Roussillon	146	1127	-813	1661	410	592	841	566	472.2
FR82	Provence-Alpes-Côte dAzur	1707	4552	-4001	5586	3950	2476	2912	2455	395.6
FR83	Corse	0	44	-34	15	4	-18	88	14	626.0
IE01	Border, Midlands and Western	3484	3598	-3137	7260	-4781	-1503	-1767	451	-115.0
IE02	Southern and Eastern	34009	14456	23599	6128	-9240	-10845	-17872	5748	-133.1
ITC1	Piemonte	1619	-970	871	1393	1498	1672	4111	1456	328.1
ITC2	Valle dAosta/ValléedAoste	11	7	-16	5	10	13	11	6	1479.7
ITC3	Liguria	1907	-116	-843	1089	-263	10	1305	441	69.3
ITC4	Lombardia	2511	209	-271	1516	2377	2582	3935	1837	218.8
ITD1	Prov. Aut. Bolzano-Bozen	83	-124	50	334	18	195	163	103	5709.5
ITD2	Prov. Aut. Trento	208	-18	94	116	-114	649	586	217	226.0
ITD3	Veneto	2141	-163	89	1095	968	3644	2011	1398	180.1
ITD4	Friuli-Venezia Giulia	510	208	-153	288	497	768	900	431	226.2
ITD5	Emilia-Romagna	75	-388	347	1453	893	2552	2663	1085	16463.3
ITE1	Toscana	628	148	-511	1849	164	1127	1699	729	1265.7
ITE2	Umbria	-13	-137	207	48	120	166	372	109	848.6
ITE3	Marche	134	190	-650	871	1619	1872	2315	907	1639.8
ITE4	Lazio	2342	-1717	-1454	3229	1234	3264	2539	1348	1029.2
ITF1	Abruzzo	317	-413	59	491	1097	339	434	332	4805.4
ITF2	Molise	229	-81	-358	131	489	318	-222	72	355.7
ITF3	Campania	306	282	-1316	3054	680	1460	3026	1070	947.5
ITF4	Puglia	-168	173	-350	823	704	395	1682	466	885.2
ITF5	Basilicata	72	46	127	1031	-805	1345	839	379	639.9
ITF6	Calabria	-130	100	34	-59	634	102	290	139	21494.5
ITG1	Sicilia	1020	-458	-523	450	112	188	894	240	3079.0
ITG2	Sardegna	167	-71	-62	318	380	418	561	244	3605.4
HU10	Közép-Magyarország	-2677	3360	-1472	-1739	6719	2039	4056	1469	1152.2
HU21	Közép-Dunántúl	688	410	-83	284	552	92	967	416	39.9
HU22	Nyugat-Dunántúl	1075	-378	222	218	160	322	913	362	31.6
HU23	Dél-Dunántúl	389	259	100	52	62	18	648	218	-21.8
HU31	Észak-Magyarország	541	-127	261	-150	222	178	786	244	15.0
HU32	Észak-Alföld	870	585	272	118	60	410	1129	492	-25.4
HU33	Dél-Alföld	426	253	207	-128	163	189	655	252	-25.6
NL11	Groningen	-37	220	1166	387	-1306	351	174	136	-121.9
NL12	Friesland	1709	429	1118	295	-100	51	-121	483	-97.1
NL13	Drenthe	213	718	1335	608	-235	752	-101	470	-66.1
NL21	Overijssel	993	899	365	-1164	994	866	-508	349	-93.8
NL22	Gelderland	2617	2817	3746	-1162	1137	745	28	1418	-93.9
NL23	Flevoland	4635	99	-862	703	-1870	-472	-780	208	-146.9
NL31	Utrecht	4178	4256	3718	-3958	3743	1973	296	2029	-87.3
NL32	Noord-Holland	18596	8484	4304	2214	4841	1106	-62	5641	-80.6
NL33	Zuid-Holland	11108	26167	-5348	-1144	7323	6489	-2605	5999	-76.4
NL34	Zeeland	2851	1773	623	1872	-1288	82	-310	800	-94.9

FDI and Economic Growth

Acronym	Region	2000	2001	2002	2003	2004	2005	2006	2000-06	Growth rate
NL41	Noord-Brabant	12345	2001	-50	-3307	-1622	724	-881	1316	-126.7
NL42	Limburg	2108	1131	1889	-3358	1783	398	264	602	-113.4
AT11	Burgenland	212	233	-110	95	43	166	816	208	151.0
AT12	Niederösterreich	1169	695	-448	75	1386	761	2002	806	123.6
AT13	Wien	3838	765	3826	891	3738	3057	12284	4057	77.7
AT21	Kärnten	313	716	36	-204	261	322	917	337	-8.6
AT22	Steiermark	651	1277	-497	172	632	771	1944	707	84.5
AT31	Oberösterreich	1133	859	-151	-19	625	972	2600	860	70.2
AT32	Salzburg	352	686	-123	309	597	524	1587	562	147.3
AT33	Tirol	780	616	421	-358	174	300	1273	458	-42.6
AT34	Vorarlberg	790	783	-471	85	340	383	1271	454	41.6
PL11	Lódzkie	568	351	114	472	767	384	1022	525	92.0
PL12	Mazowieckie	4801	3443	-4861	-554	4722	1876	3698	1875	116.0
PL21	Malopolskie	938	41	1181	772	1307	-118	2145	895	42.6
PL22	Slaskie	-133	707	939	972	3272	9	2334	1157	226.5
PL31	Lubelskie	157	425	3	-155	569	299	68	195	0.2
PL32	Podkarpackie	37	140	366	539	369	379	384	316	131.0
PL33	Swietokrzyskie	97	67	456	178	137	464	-145	179	-23.1
PL34	Podlaskie	140	84	139	226	69	245	320	175	78.1
PL41	Wielkopolskie	45	780	129	1815	-295	676	1244	628	170.5
PL42	Zachodniopomorskie	397	25	215	-82	532	169	391	235	18.8
PL43	Lubuskie	115	41	240	180	665	-35	157	195	83.3
PL51	Dolnoslaskie	-44	492	-235	720	1553	444	896	547	1173.9
PL52	Opolskie	303	-39	19	141	815	205	206	236	262.8
PL61	Kujawsko-Pomorskie	385	12	196	-44	487	-113	232	165	-29.0
PL62	Warminsko-Mazurskie	52	182	180	177	147	109	368	174	45.6
PL63	Pomorskie	555	-300	895	-152	1079	28	819	417	15.7
PT11	Norte	883	1535	564	787	-489	539	2492	902	-16.3
PT15	Algarve	131	37	83	428	106	16	128	133	103.3
PT16	Centro	791	646	668	911	-159	-141	1544	609	-23.2
PT17	Lisboa	5222	3487	-994	3327	1052	2909	6361	3052	32.7
PT18	Alentejo	822	70	40	-236	211	-42	294	166	-81.7
RO11	Nord-Vest	16	55	-60	47	460	-75	268	101	4695.3
RO12	Centru	-2	43	-70	83	479	-36	239	105	2117.2
RO21	Nord-Est	-20	112	-119	14	106	-24	235	44	1039.0
RO22	Sud-Est	30	-31	5	-1	85	64	228	54	8034.7
RO31	Sud - Muntenia	-5	-23	-11	-10	166	30	137	41	726.1
RO32	Bucuresti - Ilfov	31	787	-976	2435	2598	2261	4866	1715	5880.4
RO41	Sud-Vest Oltenia	1	13	-11	-23	202	66	53	43	7493.3
RO42	Vest	13	91	-136	65	108	-61	90	24	570.4
SK01	Bratislavskýkraj	985	641	1923	1705	2364	3061	3109	1970	116.4
SK02	ZápadnéSlovensko	168	242	53	650	-37	390	396	266	126.7
SK03	StrednéSlovensko	191	98	75	453	134	589	265	258	197.6
SK04	VýchodnéSlovensko	86	377	-112	839	45	267	696	314	295.5
FI13	Itä-Suomi	405	27	132	567	52	541	577	329	130.8
FI18	Etelä-Suomi	5669	1121	4700	6241	3155	3769	6232	4412	26.6
FI19	Länsi-Suomi	1229	567	538	1163	579	1758	1225	1009	51.8
FI1A	Pohjois-Suomi	875	-482	683	1250	-159	447	646	466	52.3
FI2	Aland	19	9	8	18	9	27	19	15	51.8
SE11	Stockholm	13109	-5879	15486	5073	25580	131	13024	9504	44.6
SE12	ÖstraMellansverige	2580	2972	-489	1418	1100	813	1959	1479	-21.6
SE32	Småland med öarna	1475	1859	-378	595	226	81	812	667	-56.5
SE21	Sydsverige	666	5072	479	1905	707	-437	1365	1394	-57.3
SE33	Västsverige	5399	6104	-2871	3283	-1584	531	3393	2036	-51.1
SE22	NorraMellansverige	541	1526	-26	1123	518	-15	1096	680	0.0

(Continued0)

Acronym	Region	2000	2001	2002	2003	2004	2005	2006	2000-06	Growth rate
SE23	MellerstaNorrland	853	1370	-653	209	931	37	460	458	-21.8
SE31	ÖvreNorrland	471	469	153	405	421	-35	216	300	-31.0
UKC1	Tees Valley and Durham	151	1289	-392	2206	766	2512	2220	1250	451.5
UKC2	Northumberland, Tyne and Wear	506	2849	-1043	1069	-388	3061	2546	1228	103.9
UKD1	Cumbria	-262	627	-489	26	-62	456	590	127	710.1
UKD2	Cheshire	-217	4381	-4753	1071	1285	4936	2269	1282	1317.1
UKD3	Greater Manchester	1747	3767	-2084	150	744	3714	2618	1522	58.0
UKD4	Lancashire	1445	4007	-3158	2179	2529	4958	1354	1902	260.2
UKD5	Merseyside	549	2045	-866	1170	325	2606	1472	1043	142.0
UKE1	East Riding and North Lincolnshire	180	1634	-619	386	15	1090	1063	536	60.3
UKE2	North Yorkshire	334	601	-607	-32	224	1102	117	248	223.7
UKE3	South Yorkshire	903	1803	-42	46	450	1189	1099	778	-21.6
UKE4	West Yorkshire	1314	3156	-2183	229	35	3207	1506	1038	63.2
UKF1	Derbyshire and Nottinghamshire	2365	2374	-3269	2393	1591	5418	4397	2181	604.0
UKF2	Leicestershire, Rutland and Northants	1242	4139	-789	-1412	1072	1611	1899	1109	-48.2
UKF3	Lincolnshire	42	386	-255	183	-161	360	204	108	155.7
UKG1	Herefordshire, Worcestershire, Warks	3050	2456	-1256	-916	604	2656	3017	1373	-5.4
UKG2	Shropshire and Staffordshire	1037	1490	-206	720	586	2423	2069	1160	87.4
UKG3	West Midlands	9814	8212	-4213	2665	989	18977	7809	6322	65.3
UKH1	East Anglia	1168	2348	-1464	912	867	3943	1826	1372	175.9
UKH2	Bedfordshire, Hertfordshire	443	4885	-2564	-780	746	6122	2128	1569	123.0
UKH3	Essex	2296	2529	-2130	1400	-372	4629	1080	1347	87.5
UKI1	Inner London	3223	8999	-13693	4982	1716	21833	14250	5902	2281.5
UKI2	Outer London	5069	9654	-8044	-737	-1855	12092	8533	3530	102.5
UKJ1	Berkshire, Bucks and Oxfordshire	1386	3637	1606	2469	1174	5742	2683	2671	36.5
UKJ2	Surrey, East and West Sussex	1960	2378	-506	-812	805	6642	1283	1679	55.0
UKJ3	Hampshire and Isle of Wight	-287	5771	-5897	6185	-238	5175	6117	2404	3229.4
UKJ4	Kent	3349	1115	986	1246	-995	2693	1831	1461	-34.3
UKK1	Gloucestershire, Wiltshire, N. Somerset	3964	8202	-4505	3581	3243	12595	8561	5092	173.9
UKK2	Dorset and Somerset	-195	3643	-241	-348	-30	2399	2671	1128	9.7
UKK3	Cornwall and Isles of Scilly	50	479	-113	427	-43	-157	701	192	66.9
UKK4	Devon	205	2210	-499	297	-931	911	2091	612	-7.4
UKL1	West Wales and The Valleys	-232	1250	-599	664	-1	1236	1036	479	425.5
UKL2	East Wales	-139	2272	-1335	1084	1382	10	1978	750	319.1
UKM3	Eastern Scotland	794	1824	-1368	1218	283	1267	2387	915	209.4
UKM5	South Western Scotland	113	4292	-1499	1922	2203	4893	4936	2409	260.0
UKM2	North Eastern Scotland	649	821	-483	-98	386	875	1085	462	70.7
UKM6	Highlands and Islands	-37	15	-10	79	154	-117	73	23	547.6
UKN0	Northern Ireland	1868	2416	-677	164	1179	2989	1589	1361	23.1
CY00	Cyprus	722	848	947	640	615	681	2638	1013	36.3
LU00	Luxembourg	4989	3549	4352	-601	4906	-435	5922	3240	-43.0
MT00	Malta	583	342	-617	259	358	630	1283	405	516.3
SI00	Slovenia	503	-216	751	1136	622	623	704	589	122.8
EE00	Estonia	245	554	321	1258	1889	1646	-44	838	218.0
LV00	Latvia	290	425	85	219	659	799	1041	503	154.9
LT00	Lithuania	24	464	833	165	455	1794	1052	684	96.7

Note: Levels in 2000m euros; growth rates between sub-periods 2000-02 and 2003-06 in %.
Source: Own elaboration

REFERENCES

Alfaro, L., Chanda, A., Kalemli-Ozcan, S. and Sayek, S. (2004): "FDI and economic growth: the role of local financial markets", *Journal of International Economics*, 64, 89-112.

Alfaro, L. and Charlton, A. (2007): *"Growth and the quality of foreign direct investment: Is all FDI equal?"*, Harvard Business School and NBER, London School of Economics.

Alfaro, L., Chanda, A., Kalemli-Ozcan, S. and Sayek, S. (2010): "Does foreign direct investment promote growth? Exploring the role of financial markets on linkages", *Journal of Development Economics, Elsevier*, 91 (2), 242-256.

Allard, G. and Pampillón, R. (2005): *"The impact of US foreign direct investment in Spain"*, Real Instituto Elcano, WP/19/2005

Argiro (2001): "Foreign direct investment and economic growth evidence from 14 European Union countries", TEI of Crete, 1-19.

Bajo-Rubio, O. and Sosvilla-Rivero, S. (1994): "An econometric analysis of foreign direct investment in Spain", *Southern Economic Journal*, 61, 104-20.

Bajo-Rubio, O., Díaz-Mora, C. and Díaz-Roldán, C. (2010): "Foreign direct investment and regional growth: An analysis of the Spanish case", *Regional Studies*, 44 (3), 373-382.

Balasubramanyam, V. N., Salisu, M. and Sapsford, D. (1996): "Foreign direct investment and growth in EP and IS countries", *The Economic Journal*, 106, 92-105.

Barba, G. and Venables, A. (2004): *Multinational firms in the world economy*, Princeton, Princeton University Press.

Barrios, S. and Strobl, E. (2002): *"Foreign direct investment and productivity spillovers: Evidence from the Spanish experience"*, Weltwirtschaftsliches Archiv, 138(3).

Barrios, S., Dimelis, S., Louri, H. and Strobl, E. (2004): *"Efficiency spillovers from foreign direct investment in the EU periphery: A comparative study of Greece, Ireland, and Spain"*, CORE, Université Catholique de Louvaine, Athens School of Economics and Business.

Barro, R. J. and Sala-i-Martin, X. (1992): "Convergence", *Journal of Political Economy*, 100 (21), 223-251.

Barro, R. J. and Sala-i-Martín (1995): *Economic growth*, New York, McGraw-Hill.

Blomström, M. and Kokko, A. (1998): "Multinationals corporations and spillovers", *Journal of Economic Surveys*, 12 (3), 247-277.

Bode, E. and Nunnenkamp, P. (2011): "Does foreign direct investment promote regional development countries? A Markov chain approach for US states", *Review World Economics*, 147 (2), 351-383.

Borenzstein, E., De Gregorio, J and Lee J-W. (1998): "How does foreign direct investment affect economic growth?", *Journal of International Economics*, 45, 115-135.

Borghesi, S. and Giovannetti, G. (2003): *"The role of institutional set-up in the success of FDI: do countries attracting FDI grow at higher rates?"*, Preliminary draft.

Busse, M. and Groizard, J. L. (2008): *"Foreign direct investment, regulations and growth"*, The World Economy, 31(7), 861-886.

Castellani, D. and Pieri, F. (2011): *"Foreign investments and productivity evidence from European regions"*, Department of Economics, 83, Finance and Statistics, University of Perugia.

Cipollina, M., Giovannetti, G., Pietrovito, F. and Pozzolo, A. F. (2012): "FDI and growth: What cross-country industry data say?", *The World Economy,* 35 (11), 1599-1629.

Dabla-Norris, E., Honda, J., Lahreche, A. and Verdier, G. (2010): "FDI flows to low-income countries: Global drivers and growth implications", *International Monetary Fund,* WP/10/132.

Dang, X. (2008): *"Foreign direct investment in China",* North Western University, Xian, China.

De Mello, L. R. (1996a): *"Foreign direct investment, international knowledge transfers and endogenous growth: Time series evidence",* Studies of Economics 9610, Department of Economics, University of Kent, UK.

De Mello, L. R. (1996b): "Foreign direct investment and endogenous growth: Evidence from time series and panel data", *Studies of Economics 9615,* Department of Economics, University of Kent, UK.

De Mello, L. R. (1997): "Foreign direct investment in developing countries and growth: A selective survey", *The Journal of Development Studies,* 34 (1), 1-34.

Elsadig, M. A. (2012): "Are the FDI inflow spillover effects on Malaysia´s economic growth input driven?", *Economic Modelling,* 29, 1498-1504.

Ewe-Ghee, L. (2001): "Determinants of, and the relation between, foreign direct investment and growth: A summary of the recent literature", *International Monetary Fund,* WP/01/175.

Hansen, H. and Rand, J. (2004): *"On the causal links between FDI and growth in developing countries",* Institute of Economics, University of Copenhagen, Development Economics Research Group.

Haskel, J. E., Pereira, S. C. and Slaughter, M. J. (2007): "Does inward foreign direct investment boost the productivity of domestic firms?", *The Review of Economics and Statistics,* 89, 482-496.

Herzer, D. (2012): "How does foreign direct investment really affect developing countries´ growth?", *Review of International Economics,* 20 (2), 396-414.

Johnson, A. (2006): "The effects of FDI inflows on host country economic growth", *Centre of Excellence for Science and Innovation Studies,* Electronic Working Paper Series, 58.

Kholdy, S. (1995): *"Causality between foreign investment and spillover efficiency",* Applied Economics, 27, 745-9.

Laurenceson, J. and Tang, K. K. (2007): *"The FDI-income growth nexus: A review of the Chinese experience",* East Asia Economic Research Group, Discussion Paper, 9.

Lee, J.Y. and Mansfield (1996): *"Intellectual property protection and US foreign direct investment",* Review of Economics and Statistics, 78, 181-186.

Lin, A. L. (1995): *"Trade effects of foreign direct investment: Evidence from Taiwan with four ASEAN countries",* Weltwirtschaftsliches Archiv, 131, 737-47.

Lipsey, R. (2002): Home and host country effects of FDI. *Paper for ISIT Conference on Challenges to Globalization,* Lidingö, Sweden.

Mullen, J. K. and Williams, M. (2005): "Foreign direct investment and regional economic performance", *Kyklos,* 58 (2), 265-282.

Ozturk, I. (2007): "Foreign direct investment-growth nexus: A review of the recent literature", *International Journal of Applied Econometrics and Quantitative Studies*, 4 (2), 79-98.

Pfaffermayr, M. (1994): "Foreign direct investment and exports: A time series approach", *Applied Economics,* 26, 337-51.

Romer, P. M. (1990): "Endogenous technological change", *Journal of Political Economy,* 98, 71-102.

Silverman BW. (1986): *Density estimation for statistics and data analysis.* London, Chapman and Hall.

Solow, R. M. (1956): "A contributional to the theory of economic growth", *Quarterly Journal of Economics,* 70, 65-94.

Tang, S. and Selvanathan, S. (2005): *"Foreign direct investment and regional income inequality in China",* Griffith University, Nathan, Queensland, Australia.

UNCTAD (2002): World Investment Report, 2002. New York and Geneva, United Nations.

Villaverde, J. and Maza, A. (2012): *"Inward foreign direct investment in the European Union: Regional distribution and determinants",* SIEPS report, 2012:6.

Wheeler, D. and Mody, A. (1992): "International investment location decisions. The case of US firms", *Journal of International Economics,* 33 (1-2), 57-76.

Zhang, K. H. (2001): "Does foreign direct investment promote economic growth? Evidence from East Asia and Latin America", *Contemporary Economic Policy,* 19 (2), 175-185.

In: Foreign Direct Investment (FDI)
Editors: Enzo Guillon and Lucas Chauvet

ISBN: 978-1-62808-403-0
© 2013 Nova Science Publishers, Inc.

Chapter 4

OUTWARD FDI TO CHINA AND THE PARENT FIRM'S ABILITY TO CREATE VALUE ADDED PER WORKER

Shu-Chin Huang[*a] *and Chang-Ching Lin*[†]
[a]Department of Economics, Ming Chuan University, Taiwan
[b]The Institute of Economics, Academia Sinica, Taiwan

ABSTRACT

The force of globalization has forced Taiwanese Information and Electronics suppliers to invest in mainland China. Traditionally, increases in a company's value added per worker were commonly associated with changes in physical capital, human capital and production technologies. However, changes in value added can also be the result of outward FDI because of capital leakage, export substitution, import penetration, technology transfer, and higher earnings from the subsidiary than the parent company, which further encourages firms to lower domestic production. This paper estimates the impact of outward FDI in mainland China on parent firms' abilities to create domestic value added per worker in the Information and Electronics sector in Taiwan using samples from 1991 to 2006. The results show that outward FDI in China lowers parent firms' value added per worker in Taiwan during this period. It implies that the government should develop strategies to increase domestic productivity while opening cross-strait investment.

JEL classification: F21; F23, O24, J24

Keywords: Factor movement policy, international investment, information and electronics industry, labor productivity, R&D, multinational firms

---

[*] schuang@mail.mcu.edu.tw
[†] lincc@econ.sinica.edu.tw

1. INTRODUCTION

To attain an economically advantageous position, many Taiwanese Information and Electronics (IE) firms[1] conducted outward foreign direct investments (OFDI) in mainland China. According to a report by AFX News Limited (2006), over 80 percent of Taiwan manufacturers had invested in China by 2005. One official report shows that the Taiwan government approved mainland China investment of Taiwanese firms was US$64.9 billion in 1991-2007 with about one-third of that investment in the IE industry (MOEAIC, 2008). This amount was larger than the total of US$55.3 billion of OFDI by Taiwanese firms in all other countries between 1952 and 2007, and more than twice of the investment of US$8.5 billion by Taiwanese in the IE industry in all other countries in the same period. It appears to show that Taiwan's IE producers play an important role in Taiwanese OFDI and they are more interdependent with China subsidiaries than with subsidiaries in other nations.

Labor productivity links directly with a nation's income and its people's living standard. Taiwanese IE suppliers with OFDI in China, on average, had higher labor productivity (defined as the value-added per real employee) than non-OFDI to China firms in 1991-2006 (Table 1). However, their growth in the labor productivity was significantly lower than firms without OFDI to China. The averaged annual change in the productivity was about eighty-five thousand New Taiwan Dollars (NT$85,000) for the former and NT$128,000 for the latter. We wonder whether there is a linkage between OFDI in China and labor productivity in the Taiwan IE sector. In the UK, Singh (1977) argued that OFDI was the core cause of the industrial decline in that country because overseas investments sometimes displace domestic investments and consequently lower the competitiveness of the domestic industry. In the USA, several studies pointed out that imports from offshore assembly plants have increased and caused domestic low-skilled worker dislocation, while some studies argued that the loss in unskilled jobs was offset by the increase in high-skilled jobs and benefit US consumers with lower prices, stockholders in higher profits and businesses in efficiency, productivity and global competitiveness (Marchant and Kumar, 2005). Nevertheless, the US trade deficit did not improve but worsened with the increase of US OFDI until the American reduced consumptions during the recent financial crisis (McMullen, 2009).

The debate on the effect of OFDI on domestic industries has been continued for decades. Several studies show that mainland China received foreign investments which improved technologies and productivities in China industries (Buckley, et al., 2007). On the other hand, there are reports showing job losses and the loss of global competitiveness in several Taiwan industries (Taiwan Advocates, 2002; Wu, 2001). The IE industry is of great concern to Taiwan because it accounts for more than one-third of Taiwan manufacturing activities[2]. It is also the major high-tech industry in which Taiwan has a strong international presence. Given the importance of the IE industry in the Taiwanese economy and the significant amount of the

---

[1] According to the industrial classification of the Taiwan Stock Exchange Corporation (TSEC), the information and electronics industry includes classification numbers from 2324 to 2331, which are manufacturers of semiconductors, computers and their peripherals, optical electronics, telecommunications networks and electronic components, and services of electronic products, information and other electronic products (TEJ, 2007).

[2] In Taiwan, the service sector accounted for about 67 percent of the GDP and the manufacturing sector accounted for less than 27 percent of the GDP in 2007. The value added produced by the Taiwan IE industry was about 11 percent of the Taiwan GDP in 2007 (National Statistics, 2008).

industry's outward direct investments to China, it is urgently necessary for Taiwanese leadership to know the possible impact of OFDI in China on domestic value creation in the IE industry. However, although there have been some studies attempted to estimate the effects of OFDI in China on Taiwan employment, industrial growth and structural changes (Ku, 1998; Chen and Ku, 2000; Chen and Ku, 2003; Chang, 2006; Li and Row, 2008), as far as the authors are aware, no studies have been performed on labor productivity side.

Table 1. A comparison between firms with and without OFDI in China, 1991-2006.

Variable	Firms without OFDI to China Mean I (obs.)	Firms with OFDI to China Mean II (obs.)	Two-sample t test: Mean I − Mean II H0: diff = 0 t statistics (d.f.)
Employment	587 persons (3876)	810 persons (3024)	-4.82 (6898)***
Sales per employee	NT$7.23 million (3867)	NT$15.97 million (3024)	-18.30 (6889)***
Labor productivity	NT$0.907 million (3307)	NT$1.332(2952)	-10.80 (6257)***
RD stocks per employee	NT$0.574 million (3722)	NT$1.185 million (3006)	-14.53 (6726)***
Capital stocks per employee	NT$1.819 million (3858)	NT$1.717 million (3017)	1.87 (6873)*
Unskilled human capital indicator	0.329 (3284)	0.297 (2947)	4.89 (6229)***
Annual change in labor productivity	NT$0.128 million (2729)	NT$0.085 (2878)	1.96 (5605)**
Growth rate of labor productivity (firms with positive value-added)	0.166 (2245)	0.130 (2511)	2.48 (4754)***
Growth rate of capital stocks per emp.	0.386 (3211)	0.125 (2992)	3.55 (6201)***
	SMEs	**Large firms**	
Labor productivity	NT$1.272 million (2509)	NT$0.997 million (3765)	-6.81 (6272)***
OFDI China's stocks per employee	NT$0.500 million (2826)	NT$ 0.358 million (3670)	-5.44 (6494)***
RD stocks per employee	NT$1.020 million (2882)	NT$0.739 million (3861)	-6.03 (6741)***
Unskilled human capital indicator	0.187 (2508)	0.397 (3760)	34.33 (6266)***
Capital stocks per employee	NT$1.430 million (3011)	NT$2.041 million (3879)	11.29 (6888)***
	Labor intensive firms	**Non-labor intensive firms**	
Labor productivity	NT$0.643 million (2841)	NT$1.493 million (3427)	22.13 (6266)***
OFDI China's stocks per employee	NT$0.248 million (2666)	NT$0.613 million (3269)	13.22 (5933)***
RD stocks per employee	NT$0.469 million (2859)	NT$1.264 million (3436)	16.43 (6293)***
Unskilled human capital indicator	0.399 (2908)	0.241 (3444)	-25.46 (6350)***
Capital stocks per employee	NT$1.741 million (2856)	NT$1.920 million (3418)	3.08 (6272)***

Notes: Employment, wages, sales revenues, capital stocks are in real terms as explained in Appendix 1.
*, ** and *** denote 10%, 5% and 1% of significant level, respectively.

This paper investigates the impact of OFDI in China on parent firms' labor productivity in the Taiwan IE industry by applying the System Generalized Method of Moments (GMM) and using firm level data in 1991−2006. The contribution of this paper is threefold. First, we estimate the impact of OFDI in China on the labor productivity from two aspects, net cumulated capital outflow from Taiwan to China (OFDI in China stocks) and earnings from Chinese investment against earnings from a Taiwanese parent company. The investigation is necessary because the initial capital outflow from Taiwan to China may produce negative effects on domestic productivity due to capital leakages, but in the longer term, earnings from China subsidiaries may bring incomes to the parent company and benefit labor productivity in the parent company. Second, we estimate the impact of OFDI in China on domestic labor productivity within different groups of firms. Firm specific characteristics such as firm size and labor-intensity can possibly affect firms' decisions in the allocation of production when they make OFDI abroad, and thus affect labor productivity in the parent company. The finding can provide important implications for strategic policy setting to regulate FDI outflow. Third, perhaps the most important contribution, we not only investigate the short-run impact of OFDI in China, but also estimate its long run effects on domestic labor productivity. The impact of OFDI on domestic labor productivity can fluctuate in the short run. Therefore it would be misleading if one evaluates its effect on a parent company by only looking at its short-run shocks.

This paper consists of 5 sections including the Introduction. Section 2 explains theories and models used for the estimation. Section 3 discusses the data used for the estimation and analyzes differences between OFDI and non-OFDI firms, large and small and medium enterprises (SMEs) and labor intensive and non-labor intensive firms. Section 4 shows some specification tests and estimation results. Finally, Section 5 concludes the study and outlines directions for future research.

2. THEORIES AND MODELS USED FOR REGRESSIONS

2.1. The Labor Productivity Model

We use a labor productivity model comprised of supply, demand and institutional factors affecting labor productivity in firms to estimate the impact of OFDI in China on Taiwanese parent firms' productivity in the IE sector. The analysis treats OFDI in China stocks as a capital leakage from Taiwan to mainland China. Hence, OFDI in China stocks becomes another input in the labor production function as presented in Model (1).

$$\frac{Q}{L} = A \times F\left(\frac{K}{L}, \frac{OFDI}{L}, \frac{RD}{L}, \frac{H}{L}, Inst, Dshock\right)$$

where Q is the value added produced by the parent firm, L is the labor input, A represents exogenous factors of production technologies that can not be controlled by the parent firm, K denotes fixed capital stocks available for production, $OFDI$ denotes the net cumulated amount of outward foreign direct investments leaking from the parent company, RD is R&D capital stocks symbolizing the firm's internal cumulated technological knowledge available for production, H is human capital per labor used for production, $Inst$ represents institutional factors affecting labor productivity such as the export share of sales, the relative size of earnings from OFDI and from the parent company, firm size, labor intensity, etc., and $Dshock$

indicates demand shocks at firm, industrial and aggregate level influencing the value-added revenue per labor unit (Appendix 1).

The skeleton format of the model is derived from a Cobb-Douglas production function but we incorporated the idea of an endogenous growth model in which a firm's R&D capital stocks and human capital are treated as endogenous rather than exogenous factors of technological changes. In addition, we add demand and institutional factors to allow labor productivities to vary with firm specific intuitional factors and demand shocks. Importantly, given the important effect of OFDI on domestic production in the Taiwan IE sector, we also include OFDI relevant variables and firm specific characteristics in the model to explain labor productivities.

Furthermore, considering the possibility of the dynamic nature between some inputs and labor productivity, we develop the model into a dynamic format for the empirical study as depicted in Model (2):

$$(2)\ P_{it} = \alpha_0 + \alpha_1 P_{i,t-1} + \beta(L)X_{it} + \lambda_i + \mu_t + \varepsilon_{it}\ (t = 2, ..., T_i\ ; i = 1, ..., N)$$

where P_{it} is the labor productivity (defined as value-added per labor) of firm i in time t, α_0 is a constant, X_{it} shows a vector of explanatory variables determining the firm's productivity level, $\beta(L)$ is a vector of associated polynomials in the lag operator, λ_i and μ_t are respectively individual-specific and annual time effects, and ε_{it} is serially uncorrelated and independent across firms. Due to the small amount of annual data available for use, the lag structure of the model is limited to a maximum of 2 periods for sensitivity analysis.

Model (2) states that a company's labor productivity at time t is explained by its past level of productivity and a group of explanatory variables including a constant, the supply factor, the institutional factor and demand shocks. Individual specific intercepts will capture time invariant effects which are not explained by other explanatory variables in the equation, including exogenous technologies used in the production.

OFDI, Profits Earned from OFDI vs. Domestic Labor Productivity

OFDI can affect the parent company's labor productivity through four important channels. First, OFDI may benefit home productivity if the overseas investment promotes exports to create value added for the parent company (Kojima, 1973; Lipsey and Weiss, 1981; Deutsche Bundesbank, 2006). Conversely, if OFDI results in an export substitution or an increase in imports from foreign subsidiaries to substitute domestic production, then it can reduce the value added revenue for the parent company (Hsu and Liu, 2002: 2; Chen, 2003; Hudson, et al., 2005; Liu and Huang, 2005; Tsai and Huang, 2007; Chiang, 2008; Li and Roe, 2008: 97). Whether OFDI produces a positive or a negative effect on the parent firm's value added revenue is largely determined by the two sides of forces.

Second, the direction of technological spillovers is not only from the parent company to foreign subsidiaries but also from foreign subsidiaries to the parent company. According to one official survey, about 89 percent of foreign subsidiaries received production technologies from Taiwan parent firms, about 9 percent of them obtained technologies through joint R&D projects with parent firms and others, and about 22 percent of them made innovations independently in the IE sector in 2006 (MOEA, 2007:A7-1). If the feedback flow of technological knowledge increases innovations in the parent company, then we expect that OFDI stocks have positive effects on the parent company's productivity. By contrast, if R&D activities in the foreign subsidiary substitute innovations in the parent company, then OFDI stocks can lower the parent company's productivity.

Third, OFDI stocks are capital leakages from the parent company. It can thus reduce domestic productivity. An empirical study by Bitzer and Görg (2009) using industry and country-level data for 17 OECD countries over the period 1973 to 2001 and found that a country's OFDI stocks are, on average, negatively related to productivity. On the other hand, a parent company may expand domestic investment to support the foreign operation, if a successful overseas investment increases profits for the parent company. In this case, OFDI can positively affect the parent company's productivity. A review done by Lipsey (1994, p. 35) showed a positive relationship over time between domestic and foreign investment. Some observers even argued that there is a linkage between OFDI and a more competitive and dynamic Canada (Hirshhorn, 1998: 8).

Fourth, profits earned from investments in China add incomes for the parent company and thus increase the value added for the parent company. The positive effect of OFDI on domestic income was supported by a study for Canada, which showed that income receipts from Canada's growing stock of OFDI made a contribution to income growth and to improvements to the current account balance in Canada during the 1980s (Hirshhorn, 1998). From this viewpoint, we expect that labor productivity in the Taiwan parent company will be increased as profits earned from China investments increase.

Firm Size, Labor-Intensity vs. Productivity

It is well documented that firm size and labor-intensity can affect labor productivity, but whether these firm specific characteristics can interact with OFDI to influence a parent company's productivity is unknown and requires further investigation. For example, there are concerns that small and medium enterprises (SMEs) face larger financial and capacity problems compared with large firms in making OFDI. Thus, once SMEs invest abroad, they are more likely to substitute low-cost foreign production for domestic production than large firms (Chen and Ku, 2003: 10-11). Consequently, SMEs directly investing abroad can produce more detrimental effects on domestic outputs and therefore more significantly reduce the labor productivity in the parent company than that of the large company. However, a study of Central Eastern European companies, Svetličič, et al. (2007) argued that SMEs frequently target specialized niches with competitive advantages in technological know-how, organizational flexibility and closer relationships with their customers; thus home country employment effects of SMEs are positive and larger than they are for large companies.

The argument for labor-intensity is relevant to a firm's labor-cost share of production. As is shown in Section 2, labor-intensive firms require more direct labor force for production than non-labor intensive firms. Moreover, their employees, on average, have less physical and R&D knowledge capitals available for production. These companies can switch more home production to low labor-cost China subsidiaries and thus reduce more labor productivity in the Taiwan parent company than that of non-labor-intensive firms. Moreover, most information and electronics products are not heavy. Labor-intensive producers can ship components from Taiwan to China and employ low-cost laborers in China for assembling and producing low-end products to serve the global market. In the longer term, the Chinese subsidiary can become more capable in production and doing R&D independently. If the parent firm does not invest substantially in physical as well as R&D capitals in Taiwan to upgrade its Taiwanese production, then the labor intensive company can significantly lower its business activities in Taiwan and greatly reduce its labor productivity in Taiwan in the long-run.

Kojima (1973), however, studied Japanese multinationals and argued that their overseas investments were in line with the host country's comparative advantage and thus promoted trade for Japan. We are not sure whether the argument still holds if one uses a longer period of data to test the hypothesis. Chiang (2008) studied the IT industry which was first developed in the US and then transmitted to Japan and hence to Taiwan, South Korea and China. The author argued that the US has already reached the reverse import stage for IT goods while East Asian economies are at the export stage. Luckily, the US is now able to export IT services to the other four countries, otherwise the trade deficit in the IT goods signals a relative incompetence of US producers to producers in the other four nations. Returning to the Taiwanese case, China was then and still is teeming with labor resources and her labor costs were relatively cheap compared with Taiwan labor costs during 1991−2006. China had the comparative advantage in labor supply and that made China the world production base during the study period. Unless Taiwanese labor intensive firms increase investments in Taiwan to improve Taiwan operations when they are directly investing in China, we expect that labor intensive firms OFDI in China produce more negative effects on domestic outputs and thus less value added revenue per employee.

To estimate the effects of OFDI in China and firm specific characteristics (e.g., firm size and labor intensity) on domestic labor productivity, we will explicitly introduce the interaction terms, (OFDI in China stocks per employee × SME) and (OFDI in China stocks per employee × labor-intensity), into a regression model. If the coefficient of the first interaction term is negative, then SMEs conducting OFDI in China produce a more detrimental effect on the productivity of parent firms than large firms and vice versa. If the coefficient of the second interaction term is negative, then labor-intensive firms investing in China reduce a larger amount of productivity in Taiwanese parent firms than non-labor intensive firms and vice versa.

Capital Stocks, R and D, Human Capital vs. Labor Productivity

In the traditional supply side growth model, an increase in capital stocks will increase output, and thus an increase in capital stocks per labor will raise output per labor. However, the argument may not hold at the firm level if the demand side factor is also considered in the model. Given the quantity demanded remains unchanged, there is no reason that an increase in capital stocks per labor unit will increase output per labor unit. This is particularly true in consumer product industries in which fixed capitals are not part of its output. In this aspect, we expect that the coefficient of capital stocks per employee in the labor productivity function is insignificant. However, if the new machinery contains new technologies to improve productivity, then, other things being equal, increases in capital stocks per labor will increase output per labor.

Non-embodied technologies such as production process, know-how, new product design, etc., are mostly generated by the firm's R&D efforts or buy in from others. With all other things being equal, increases in these types of technologies can increase output or the company's value added. Thus, we expect that with more R&D capital stocks per labor unit the more value added revenue per labor unit.

Next, human capital is separated from physical labor inputs in the endogenous growth model. Skilled workers have higher human capital and thus they are expected to produce more value added revenue for a company than unskilled workers. Limited by available data, we use the share of direct labor costs in the total labor compensation in a firm to approximately indicate the level of human capital used in the company. The share is between 0 and 1. A higher share implies a lower human capital used for production because direct laborers usually work mechanically and use less skills in production than indirect laborers. Thus, we expect that the coefficient of the unskilled human capital indicator is negative in the labor productivity equation.

Export Share and Labor Productivity

Export share expresses the openness of a company. It is constructed by exports divided by firm-specific total sales, including domestic and foreign sales. We do not consider imports because import data are unavailable at the firm level. A higher export share implies that the firm has more interactions with the international market. It is well documented that trade is an important channel for cross border technology transfers (Coe and Helpman, 1995). We expect that exchanges between Taiwanese producers and their foreign customers improve production technologies for Taiwanese companies and thus positively affect labor productivity of Taiwanese producers.

Demand Shocks and Labor Productivity

Labor productivity growth has a major cyclical component which is relevant to demand shocks. For example, some studies show that the significant growth in labor productivity in the US during the second half of the 1990s was a reflection of the strengthening of aggregate demand rather than a fundamental improvement in physical capital or technologies (Steindel and Stiroh, 2001: 26-27). Hence, it is important to include the demand factor into the labor productivity function to allow productivities to vary with demand shocks. In practice, we use sales gaps, industrial growth rates and year dummies to capture demand shocks at the firm, industrial and aggregate levels.

Finally, we expect labor productivity to adjust with delay to changes in some of the factors mentioned above. The process of adjustment to changes in these factors may depend on the passage of time, which argues for including lags of these factors as regressors. Furthermore, the process of adjustment can depend on the difference between equilibrium productivity level and the previous year's actual level; thus it calls for a dynamic model in which lags of the dependent variable are included as explanatory variables.

2.2. Estimation Strategies

Due to firm-specific fixed effects and lagged dependent variables in the panel regression of interest and the potential existence of endogeneity in explanatory variables, we adopt the one-step system GMM designed by Blundell and Bond (1998). The advantages of using the one-step system GMM are threefold. First, the system GMM is more efficient than the conventional first difference GMM. In addition to exogenous variables, we use the levels and the first differences of lagged dependent and endogenous explanatory variables as instruments. Particularly, the system GMM considers not only the moment conditions in differenced errors equations as imposed by Arellano and Bond (1991) but also the moment conditions that the first differences of lagged dependent variables and lagged explanatory variables should be uncorrelated with the errors and individual effects. Hayakawa (2007) also showed that the system GMM delivers less biased estimates than the level and difference GMMs. Second, the system GMM can allow for endogenous explanatory variables other than lagged dependent variables without using extra instruments variables. Third, the one-step rather than two-step system GMM is used for the estimation because simulation studies have suggested very modest efficiency gains from using the two-step version, but a high instrument count can result in a downward-bias for coefficient standard errors in two-step GMM (Roodman, 2007: 8-9; Bond, 2002: 9-10). For further details of the technique used in the system GMM, please refer to Blundell and Bond (1998) and Roodman (2006). The detailed discussions on the analysis of endogenous variables and the instruments used in our estimation are described in Section 4.1.

To reduce the impacts of heterogeneities across hundreds of firms, we further adopt robust standard errors in our estimation. Moreover, it is worth pointing out that we cannot introduce extra time-invariant variables (e.g., firm size dummy or labor-intensive dummy variables) in the model due to fixed effects. Alternatively, to tackle the impact of OFDI in China on productivity, we allow the slope coefficients of OFDI to be group-specific across firms. Finally, firm level time series data for OFDI in China are available in 1991-2006 according to the companies' annual financial reports. Yet, firm level data for OFDI in other countries are unavailable. Thus, when we estimate the impact of OFDI in China on a parent company's labor productivity, we use the firm-specific fixed effects to control other firm-specific effects including OFDI to other countries.

3. DATA

We collected data from 668 Taiwan IE firms which were either listed on the Taiwan Stock Exchange (TSE) or as Over-the-Counter (OTC) in Taiwan from 1991 to 2006. These firms were classified by the Taiwan Stock Exchange Corporation (TSEC) under the IE industrial group (code: M2300) and included IE manufacturers and services providers. The total net sales of these firms was about NT$8,047 billion in 2006, and it accounted for about 55.8 percent of the total sales of all Taiwanese TSE and OTC firms in the year. Among these firms, 642 firms had completed data for regressions and 539 firms had direct investments in mainland China. In 2006, there were 263 firms in our data set with employment fewer than 200 persons, which were, by definition[3], SMEs in Taiwan. Our data are imbalanced from

---

[3] The MOEA defines SMEs if firms with employment less than 200 persons or received capital less than NT$80 million. The definition of SME is various across countries mainly because of the wide diversity of businesses. For example, a SME is defined as any business which employees fewer than 250 full-time employees and turnover below €50 million in the EU, any manufacturing business employees fewer than 100 people in Hong Kong, and any business establishment with less than 500 employees and less than CAD50 million in gross revenues in Canada. We adopt the MOEA definition to fit the Taiwanese situation. Moreover, we do not assign a SME-status to a firm according to the firm's initial employment, but use the MOEA definition to

1991 to 2006 with the earliest investments by some IE firms to China in 1997. We use data from 1991 rather than from 1997 to preserve information about firms' performance before and after conducting OFDI in China, because the formal regulation for Taiwanese engaging in the indirect investment or technical collaboration with people in mainland China was set in October, 1990. Note that for non-OFDI in China observations, their net cumulated amounts of OFDI in China (briefly noted as 'OFDI China's stocks') are zero.[4] Firm level data used in this study come from the Taiwan Economic Journal (TEJ). Industries' value-added indices and price indices are obtained from the National Statistics of Executive Yuan in Taiwan. The statistical descriptions of the variables considered are summarized in Appendix 1.

3.1. Data Analysis by OFDI in China

As mentioned earlier, most Taiwan IE producers have invested in mainland China before 2006. It is interesting to know whether there are significant differences in firm characteristics between the OFDI and non-OFDI in China producers. Thus, we conduct two-sample t tests on the two groups of firms (Table 1). We find that in the sample of 1991-2006, firms with OFDI in China had significantly larger employment than firms without OFDI in China (810 vs. 587 persons). Moreover, their labor productivity (defined as value-added revenue per employee) and R&D capital stocks per employee were on average higher than firms without OFDI to China (NT$1.3 vs. 0.9 million and NT$1.2 vs. 0.6 billion, respectively). Further, the unskilled human capital indicator (defined as direct labor costs / total labor compensation) was lower for the former than the latter (29.7 vs. 32.9 percent). The data depict that firms with OFDI to China were on average larger, more productive, more knowledge intensive and less dependent on direct labor force used for their business operations in Taiwan than firms without OFDI to China in the IE sector. However, in terms of growth rates, OFDI to China firms were lower than non-OFDI to China firms in labor productivity, sales per employee and capital stocks per employee. The respective averaged annual growth rates are 28, 24 and 13 percents versus 42, 37 and 39 percents. The relatively slow growth of firms with OFDI in China signals the possibility that OFDI in China negatively affects Taiwan IE industry. Nevertheless, the significant difference may be partly due to firm sizes, since OFDI in China firms are relatively large which may produce smaller growth rates than SMEs. Thus, a further investigation on firm size is necessary.

---

identify a SME through the whole sample period. In other words, some firms can be SMEs in the early 1990s, while becoming large firms in the 2000s. We do not use the initial number of employment to fix firm size because our sample period is long (a maximum period of 16 years) and our data are unbalanced. Many of our sample firms started business after 1991, and some of them became large firms before 2006. Most Taiwanese IE firms are young, and so do firms in our sample. The average firm age in our sample is about 13.4 years. It is no reason that we estimate their behaviors by assuming that they were small firms when they had already become large firms.

[4] For robustness, we also conducted similar estimations using the post-Asia-financial-crisis sample, the sample from 1998 to 2006. As it is shown in Appendix 3, the main results are qualitatively consistent with the results from the 1991-2006 samples.

3.2. Data Analysis by Firm Size

Next, let us consider the differences between large firms and SMEs. As shown in Table 1, SMEs did significantly differ from large firms in several aspects. Particularly, SMEs tended to have more labor productivity. Although each worker had less physical capital stocks to use for production in the SME than in the large firm, most workers in the SME were indirect workers with higher human capital than the average in the large company (unskilled human capital indicator was 0.19 in the SME vs. 0.40 in the large firm). Importantly, though the amount of capital invested in China by the SME was lower than by the large company, OFDI in China stocks per employee was higher for the SME than for the large company. It shows that the average SME was more dependent on their China subseries than the large company.

3.3 Data Analysis by Labor Intensity

We further classified our samples based on their labor intensity. The firms are referred to as labor-intensive firms if their labor-costs as a share of sales were above the sample mean, 8.1 percent; otherwise firms were referred as the non-labor-intensive firms. Labor intensive firms on average had lower labor productivity as well as capital stocks and R&D capital stocks per employee than non-labor intensive firms. It shows that there was less physical capital and technological knowledge available for each worker in a labor intensive firm. Moreover, data show that labor-intensive firms had a higher share of direct labor costs in total labor compensation. It may imply that the company was more dependent on unskilled laborers for production than non-labor intensive firms. Finally, OFDI in China stocks per employee was lower in labor-intensive firms than in non-labor-intensive firms and contradicts conventional impressions that labor-intensive firms would have invested more in China than that of non-labor-intensive firms partially because low-cost labor inputs might be more important to them than to non-labor-intensive firms.

4. REGRESSION RESULTS

The above data analyses disclose that firms with and without OFDI in China are different in the level and growth of labor productivity. Moreover, the differences also appear between SMEs and large firms, and labor intensive and non-labor intensive firms. Next, we take a further step to estimate whether the difference is a result of OFDI in China or not, by using a one-step system GMM and available data of 642 IE firms from 1991-2006. The GMM results show short-run effects, and then, based on the short-run results, we use the non-linear combinations of estimators (NLCOE) to compute the long-run estimates after GMM estimation command in Stata. The calculations are based on the "delta method", which is an approximation appropriate in large samples (Stata, 2005). The formula for a long-run estimate is $\sum_{j=1}^{J} \hat{\beta}_{k,j}/(1-\alpha_1)$, where $J = 1$ + maximum lagged order of an interest variable x_k, $\hat{\beta}_{k,j}, j=1,(2,...)$ are the estimated coefficients of current (and lagged, if any) x_k, and $\hat{\alpha}_1$ is the estimated coefficient of lagged labor productivity. Short-run results are reported in Table 3 and long-run estimates are reported in Table 4. For comparison, the results generated from OLS and Fixed Effects (FE) estimations are reported in the tables as well.

4.1. Exogeneity, Causality, Over-Identification, and Serial Correlations Tests

We applied a regression based Hausman test suggested by Wooldridge (2002: 118-122) to detect whether any of our explanatory variables is endogenous and found that lagged labor productivity, OFDI China stocks per employee and R&D stocks per employee are endogenous in the labor productivity equation as reported in Table 2. The result indicates that these three variables have dynamic relationships with labor productivity. Other variables in the equations are exogenous. It is not surprising that lagged labor productivity is endogenous due to the dynamic settings with firm-specific fixed effects. The finding also supports Li and Roe (2008: 92) who argued that OFDI flows are endogenous in an aggregate growth model. Furthermore, we found that R&D capital stocks per employee is also endogenous, a finding neglected by previous studies.

Table 2. Results of exogeneity tests.

The overall error component of instrumented explanatory variable	Labor Productivity
(Labor productivity)$_{t-1}$	1.10(13.3)***
(Capital stocks per employee)$_t$	-0.03(0.6)
(OFDI China's stocks per emp.)$_t$	-0.27(3.1)***
(RD stocks per employee)$_t$	0.48(4.6)***
(Unskilled human capital indicator)$_t$	0.11(0.3)
(China gains / Taiwan gains)$_t$	-0.05(1.0)
Total observations	3691
R-sq. within	0.53
Corr(u_i, Xb)	-0.48
Sigma u (the fixed effect error component)	1.74
Sigma e (the overall error component)	0.67
Rho (fraction of variance due to u)	0.87
F test (d.f.)	(28, 3032) = 24.8***

Notes: The t-ratio is behind each coefficient within parentheses. *, ** and *** denote 10%, 5% and 1% of significant level, respectively. In the labor productivity equation, explanatory variables include the respectively instrument variables and their error components and some exogenous variables, including the growth rate of industrial value-added revenue, company sales gap, export share of sales, company's corporate income tax rate, firm age, time trend and a constant. For each instrumented variable, we use instrumental variables including the first difference of the dependent variable in periods of t-1 and t-2 and some relevant strictly exogenous variables. For details of the methodology, please refer to Wooldridge (2002: 118-122).

Table 3. Short-run labor productivity equations, 1991-2006
Dependent variable: labor productivity

Explanatory variable	One-step system GMM (A)	(B)	Fixed Effects (C)	OLS (D)
Labor productivity				
Lag 1	0.677(16.3)***	0.685(16.3)***	0.448(12.1)***	0.810(26.3)***
Capital stocks per employee	0.111(0.8)	0.009(0.6)	0.1016(0.6)	0.007(0.6)
OFDI China's stocks per emp.	0.208(2.8)***	0.081(1.5)	0.158(1.8)*	0.025(0.3)
Lag 1	-0.237(1.9)*	-0.044(0.5)	-0.075(0.7)	-0.021(0.2)
Lag 2	-0.144(1.5)	-0.146(1.7)*	-0.130(1.5)	-0.111(1.2)
OFDI China's stocks per emp. × SME		0.159(2.2)**	0.164(2.2)**	0.178(2.5)***
Lag 1		-0.182(2.0)**	-0.087(1.1)	-0.146(1.9)*
OFDI China's sto. per emp. × labor int.		-0.119(2.8)***	-0.136(2.9)***	-0.096(2.5)***
Unskilled human capital indicator	-0.335(2.8)***	-0.280(2.4)**	0.055(0.3)	-0.206(2.8)***
RD stocks per employee	-0.305(2.6)***	-0.312(2.7)***	-0.347(3.3)***	0.276(2.8)***
Lag 1	0.387(3.2)***	0.395(3.32)***	0.427(3.7)***	0.353(3.1)***
China gains / Taiwan gains	0.017(0.5)	0.012(0.4)	0.017(0.9)	0.009(0.4)
Lag 1	0.112(0.5)	0.141(1.3)	0.026(1.0)	0.032(1.3)
Industrial growth rates	0.914(4.3)***	0.950(4.4)***	0.530(2.5)***	0.855(4.7)***
Sales gap	1.77(2.0)**	1.666(1.9)*	6.378(11.3)***	0.859(4.7)***
Export share	0.217(2.8)***	0.191(2.7)***	0.277(2.5)***	0.137(2.7)***
Constant	0.075(0.8)	0.059(0.7)	0.523(3.7)***	-0.013(0.2)
1994 year dummy	0.054(0.8)	0.053(0.7)	0.019(0.2)	0.071(0.9)
1995 year dummy	0.027(0.3)	0.019(0.2)	-0.076(0.6)	0.001(0.0)
1996 year dummy	-0.125(1.6)	-0.128(1.6)	-0.287(2.5)***	-0.139(1.6)
1997 year dummy	-0.054(0.6)	-0.047(0.6)	-0.307(2.6)***	-0.023(0.3)
1998 year dummy	-0.105(1.2)	-0.103(1.2)	-0.391(3.4)***	-0.084(1.1)
1999 year dummy	0.051(0.5)	0.063(0.7)	-0.330(2.6)***	0.093(1.1)
2000 year dummy	0.101(0.9)	0.105(0.9)	-0.292(2.2)**	0.140(1.6)
2001 year dummy	0.076(0.8)	0.096(1.0)	-0.384(2.8)***	0.045(0.5)
2002 year dummy	0.175(1.9)*	0.188(2.0)**	-0.289(2.2)**	0.182(2.1)**
2003 year dummy	0.353(3.6)***	0.361(3.7)***	-0.111(0.9)	0.317(3.6)***
2004 year dummy	0.349(3.2)***	0.354(3.3)***	-0.066(0.5)	0.277(3.1)***
2005 year dummy	0.245(2.3)**	0.236(2.3)**	-0.089(0.7)	0.136(1.4)
2006 year dummy	0.472(4.3)***	0.456(4.2)***	0.174(1.3)	0.347(3.6)***
Wald: Chi2(d.f.)	(26)=1,125***	(29)=1,239***		
Hansen: Chi2(d.f.)	(322)=345(0.18)	(426)=452(0.19)		
Arellano-Bond AR(1) 1st dif.: z	-7.39(0.00)***	-7.41(0.00)***		
Arellano-Bond AR(2) 1st dif.: z	-0.09(0.93)	-0.10(0.92)		
F test			(29, 3988) = 21.7***	(39, 4629) = 6.8***
R^2			0.35 (within)	0.60
Number of instruments	349	456		
Number of firms	642	642	642	642
Number of observations	4,659	4,659	4,659	4,659

Notes: Here, we only have 13 year dummies because the maximal lagged order of dependent variables is 2 and the GMM takes the first-difference. Behind each coefficient is the t-ratio. *, ** and *** denote 10%, 5% and 1% of significant level, respectively. For a Hansen test of over-identification, Arellano-Bond tests for AR(1) and AR(2), P-values are in parentheses. In Columns (A) — (B), the lagged dependent variable, OFDI China stocks per employee, (OFDI China stocks per employee × SME), (OFDI china stocks per employee × Labor intensive), and RD stocks per employee are predetermined variables as suggested by the data. Their first differences are used as instruments for level GMM equations and their lags are used as instruments for first differences GMM equations as Blundell and Bond (1998) in addition to all exogenous variables included in the equations and a time trend.

To further check whether the endogenous variables depend on the past values of labor productivity, we conduct Granger causality tests and found that labor productivity did Granger-cause OFDI to China stocks per employee and R&D stocks per employee during the period of interest (Appendix 2). The results suggest that OFDI to China stocks per employee and R&D stocks per employee are affected by the past values of labor productivity.

To take the endogenous and causality problems into account, we use instrumental variables. Following Blundell and Bond (1998: 137) and Roodman (2006: 22), in addition to exogenous variables used in the equation, we not only use instruments of the differences of the lagged dependent variable, OFDI China stocks per employee, and R&D stocks per employee in level GMM equations, but also the instruments of the second or higher older lagged dependent variable and first and higher older lagged levels of OFDI China stocks per employee and R&D stocks per employee in the difference GMM equations. To be valid, we investigate whether over-identification test is passed or not when we use these instruments. As reported in Table 3, Hansen's over-identification test suggests that there is no over-identification in our estimation. Moreover, the assumption of serially uncorrelated errors is curial to make the system GMM estimation valid. We, therefore, conduct the Arellano-Bond test and it appears to show that all system GMM estimations listed in Table 3 have satisfactory statistics to reject the null hypothesis that the first differenced errors have zero autocorrelation (AR(1)) while not reject that the second-order autocorrelation (AR(2)) is zero, which indirectly provides an evidence that the errors are not serially correlated at the second order.

4.2. Regression Results

Accounting for Labor Productivity in Taiwanese IE firms

Our results show that labor productivity in the current year is moderately relevant to the firm's labor productivity in the previous year in the short-run. The estimated coefficients of the lagging one-year dependent variable are about 0.68 (Table 3, Eq. (A) and (B)). It is a good estimate which falls between the OLS estimate 0.81 and the FE estimate 0.45 (Eq. (C) & (D)).[5] In the long-run, the negative factors to reduce value added per employee (labor productivity) in Taiwanese parent firms are OFDI in China stocks per employee and unskilled human capital indicator (Table 4). Conversely, value added per employee in the parent firms is positively associated with RD capital stocks per employee, industrial growth rates, sales gap, and export share.

---

[5] As it is pointed out by Bond (2002: 4-5), when one uses panel data with endogeneity, the OLS estimator of the lagged dependent variable is inconsistent and biased upwards while the Fixed Effects estimator is biased downwards. Thus, a candidate consistent estimator should lie between the OLS and FE estimates, or at least not be significantly higher than the former or significantly lower than the latter. Therefore, a robustness check of the estimated system GMM results is to look at the estimated coefficient on the lagged dependent variable. A good estimate should fall between the OLS and the FE estimates.

Table 4. Long-run effects on Taiwan parent firms' labor productivity in the IE sector Dependent variable: labor productivity.

Explanatory variable	One-step system GMM (A)	(B)	Fixed Effects (C)	OLS (D)
Capital Stocks per employee	0.035(0.8)	0.028(0.6)	0.029(0.6)	0.038(0.6)
OFDI China stocks per employee	-0.537(2.6)***	-0.344(1.5)	-0.085(0.7)	-0.560(2.3)**
OFDI China stocks per emp. × SME		-0.072(0.3)	0.139(1.1)	0.170(0.7)
OFDI China stocks per emp. × labor int.		-0.378(2.9)***	-0.247(2.9)***	-0.505(2.4)**
Unskilled human capital indicator	-1.039(3.1)***	-0.887(2.6)***	0.100(0.3)	-1.084(2.9)***
RD stocks per employee	0.252(2.0)**	0.263(2.1)**	0.146(2.3)**	0.405(2.5)***
China gains / Taiwan gains	0.401(0.5)	0.487(1.2)	0.078(1.4)	0.212(1.4)
Industrial growth rates	2.834(4.0)***	3.011(4.0)***	0.962(2.5)***	4.504(3.9)***
Sales gap	5.491(2.0)**	5.282(1.9)*	11.564(9.9)***	4.527(3.8)***
Export share	0.672(3.0)***	0.606(2.9)***	0.502(2.4)**	0.722(2.6)***

Notes: These long-run effects are estimated using Non-linear Combinations of Estimators based on estimates from the system GMM, the Fixed Effects regression and the OLS listed in Table 3. The t-ratio is behind each coefficient within parentheses. *, ** and *** denote 10%, 5% and 1% of significant level, respectively.

OFDI in China as. Labor Productivity

OFDI in China has negative effects on home labor productivity starting from one-year lag (Table 3, Eq. (A)). A NT$1 million increase in OFDI-China stocks per employee lowers labor productivity in the Taiwan parent firm for about NT$0.54 million in the long run (Table 4, Eq. (A)). However, in contrast to OFDI in China stocks, earnings from the China investment raise labor productivity in Taiwan in both the short and long run, though it is still insignificant (Eq. (A)). Our estimated size of effect, however, does differ from Chang (2005) who studied the Taiwan aggregate economy and found OFDI had a negative but insignificant effect in GDP over 1981-2003. It also differs from Chen and Ku (2000) who argued that OFDI by Taiwanese companies in low income countries produced insignificant impact on firm growth in 1986-1994. On the other hand, our results support Lie and Roe (2008) who used Taiwanese aggregate data and argued that there is a lag negative effect on Taiwan economy due to OFDI in China. The difference in findings can be explained by the specificity of our study to the IE industry, our larger panel sample size, more up-to-date study period, and more comprehensive equation.

We also find that, when a company invests directly in China, its degree of labor-intensity does significantly affect labor productivity in both the short- and long-run (Tables 3 and 4, Eq. (B)). The short-run result indicates that when labor-intensive firms conducted OFDI in China, it lowered the parent company's labor productivity in the same year. In the long-run, labor intensive firms conducting OFDI in China significantly reduced the parent company's labor productivity and the reduction is significantly higher than that produced by non-labor intensive firms investing in China. Specifically, in the long-run when a labor-intensive company increases the cumulated amount of OFDI to China per employee by NT$1 million, it reduces its Taiwan labor productivity for about NT$0.72 million which is significantly larger than NT$0.34 million produced by a non-labor intensive firm. The finding has some implications to policy making. Because OFDI to China by labor intensive firms are particularly detrimental on Taiwanese labor productivity, it is necessary for the government to have a good strategy to encourage them to upgrade themselves in Taiwan rather than to invest in China. The finding also casts the doubt on Kojima (1973) arguing that OFDI in line with the host country's comparative advantage would benefit the home country. China has the comparative advantage in labor costs; however, evidence provided by this study shows that not only non-labor intensive firms but also labor-intensive firms investing in China produced negative effects on the parent company's labor productivity from 1991 to 2006.

Turning to firm size, while our result shows that the negative impact on home labor productivity is insignificantly different between large firms and SMEs in the long-run, the short-run effect is quite different. SMEs tend to have more contemporary positive impacts of OFDI on labor productivity than large firms, but the positive effect turns into a negative effect after a one year lag. Overall, the effect is insignificant in the long-run. The phenomenon that labor productivities in SMEs are dramatically changed after OFDI in China partially reflects the fact that production scales in SMEs are not sufficiently large to retain production sites both in China and in Taiwan. Consequentially, SMEs depend upon the employees in Taiwan to share their experiences and technology with Chinese workers at the beginning stages of production and over time, tend to relocate their major production sites from Taiwan to China after these skills are transferred.

Capital Stocks, R and D, Export Share vs. Labor Productivity

As expected, changes in capital stocks per employee do have positive effects on labor productivity but it is insignificant in both the short and long run. On the other hand, the increase in R&D capital stocks per employee significantly improves labor productivities for IE firms in the long run. If the firm increased NT$1 million more in R&D capital stocks per employee, labor productivity is predicted to be about NT$0.26 million more in the long run and shows that innovations in product and process technologies do improve labor productivity in IE firms. Exports also play an important role to improve the labor productivity for IE firms in both the short and long run. We find that a one percent increase in export share raises long-run labor productivity by about NT$0.6 million.

Sales Gap, Industrial Growth Rates and Aggregate Demand Shocks

Labor productivities in Taiwan IE firms are significantly affected by demand factors. A one percent increase in the industrial growth rate in the value added revenue increased the labor productivity in an average IE company by about NT$0.03 million in the long-run. In addition, a company's sales gap significantly influences labor productivities in both the short and long run. In the long run, a one percent increase from the normal trend in the company's sales increased the labor productivity by about NT$0.05 million. Finally, aggregate demand shocks also significantly affect the labor productivity in the sample period. Coefficients of year dummies from 2002 to 2006 are positive and significant. This implies that aggregate demand shocks in this period have positive contributions to the labor productivity in Taiwanese IE firms.

5. CONCLUSION AND POLICY IMPLICATIONS

Forced by international competition, many Taiwanese suppliers in the IE industry carried out their first time overseas production in mainland China in 1991-2006. Our estimated results show that OFDI into China significantly lowered labor productivity in the parent company in the industry during the sample period. This implies that the parent firm's ability to create value added per worker was hurt by the overseas production. In the long-run, the negative impact was particularly significant for labor intensive firms. It is a warning to policy makers in Taiwan when they are contemplating further liberalization for IE firms to invest in mainland China. On the other hand, results show that the increase in R&D stocks and the lower in the use of unskilled laborers in the parent company significantly raised labor productivities in the parent company. Thus, we urge the government to make further efforts to promote domestic investments in R&D and training to increase domestic labor productivities. Furthermore, results indicate that demand factors, such as a company's sales gap and the industrial growth, have important positive effects on a parent company's labor productivity. This implies that demand played a strong pull-role in lifting labor productivity in the Taiwanese IE sector. Besides, foreign markets as indicated by export share had significantly positive contributions to domestic labor productivity. These finding suggests that it is unlikely that Taiwan can effectively increase domestic labor productivity simply by government investments in domestic R&D and training while sacrificing the foreign market. In other words, an inward-trade policy cannot be a successful strategy.

Given the importance of the China market, the comparative advantage of Chinese in labor, land and natural resources, and tax incentives provided by China governments to Taiwan investors, it is difficult for the Taiwan government to restrict IE firms to invest in China. Meanwhile, China is cooperating with other nations to form free trade areas which provide firms with an even greater demand incentive, whereas political constraints have prevented Taiwan from engaging in these trade talks. Thus, strategic policies, as it is suggested by the findings of this study, would be to require Taiwanese firms to invest a certain amount of domestic R&D and retain headquarters in Taiwan when they are applying overseas investments. In the meantime, an improvement in the domestic investment environment, in particularly by enlarging the demand size (including domestic and foreign markets) is decisive to attract both domestic and foreign companies to invest in Taiwan, and therefore creates value added in the nation.

Finally, more work is needed to enable us to fully understand and appropriately react to the challenge in OFDI. As this study concentrates upon the Taiwan IE sector, our findings may not represent all industries. Further research is needed to examine the impact of such investment in other industries. Nevertheless, this paper shows the different characteristics of firms with and without OFDI in mainland China in the IE industry. Moreover, this is the first paper to apply the system GMM to investigate the relationship between OFDI in China and the ability of the parent firm to create value added per worker in the Taiwan IE industry. Furthermore, we show the different OFDI impacts on large firms and SMEs, as well as on labor intensive and non-intensive firms. The research results have important implications in OFDI policy.

ACKNOWLEDGMENTS

The authors appreciate the valuable suggestions and comments received from participants at the Tenth Annual Conference on Empirical Economics (National Chung Cheng University, Taiwan) on the early draft of this paper. We are also grateful to the Taiwan Economic Journal (TEJ) for providing the data.

REFERENCES

AFX – Asia (2006) Taiwan indictment of UMC executives may backfire – analysts, *AFX News Limited*, 10 January 2006.

Arellano, M. and Bond, S. (1991), "Some tests of specification for panel data: Monte Carlo Evidence and an application to employment equations," *Review of Economic Studies*, 58, 277-97.

Bitzer, J, Görg, H. (2009), "Foreign direct investment, competition and industry performance," *The World Economy*, 32: 2, 221-233.

Blomstrom, M., Fors, G. and Lipsey, R. (1997), "Foreign Direct Investment and Employment: Home Country Experience in the United States and Sweden," *Economic Journal*, 107: 445, 1787-1797.

Blundell, R. and Bond, S. (1998), "Initial Conditions and Moment Restrictions in Dynamic Panel Data Models", *Journal of Econometrics*, 87, 115-43.

Bond, S. (2002), "Dynamic panel data models: A guide to micro data methods and practice," Centre for Micro Data Methods and Practice Working Paper No. CWP09/02.

Buckley, P.J., Clegg, L.J., Cross, A.R., Liu, X., Voss, H. and Zheng, P. (2007), "The Determinants of Chinese Outward Foreign Direct Investment," *Journal of International Business Studies*, 38: 4, 499-518.

Chang, S-C. (2005), "The Dynamic Interactions among Foreign Direct Investment, Economic Growth, Exports and Unemployment: Evidence from Taiwan," *Economic Change and Restructuring*, 38, 235-256.

Chen, T-J. (2003), "Will Taiwan Be Marginalized by China?" Asian Economic Papers, 2(2), 78-97.

Chen, T-J. and Y-H Ku (2000), "The Effect of Foreign Direct Investment on Firm Growth: the Case of Taiwan's Manufacturers", Japan and the World Economy, 12, 153-72.

Chen, T-J and Y-H Ku (2003), "The Effects of Overseas Investment on Domestic Employment," *NBER Working Papers* No. 10156.

Chiang, H. H. (2008), "The 'Flying Geese Development' model of the IT industry in East Asia", *Journal of the Asia Pacific Economy*, 13: 2, 227-242.

Coe, D. T. and Helpman, E. (1995), "International R&D spillovers," *European Economic Review* 39, 859-887.

Deutsche Bundesbank (2006), "German Foreign Direct Investment Relationships: Recent Trends and Macroeconomic Effects," in *Monthly Report of the Deutsche Bundesbank*, 58: 9, 43-58.

Griliches, Z. (1980), "Returns to research and development expenditures," in J. W. Kendrick and B. N. Vaccara, eds., *New Developments in Productivity Measurement and Analysis*, London: University of Chicago Press.

Hayakawa, K. (2007), "Small sample bias properties of the system GMM estimator in dynamic panel data models," *Economics Letters*, 95: 1, 32-38.

Hirshhorn, R. (1998), "Investment research at Industry Canada," *Micro: the Micro-Economic Research Bulletin*, 4, 8-10.

Hsu, C-M and Liu, W-C (2002), "The Role of Taiwanese Foreign Direct Investment in China: Economic Integration or Hollowing-Out?" National Policy Foundation Research Report No. Finance (Research) 091-071, 1-23.

Hudson, D., T. Xia and O. Yeboah (2005), "Foreign Direct Investment and Domestic Industries: market Expansion or Outsourcing?" *Review of Agricultural Economics*, 27: 3, 387-393.

Investment Commission, the Ministry of Economic Affairs of the Republic of China (MOEAIC) (2002), *Regulation for Approval and Consideration of Foreign Investment or Technical Cooperation*, Taipei: MOEAIC.

_____ (2008) *Yearly Report on Foreign Direct Investment, 2007*, Taipei: MOEAIC.

Kojima, K. (1973), "A Macroeconomic Approach to Foreign Direct Investment," *Hitotsubashi Journal of Economics*, 14, 1-21.

Ku, Y. H. (1998), "Foreign Direct Investment and Industrial Structural Adjustment: An Empirical Study on Taiwan Electronics Industry", *Taiwan Economic Review*, 26: 4, 459-486.

LEDinside (2008), "Many Taiwan Producers Enter the Chongqing Xiyong Microelectronics Industrial Park," http://www.ledinside.com/tw.news_Chongquing_LED_20080801.

Li, N. C. and T. L. Roe (2008), "Taiwanese Outward Investment: Economic Bane or Boon?" *Taiwan Economic Forecast and Policy*, 38: 2, 73-109.

Lipsey, R. (1994), "Outward Direct Investment and the US Economy," *NBER Working Paper* No. 4691.

Lipsey, R. and M. Y. Weiss (1981), "Foreign Production and Exports in Manufacturing Industries," *Review of Economics and Statistics*, LXIII: 4, 488-494.

Liu, B. J. and F-M Huang (2005), "Outward Direct Investment, Reverse Import, and Domestic Production: Evidence from Taiwanese Manufacturing Firms," *Hitotsubashi Journal of Economics*, 46: 1, 65-84.

Marchant, M. A. and Kumar, S. (2005), "An Overview of U.S. foreign Direct Investment and Outsourcing," *Review of Agricultural Economics*, 27: 3, 379-386.

McMullen, A. (2009), "Mild Increase in U.S. Trade Deficit a 'Good Thing,'" *Financial Post*, 2009/05/13 (http://www.canada.com/business/).

Ministry of Economic Affairs (MOEA) (2007), *Survey on Foreign Investment by Manufacturers,* Taipei: MOEA.

National Statistics (2008), *Statistics Tables for Real Gross Domestic Product,* Taipei: National Statistics, R.O.C.

Roodman, D. (2006), "How to do xtabond2: An introduction to 'Difference' and 'System' GMM in Stata," Center for Global Development Working Paper No. 103.

Roodman, D. (2007), "A Short Note on the Theme of Too Many Instruments," Center for Global Development Working Paper No. 125.

Singh, A. (1977), "UK industry and the world economy: a case of deindustrialization?" *Cambridge Journal of Economics*, 1, 113-134.

StataCorp (2005), Stata Statistical Software: Release 9. College Station, Texas: StatCorp LP.

Steindel, C. and K. J. Stiroh (2001), "Productivity: What Is It, and Why Do We Care About It?" *Business Economics*, 36: 4, 13-31.

Svetličič, M., A. Jaklič, and A. Burger (2007), "Internationalization of Small and Medium-Size Enterprises from Selected Central European Economies," *Eastern European Economics*, 45: 4, 36-65.

Taiwan Advocates (2002), "Public Opinion on the Cause of High Unemployment Rate," Taipei: Research, Development and Evaluation Commission, Executive Yuan.

Tsai, P-L and C-H Huang (2007). "Openness, Growth and Poverty: The Case of Taiwan". *World Development*, 35:11, 1858–1871.

Wooldridge, J. (2002), *Econometric Analysis of Cross Section and Panel Data*, Massachusetts: The MIT Press.

Wu, Z. J. (2001), "Unemployment rate is difficult to fall because of the sluggish adjustment in the structure of labor force," NFP Commentary, Society (comment) No. 090-05, 1-4.

Appendix 1. Statistical descriptions and variable definitions

Variable	Obs.	Mean	Sta. dev.	Min.	Max.
Employment (person) [b]	6,922	4.50	0.69	0.43	6.77
Labor productivity (NT$ million) [c]	6,406	1.09	1.57	-12.79	19.57
Capital stocks per employee (NT$ million) [d]	6,890	1.77	2.25	0.002	19.96
OFDI China stocks per employee (NT$ million) [e]	6,910	2.59	3.11	0	9.82
Unskilled human capital indicator (ratio) [f]	6,471	0.31	0.26	0	0.97
RD stocks per employee (NT$ million) [g]	6,743	0.86	1.90	0	62.76
Export share (ratio) [h]	6,683	0.52	0.34	0	1
China gains / Taiwan gains (ratio) [i]	6,911	0.005	0.45	-9.85	8.50
Industrial growth rate (ratio) [j]	6,829	0.17	0.11	-0.14	0.37
Sales gap (ratio) [k]	7,801	0.0002	0.08	-1	0.25
R&D intensity (ratio) [l]	6,415	0.04	0.07	0	0.98
Corp. income tax rate (ratio) [m]	6,129	0.11	0.12	0	0.98
Labor intensive dummy [n]	6,413	0.46	0.50	0	1
SME dummy [o]	6,909	0.44	0.50	0	1
Firm age [p]	8,680	13.39	8.40	2	56

Notes:
- a. The first year data of new establishments are deleted.
- b. Real employment, employment deflated by industrial average monthly hours worked.
- c. Real value-added / Real employment in the parent firm. Value-added are deflected by using industrial wholesale price index, 2001=100. Outliners above ±20 are eliminated.
- d. Gross fixed capital stocks / Real employment; gross fixed capital stocks are stocks at the end period in the Taiwan parent company and deflated by using fixed capital formation price index, 2001 = 100.
- e. Real OFDI in China stocks / Real employment; outliners with the number greater than NT$20 million per employee are deleted. OFDI China stocks are the net cumulated amount of OFDI in China deflated by fixed capital formation prices, 2001 = 100. For non-OFDI in China observations, the value is zero.
- f. Direct labor costs / Total labor compensation.
- g. Real RD stocks / Real employment; RD stocks are estimated by using the perpetual inventory model if a firm is older than 5 years old, otherwise they are the sum of annual R&D expenditures. Following the approach suggested by Griliches (1980), a 15 percent of depreciation rate is assumed for R&D stocks and the benchmark for the initial RD stocks is computed by using the formula: $RDstocks_0 = RDexpenditures_1 / (g+0.15)$, where g is the average growth rate of available annual R&D expenditures.
- h. Export share = [exports / (exports + sales in the Taiwan market)]
- i. (Profits earned from OFDI in China / the Taiwan parent company's net income before tax); outliners with values greater than ±20 were deleted.
- j. The growth rate of real industrial value-added.
- k. Sales gap = [(Actual sales / Trend sales). Sales are deflated by industrial wholesale prices and in the natural logarithm. Trend sales are computed by applying the Hodrick-Prescott filter. We use Sales gap rather than Output gap to capture demand fluctuations, because many firms do buy goods from others for sale and on the other hand, some firms reduce outputs because of outsourcing.
- l. R&D intensity = (R&D expenditures / sales). Some startups have very high R&D intensities in our data set. Outliners with value above 1 were deleted.
- m. Business income tax rates paid with adjustments of tax losses and gains of previous periods.
- n. A dummy variable with the (labor costs / sales) ratio greater than the median 8.14 percent of total observations equal 1, otherwise equal 0.
- o. Firms with employment less than 200 people equal 1, otherwise equal 0.

Appendix 2. Results of Granger non-causality test.

Explanatory variable	OFDI China's stocks per employee	RD stocks per employee
OFDI China's stocks per employee		
Lag 1	0.900(8.3)***	0.177(0.8)
Lag 2	0.086(0.8)	-0.172(0.9)
Lag 3	0.001(0.0)	0.041(0.3)
Lag 4	-0.033(0.5)	0.064(0.8)
Labor productivity		
Lag 1	0.032(1.8)*	-0.193(2.9)***
Lag 2	-0.027(2.0)**	0.156(2.0)**
Lag 3	0.005(0.3)	0.018(0.4)
Lag 4	0.006(0.3)	0.064(0.8)
RD stocks per employee		
Lag 1		
Lag 2	0.054(1.3)	1.278(5.4)***
Lag 3		
Lag 2	-0.087(1.5)	-0.502(2.1)**
Lag 3	-0.067(0.8)	0.029(0.1)
Lag 4	0.117(1.3)	0.076(0.4)
Granger causality statistic:		
Coef. of labor pro. lag1-lag4 = 0	F(4, 2620)=1.50(0.20)	F(4, 2629)=2.16(0.07)*
Coef. of RD st. per emp. lag1-lag4 = 0	F(4, 2620)=1.85(0.12)	
Coef. of OFDI Ch. per emp. lag1-lag4 = 0		F(4, 2629)=0.29(0.89)
Total observations	3,261	3,273
R-sq. within	0.70	621
Corr(u_i, Xb)	0.51	0.41
Sigma u (the fixed effect error component)	0.38	0.85
Sigma e (the overall error component)	0.48	1.04
Rho (fraction of variance due to u)	0.38	0.40
F test (d.f.)	(23, 2620)=93.85***	(23, 2629)=66.29***

Notes: Firm specific dummy variables and year dummy variables from 1996 to 2006 are included in the estimations. The t-ratio is behind each coefficient within parentheses. For Granger causality statistic, P-values are in parentheses. *, ** and *** denote 10%, 5% and 1% of significant level, respectively.

Appendix 3. GMM results for 1998-2006 Dependent variable: labor productivity.

Explanatory variable	One-step system GMM		Long-run estimators	
	OFDI and non-OFDI China firms (E)	OFDI China firms (F)	OFDI and non-OFDI China firms (E)	OFDI China firms (F)
Labor productivity				
Lag 1	0.663(12.7)***	0.748(13.3)***		
Capital stocks per employee	0.020(1.2)	0.026(0.9)	0.060(1.2)	0.10(0.9)
OFDI China's stocks per emp.	0.382(4.1)***	0.161(1.6)	-0.645(3.6)***	-0.451(2.2)**
Lag 1	-0.599(4.6)***	-0.274(2.1)**		
Unskilled human capital	-0.454(2.9)***	-0.252(1.6)*	-1.348(3.4)***	-1.000(1.6)
RD stocks per employee	-0.591(3.3)***	-0.236(1.7)*	0.328(2.4)**	0.324(1.8)*
Lag 1	0.702(3.7)***	0.318(1.8)*		
China gains / Taiwan gains	0.007(0.3)	0.017(0.5)	0.021(0.3)	1.008(1.4)
Lag 1		0.237(1.5)		
Industrial growth rates	0.862(4.0)***	0.652(2.6)***	2.560(3.5)***	2.590(2.4)**
Sales gap	2.556(2.2)**	1.26(1.8)*	7.589(2.1)**	5.018(1.7)*
Export share	0.314(3.7)***	0.164(2.0)**	0.933(3.9)***	0.652(1.7)*
Constant	0.160(1.8)*	0.120(0.9)	0.474(2.0)**	-0.475(0.9)
2000 year dummy	0.028(0.5)	0.198(2.0)**		
2001 year dummy	0.022(0.3)	0.244(1.9)*		
2002 year dummy	0.122(1.9)*	0.321(2.6)***		
2003 year dummy	0.295(3.8)***	0.412(3.5)***		
2004 year dummy	0.296(3.1)***	0.447(3.7)***		
2005 year dummy	0.201(2.1)**	0.388(3.5)***		
2006 year dummy	0.464(4.2)***	0.536(4.7)***		
Wald: Chi2(d.f.)	(18)=675***	(19)=665***		
Hansen: Chi2(d.f.)	(108)=124(0.14)	(107)=119(0.21)		
Arellano-Bond AR(1) 1st dif.: z	-7.45(0.00)***	-5.04(0.00)***		
Arellano-Bond AR(2) 1st dif.: z	0.19(0.85)	-0.47(0.64)		
F test				
R^2				
Number of instruments	127	127		
Number of firms	646	507		
Number of observations	4,151	2,292		

Notes: Behind each coefficient is the t-ratio. *, ** and *** denote 10%, 5% and 1% of significant level, respectively. For a Hansen test of over-identification, Arellano-Bond AR(1) and AR(2) tests, P-values are in parentheses. In Columns (E) — (F), the lagged dependent variable, OFDI China stocks per employee, and RD stocks per employee are non-strictly exogenous variables as suggested by the data. Instrumental variables are used for these variables.

In: Foreign Direct Investment (FDI)
Editors: Enzo Guillon and Lucas Chauvet

ISBN: 978-1-62808-403-0
© 2013 Nova Science Publishers, Inc.

Chapter 5

FOREIGN DIRECT INVESTMENT ON ASEAN'S INCOME INEQUALITY REVISITED: A SPATIAL PANEL DATA MODEL APPROACH

Nathapornpan Piyaareekul Uttama[*]
Economics Program, School of Management, Mae Fah Luang University, Tasud, Muang, Chiang Rai, Thailand

ABSTRACT

The Association of Southeast Asian Nations (ASEAN) is recognized as one of the most attractive regions to foreign investors, according to the declaration to create ASEAN Economic Community in 2003. It was commonly believed that the investment liberalization will help to foster economic growth and development and income inequality reduction in ASEAN member countries.

However, from World Bank database, the income inequalities are raising in most of the ASEAN member countries; this phenomenon exhibits serious concerns for policymakers in this region.

This chapter revisits the impact of foreign direct investment (FDI) on income inequalities for selected Asian countries (Indonesia, Malaysia, Philippines, Singapore, Thailand and Vietnam) during the period 1985-2011. A FDI-led inequality model is developed by incorporating trade, economic integration, financial development and spatial effect as proxy for economic geography in the model specification and a spatial fixed effect model is used to estimate the model.

The estimated results reveal that income inequality is negatively affected by an increase in bilateral trade and financial development, whereas bilateral FDI and economic integration stimulate income inequality in ASEAN. The results also indicate that third-country (spatial) effects of income inequality, trade and financial development have positive relationships with income inequality in such ASEAN countries, whereas spatial effects of FDI and economic integration are important determinants to reduce the inequality gap in ASEAN.

---

[*] E-mail: nathapornpan@mfu.ac.th, n_piyaareekul@hotmail.com.

Thus, the ASEAN economic agreements and policies should be tailored, integrated and harmonized in order to achieve the desired outcome of becoming ASEAN Economic Community and to foster the sustainable and equitable economic development in ASEAN.

Keywords: Foreign direct investment; Income inequality; ASEAN; Spatial econometric model

JEL: C31, F21, F15, O1

1. INTRODUCTION

The rapid growth of foreign direct investment (FDI) in the Association of Southeast Asian Nations (ASEAN) has been surprised by widening income inequality after the declaration of ASEAN Economic Community (AEC) in 2003. Whilst inward FDI (both intra- and extra-ASEAN FDI) to ASEAN in 2011 increased by 23% (ASEAN, 2013a), GINI income inequality indexes were also growing in most countries of ASEAN (World Bank, 2013). This FDI-inequality nexus points out the paradox of the AEC paradigm and the failure of the implementation of AEC roadmap, even though economic difference between ASEAN's middle and low income countries was gradually diminishing (World Bank, 2013). Under the AEC blueprint, ASEAN region becomes a single market where free flows of goods, services, investment and skilled labor, freer flow of capital, equitable economic development, and reduction in poverty and socio-economic disparities could be ensured by the year 2015. Importantly, there is no reasonable conclusive evidence for explaining this puzzle to appear. With the background in mind, there are three driving forces behind a positive linkage between ASEAN's income inequality and FDI: regional economic integration, FDI attractiveness and spatial effects. The regional economic integration in ASEAN has evidently been seen after Asian financial crisis in year 1997. Meanwhile, ASEAN has been transiting from an international market-driven economy to a regional market-driven economy. The geographical aspect of economic growth and development has become a mainstream concern nowadays. It is believed that the proximity to ASEAN member countries (spatial effect) encourages the flux of FDI and trade that lead to reduce an economic development gap and together enhances the economic growth. However, the spatial effect of inequality has been rarely studied, and the relevant importance of the factors underlying regional income inequality in ASEAN is still unclear. As a matter of fact, income inequality becomes a hot issue of economists, geographers and policy makers.

Currently, there were a number of empirical studies on the impact of FDI on income inequality, but most of all have improved to analyze national inequality from FDI inflows and very few studies exist for regional inequality. For example, Wei et al. (2009), Yu et al. (2011), Herzer and Nunnenkamp (2011) and Chintrakarn et al. (2012) showed empirical evidence to support the fact that an increase in FDI decreases income inequality, whereas Choi (2006), Basu and Guariglia (2007) and Shahbaz (2010) consistently found the positive relationship between FDI and inequality. These studies showed in particular that foreign direct investment speeds up the income inequality. Moreover, some empirical evidence suggested the relationship between economic integration and income inequality such as Barro

(2008), Barrios and Strobl (2009), Jalil (2012) and Jaumotte et al. (2008). The results of first two studies showed the positive relationship between economic integration and income inequality, whereas the last two studies confirmed the negative relation between these two determinants. Until now, there has been extensive research on the spatial effects on income inequality e.g. Li and Wei (2010), Portnov and Felsenstein (2010), Gravier-Rymaszewska et al. (2010) and Liao and Wei (2012); it is still no relative evidence of spatial effects on ASEAN's income inequality. The impacts of international economic activities such as FDI, economic integration and economic geography on ASEAN's income inequality deserve more research efforts. Particularly, the question is whether inward FDI improves or worsens income inequality in both individual ASEAN economies and ASEAN as a whole. Thus, in order to fill this gap, this chapter mainly focuses on the impacts of FDI, economic integration and spatial effects on inequality development in the ASEAN economy.

The remainder of this chapter is organized as follows. Section 2 presents the stylized facts of FDI and income inequality in ASEAN. Section 3 reviews the existing empirical evidence concerning the link between income inequality and international economic activities to illustrate the main mainstreams at hand. The empirical approach along with the description of data is presented in section 4. Section 5 is contributed to a discussion of the estimation results and the last section summarizes the findings and discusses some policy implications.

2. STYLIZED FACTS OF FDI AND INCOME INEQUALITY

Since the Association of Southeast Asian Nations lifted the restrictions on FDI through the 1998 Framework Agreement on the ASEAN Investment Area (AIA) and the 2009 ASEAN Comprehensive Investment Agreement (ACIA)[1], FDI inflows to ASEAN have increased very rapidly. From ASEAN (2013a), the ASEAN has seen a faster increase in both extra-ASEAN FDI and intra-ASEAN FDI by 181% and 15%, respectively, from 2000 to 2010. Data also indicated that more than 35% of inward FDI went to the manufacturing sector in 2005, but approximately 27% of FDI in the manufacturing sector in 2010. Meanwhile the share of FDI going to the real estate sector increased sharply from 15% in 2005 to 21% in 2010. With the high average growth in extra- and intra-ASEAN FDI, it implies its importance itself to ASEAN economic growth and development. Inward FDI is not only a driver of economic growth and development in ASEAN, but also a potential engine in increasing the economic security in ASEAN.

More importantly, the ACIA is one of the key successes of building ASEAN Economic Community in 2015, as well as the ASEAN Trade in Goods Agreement (ATIGA), ASEAN Framework Agreement on Services (AFAS), and ASEAN Finance Cooperation through Chiang Mai Initiative Multilateralism (CMIM) with China, Japan and the Republic of Korea, and Asian Bond Markets Initiative (ABMI). It might be said that trade, investment and financial liberalization can attract more FDI to ASEAN. Also it is believed that higher FDI flows encourage economic growth, then, the income equality in ASEAN will come true.

---

[1] The ACIA was accredited as the accession of ASEAN investors and foreign-owned ASEAN-based investors into "a more liberal, facilitative, transparent and competitive investment destination" (ASEAN, 2013b). Indeed, the ACIA was revised and enlarged from the existing investment agreements: the 1998 Framework Agreement on the ASEAN Investment Area and the 1987 ASEAN Agreement for the Promotion and Protection of Investments.

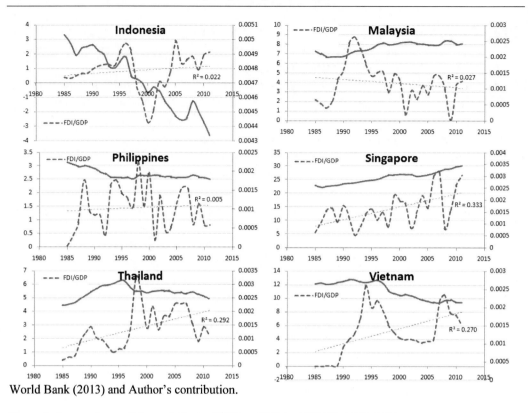

World Bank (2013) and Author's contribution.

Figure 1. Income Inequalities and Share of FDI to GDP in ASEAN, 1985-2011.

However, the relation between FDI inflows and income inequality in ASEAN has been very unnoticeable.

In an attempt to analyze this relationship, we compare the two variables: GINI income inequality index and the share of FDI as a percentage of GDP within each of the six selected ASEAN countries from the period 1985-2011 (Figure 1).

Graphical results reveal that these two variables seemingly demonstrate the same trend for Singapore, Thailand and Philippines. This may lead one to conclude that inward FDI has contributed to widening income inequalities in Singapore, Thailand and Philippines. However, since the declaration of the ASEAN investment agreement in 1998, FDI inflows to Indonesia and Vietnam have been increasing; their income inequalities have been decreasing. On the contrary, during 1998-2011, Malaysia's FDI inflows have been decreasing, its income inequality has been increasing. The seemingly negative correlation between the two series suggests that FDI might not have led to an increase in income inequality in Indonesia, Malaysia and Vietnam. From these contradictory results, it is necessary to study deeper the impact of FDI on income inequality in ASEAN.

Figure 2 depicts the linkages of ASEAN's GINI income inequality index and trade openness during the period 1998-2008. After the initiation of AIA in 1998, the time trends of income inequality and economic integration for Malaysia, Philippines, Singapore and Thailand are consistent and indicate a significant upward trend. It implies that a deeper economic integration might have rendered widening income inequality in all these four ASEAN countries.

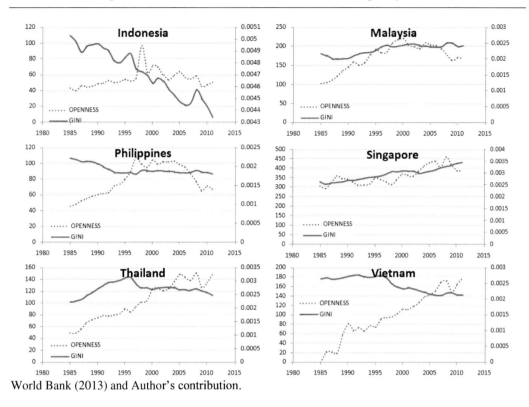
World Bank (2013) and Author's contribution.

Figure 2. Income Inequalities and Economic Integration in ASEAN, 1985-2011.

Conversely, these two variables seemingly also illustrate the same trend for Indonesia, but point out a significant downward trend.

Moreover, graphical relationship between Vietnam's income inequality and economic integration reveals that these two variables seem to have the opposite trend. This may lead one to conclude that economic integration has not contributed to widening income inequalities in Vietnam. However, the different results about the relationship between income inequality and economic integration in ASEAN member countries make any doubts in the efficiency and effectiveness of the implementation of the ASEAN economic agreements. Therefore, it is very important to prove this fact. The outcome could help to indicate the future of the ASEAN whether ASEAN should fight hard to achieve the goals of ASEAN Economic Community, especially an advocate in equitable development.

Summing up, it is commonly believed that investment liberalization and facilitation encourage foreign investment flows to ASEAN; and then it leads to foster economic growth and development, improve the well-being, and reduce an income inequality in ASEAN countries. However, the contradiction between the two cases shown above entails further investigation of the impacts of FDI and economic integration on income inequality in ASEAN. Therefore, in the next section, we demonstrate whether FDI and economic integration cause an income inequality in ASEAN.

3. LITERATURE REVIEW AND ANALYTICAL FRAMEWORK

In fact, income inequality analysis is a comparatively serious issue. Numerous studies have estimated the impacts on income inequality in many contexts, for instance, how change in inequality over time; how inequality is affected by economic growth, socio-economic development and globalization; and how to reduce inequality gap between countries. Most of these studies provided a solid foundation for further studies in different regions in the world. In this chapter, the literature on the globalization-inequality nexus is focused. Generally, there were three main perspectives in the relationship between globalization and inequality.

First, the empirical literature on the relationship between foreign direct investment and income inequality is rather large and still expanding. Generally, there is empirical evidence to support the fact that an increase in FDI decreases income inequality such as Wei et al. (2009), Yu et al. (2011), Herzer and Nunnenkamp (2011) and Chintrakarn et al. (2012), whereas the contradictory results of the relationship between FDI and inequality are found consistently in Choi (2006), Basu and Guariglia (2007) and Shahbaz (2010). Wei et al. (2009) investigated the impacts of FDI on regional growth and inequality in three Chinese regions (inter-province, intra-region, inter-region) during 1979-2003 using cross-section and panel data techniques. Their results indicated that FDI plays a consistent and positive effect on economic growth in China while the uneven distribution of FDI causes regional income inequality in China. They also suggested that "FDI should not be blamed for raising regional inequality. It is the uneven distribution of FDI instead of FDI itself that has been responsible for China's regional growth differences." Likewise, Yu et al. (2011) explored the relationship between FDI and income inequality in 29 Chinese provinces over the period 1990-2005 using the Shapley value regression-based decomposition approach. They seemed to find the optimistic impact on FDI and regional inequality and suggested that "FDI stock should not be viewed as the cause of China's widening regional income inequality". Moreover, Herzer and Nunnenkamp (2011) performed panel cointegration and causality techniques across European countries during the period 1980 to 2000 and proved that FDI had a negative long-run impact on income inequality. Chintrakarn et al. (2012) analyzed state-level panel data on FDI and income inequality for the U.S. over the period 1977 to 2001 using panel cointegration techniques. The result showed that FDI is inversely linked with income inequality. However, some empirical studies tend to confirm the positive relationship between FDI and income inequality. Choi (2006) evaluated FDI-inequality nexus for 119 countries from 1993 and 2002 using pooled OLS. It was posited that GINI index as proxy for income inequality increases as FDI as a percentage of GDP increase. Basu and Guariglia (2007) re-estimated long-run relationship between the infusion of foreign capital and human capital inequality for 119 developing countries over the period 1970–1999. The results indicated that FDI tended to promote inequality and growth, but reduced the share of agriculture to GDP in the long run. Similarly, Shahbaz (2010) tested the alliance between FDI and income inequality for Pakistan. Using time series data over the period 1971 to 2005, the estimated results on autoregressive distributed lag model (ARDL) indicated that FDI favors income inequality in Pakistan.

Second, some researchers investigated the relationship between trade and some contributing trade factors and income inequality such as regional economic integration. For example, Wan et al. (2006) employed the polynomial inverse lag framework in order to investigate the impacts of inequality on investment, education, trade and growth for China during the period 1987 to 2001. Focusing on the trade-inequality relationship, the results showed that trade as a percentage of GDP is found to cause more income inequality. It is also agreed with their expectations. Barro (2008) primarily explored and confirmed the presence of the Kuznets curve from the 1960s into the 2000s that is an inverse-U shape relationship between income inequality and per capita GDP. In addition, he also incorporated country's openness variable into the estimated model. His findings showed a significantly positive relationship between international openness and income inequality and a surprisingly negative effect of income inequality on economic growth.

Likewise, Barrios and Strobl (2009) investigated the relationship between GDP per capita and regional inequality for a number of European countries during the period 1975-2000. Using a flexible-semi-parametric estimator, the empirical results showed that the linkage between GDP per capita and regional inequality is in type of a bell-shaped relationship. It implies that regional inequality rises with an increase in GDP per capita and falls as GDP per capita continues to rise.

Moreover, they also examined the impacts of structural funds, fiscal decentralization, openness and dissimilarity on regional inequality. Their findings indicated the significantly positive relationship between real openness and regional inequality. Jalil (2012) used the Kuznets curve framework to determine the openness–inequality nexus for China during the period 1952 to 2009. Using the auto regressive distributed lag model estimator, the results revealed a curvilinear relationship between openness and income inequality, as in the line with the Kuznets hypothesis. Income inequality increases in accordance with an increase in openness and declines after a certain critical point. Jaumotte et al. (2008) re-examined the impacts of trade globalization e.g. the share of export and import to GDP, financial globalization e.g. the share of FDI and portfolio investment to GDP, ICT capital, private credit and education on income inequality for 20 advanced countries and 31 developing and emerging market countries during the period 1981-2003. The main results showed that income inequality declines with trade liberalization and export growth, whereas it is found to be higher with an increase in financial globalization and private credit.

Moreover, Zeng and Zhao (2010) theoretically examined the effects of domestic transport costs and international trade costs on interregional and international inequalities using a footloose-capital model of two countries and four regions. They found that smaller international trade costs lead to a larger national manufacturing share, and subsequently, a smaller interregional inequality.

Third, in general, the financial development is an important factor for driving economic growth and development. There are some variables employed to proxy for financial development such as the ratio of deposit money bank, the ratio of liquid liabilities to GDP, the private credit by deposit money banks to GDP, the private credit by deposit money banks and other financial institutions to GDP, the value of listed shares to GDP and total shares traded on the stock market exchange to GDP.

As far as the impacts on income inequality are concerned, Jaumotte et al. (2008) and Jalil (2012) considered the impacts of financial development on income inequality. The former findings posited the significantly positive relationship between private credit as a proxy for financial development and income inequality. The latter showed the contradictory result of the linkage between inequality and financial development that is the significantly negative relationship between them. An increase in financial development (calculated as a single index based on the principal components) alleviates the income inequality.

Finally, recently the international economics literature has often observed the spatial factor for explaining the effects of economic geography and country's characteristics on international economic activities e.g. trade, FDI and international finance. Although there has been extensive research on the spatial effects on improving regional inequality, the relative importance of these contributing factors in various regions in the global world is still lacked currently. The literature on regional inequality have displayed their own characteristics and proposed some new analytical frameworks such as Li and Wei (2010). In fact, they have developed new explanations and proposed new processes that are responsible for regional inequality. Employed the multi-scale and multi-mechanism framework on regional inequality, they examined the linkages between regional inequality and geographical scales which are different aspects of the same underlying inequality studies. The findings pointed out that regional inequality declines with geographical scale and FDI growth. Some spatial studies on inequality concerned about the question how differences in inequality across regions such as Portnov and Felsenstein (2010), Gravier-Rymaszewska et al. (2010) and Liao and Wei (2012).

In addition, the existing studies on inequality have been also considered in other contexts. For example, Zhang and Eriksson (2010) indicated that an increase in income inequality mirrors an increase in inequality of opportunity.

According to Taylor and Driffield (2005), Driffield et al. (2010) and Sahu (2010), the relationship between wage inequality and FDI was negative whether inward FDI has contributed to increasing wage inequality. This study is supported by Anwar and Sun (2012) which argued that trade liberalization and market competition can affect an increase in the level of skilled-unskilled wage inequality. Researchers have investigated the effects of household poverty and district-level consumption inequality e.g. Annim et al. (2012) and Goh et al. (2009), physical, human and infrastructure capital e.g. Fleisher et al. (2010), capital income e.g. Chi (2011), technology spillovers e.g. Clark et al. (2011), economic growth e.g. Gravier-Rymaszewska et al. (2010), Wan et al. (2006), Barro (2008) and Berg et al. (2011), income per capita e.g. Bouvet (2010), and policy bias e.g. Jones et al. (2003) and Castro (2011).

Until now, there were a number of studies on the impact of FDI on inequality, but most of all have analyzed national inequality from the entry of FDI and very few studies exist for regional inequality.

Likewise, the prior studies provided much progress in understanding the inequality from trade, economic integration and financial development, but there is still no any evidence on regional inequality from the ASEAN region. Particularly, the question is whether foreign direct investment improves or worsens income inequality in ASEAN, whether investment liberalization under the AEC leads to a decline in regional inequality in the ASEAN's economy, which additional international economic factors influence income inequality, and how important in the spatial effects on inequality in ASEAN. This also challenges the search for the counterfactual effects of regional economic integration under the ASEAN Economic Community whether it can stimulate economic development more than what individual ASEAN member economies could achieve without integration.

Therefore, the interactions between international economic activities and their spatial effect on income inequality deserve more research efforts. In order to fill this gap, this chapter focuses on the impacts of foreign direct investment, trade, financial development, regional economic integration and spatial factors on regional income inequalities in ASEAN (Figure 3). According to the literature review mentioned above, our empirical analysis is conducted under the specific hypotheses as shown in the following table.

4. Empirical Approach

This section presents the research methodology framework for analyzing empirically the impacts of FDI, trade, regional economic integration, financial development and spatial effects on income inequalities in ASEAN.

It starts with the empirical model construction, econometric tool selection and data collection.

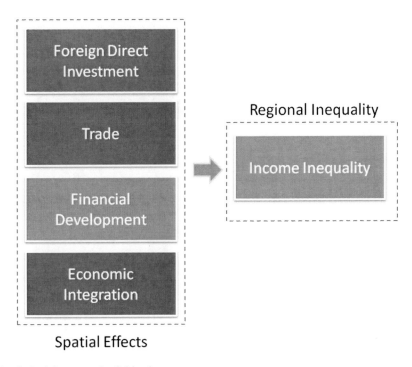

Figure 3. Analytical framework of this chapter.

Table 1. Hypotheses on Income Inequality

Parameters	Expected sign	Source
Foreign direct investment	+/-	Positive sign: Choi (2006), Basu and Guariglia (2007), Shahbaz (2010) Negative sign: Wei et al. (2009), Yu et al. (2011), Herzer and Nunnenkamp (2011), Chintrakarn et al. (2012)
Trade	+/-	Positive sign: Wan et al. (2006) Negative sign: Jaumotte et al. (2008)
Economic integration	+/-	Positive sign: Barro (2008), Barrios and Strobl (2009) Negative sign: Zeng and Zhao (2010), Jalil (2012)
Financial development	+/-	Positive sign: Jaumotte et al. (2008) Negative sign: Jalil (2012)
Spatial effects	-	Li and Wei (2010)

4.1. Empirical Model

In the light of the literature review, the well suited model specification to capture the empirical impacts of FDI, trade, economic integration and financial development and their spatial effects on ASEAN's income inequality is shown in the following threshold specification:

$$INEQ_{it} = \beta_0 + \beta_1 FDI_{it} + \beta_2 TRADE_{it} + \beta_3 REI_{it} + \beta_4 FIN_{it} + \alpha_1 WINEQ_{it} + \alpha_2 WFDI_{it} + \alpha_3 WTRADE_{it} + \alpha_4 WREI_{it} + \alpha_5 WFIN_{it} + u_{ijt} \quad (1)$$

where i=1,2,...,n is the country index, t=1,2,...,T is the time index. The dependent variable, INEQ is country i's income inequality measured by the weighted GINI index, G_w, (Shankar and Shah, 2003) and the Theil index, T, (Theil, 1967):

$$G_w = \left(\frac{1}{2\bar{y}}\right) \sum_i^n \sum_j^n |y_i - y_j| \frac{p_i p_j}{P^2} \quad (2)$$

where $\bar{y}$ is national mean per capita GDP; p_i and p_j are population of regions i and j, respectively; P is total population; and n the numbers of the regions;

$$T = \sum_i Y_i \log \frac{Y_i}{P_i} \quad (3)$$

where Y is GDP share of region i; P is population share of region i. The independent variable, FDI stands for inward foreign direct investment measured in term of the percentage share of FDI in GDP. TRADE is expressed as trade balance (TB) and term of trade (TOT). REI denotes regional economic integration divided in openness index (OPEN) and average tariff rates (TARS). FIN represents financial development proxied by the percentage share of domestic credit in private sector (PRC) and the percentage share of market capitalization in GDP (CAP). All variables are in natural logarithms.

Moreover, our model specification is also allowed for a model with spatial dependence across spatial units at each point in time. WINEQ, WFDI, WTRADE, WREI and WFIN are the spatial lagged variables of income inequality, foreign direct investment, trade, economic integration and financial development, introduced to capture the economic geographic relationship among countries (spatial units).

They are obtained by multiplying spatially weighted matrix, based on the distance (d) between the capital of destination country (i) and third country (j) with the values of INEQ, FDI, TRADE, REI and FIN.

The spatially weighting matrix W_N is $N_t \times N_t$ where N is the number of cross-sectional units that is row-normalized with typical elements w_{ij}. Based on Baltagi et al. (2007), w_{ij} is calculated using a simple inverse distance:

$$w_{ij} = \begin{cases} \dfrac{d_{ij}^{-1}}{\sum_{j=1}^{N} d_{ij}^{-1}} & if\ i \neq j \\ 0 & if\ i = j \end{cases} \qquad (4)$$

and

$$W = \begin{bmatrix} 0 & w_{2,1} & \cdots & w_{n,1} \\ w_{1,2} & 0 & \cdots & w_{n,2} \\ \cdots & \cdots & 0 & \cdots \\ w_{1,n} & w_{2,n} & \cdots & 0 \end{bmatrix} \qquad (5)$$

where W is as a block-diagonal n x n matrix with W_{N_t} where $n = \sum_{t=1}^{T} N_t$. When a row-standardized weighting matrix is performed, W is normalized so that each row sums to unity.

The error term u_{ijt} is shown by a spatial error model of the form:

$$u_{it} = \rho W_{N_t} u_{it} + \varepsilon_{it} \quad with\ |\rho| < 1 \qquad (6)$$

$$\varepsilon_{it} = \mu_i + \delta_t + \gamma_{it} \qquad (7)$$

The term μ_i is considered as country fixed effects to be spatially correlated reflecting any time-invariant heterogeneity effects; δ_t is represented as time fixed effects in order to capture the impacts of all individual-invariant variables; and $u_{it} = \rho W_{N_t} u_{it} + \varepsilon_{it}$ is the spatial error term, where ρ is a coefficient on the spatially correlated errors which measures how spatial-weighted variables affect the dependent variable; and ε is the classical error term.

4.2. Econometric Methodology

In this chapter, we incorporate the spatial-weighted independent variables into the empirical model which can lead to the presence of spatial autocorrelation. Therefore, our model specification will be constructed by taking into account the spatial autocorrelation into the model, so-called spatial model with spatially correlated residual (Anselin, 1999). This model is given by

$$Y = \beta X + W X \delta + u \qquad (8)$$

$$u = \rho W u + \epsilon \qquad (9)$$

The term *Y* represents the *n x 1* vector of observations on the dependent variable with *n=NT* denoting the number of observations where *N* is the number of unique cross-sectional units and *T* is the number of time periods. The term *X* is the *n x K* matrix of observations on the set of exogenous variables and *β* is the *K x 1* vector of regression parameters.

The term *WX* is the spatially lagged exogenous variable where *W* is an *N x N* spatial weighting matrix of known constants that captures the location of recipient countries with respect to other recipient countries. δ is the *K x 1* vector of additional parameters, or alternatively, spatial autoregressive parameters which measure how the exogenous variable *X* is spatially influenced.

The term *u* is spatially correlated with the spatial weighted matrix W_n for each time period. $W = (I_T \otimes W_N)$ where I_T is an identity matrix of dimension *T*, and the *N x N* spatial weight matrix W_N has zero diagonal elements which is row-normalized with its entries usually declining with distance. ρ is a spatial autocorrelation parameter assumed to be bounded in absolute value $|\rho| < 1$. In the model with spatially correlated residuals, the error for one observation depends on a weighted average of the errors for neighboring observations, with ρ measuring the strength of this relationship. When $\rho=0$, there is no spatial correlation.

To obtain the concrete empirical results, the diagnostic tests are first conducted to choose an appropriate estimator and to define the quality of the empirical model. The Moran's I test is used to check for spatial autocorrelation in residuals; the Breusch-Pagan test is used for identifying the heteroskedasticity; the Jarque-Bera test is used for indicating the normality; and the variance inflation factor is used for checking the multicollinearity. Finally, if the spatial panel data model is estimated by the chosen estimators, it is estimated using the Maximum Likelihood (ML) estimator on fixed effect model (FEM) and random effect model (REM) to indicate the impacts of FDI, trade, economic integration and financial development and their spatial effects on economic inequality. The spatial panel data model is estimated using the spatial econometrics toolbox. All estimated results are computed on mathematical program and simultaneously interpret with the qualitative results.

First, it is the diagnostic test for the presence of spatial autocorrelation, representing the presence of spatial effects in the residuals or error terms from a panel data model analysis. The presence of spatial autocorrelation causes misspecification and measurement errors (Anselin, 1999; 2001). Ignoring spatially correlated errors can lead to a problem of efficiency, whereas the coefficient standard error estimates are biased but the coefficient estimates remain unbiased. In addition, the occurrence of spatial autocorrelation indicates that the ordinary least square (OLS) estimator loses its property of efficiency and becomes an inappropriate estimator for a model with a spatial error model (Elhorst, 2001). In fact, it is common practice to detect the spatial autocorrelation using Moran's I statistic computed from the residuals. The null hypothesis of no spatial autocorrelation is tested against the alternative hypothesis of spatial autocorrelation. When spatial autocorrelation is detected in the residuals from a panel data model analysis, the spatial effect must be accounted for in the model for the accurate estimation of the estimated coefficients and their associated variances. In this case, a model with spatially correlated residuals is fit to the data instead of a model with spatially uncorrelated residuals.

Second, the diagnostic test is to detect a model misspecification in the form of heteroskedasticity. Indeed, heteroskedasticity is often associated with cross-sectional data where the units vary significantly in size; it occurs when the variance of the error term varies across different values of the independent variables: $Var(u_i|X_i) = \sigma_i^2$. Ignoring the presence of heteroskedasticity might result in the biased variance of the estimated parameters in which misleading conclusions can be made, but does not result in the biased parameter estimates (Wooldridge, 2001). The Breusch-Pagan test is most often used to detect the misspecification in term of heteroskedasticity. The null hypothesis of homosedasticity that the variance of the error term is constant is tested against the alternative hypothesis of heteroskedasticity.

Third, the diagnostic test is to warrant the quality of the estimated model: the normality test. It is used to determine whether a random variable is normally distributed. In many statistical analyses, the normality is often assumed without any empirical evidence or test. If the normality test assumption is violated, interpretation and inference are not reliable or valid. Particularly in the maximum likelihood estimation, the assumption of normality of the regression error terms is needed. Moreover, in the presence of spatial autocorrelation and heteroskedasticity, the normality test helps to safely interpret the result of the misspecification test. It is a common practice to examine the normality using the Jarque-Bera test which is the most popular normality test in the econometric literature (Thadewald and Büning, 2007). The null hypothesis of a normal distribution of residuals in the model is tested against the alternative hypothesis of non-normal distribution. The low probability of the test score indicates non-normal distribution of the error term.

Fourth, it is the diagnostic test for multicollinearity provided to ensure a precision of predictions in a multiple regression model. The presence of multicollinearity among variables leads to bias econometric results i.e. unreasonable coefficient estimates, wrongly higher standard errors and consequently insignificant interpretation and inference. Ignoring the effects of multicollinearity can lead to model misspecification. To detect the multicollinearity, the variance inflation factors (VIF) method is used to calculate an index which measures how much the variance of a coefficient is increased due to multicollinearity. In practice, a VIF greater than 10 would indicate a presence of multicollinearity, whereas a VIF greater than 30 becomes potentially problematic requiring specific corrections (Kennedy, 2003).

Finally, as an important step, if the Moran's I statistic indicates the presence of spatial autocorrelation, a spatial model with spatially correlated residuals should be estimated with the appropriate estimator. To eliminate the biases arising from omitted variables, the fixed effect model and random effect model estimation are used in panel data model analysis in order to control for unobservable heterogeneity.[2] The FEM gives consistent estimates if the individual effect is correlated with explanatory variables, whereas the REM gives consistent estimates when the individual effect does not correlate with explanatory variables. In fact, the REM approach has more advantage than the FEM approach. The REM allows for estimating parameters corresponding with individual-specific time-invariant variables but does not allow in the FEM. In the common practice, a Maximum Likelihood (ML) estimator is widely used to estimate a model with spatial autocorrelation error terms. The idea behind the ML estimation is to maximize the concentrated log-likelihood in the spatial error parameter. Conditionally upon the asymptotic normality, the ML estimator is considered to be robust and yields consistent and efficient parameter estimates. However, the ML has important limitation of estimated results. The ML estimator is computationally infeasible in case involving large sample sizes in a single cross section data set (Kelejian and Prucha, 1999). After running the FEM and REM, some appropriate hypothesis tests are made to select the best formulation in

---

[2] (Baltagi, 2005, p.4-7) stated that "the panel data model has more important advantages than pooled cross-section time-series data: (1) it can control for individual heterogeneity, (2) it gives more informative data, more variability, less collinearity among the variables, (3) it allows for constructing and testing more complicated behavioral models, and (4) it provides more efficient parameter estimates".

dealing with the unobservable individual effects. The Hausman specification test is the test of whether the fixed or random effect model should be used in our panel-data setting. The question is whether there is significant correlation (heterogeneity) between the unobserved individual-specific time-invariant effects and the regressors of interest. The null hypothesis of uncorrelated heterogeneity is tested against the alternative hypothesis of correlated heterogeneity. Under the null hypothesis, the REM is consistent and efficient, but under the alternative hypothesis, it produces biased estimators and the FEM would be preferred.

4.3. Data Source

The data set consists of cross-country observations for six ASEAN member countries (Indonesia, Malaysia, Philippines, Singapore, Thailand and Vietnam) during the period 1985 to 2011. GDP, GDP per capita and population exploited to measure income inequality index are extracted from the World Development Indicators as well as share of FDI in GDP, share of gross fixed capital formation in GDP, trade balance, term of trade, trade openness and average tariff rates. Meanwhile the variables proxies for financial development, the percentage share of domestic credit in private sector and the percentage share of market capitalization in GDP, are taken from Financial Structure Dataset of World Bank. Table 2 exhibits the descriptive statistics.

5. EMPIRICAL RESULTS

The empirical results of the effects of FDI, trade, economic integration, financial development and spatial effects on ASEAN's income inequality are presented in this section.

In the estimation, we divide income inequality into two different measures: GINI index and Theil index, meanwhile, the estimated results are provided in eight different model aspects.

Table 2. Descriptive Statistics

Bilateral Variables	Mean	Standard Deviation	Minimum	Maximum
GINI	0.0028	0.0009	0.0018	0.0050
THEIL	0.0572	0.1319	-0.0298	0.4008
FDI	4.6797	5.4642	-2.7574	27.8624
TB	0.0502	0.1083	-0.1966	0.3441
TOT	0.0076	0.0032	-0.0025	0.0045
OPEN	-145.1312	108.9019	0.0000	460.4711
TARS	4.0634	6.58335	0.0000	34.9700
PRC	68.9446	42.6029	0.0000	165.7191
CAP	66.6795	72.3164	0.0000	328.8763

Note: The number of observations is 162 followed by 6 countries over 27 time periods (1985-2011).

Table 3A. Fixed Effect Model and Random Effect Model of GINI Coefficient Index

	Model 1		Model 2		Model 3		Model 4	
	FEM (1)	REM (2)	FEM (3)	REM (4)	FEM (5)	REM (6)	FEM (7)	REM (8)
FDI	0.009	-0.001	0.001	-0.001	0.001***	0.002	0.011	-0.001
TB	-0.001	0.001***	-0.001	0.001	0.005	-0.002	-0.001	-0.001
TOT								
OPEN	0.002***	-0.004*	0.001	0.001				
TARS					-0.002	-0.003*	-0.001	0.001
PRC	-0.004*	0.998*			-0.003*	0.998*		
CAP			0.001	0.998*			0.001	0.998*
WGINI	0.997*	-0.001	0.996*	-0.001	0.996*	-0.001***	0.996*	-0.001
WFDI	-0.009	0.001	-0.001	0.001	-0.014***	-0.001	-0.011	0.001
WTB	0.001	-0.001***	0.001	-0.001	-0.041	0.002	0.012	0.001
WTOT								
WOPEN	-0.002***	0.004*	-0.001	-0.001				
WTARS					0.002	0.003*	0.001	-0.001
WPRC	0.004*	-0.007			0.003*	-0.009		
WCAP			-0.001	-0.003			-0.001	0.009
Rho	-0.779*	-0.773*	-0.741*	-0.739*	-0.755*	-0.762*	-0.743*	-0.741*
Constant		0.001		0.001		0.001***		0.001
Goodness of fit:								
Observations	162	162	162	162	162	162	162	162
Adj.R^2	0.930	0.997	0.925	0.997	0.928	0.997	0.925	0.997
Log Likelihood	1114.658		1109.946		1113.165		1109.968	
Variance σ_v^2	0.001		0.001		0.001		0.001	
Diagnostic tests:								
Jarque-Bera	1678.00*		2273.00*		1607.00*		2317.00*	
VIF	8.93		7.79		3.35		3.48	
Breusch-Pagan	135.95*		206.75*		92.84*		205.53*	
Moran's I	0.9796*		0.8874*		1.0264*		0.8767*	
LM test	12.00*		14.22*		12.93*		14.06*	
Hausman test		289.35*		391.95*		324.20*		399.55*

Note: The subscripts *, ** and *** denote the 1%, 5% and 10% significance levels respectively.

5.1. Estimation Results of GINI Index

Based on Equation (1), the estimation results of GINI coefficient index as proxy for income inequality are shown in Table 3 (3A and 3B). There are eight models (Model 1 to Model 8) that estimate the impacts of income inequality in the same way but different in the proxy explanatory variables.

The specification and diagnostic test results in all of the models are quite similar. The Jarque-Bera test statistic indicates that the error term is normally distributed, whereas the Breusch-Pagan test statistic exhibits that the hypothesis of homoskedasticity is not rejected. The VIF index confirms the absence of multicollinearity. The Moran's I test statistic shows that there is an evidence of the presence of spatial autocorrelation in the model. It implies that a spatial estimation model with spatially autocorrelation errors is appropriate. Ignoring the possibility of spatial autocorrelation in the error term leads to seriously biased parameter estimates and makes misleading inferences. As for this matter, the spatial FEM and REM estimators are applied here.

Moreover, Table 3 compares the estimated results with FEM and REM estimator for eight models. In order to make better approximation, the Hausman test is taken and its statistic confirms the presence of a correlation between individual effects and explanatory variables.

The estimated results from FEM are explained here. Almost results are consistent with theoretical expectations and empirical findings in the income inequality literature that provide support for the hypotheses of this study.

Column 1 of Table 3A shows both bilateral and third-country (spatial) effects on income inequality. In the bilateral parameters, the coefficient of the FDI-GDP ratio is positive but insignificant, and the coefficient of the openness index (proxy for economic integration) is significant positive. Moreover, the coefficient of trade balance is negative but insignificant, while the coefficient of the private credit (proxy for financial development) is significant negative.

This suggests that an increase in *FDI* and *economic integration* in the individual ASEAN economies are positively related to an increase in income inequality in ASEAN countries. On the contrary, an increase in *trade* and *financial development* is related to a decline in income inequality in ASEAN economies.

Specifically, in the spatial parameters, the coefficient of trade balance is positive but insignificant, and the coefficients of GINI and private credit are significant positive. In addition, the coefficient of FDI is negative but insignificant, and the coefficient of openness is significant negative. This implies that an increase in *income inequality, trade* and *financial development* in other ASEAN economies are positively related to an increase in income inequality in the individual ASEAN countries. Conversely, an increase in *FDI* and *economic integration* in other ASEAN economies is related to a decline in income inequality in that individual ASEAN economy.

Comparing the estimated results of GINI index (Model 1-8) in the bilateral aspects, income inequality in individual ASEAN economies is positively influenced by FDI and economic integration, whereas it is negatively influenced by trade and financial development. In the spatial aspects, income inequality in individual ASEAN countries is positively influenced by trade and financial development, whereas it is negatively influenced by FDI and economic integration.

Although FDI is found to cause a larger income inequality in individual ASEAN countries, but an increase in FDI as a whole ASEAN countries fosters a decline in income inequality in this region.

It implies that the inequality gap can reduce with the spatial distribution of FDI in favor of the ASEAN economies, then, the equality development in ASEAN can reach. Likewise, ASEAN should encourage deeper economic integration among member countries and should strengthen through preferential policies regarding human development, trade and investment facilitation improvement and infrastructure development in order to promote intra-economic activities.

Table 3B. Fixed Effect Model and Random Effect Model of GINI Coefficient Index

	Model 5		Model 6		Model 7		Model 8	
	FEM (1)	REM (2)	FEM (3)	REM (4)	FEM (5)	REM (6)	FEM (7)	REM (8)
FDI	0.005	-0.001*	0.001***	-0.001*	0.001**	-0.001*	0.011**	-0.001*
TB								
TOT	-0.001*	0.002*	-0.001*	0.001	-0.001*	-0.002	-0.001*	-0.002
OPEN	0.002*	-0.001	0.001	-0.001				
TARS					-0.002	0.001	-0.002	-0.001
PRC	-0.001	0.998*			0.001	0.998*		
CAP			-0.001	0.995*			-0.001	0.998*
WGINI	0.997*	-0.005	0.998*	-0.001*	0.997*	-0.001**	0.998*	-0.001**
WFDI	-0.005	0.001*	-0.013*	0.001*	-0.001***	0.001*	-0.011**	0.001*
WTB								
WTOT	0.001*	-0.002*	0.001*	0.001	0.001*	0.002	0.001*	0.002
WOPEN	-0.002*	0.001	0.001	0.001				
WTARS					0.002	-0.001	0.002	0.001
WPRC	0.001	0.001			-0.001	-0.003		
WCAP			0.001	0.009			0.001	-0.002
Rho	-0.985*	-1.088*	-0.988*	-1.071*	-0.988*	-1.068*	-0.988*	-1.074*
Constant		0.005		0.001		0.001		0.001*
Goodness of fit:								
Observations	162	162	162	162	162	162	162	162
Adj.R^2	0.973	0.999	0.972	0.999	0.971	0.999	0.972	0.999
Log Likelihood	1185.243		1181.237		1180.263		1180.901	
Variance σ_v^2	0.001		0.001		0.001		0.001	
Diagnostic tests:								
Jarque-Bera	450.90*		523.20*		429.20*		454.40*	
VIF	7.62		6.69		2.71		2.66	
Breusch-Pagan	299.81*		338.24*		293.17*		314.73*	
Moran's I	-0.9270*		-0.5818*		-0.2303*		-0.2443*	
LM test	1.17		0.99		1.73		1.48	
Hausman test		177.12*		196.12*		177.49*		19.377*

Note: The subscripts *, ** and *** denote the 1%, 5% and 10% significance levels respectively.

5.2. Estimation Results of Theil Index

This section presents the empirical results of Theil income inequality index which are estimated as similar as the previous one. Table 4 (4A and 4B) shows the impacts on income inequality in eight different models (Model 1-8). Unsurprisingly, the specification and diagnostic test results in eight models are the same. The error term is normally distributed (Jarque-Bera test statistic) and there is the presence of the heteroskedasticity (Breusch-Pagan test statistic).

The VIF statistic shows the absence of multicollinearity, whereas the Moran's I test shows that there is an evidence of the presence of spatial autocorrelation in the model. According to the Hausman test statistic, the best spatial panel data estimator is the spatial FEM.

The estimated results from FEM in Table 4 exhibit that most results are consistent with theoretical and empirical literature, as shown in the previous section. These results are also similar to the GINI index model.

Table 4A. Fixed Effect Model and Random Effect Model of Theil Coefficient Index

	Model 1 FEM (1)	REM (2)	Model 2 FEM (3)	REM (4)	Model 3 FEM (5)	REM (6)	Model 4 FEM (7)	REM (8)
FDI	0.003	-0.046	0.009***	-0.054	0.002*	0.053	0.003*	0.068
TB	-0.053	0.008*	-0.060***	0.007*	0.045	-0.001	0.055	-0.001
TOT								
OPEN	0.008*	-0.003*	0.007*	-0.001*				
TARS					-0.002	0.004*	-0.002	-0.002*
PRC	-0.003*	1.008*			0.003*	0.996*		
CAP			-0.001*	1.007*			-0.002*	0.995*
WGINI	0.996*	-0.004	0.995*	-0.001	0.996*	-0.002*	0.996*	-0.003*
WFDI	-0.004	0.045	-0.001	0.055	-0.002*	-0.051	-0.003*	-0.065
WTB	0.051	-0.008*	0.060***	-0.007*	-0.043	0.001	-0.052	0.001
WTOT								
WOPEN	-0.008*	0.003*	-0.007*	0.001*				
WTARS					0.002	-0.004*	0.002	0.001*
WPRC	0.003*	0.008			-0.003*	-0.003		
WCAP			0.001*	-0.003			0.001*	0.001
Rho	-0.820*	-0.813*	-0.810*	-0.805*	-0.603*	-0.594*	-0.615*	-0.620*
Constant		0.004		0.001***		0.002*		0.003*
Goodness of fit:								
Observations	162	162	162	162	162	162	162	162
Adj.R^2	0.982	0.995	0.982	0.995	0.957	0.986	0.957	0.986
Log Likelihood	422.428		423.036		355.923		355.131	
Variance σ_v^2	0.003		0.003		0.007		0.007	
Diagnostic tests:								
Jarque-Bera	43.97*		62.37*		1192.00*		1218.00*	
VIF	10.26		8.78		4.01		4.00	
Breusch-Pagan	80.81*		100.41*		124.59*		159.62*	
Moran's I	1.0290*		1.0431*		1.0372*		0.9380*	
LM test	0.09		0.06		6.31*		4.93**	
Hausman test		300.87*		289.24*		730.20*		636.61*

Note: The subscripts *, ** and *** denote the 1%, 5% and 10% significance levels respectively.

Table 4B. Fixed Effect Model and Random Effect Model of Theil Coefficient Index

	Model 5		Model 6		Model 7		Model 8	
	FEM (1)	REM (2)	FEM (3)	REM (4)	FEM (5)	REM (6)	FEM (7)	REM (8)
FDI	0.003	-0.001	0.012***	-0.001	0.002*	-0.001	0.003*	0.001
TB								
TOT	-0.001	0.008*	-0.001	0.004*	-0.001	-0.001	0.001	-0.001
OPEN	0.008*	-0.002*	0.005*	-0.001*				
TARS					-0.002	0.004*	-0.002	-0.002*
PRC	-0.002*	0.999*			0.004*	0.997*		
CAP			-0.018*	0.856*			-0.002*	0.997*
WGINI	0.994*	-0.004	0.794*	-0.004*	0.997*	-0.002*	0.997*	-0.003*
WFDI	-0.003	0.001	-0.004*	0.001	-0.002*	0.001	-0.003*	-0.001
WTB								
WTOT	0.001	-0.008*	-0.001	0.004	0.001	0.001	0.001	0.001
WOPEN	-0.008*	0.002*	0.009	-0.005				
WTARS					0.001	-0.004*	0.002	0.001*
WPRC	0.002*	0.001			-0.004*	-0.002		
WCAP			-0.001***	1.232*			0.001*	0.001
Rho	-0.823*	-0.821*	0.241*	0.055	-0.600*	-0.597*	-0.618*	-0.617*
Constant		0.003***		0.001*		0.002*		0.003*
Goodness of fit:								
Observations	162	162	162	162	162	162	162	162
Adj.R^2	0.982	0.995	0.966	0.963	0.957	0.986	0.957	0.986
Log Likelihood	421.866		380.458		355.593		354.588	
Variance σ_v^2	0.003		0.005		0.007		0.007	
Diagnostic tests:								
Jarque-Bera	49.48*		64.06*		1272.00*		1344.00*	
VIF	9.20		7.95		3.32		3.23	
Breusch-Pagan	77.79*		94.28*		101.83*		171.94*	
Moran's I	1.0231*		0.3493*		0.9678*		0.9903*	
LM test	0.08		0.01		6.37*		5.74*	
Hausman test		281.91*		278.55*		774.88*		803.45*

Note: The subscripts *, ** and *** denote the 1%, 5% and 10% significance levels respectively.

Going more into detail, a look at the bilateral determinants of income inequality in column 1 of Table 4A displays that FDI has a positive and insignificant sign, whereas economic integration has a positive and significant sign.

Meanwhile trade has a negative and insignificant sign, and financial development has a negative and significant sign. The spatial effects rarely correlate with the bilateral conclusion. Indeed, the negative signs obtained for FDI and economic integration tend to support the income inequality.

Similarly, the positive sign recorded for third-country income inequality, trade and financial development are in favor of income inequality. Considering the results in all eight models, the sign of the parameters tend to show that the bilateral FDI and economic integration encourage income inequality, whereas trade and financial development tend to discourage income inequality.

In addition, the spatial effects of trade and financial development tend to encourage income inequality, whereas income inequality is discouraged by the spatial FDI and economic integration.

Intuitively, although the surge of FDI tends to obstruct the equality development in such ASEAN countries, if all ASEAN countries commonly promote more FDI, it tends to reduce their income inequality.

5.3. Robustness Check

In order to check the sensitivity of our estimated results, the robustness with respect to alternative spatial-weighted schemes for third-country (spatial) effects is provided. In this regard, there are two alternative weighted schemes implemented:

Inverse squared bilateral distance: $w_{ij} = \left(\frac{1}{d_{ij}}\right)^2$ $\forall\, i \neq j$ which implies a faster spatial effect.

Inverse square roots of bilateral distance: $w_{ij} = \left(\frac{1}{d_{ij}}\right)^{\frac{1}{2}}$ $\forall\, i \neq j$ which implies a slower spatial effect.

The diagnostic tests and the estimated results with these alternative weighted schemes are illustrated in Table 5 and 6. We start with the diagnostic tests for income inequality. The Moran's I test indicates the presence of spatial correlation of the residuals in the data which suggests that the spatial regression model with spatially correlated residuals should be provided.

The complementary tests exhibit that the error term is normally distributed (Jarque-Bera), the hypothesis of homoskedasticity is not rejected (Breusch and Pagan), and the VIF statistic indicates no multicolinearity problems.

Moreover, the empirical results illustrate that almost significant explanatory variables are in line with the theoretical hypotheses. In the discussion of the results, we focus on the FEM estimates because the Hausman test rejects the REM. the expected signs in these estimated results are very similar to those obtained in Table 3 and 4.

Following column 1 of Table 5, first of all, there is indeed positive relationship between FDI and income inequality in ASEAN. The results also indicate that economic integration exhibits positive and insignificant sign. In addition, the estimated coefficients in trade and financial development are negative and significant signs.

Finally, the estimated coefficients in spatial effects of FDI and economic integration are insignificant and negative. However, at least two of the estimated coefficients in spatial effects of income inequality and financial development are positively significant.

Although almost estimated coefficients in bilateral and third-country determinants in column 1 of Table 6 are insignificant, these parameters show the same expected signs to the previous one.

This suggests that the estimated results are fairly robust with respect to the alternative spatial weighting schemes.

Table 5A. Fixed Effect Model and Random Effect Model of GINI Index (Weighted Scheme I)

	Model 1		Model 2		Model 3		Model 4	
	FEM (1)	REM (2)	FEM (3)	REM (4)	FEM (5)	REM (6)	FEM (7)	REM (8)
FDI	0.001	-0.006	0.001	-0.005	0.001**	-0.004	0.001***	-0.004
TB	-0.006	0.001	-0.004	0.001	-0.004	-0.004	-0.003	-0.003
TOT								
OPEN	0.001	-0.003**	0.001	0.001				
TARS					-0.004	-0.002**	-0.004	-0.001
PRC	-0.003**	1.002*			-0.002**	1.001*		
CAP			0.001	1.001*			0.001	1.001*
WGINI	0.999*	-0.001	0.999*	-0.001	1.001*	-0.001***	1.005*	-0.001
WFDI	-0.001	0.006	-0.001	0.005	-0.001**	0.004	-0.001***	0.004
WTB	0.006	-0.001	0.004	-0.001	0.003	0.005***	0.003	0.003
WTOT								
WOPEN	-0.001	0.003**	-0.001	-0.001				
WTARS					0.005***	0.002**	0.004	-0.001
WPRC	0.003**	-0.001			0.002**	0.002		
WCAP			-0.001	-0.001			-0.001	0.007
Rho	-0.833*	-0.838*	-0.838*	-0.843*	-0.836*	-0.842*	-0.847*	-0.845*
Constant		0.001		0.001		0.001***		0.001
Goodness of fit:								
Observations	162	162	162	162	162	162	162	162
Adj.R^2	0.972	0.999	0.971	0.998	0.972	0.999	0.972	0.999
Log Likelihood	1140.678		1138.525		1141.181		1139.478	
Variance σ_v^2	0.001		0.001		0.001		0.001	
Diagnostic tests:								
Jarque-Bera	1191.00*		1895.00*		1087.00*		1919.00*	
VIF	5.24		4.52		2.47		2.58	
Breusch-Pagan	101.57*		148.01*		71.31*		151.90*	
Moran's I	-0.6603*		-0.1655*		0.1225*		-0.1151*	
LM test	72.01*		81.36*		75.84*		75.27*	
Hausman test		5142.35*		977.12*		2678.39*		1062.98*

Note: a. The subscripts *, ** and *** denote the 1%, 5% and 10% significance levels respectively.
b. Weighting Scheme I denotes the inverse squared distance weighting scheme.

Table 5B. Fixed Effect Model and Random Effect Model of GINI Index (Weighted Scheme I)

	Model 5		Model 6		Model 7		Model 8	
	FEM (1)	REM (2)	FEM (3)	REM (4)	FEM (5)	REM (6)	FEM (7)	REM (8)
FDI	0.007	-0.001*	0.007	-0.001*	0.001**	-0.001*	0.001**	-0.001*
TB								
TOT	-0.001*	0.001*	-0.001*	0.001**	-0.001*	-0.003	-0.001*	-0.003
OPEN	0.001*	-0.001	0.001**	-0.001				
TARS					-0.003	-0.001	-0.003	-0.001
PRC	-0.001	1.003*			-0.001	1.001*		
CAP			0.001	1.003*			0.001	1.003*
WGINI	1.009*	-0.007	0.999*	-0.007	0.999*	-0.001**	0.998*	-0.001***
WFDI	-0.007	0.001*	-0.008	0.001*	-0.001**	0.001*	-0.001**	0.001*
WTB								
WTOT	0.001*	-0.001*	0.001*	-0.001***	0.001*	0.003	0.001*	0.003
WOPEN	-0.002*	0.001	-0.001**	0.001				
WTARS					0.003	0.001	0.003	-0.001
WPRC	0.001	0.001			0.001	-0.002		
WCAP			-0.001	-0.001			-0.001	-0.001
Rho	-0.666*	-0.658*	-0.667*	-0.661*	-0.690*	-0.692*	-0.694*	-0.689*
Constant		0.007		0.006		0.001**		0.001**
Goodness of fit:								
Observations	162	162	162	162	162	162	162	162
Adj.R^2	0.976	0.998	0.976	0.998	0.976	0.999	0.977	0.999
Log Likelihood	1180.449		1179.450		1178.099		1178.152	
Variance σ_v^2	0.001		0.001		0.001		0.001	
Diagnostic tests:								
Jarque-Bera	167.20*		283.30*		189.40*		203.90*	
VIF	4.31		3.64		1.84		1.82	
Breusch-Pagan	120.14*		161.05*		108.33*		123.94*	
Moran's I	-0.3714*		0.8414*		0.6395*		0.4941*	
LM test	0.30		0.29		2.40		1.70	
Hausman test		121.94*		166.03*		158.15*		185.45*

Note: a. The subscripts *, ** and *** denote the 1%, 5% and 10% significance levels respectively.
b. Weighting Scheme I denotes the inverse squared distance weighting scheme.

Table 6A. Fixed Effect Model and Random Effect Model of GINI Index (Weighted Scheme II)

	Model 1		Model 2		Model 3		Model 4	
	FEM (1)	REM (2)	FEM (3)	REM (4)	FEM (5)	REM (6)	FEM (7)	REM (8)
FDI	0.006	-0.005	0.006	-0.004	0.008	-0.004	0.006	-0.004
TB	-0.005	0.001	-0.005	-0.001	-0.004	-0.001	-0.004	-0.001
TOT								
OPEN	0.001	-0.002***	0.001	0.001				
TARS					-0.001	-0.002***	-0.001	0.001
PRC	-0.002***	1.004*			-0.001	0.999*		
CAP			0.001	1.003*			0.001	0.999*
WGINI	0.997*	-0.006	0.996*	-0.007	0.996*	-0.009	0.996*	-0.007

	Model 1		Model 2		Model 3		Model 4	
	FEM (1)	REM (2)	FEM (3)	REM (4)	FEM (5)	REM (6)	FEM (7)	REM (8)
WFDI	-0.006	0.005	-0.006	0.004	-0.008	0.004	-0.006	0.004
WTB	0.005	-0.001	0.005	0.001	0.004	0.001	0.005	0.001
WTOT								
WOPEN	-0.001	0.002***	-0.001	-0.001				
WTARS					0.002	0.002***	0.002	-0.001
WPRC	0.002	0.001			0.001	-0.003		
WCAP			-0.001	-0.001			-0.001	-0.003
Rho	-0.742*	-1.670*	-0.738*	-1.684*	-0.739*	-1.673*	-0.742*	-1.684*
Constant		0.006		0.006		0.009		0.006
Goodness of fit:								
Observations	162	162	162	162	162	162	162	162
Adj.R^2	0.962	0.999	0.965	0.999	0.965	0.999	0.965	0.999
Log Likelihood	1139.497		1138.372		1139.263		1138.530	
Variance σ_v^2	0.001		0.001		0.001		0.001	
Diagnostic tests:								
Jarque-Bera	1184.00*		1801.00*		1085.00*		1821.00*	
VIF	7.31		6.35		3.17		3.32	
Breusch-Pagan	128.15*		196.70*		97.84*		210.06*	
Moran's I	0.6226*		0.5963*		0.7809*		0.6104*	
LM test	28.99*		33.49*		30.73*		31.71*	
Hausman test		595.27*		1537.01*		674.44*		973.38*

Note: a. The subscripts *, ** and *** denote the 1%, 5% and 10% significance levels respectively.
b. Weighting Scheme II denotes the inverse squared root distance weighting scheme.

Table 6B. Fixed Effect Model and Random Effect Model of GINI Index (Weighted Scheme II)

	Model 5		Model 6		Model 7		Model 8	
	FEM (1)	REM (2)	FEM (3)	REM (4)	FEM (5)	REM (6)	FEM (7)	REM (8)
FDI	0.004	-0.001*	0.004	-0.001*	0.008	-0.001*	0.008	-0.001*
TB								
TOT	-0.001*	0.001***	-0.001*	0.001	-0.001*	-0.002	-0.001*	-0.002
OPEN	0.001**	-0.001	0.001**	-0.001				
TARS					-0.001	-0.001	-0.001	-0.001
PRC	-0.001	1.009*			-0.001	1.005*		
CAP			0.001	1.008*			0.001	1.007*
WGINI	1.004*	-0.005	1.004*	-0.005	1.005*	-0.005	1.007*	-0.008
WFDI	-0.005	0.001*	-0.005	0.001*	-0.008	0.001*	-0.008	0.001*
WTB								
WTOT	0.001*	-0.001***	0.001*	-0.001	0.001*	0.002	0.001*	0.002
WOPEN	-0.001**	0.001	-0.001***	0.001				
WTARS					0.002	0.001	0.002	0.001
WPRC	0.001	-0.004			0.001	0.008		
WCAP			-0.001	0.001			-0.001	0.008
Rho	-0.473*	-1.228*	-0.473*	-1.235*	-0.513*	-1.279*	-0.512*	-1.273*
Constant		0.004		0.005		0.008		0.008
Goodness of fit:								

Table 6B. Fixed Effect Model and Random Effect Model of GINI Index
(Weighted Scheme II)
(continued)

	Model 5		Model 6		Model 7		Model 8	
	FEM (1)	REM (2)	FEM (3)	REM (4)	FEM (5)	REM (6)	FEM (7)	REM (8)
Observations	162	162	162	162	162	162	162	162
Adj.R^2	0.966	0.999	0.966	0.999	0.967	0.999	0.967	0.999
Log Likelihood	1166.794		1166.252		1164.689		1164.698	
Variance σ_v^2	0.001		0.001		0.001		0.001	
Diagnostic tests:								
Jarque-Bera	387.80*		526.70*		366.70*		393.80*	
VIF	6.08		5.22		2.37		2.34	
Breusch-Pagan	202.47*		243.39*		190.85*		209.08*	
Moran's I	0.6349*		0.6877*		0.7145*		0.7314*	
LM test	0.15		0.24		1.06		0.81	
Hausman test		124.73*		159.43		137.26*		161.05*

Note: a. The subscripts *, ** and *** denote the 1%, 5% and 10% significance levels respectively.
b. Weighting Scheme II denotes the inverse squared root distance weighting scheme.

CONCLUSION

This chapter mainly focuses on the impacts of foreign direct investment, regional economic integration and spatial effects on income inequality in ASEAN. The spatial panel data model techniques are used to investigate these impacts. Data at the country level for six ASEAN economies over the period of 1985-2011 are employed. The primary estimated results reveal that bilateral economic integration and FDI have positive relationships with income inequality, on the contrary, bilateral trade and financial development.

Moreover, the spatial effects of FDI and economic integration have negative relationships with income inequality, whereas spatial effects of income inequality, trade and financial development have positive relationships. These estimated results are in line with the theoretical predictions.

Arguably the findings have important policy implications. For example, in terms of ASEAN Economic Community, which has been aimed at boosting foreign direct investment, the evidence exhibited here suggests that widening income inequality may be unavoidable. As argued in this chapter, the main reason for this is the common spatial distribution of FDI because it is unlikely to appear every ASEAN countries at the same time.

Therefore, one may argue that regional investment policies should aim at fostering intra-ASEAN FDI in order to guarantee greater prosperity at the reduction in income inequality in ASEAN, especially the newest ASEAN member countries lie well below ASEAN GDP per capita levels. Accordingly, specific policies on trade and investment liberalization and facilitation, monetary and financial security, and transportation and communication stability should be tailored, integrated and harmonized in order to achieve the desired goals of becoming ASEAN economic community. These are indeed beneficial to boost economic growth and sustainable development in the ASEAN.

REFERENCES

Annim, S. K., Mariwah, S., and Sebu, J. (2012). Spatial inequality and household poverty in Ghana. *Economic Systems*, *36*(4), 487–505.

Anselin, L. (1999). Spatial econometrics. Technical Report. Bruton Center, University of Texas, Dallas.

Anselin, L. (2001). Spatial Econometrics. In A Companion to Theoretical Econometrics, pp. 310–330. Blackwell Publishing.

Anwar, S., and Sun, S. (2012). Trade liberalisation, market competition and wage inequality in China's manufacturing sector. *Economic Modelling*, *29*(4), 1268–1277.

ASEAN (2013a). ASEAN Statistics. Available from http://www.asean.org/resources/ 2012-02-10-08-47-55.

ASEAN (2013b). Fact Sheets: ASEAN Economic Community - Investment. Available from http://www.asean.org/images/2012/publications/FactSheet/Investment.pdf.

Baltagi, B. H. (2005). Econometric Analysis of Panel Data (3rd ed.). John Wiley and Sons.

Barrios, S., and Strobl, E. (2009). The dynamics of regional inequalities. *Regional Science and Urban Economics*, *39*(5), 575–591.

Barro, R. J. (2008). Inequality and Growth Revisited , Working Papers on Regional Economic Integration No. 11. Asian Development Bank.

Basu, P., and Guariglia, A. (2007). Foreign Direct Investment, inequality, and growth. *Journal of Macroeconomics*, *29*(4), 824–839.

Berg, A., Ostry, J. D., and International Monetary Fund. (2011). Inequality and unsustainable growth two sides of the same coin? International Monetary Fund.

Bouvet, F. (2010). EMU and the dynamics of regional per capita income inequality in Europe. *The Journal of Economic Inequality*, *8*(3), 323–344.

Castro, G. Á. (2011). The Effect of Trade and Foreign Direct Investment on Inequality: Do Governance and Macroeconomic Stability Matter? *Economia Mexicana NUEVA EPOCA*, *XX*(1), 181–219.

Chi, W. (2011). Capital Income and Income Inequality: Evidence from Urban China. Munich Personal RePEc Archive (MPRA).

Chintrakarn, P., Herzer, D., and Nunnenkamp, P. (2012). FDI and Income Inequality: Evidence from a Panel of U.S. States. *Economic Inquiry*, *50*(3), 788–801.

Choi, C. (2006). Does foreign direct investment affect domestic income inequality? *Applied Economics Letters*, *13*(12), 811–814.

Clark, D. P., Highfill, J., Campino, J. de O., and Rehman, S. S. (2011). FDI, Technology Spillovers, Growth, and Income Inequality: A Selective Survey. *Global Economy Journal*, *11*(2).

Driffield, N., Girma, S., Henry, M., and Taylor, K. (2010). Wage Inequality, Linkages and FDI, IZA Discussion Paper No. 4722. Institute for the Study of Labor (IZA).

Elhorst, J. P. (2001). Panel data models extended to spatial error autocorrelation or a spatially lagged dependent variable, Research Report 01C05. Research Institute SOM (Systems, Organizations and Management). University of Groningen.

Fleisher, B., Li, H., and Zhao, M. Q. (2010). Human capital, economic growth, and regional inequality in China. *Journal of Development Economics*, *92*(2), 215–231.

Goh, C., Luo, X., and Zhu, N. (2009). Income growth, inequality and poverty reduction: A case study of eight provinces in China. *China Economic Review*, *20*(3), 485–496.

Gravier-Rymaszewska, J., Tyrowicz, J., and Kochanowicz, J. (2010). Intra-provincial inequalities and economic growth in China. *Economic Systems*, *34*(3), 237–258.

Herzer, D., and Nunnenkamp, P. (2011). FDI and Income Inequality: Evidence from Europe, Kiel Working Paper. Kiel Institute for the World Economy.

Jalil, A. (2012). Modeling income inequality and openness in the framework of Kuznets curve: New evidence from China. *Economic Modelling*, *29*(2), 309–315.

Jaumotte, F., Papageorgiou, C., and Lall, S. (2008). Rising Income Inequality: Technology, or Trade and Financial Globalization?, SSRN Scholarly Paper No. ID 1175363. Social Science Research Network.

Jones, D. C., Li, C., and Owen, A. L. (2003). Growth and regional inequality in China during the reform era. *China Economic Review*, *14*(2), 186–200.

Kelejian, H. H., and Prucha, I. R. (1999). A Generalized Moments Estimator for the Autoregressive Parameter in a Spatial Model. *International Economic Review*, *40*(2), 509–533.

Kennedy, P. (2003). A Guide to Econometrics (5th ed.). The MIT Press.

Li, Y., and Wei, Y. H. D. (2010). The spatial-temporal hierarchy of regional inequality of China. *Applied Geography*, *30*(3), 303–316.

Liao, F. H. F., and Wei, Y. D. (2012). Dynamics, space, and regional inequality in provincial China: A case study of Guangdong province. *Applied Geography*, *35*(1–2), 71–83.

Portnov, B. A., and Felsenstein, D. (2010). On the suitability of income inequality measures for regional analysis: Some evidence from simulation analysis and bootstrapping tests. *Socio-Economic Planning Sciences*, *44*(4), 212–219.

Sahu, P. K. (2010). FDI, wage inequality and employment in emerging economies: recent evidence from Indian manufacturing. Munich Personal RePEc Archive (MPRA).

Shahbaz, M. (2010). Income inequality-economic growth and non-linearity: a case of Pakistan. *International Journal of Social Economics*, *37*(8), 613–636.

Shankar, R., and Shah, A. (2003). Bridging the Economic Divide Within Countries: A Scorecard on the Performance of Regional Policies in Reducing Regional Income Disparities. *World Development*, *31*(8), 1421–1441.

Taylor, K., and Driffield, N. (2005). Wage inequality and the role of multinationals: evidence from UK panel data. *Labour Economics*, *12*(2), 223–249.

Thadewald, T., and Büning, H. (2007). Jarque-Bera test and its competitors for testing normality : a power comparison. *Journal of Applied Statistics*, *34*(1), 87–105.

Theil, H. (1967). Economics and Information Theory. Amsterdam, Netherlands: North-Holland Publishing Company.

Wan, G., Lu, M., and Chen, Z. (2006). The inequality–growth nexus in the short and long run: Empirical evidence from China. *Journal of Comparative Economics*, *34*(4), 654–667.

Wei, K., Yao, S., and Liu, A. (2009). Foreign Direct Investment and Regional Inequality in China. *Review of Development Economics*, *13*(4), 778–791.

Wooldridge, J. M. (2001). Econometric Analysis of Cross Section and Panel Data. The MIT Press.

World Bank (2013) World DataBank : World Development Indicators (WDI). Available from http://databank.worldbank.org/ddp/home.do?Step=1andid=4

Yu, K., Xin, X., Guo, P., and Liu, X. (2011). Foreign direct investment and China's regional income inequality. *Economic Modelling*, *28*(3), 1348–1353.

Zeng, D.-Z., and Zhao, L. (2010). Globalization, interregional and international inequalities. *Journal of Urban Economics*, *67*(3), 352–361.

Zhang, Y., and Eriksson, T. (2010). Inequality of opportunity and income inequality in nine Chinese provinces, 1989–2006. *China Economic Review*, *21*(4), 607–616.

In: Foreign Direct Investment (FDI)
Editors: Enzo Guillon and Lucas Chauvet

ISBN: 978-1-62808-403-0
© 2013 Nova Science Publishers, Inc.

Chapter 6

GLOBAL TRENDS IN R AND D-INTENSIVE FDI: OPPORTUNITIES AND CHALLENGES FOR DEVELOPING COUNTRIES

José Guimón[*]

Department of Economic Structure and Development Economics,
Autonomous University of Madrid, Madrid, Spain

ABSTRACT

The available evidence shows that the geography of corporate research and development (R and D) is becoming more multi-polar, which brings along new opportunities for some developing countries. However, global competition to attract FDI in R and D has become very intense, and developing countries that fail to raise their technological capabilities in line with the needs of multinational companies will remain marginalized from global innovation networks. Building on a critical review of the existing literature and on a variety of country-specific examples, the aim of this chapter is to unveil the policy options available for developing countries to attract R and D-intensive FDI.

1. INTRODUCTION

The growing relevance of R and D-intensive FDI reflects wider trends in the global economy. Multinational companies (MNC) are gradually modifying their strategies and spatial organization, involving an on-going fragmentation of their international value chains in the search of sustainable competitiveness. This applies to their manufacturing, logistics, sales or administrative functions, and increasingly also to R and D activities (Schmitz and Strambach, 2009). Through R and D internationalization, MNCs aim at tapping into resources and capabilities from multiple local contexts in order to integrate and leverage them into competitive advantages (Meyer *et al.*, 2011).

---

[*] Corresponding author: José Guimón. E-mail: jose.guimon@uam.es.

Indeed, corporate R and D shows signs of evolution from a centralized and hierarchical node of global supply chains towards one that builds upon an open network of geographically dispersed R and D centers.

As a result, R and D-intensive FDI has grown substantially since the early 1990s, albeit with significant differences across industries and countries. A study by Booz Allen Hamilton, a consulting firm, shows that the largest 1000 companies by R and D expenditure allocate on average 55 percent of their R and D budget outside the countries where they are headquartered (Jaruzelski and Dehoff, 2008). Ninety-nine percent of these firms conduct some R and D in their subsidiaries abroad and their total number of overseas R and D sites increased by 6 percent from 2004 to 2007. The annual R and D investments by foreign subsidiaries in the OECD area more than doubled between 1997 and 2007, reaching USD 89.3 billion (OECD, 2011). Foreign subsidiaries contribute with around one third of total business expenditure in R and D on average in European Union countries, around 15% in the US and around 5% in Japan, reaching over 60% in some small economies like Slovakia and Ireland (OECD, 2011).

But R and D-intensive FDI is a very heterogeneous phenomenon and it is necessary to consider the different strategic motivations and entry modes in order to better frame its developmental impact and the policy implications for host economies. R and D-intensive FDI can be defined as an investment involving a lasting interest and control by a resident entity in one economy in an enterprise resident in another economy for the purpose of conducting R and D activities. This may occur through greenfield investments (creation of a new R and D center overseas by a multinational company or expansion of an existing subsidiary), through transnational mergers and acquisitions (full or partial acquisition of a domestic company active in R and D by a foreign company) or through transnational joint ventures (joint ownership of an R and D center by foreign and domestic entities).

In addition to these different possible entry modes, there are many different types of R and D activities that MNCs may internationalize, reflecting different strategic motivations (Bas and Sierra, 2002; Florida, 1997; Kuemmerle, 1999). The R and D activities may be demand-driven, supply-driven or efficiency-seeking; global, regional or local in scope; radical or incremental; product or process oriented; autonomous or highly integrated into the global R and D value chain; and so forth. There are also significant differences in the extent and scope of R and D internationalization by industries and scientific fields (OECD, 2011).

Demand-driven R and D is associated to the adaptation of products, services or processes to overseas markets, while supply-driven R and D relates to tapping into localized knowledge and technology. The internationalization of corporate R and D was primarily demand driven in the past, following the internationalization of manufacturing and sales, but in recent years supply driven motivations are gradually growing in importance (Carlsson, 2006; Edler, 2008). Indeed, the role of subsidiaries in global innovation networks is becoming more active, involving not only incremental innovations but also multi-technology product development and basic research.

However, while the number of supply-driven R and D centers may have increased in recent years, MNCs often operate with just a few of such global R and D labs in carefully selected locations, with the historical core R and D unit in the country of origin often holding a coordinating role (Sachwald, 2008). Whatever the strategic motivations, R and D-intensive FDI normally unfolds through the upgrading of existing subsidiaries, rather than through completely new investments.

R and D mandates are often assigned through a competitive bidding process involving several potentially-capable subsidiaries of the MNC already present in different countries and regions. This kind of intra-corporate competition to attract R and D is becoming more intense as global innovation networks have become more mature and as a growing and more diverse set of locations have acquired the threshold level of technological capabilities and infrastructure required for hosting R and D facilities. MNCs are continuously rationalizing and restructuring their international network of R and D units, often resulting in an increase in R and D expenditure overseas but a reduction in the total number of R and D units, through strategies such as regional integration of R and D efforts (e.g. one dominant R and D center for Europe, with a smaller network of collaborating units).

It should also be acknowledged that MNCs may undertake other modes of innovation other than R and D, which may have an equivalent effect on learning and competence building in host economies. Under a broad view of innovation, the role of MNCs is not limited to its contribution to R and D efforts but also to human capital development; organizational change and new business models; marketing, branding and design; etc. In addition, the subject of analysis could also be extended to include other high value business functions such as advanced manufacturing, business process outsourcing, technical assistance, etc. Some agencies and analysts adopt an industrial (rather than functional) perspective, which consists in targeting the most dynamic and high technology sectors like software, electronics and telecommunications, pharmaceuticals, biotechnology, nanotechnology, or aeronautics. Others speak of "quality" FDI or of "knowledge-intensive" FDI (OECD, 2012). The logic remains the same: to use FDI as a catalyst for technological development and for upgrading in global value chains.

Moreover, R and D-intensive FDI needs to be understood as part of a wider process that can be characterized as the globalization of innovation Archibugi and Pietrobelli, 2003). This includes not only FDI but also international collaboration and strategic alliances, transnational technology contracts and licensing, international trade of high technology products, and international flows of human capital. Indeed, from a development and policy perspective the critical issue is the nature and extent of cross-border technological linkages, rather than whether these linkages are organized intra-firm (through FDI) or inter-firm (through contracts and alliances).

Developing countries are increasingly aware of the importance of R and D-intensive FDI and its role as a mechanism for technological transfer and catching-up. However, they tend to face more difficulties in attracting the R and D of MNCs than developed countries and see a higher need of government intervention because of the presence of more acute market failures and systemic inefficiencies. And even if a country manages to attract some FDI in R and D, the expected benefits for the national innovation system will not accrue automatically.

Against this background, the purpose of this paper is to explore the policy implications for developing countries of recent global trends in R and D-intensive FDI. To set the stage for the discussion, the following section summarizes the impact on host countries of this type of FDI and the reasons supporting policy intervention. Section 3 depicts the policy instruments that can be used to attract R and D-intensive FDI at the interplay between technology policies and FDI promotion policies. Section 4 focuses on describing the new role of emerging countries in global innovation networks, while Section 5 discusses the challenges associated with embedding FDI in national innovation systems.

Finally, Section 6 rounds up this chapter with an analysis on the main policy options available for developing countries to attract and embed R and D-intensive FDI.

2. IMPACT ON HOST COUNTRIES AND RATIONALES FOR POLICY INTERVENTION

Given that MNCs undertake the bulk of global R and D expenditure, their location decisions determine to a large extent the geography of R and D activity. In view of the potential benefits of innovation and FDI for growth and competitiveness, attracting R and D-intensive FDI is becoming a critical concern for national policymakers, in developed and developing countries alike (OECD, 2011; UNCTAD, 2005).

As more corporations set up R and D centers overseas, national innovation systems are becoming more linked to global networks and more dependent on foreign sources of knowledge. FDI is expected to bring significant benefits to host countries by enabling an upgrading of technological capabilities as well as a better access to international markets (Cantwell and Piscitello, 2000; Carlsson, 2006; Santangelo, 2005). The impact of R and D-intensive FDI on host countries comprises direct and indirect effects (Görg and Strobl 2001; Narula and Dunning, 2010).

Direct effects are associated with a net increase in domestic R and D activity, involving more R and D expenditure and the quick creation of job opportunities for highly skilled labor locally, which could slow down or revert brain drain. The direct benefits will be larger when the subsequent R and D activities of MNC subsidiaries complement (rather than replace) the R and D activity of local companies. Still, some extent of crowding-out of the technological activity of local firms can be expected through intensified competition for limited specialized assets, including human capital.

The risk of crowding-out is especially acute in the case of transnational MandAs, where the only short term effect for the host country is a change of ownership, while in the medium- to long-run there is a trade-off between the potential for expansion and upgrading, on the one hand, and the risk that the acquirer ends up reducing the subsidiary's R and D mandate to avoid duplicities with other pre-existing R and D centers within the MNC's global network, on the other hand.

In addition to its direct impact, R and D-intensive FDI can bring along indirect effects or *spillovers*, which refer to "productivity improvements resulting from knowledge diffusion – both in the form of unintentional transmission or intentional transfer – from multinational affiliates to domestic firms, encompassing both technology and all forms of codified and 'tacit knowledge' related to production, including management and organizational practices" (Farole and Winkler, 2012).

Indirect effects unfoald through different types of formal and informal linkages and knowledge spillovers.

Among other indirect effects, R and D-intensive FDI may enable locally produced components to be incorporated at the design stage of new products, opening up new markets for local suppliers and new opportunities to collaborate with MNCs. R and D-intensive FDI facilitates the transfer of tacit technological knowledge, which is hard to acquire by other means.

Besides collaborative agreements with local firms and research centers, knowledge spillovers also unfold through indirect employment effects, whereby the host country benefits from training provided by MNC subsidiaries to their employees, who subsequently become available to local firms through the job market or may establish new ventures themselves (Fosfuri et al., 2001). Other sources of indirect benefits include demonstration and competition effects, because the presence of innovative MNC subsidiaries spurs domestic firms to engage in R and D and enhance the efficiency of their operations to be able to compete.

However, the benefits associated with R and D-intensive FDI do not accrue automatically; a threshold level of absorptive capacity is required in order to tap into the potential externalities. Absorptive capacity can be defined as the firm's (or country's) ability to acquire, assimilate and exploit knowledge developed elsewhere (Cohen and Levinthal, 1989). Thus, besides attracting new flows of R and D-intensive FDI, a related policy objective is to reap the benefits associated with the existing R and D activity of MNC subsidiaries by stimulating their embeddedness into the national innovation system (e.g. linkages with local firms and universities) and by augmenting the absorptive capacity of domestic agents (e.g. human capital, research infrastructure, public R and D).

Government intervention to attract R and D-intensive FDI may be justified by the presence of market failures or imperfections.

For example, in the case of R and D a well known market failure is that firms are not sensitive to the positive externalities of knowledge creation and, if left to the market, they would under-invest in R and D due to appropriability concerns and to the duration and risk inherent in R and D projects. This applies arguably to a larger extent to the specific case of MNC subsidiaries, given that they are operating in more unknown markets where the risk of knowledge spillovers may be perceived as higher. With regard to FDI, an example of market failure is that those who decide the allocation of R and D centres within global innovation networks lack perfect information about all potential countries and regions, which implies that their location decisions may be biased.

In addition to market failures, the literature on innovation systems has played an important role in shaping a new policy approach, bringing along the notion of systemic failures as a rationale for innovation policies (Smith, 2000). Under this framework policy makers are expected to intervene when the system of knowledge generation and diffusion does not achieve its objectives of contributing to innovation and technological progress in an efficient manner, because of the lack of well developed networks between the different actors of the system, because of institutional weaknesses, because of an inadequate provision of research infrastructure, and so on.

Thus, the role of governments is not limited to providing funding for education and R and D, but extends further to facilitating linkages and enhancing the dynamism of the national innovation system.

The case for public intervention is sound, but governments should set realistic targets to guide their policies by coupling their country's potential location advantages with the dynamics of global innovation networks.

Attracting R and D-intensive FDI is not an easy task because it requires advanced technological infrastructure and capabilities and because competition among countries is becoming more intense, within a context of continuous restructuring and segmentation of global value chains.

3. INDUSTRIAL AND INNOVATION POLICIES TO ATTRACT R AND D-INTENSIVE FDI

There are many different policy instruments that can be used to attract R and D-intensive FDI, involving a close coordination of innovation policy and FDI policies (Table 1). On the one hand, the role of innovation policy is to improve the investment climate for R and D by identifying and acting upon the strengths and weaknesses of the national innovation system. The objective would be to provide the necessary infrastructures, public R and D, human capital, and regulatory regimes, in addition to fiscal and financial incentives to private firms undertaking R and D.

On the other hand, the role of FDI promotion policies is to improve the image of the country as an R and D location and to provide targeted services to both potential and existing foreign investors in R and D. In most countries, these kinds of policies are implemented by state-owned investment promotion agencies. The positive impact of FDI promotion policies can also be indirect, through its policy advocacy role by guiding policy reform programs towards the dynamic needs of MNCs.

When designing targeted strategies to promote R and D-intensive FDI, policymakers are confronted with the challenge of selecting the most appropriate policy mix to improve the location's attractiveness and to promote and embed the R and D of MNCs, considering the country's stage of development and institutional profile.

Specific government actions should follow from an intelligence gathering and technology foresight exercise in continuous dialogue with the private sector and the managers of existing MNC subsidiaries.

But determining the optimal policy mix is a very difficult task because it involves different government departments and agencies and because the relative efficiency of the different policy instruments is uncertain ex ante and hard to evaluate ex post. Some of the policy instruments may have a short term impact, such as fiscal and financial R and D incentives, while others such as improving the education system will only have visible effects in the long run after sustained investments.

Despite large differences, a common characteristic of the most successful countries following FDI-assisted development strategies is that they have sought to attract FDI but also to develop and upgrade domestic capabilities and location advantages in tandem.

Table 1. National policies to attract R and D-intensive FDI

Policy domain	Key policy instruments
Innovation policies	• Public R and D, universities, and scientific infrastructure • Human capital and attraction of foreign talent • Fiscal and financial incentives to corporate R and D • Clusters and linkages • Intellectual property rights regime
FDI policies	• FDI incentives and performance requirements • International marketing • Pre-investment and after-care services to foreign investors • Policy advocacy

Source: Adapted from Guimón, 2009.

The upgrading efforts require "system coordination initiatives" to improve the education system, infrastructures, and institutions, as illustrated with the case of the electronics industry in Malaysia (Rasiah, 2002).

3.1. The Case of Ireland

Ireland represents one of the most evident examples of successful FDI-assisted development. From 1995 to 2007 average annual GDP growth reached 6%, significantly above the rest of EU and OECD countries. Although there are many reasons explaining the Celtic Tiger's impressive growth, top among them has been its success in attracting FDI. However, in 2008 the Irish economy entered into a deep recession and as a consequence government finances are now under great stress, following massive banking bailouts and financial assistance received from the EU and the IMF. Despite the severe macroeconomic effects of the financial crisis, Ireland has managed to continue attracting large flows of FDI in recent years (Brennan and Verma, 2013).

The Irish government started to promote FDI proactively in the early 1970s, and from the mid-1980s it has sought to develop strong industrial clusters based on FDI in key high-technology, high growth industries (Ruane and Buckley, 2006). This included the computer industry, pharmaceuticals, and medical technology, followed later by international services. Thanks to its low corporate tax rate (12.5%) and to its well educated workforce, Ireland successfully became an attractive export-platform within the EU Single Market, especially suited for US multinationals given the common language and cultural ties.

Following an initial focus on employment-intensive manufacturing projects, in recent years the focus of FDI policies has turned to promoting the R and D activity of multinational companies, encompassing massive investments in education and scientific infrastructure, generous fiscal and financial incentives to FDI in R and D, a strong promotion of university-industry collaboration, and new forms of public-private partnerships for strategic priority setting and international promotion.

As in all other European countries, significant resources have been put to promoting R and D through investments in public research centers, technology clusters and R and D funding programs. The difference is that Irish efforts have been very tightly linked to the needs of multinational corporations.

Indeed, as the country sought to specialize in high technology sectors and higher value added activities, it made strong efforts to upgrade domestic capabilities to enable this transition by investing consistently in education and technological infrastructure. In particular, Irish education policy has been highly active in addressing the skill needs of foreign investors through a binary system of universities providing academic training and institutes of technology providing technical skills in key disciplines. As a result, the country holds amongst the highest share of young science and engineering graduates in Europe. Ireland has also successfully attracted talented scientists from abroad, offering attractive working conditions and flexible immigration procedures.

A National Technology Foresight exercise in 1998 identified ICT and biotechnology as key enabling technologies of the future, and based on this the government established Science Foundation Ireland (SFI) in 2000, modeled on the US National Science Foundation, to attract world-class research in these areas (Harris, 2006).

Recent initiatives include the Centers for Science, Engineering, and Technology (CSET) program, which connects researchers in academia and industry through grants worth as much as 20 million euro over 5 years, renewable for an additional term of up to 5 years. This kind of programs has encouraged MNC subsidiaries to engage in R and D in cooperation with universities and public research centers. Moreover, in addition to the low general corporate tax rate, in 2004 a 20% tax credit for incremental R and D was introduced, and the country also offers tax deductions for income related to patent licensing.

In parallel, the Irish government's investment promotion agency, IDA Ireland, collaborates closely with existing multinational subsidiaries offering tailored support services and financial assistance to encourage them to expand their R and D activities in the country. Every foreign subsidiary has one direct project manager and close links have been forged with the managers of MNC subsidiaries in order to facilitate their expansion and upgrading. IDA Ireland has introduced new screening systems to rate the potential for R and D expansion of the existing base of MNC subsidiaries based on different qualitative measures, in order to determine the level of "aftercare" services and incentives to offer. For the firms with the highest rankings, IDA Ireland performs a more detailed analysis of what could be done to enhance their R and D activities. Moreover, IDA Ireland has become directly involved in building new R and D infrastructure to address the needs of MNC subsidiaries. For example, in 2005 it dedicated 70 million euro to the creation of the National Institute of Bioprocessing Research and Training (NIBRT), its most costly project of that year. IDA Ireland saw bioprocessing as a strategic industry where existing MNC subsidiaries had the potential to upgrade their R and D activity, and saw the necessity to create this research and training centre in order to stimulate the upgrading process. This is a rare role for an investment promotion agency and a clear manifestation of how FDI policies and innovation policies become more closely interconnected when the focus is on attracting R and D-intensive FDI.

Ireland has a long record of successfully framing its national policies to match the current and potential needs of multinational companies with its national industrial development goals. The country reacted fast to the opportunities of specializing in new industry sectors and trends, providing Ireland with a "first-mover advantage" during the years of fast globalization that may now be hard to replicate by other countries.

4. THE GROWING ATTRACTIVENESS OF DEVELOPING COUNTRIES

In recent years global R and D networks are becoming more multi-polar, with an increasing relevance of developing countries both as destinations and as sources of R and D-intensive FDI. For example, according to data from the US Bureau of Economic Analysis, R and D expenditures of US MNCs' foreign affiliates outside Canada, Europe and Japan grew from 18% of the total in 2004 to 21% in 2008, with China's share almost doubling (from 2.2% to 4.1%). This shows that developing countries still account for a small - but increasing - share of R and D performed by MNCs.

Table 2 shows the geographical distribution of new investments by multinational companies in creating or expanding R and D centers abroad, from 2003 to 2010[1].

---

[1] The source is the fDi Markets database, which comprises greenfield FDI project announcements, excluding M and As. The data is compiled by the Financial Times Group through global, national and regional media; financial

Table 2. Distribution by region of inward R and D-intensive FDI (2003-2010)

	Number of FDI in R and D projects	Percentage of world total	Percentage of total FDI projects
Asia-Pacific	987	43.4	13.8
Western Europe	566	24.9	2.3
North America	289	12.7	7.1
Middle East	209	9.2	1.3
Rest of Europe	132	5.8	0.8
Latin America and Caribbean	68	3.0	1.3
Africa	24	1.1	0.1
World total	2275	100	2.1

Source: Author's calculations based on fDi Markets database, last accessed March 30, 2011.
Note: Based on number of greenfield FDI announcements per sector where the main business activity is R and D, without considering the quantity of the investment. MandAs are excluded.

During this period there were a total of 2275 announcements of new FDI in R and D projects in the world, out of which 43 percent were located in Asia-Pacific. Western Europe attracted almost 25 percent of all new FDI in R and D projects during that period, while the share of North America was around 13 percent. The table also indicates the share of R and D projects in total inward FDI by region. For example, in Western Europe around 2.3 percent of all new FDI projects were directly related to R and D, while in the rest of Europe the share was below 1 percent.

The large share of Asia-Pacific in global FDI in R and D flows (43%) can be largely ascribed to the increasing attractiveness of China and India. The number of R and D centers owned by foreign MNCs rose from only 100 in each of the two countries in 2001 to 1100 in China and 780 in India by the end of 2008 (Bruche, 2009).

According to Jaruzelski and Dehoff (2008) eighty-three percent of all new R and D sites opened between 2004 and 2007 by the largest 1000 MNCs by R and D expenditure were located in China or India.

The increasing attractiveness of China and India for international investment in innovation reflects that these are the largest countries in the world by population and among the countries with the highest economic growth during the last two decades. Indeed, they have opened up to the world economy and liberalized international capital flows only very recently. These factors have transformed them in the "hot spots" for international investment. Moreover, China and India have substantially expanded their pools of scientific, engineering, and math skills and are steadily increasing both their public and private R and D (Chen, 2008; Yusuf, 2012). This has enabled their specialization in manufacturing and other activities like business process outsourcing to evolve towards more knowledge intensive segments of corporate value chains, including R and D.

---

information providers (such as Reuters); corporate websites; and government websites. Despite its limitations, this is one of the few sources to identify R and D-intensive FDI projects, because it provides information not only of the sector but also of the business activity associated with each investment announcement. By selecting only the FDI projects where the business activity is R and D the flows of R and D-intensive FDI can be proxied.

In the words of Yusuf (2012), "multinational corporations are diversifying their R and D operations and transferring more of their research activities to emerging economies in order to capitalize on the elastic supply of skills and on expanding market opportunities".

In addition, this process is being supported by the development of local institutions and the adoption of a proactive policy approach to attracting R and D-intensive FDI. For example, the governments of China and India have used their large market size and attractiveness as a bargaining tool and they have coordinated procurement and technology policies with approvals for foreign investment in order to increase local capabilities (Huggins et al., 2007). They have actively encouraged foreign investors in manufacturing to open up R and D centers as well.

According to World Bank (2010), besides China and India, the main destinations for R and D-intensive FDI in developing countries are Brazil, the Czech Republic, Hungary, Malaysia, Russia and Thailand. In many cases, FDI in large-scale manufacturing activities (market-seeking or efficiency-seeking) naturally evolved over time to also include some extent of knowledge-intensive and R and D activities (competence-exploiting), like in the case of the automotive industry in Brazil or the electronics industry in China.

However, many other developing countries lack the large and dynamic markets that countries like China, India or Brazil can use as a bargaining tool to attract the R and D of MNCs, and they also lack the technological infrastructure, human capital and specialized clusters that MNCs are looking for when deciding where to locate their international R and D centers. Indeed, although the emerging new geography of corporate R and D is becoming more multi-polar, this does not necessarily imply that it will be inclusive. Competition is strong and countries that fail to raise their technological capabilities in line with MNC needs risk becoming marginalized from global innovation networks.

In general, developing countries are more likely to attract demand-driven or efficiency-seeking rather than supply-driven R and D, given their lower technological capabilities relative to the most technologically advanced developed countries. Demand-driven and efficiency-seeking R and D subsidiaries tend to focus initially in lower-end and routine R and D activities (Manning et al., 2008). Along these lines, Thursby and Thursby (2006) show that the kind of R and D activities by MNCs in emerging countries normally entails familiar science (i.e. applications of science currently used by the firm and/or its competitors) rather than new science (i.e. novel applications of science), which remains concentrated in the core developed countries. Similarly, Puga and Trefler (2010) suggest that developing economies normally engage initially only in incremental (rather than radical) R and D, related to addressing production-line bugs and suggesting minor product improvements. But these lower-end R and D activities may act as a seed in the sense that they may enable with time a shift towards higher value adding R and D activities following learning and competence building in the subsidiaries (Chaminade and Vang, 2008; Medcof, 2007). Indeed, the developmental impact of demand-driven and efficiency-seeking R and D should not be neglected. Rather, such R and D activities should be seen as an invaluable opportunity for an evolutionary upgrading of technological capabilities. Beyond mere adaptation of existing products and processes, another possible demand-driven motivation which is gaining importance in recent years is related to the design of new products for low cost manufacturing, in order to tap into the vast market of low income customers who cannot afford products such as refrigerators, washing machines, or cars within the range of existing high-end options designed for the middle classes of developed countries (Eyring et al., 2011).

5. THE CHALLENGE OF BUILDING KNOWLEDGE-INTENSIVE LINKAGES AROUND FDI IN DEVELOPING COUNTRIES

Building a dynamic national innovation system where universities and public research institutes collaborate with firms is critical to attract R and D-intensive FDI and to capture the associated knowledge spillovers. Indeed, the opportunities for upgrading and the benefits for the host country are magnified when MNC subsidiaries become embedded in the domestic milieu by collaborating with local firms, universities or business associations. The role of governments as linkage facilitators and skills coordinators is not limited to promoting linkages between MNCs and domestic suppliers or partners; it should extend further to linkages with universities and public research centers. This includes joint-research projects as well as subcontracting of certain research activities. Universities and public research centers also offer MNCs technical services for testing and consultancy.

However, there are many challenges involved in establishing knowledge-intensive linkages between MNCs and local actors, and even in some of the most successful technological clusters in developing countries like Bangalore, linkages of MNC subsidiaries and local firms or universities remain ill-developed (D'Costa, 2006). A typical challenge is that there are existing local firms which, while in the appropriate industry, do not currently meet the quality and reliability requirements of MNCs.

Thus policies to upgrade reliability and quality in local firms are of critical importance. As multinationals seek to rationalize their activities, they are increasingly adopting global sourcing strategies to rely on a handful of strategic partners to provide inputs to their global value chains, rather than on different suppliers in each individual country, especially for higher value added, strategic inputs. Therefore governments of developing countries should aim at creating incentives for the MNC to consider local partners, and not expect linkages to occur naturally.

Indeed, as argued in Section 2, a threshold level of absorptive capacity is required in order to engage into knowledge-intensive linkages with MNCs. In the absence of high quality human capital, research institutions and clusters of innovative firms, knowledge linkages between MNCs and local actors will tend to be irrelevant. The case of Costa Rica is useful to illustrate the global-local frictions inherent in attracting FDI and building knowledge-intensive linkages and dynamic local clusters around MNCs in developing country settings.

5.1. The Case of Costa Rica

Since the 1990s, Costa Rica has been very successful in attracting FDI and using it as a lever of structural change to specialize in high-technology, high-growth industries. The big quantitative and qualitative jump came in 1996 when Intel announced a US$300 million investment into the establishment of a microchip export-oriented factory in the country. This was followed by other FDI projects in that industry as well as in other high technology industries.

Costa Rica offered attractive conditions for foreign investors given its political and macroeconomic stability; geographic position; incentives to FDI; low corporate tax rate; quality of life; etc.

The incentives and public services provided to FDI through the Free Trade Zones program had a strong contribution to the attraction of large manufacturing plants of multinational companies oriented to exports of high technology products (PROCOMER, 2011).

FDI contributed to diversifying the economy out of primary products (coffee, bananas, sugar), textiles and apparel towards electronics, software, medical devices and logistics. The government successfully implemented targeted FDI policies reflecting national developmental priorities, negotiating firm-level packages and deploying specific industrial policies to promote productive linkages (Mortimore and Vergara, 2004). These proactive FDI attraction policies were supported by CINDE, a private-public agency with the national mandate of promoting FDI.

Despite the incontestable benefits of FDI for Costa Rica in terms of employment generation, diversification and economic growth, the spillovers from FDI have been weak because of limited linkages between multinational subsidiaries and local firms. Some studies show signs of a dual development of foreign-owned and national firms, and to a crowding-out effect of local firms. For example, Paus and Gallagher (2008) argues that there have been some positive spillovers from FDI through the training, education, and demonstration channels, but spillovers via backward linkages have been relatively small. Sanchez-Ancochea (2006) shows that local purchases as a percentage of total exports of multinational plants located in Costa Rican free trade zones (FTZ) decreased from around 10% in 1994 to less than 3% in 2001, a much lower figure than in countries like Korea and Taiwan, and a revised analysis by OECD (2012) does not show any significant progress during the last decade. Nicholson and Sahay (2007) suggests a crowding-out effect of FDI on local firms, especially through the labour market. The number of new jobs created by FDI rose from 7,758 in 2003-05 to 34,385 in 2009-11 (OECD, 2012), for a country with a labor force of just around 2.2 million people. Indeed, the evidence suggests that multinational subsidiaries were able to recruit trained software staff from other local firms, which together with the shortage of skilled workers in the industry led to an increase in salaries and a growing difficulty of local firms to match the conditions offered by multinationals.

According to OECD (2012) "In general, local industry is lagging, and MNCs tend to rely on local suppliers mostly for low-hand services such as security, cleaning or packaging. Even though there are interesting examples of domestic companies working as suppliers for MNCs this is not a common feature of the system and there is much room for improving the linkages between FDI and the domestic economy" (...) "On the other hand, foreign companies have demonstrated little interest to develop a network of local suppliers, for reasons of economies of scale, trust and quality control".

Against this background, the government of Costa Rica has made significant attempts to promote linkages and spillovers, for example through the Costa Rica Provee program, launched in 2001. The aim of this program was to identify potential national suppliers and turn them into actual input suppliers of multinational subsidiaries. Recent evaluations of this program (PROCOMER, 2011; Vargas et al., 2010) show that it has reached significant success and continues to expand. The number of local suppliers included in the program grew from 36 in 2004 to 573 in 2010, comprising a wide array of sectors, such as metals, plastics, equipment, packaging, software and services. Up to 2010, the program has promoted new orders worth USD 37 million made by 248 exporting companies to 331 local suppliers (PROCOMER, 2011).

This figure does not include subsequent orders placed; if we include these the figure would reach around USD 840 million for 2002-2009 (Vargas et al., 2010). Despite the difficulties of evaluating this type of programs, one more sign of success is that during the 2000s Costa Rica has improved its position relative to other countries in indicators of quantity and quality of suppliers comprised in global competitiveness rankings. For example, Costa Rica's position in the 'quality of local suppliers' index of the World Economic Forum's global competitiveness report improved significantly (from 44 in 2001 to 28 in 2010), while its position in the 'quantity of local suppliers' index improved from 55 to 44.

Since 2011, targeted FDI promotion efforts have focused on four strategic sectors: Life Sciences, Advanced Manufacturing, Services and Clean Technologies-Renewable Energy. Existing multinational subsidiaries have progressively upgraded their operations in the country, moving towards more knowledge-intensive activities within their industries. For example, Intel, which focussed initially only in manufacturing, has recently opened an engineering centre with around 300 employees dedicated to the design, development and testing of semiconductors. Beyond basic technical support and customer service centers, companies like Microsoft, Oracle, Avionics, HP, among others, have recently opened new R and D sites in the country. To support this process, the government is designing new programs to promote private sector R and D, to improve the dynamism of local clusters, and to improve the quantity and quality of highly skilled employees.

As foreign companies upgrade their activities in the country, new opportunities will become available for developing knowledge-intensive local linkages, but these will only materialize if local firms and research institutions manage to to raise their technological capabilities in tandem and to match the quality requirements of MNCs.

6. POLICY OPTIONS FOR DEVELOPING COUNTRIES

The scope of FDI policies changes throughout the different stages of a country's investment development path (IDP). The IDP envisages economic development as a succession of structural changes and contends that such economic and social transformations have a systematic relationship with the behavior of inward and outward FDI (Dunning, 1981; Dunning and Narula, 1996).

The first stage of the IDP reflects the situation in most of the least developed countries, where both inward and outward FDI are very small, often due to the combination of a limited domestic market, lack of infrastructures, low-skilled labor force and inappropriate institutions and government policies. In this context, the main role of governments is to set up the basic legal and commercial institutions and infrastructure. In the second stage of the IDP, inward FDI starts growing thanks to the development of some location specific advantages that raise the country's attractiveness to MNCs. The kind of FDI attracted is usually related to natural resource-seeking or market-seeking motivations, sometimes involving labor-intensive manufacturing. Governments normally focus on improving the business climate and attracting as much FDI as possible through deregulation, liberalization of capital flows and privatization of state-owned enterprises.

In the following stages, the quantity and quality of inward FDI increase progressively, and outward FDI also starts to grow as domestic firms build ownership advantages.

Progression through the investment development path can be conceptualized as a learning process that involves developing domestic capabilities in an appropriate sequence that creates the conditions to attract higher value-adding FDI. As countries reach a threshold level of institutions, infrastructures and technological capabilities, governments need to provide a more active kind of support through industrial and innovation policies (Narula and Dunning, 2010). This normally entails developing and fostering specific industries and technological trajectories, such that the location advantages they offer are less generic and more specific, and such that they attract high value adding activities of MNCs. In a way, this involves a shift in FDI policies, focusing more on the *quality* rather than only the *quantity* of FDI (Guimón and Filippov, 2012) and it requires a more proactive kind of policy intervention, unlike generic FDI policies which can rely largely on investment liberalization and macroeconomic stability, along with marketing and promotion.

Thus, attracting R and D-intensive FDI can be interpreted as an evolutionary and sequential process following the development of local capabilities. The objective guiding FDI policies would be to progressively attract higher value adding segments of corporate value chains, a key component of which are R and D activities. Initially, the kind of R and D being attracted will be local and incremental in scope, motivated by demand-driven or efficiency-seeking strategies. But with time these R and D mandates might expand to more sophisticated, supply-driven activities following local learning and capabilities development. This may culminate in a self-reinforcing process where dynamic and innovative clusters emerge through the upgrading of local capabilities and MNC subsidiaries' mandates in tandem, and where the subsidiaries become simultaneously deeply integrated within the MNC global structure and deeply embedded within the domestic innovation system; a situation that has been defined as dual embeddedness (Meyer et al., 2011).

To conclude, we summarize below some possible options that should be in the radar of developing country governments' aiming to attract and embed R and D-intensive FDI. In any case, governments of developing countries should set realistic targets to guide their policies by coupling their country's potential location advantages with the dynamics of global innovation networks.

Attracting R and D-intensive FDI is not an easy task because it requires advanced technological infrastructure and capabilities and because competition among countries is becoming more intense, within a context of continuous restructuring and segmentation of global value chains.

I) Public R and D, Universities, and Scientific Infrastructure

A key challenge for developing countries is to strengthen their universities and public research institutes by recruiting adequate staff and providing them with adequate funding and equipment to carry out R and D and provide postgraduate education in science and technology subjects, which is a necessary condition for promoting private investment in R and D. It is critical that public R and D centers comply with the standard requirements of MNCs.

For example, Russia is known for holding high quality R and D centers, but they often lack the quality assurance, accreditations and experience with contractual research that enables the formation of linkages with MNCs (Narula and Jormanainen, 2008).

In addition to universities and public R and D labs, science and technology parks may be attractive for MNCs as they facilitate networking with other firms and research centers, provide the necessary infrastructure and administrative support, and offer a pleasant working and living environment. Thus a possible policy instrument to attract R and D-intensive FDI is to offer "research hosting" services to foreign firms through science and technology parks, which may include subsidized office space, access to R and D infrastructure and equipment, administrative services, and support in applying for R and D incentives.

II) Human Capital

The availability of world-class scientists and engineers is another critical location driver for R and D-intensive FDI. This calls for policies to increase the number of scientists and engineers by encouraging the younger generations to choose a career in science and engineering, by offering grants and increasing the budgets of universities and research centers, and by facilitating the exchange of researchers between the public and the private spheres and the mechanisms for life-long learning.

Innovation requires not only engineers and scientists, but rather a broad range of qualifications, including technicians, administrative staff and skilled workers. Tertiary education institutions should focus on all of these different levels, and specific programs should be developed in the appropriate industries and specializations for which demand exists, in addition to generic subject areas. Policymakers should aim at addressing innovation skills gaps across these different levels.

Building a strong human capital base is not only about growing indigenous talent, but also about attracting and retaining talent.

Thus the inflow of highly-skilled researchers from abroad should be facilitated, in order to enlarge the home talent base and to enable flexible intra-firm employee mobility as demanded by foreign investors.

This can be encouraged through different policies, such as making the conditions of local researchers and university professors more attractive to foreign candidates; reforming the immigration legislation and procedures; reducing income taxation for high-skilled immigrants; or facilitating the accreditation of foreign qualifications. For example, many countries, such as Germany, Spain and the UK, have recently introduced fast track visa procedures for highly skilled immigrants and intra-company transfers.

Policy initiatives should also be directed towards providing incentives for the return of national researchers located abroad, with the aim of transforming the original brain drain into a brain circulation with benefits for the national innovation system.

Moreover, building linkages with the diaspora of national scientists and business managers working in foreign countries may be a useful mechanism for investment promotion purposes, as demonstrated by the successful experience of China and India in this front. Similarly, in Chile, an initiative called Chile Global[2] was established to create a network of successful Chilean businessmen abroad aimed at promoting knowledge-intensive businesses and partnerships, enhancing technological transfer, and increasing the supply of investment projects.

---

[2] http://www.chileglobal.net.

III) Financial and Fiscal Incentives to Business R and D

Fiscal incentives consist in a favorable tax treatment to R and D expenditure and may take the form of accelerated depreciation, tax holidays, tax credits or import tariff exemptions, while financial incentives refer to the direct funding of business R and D projects by the government through grants or subsidies, preferential loans (including interest allowances) or equity stakes.

The specialized literature suggests that incentives can influence the final R and D location decision when competing locations rate similarly in the rest of attraction factors (OECD, 2011). In any case, incentives cannot compensate for a country's weaknesses in other more important location factors such as the quality of universities and the availability of well trained engineers and scientists. During the last years there has been a widespread increase in the use by governments of incentives to corporate R and D, including in many developing countries like Brazil, India, Malaysia, Mexico and South Africa (UNCTAD, 2005). However, incentives should be offered cautiously, after carefully considering the potential spillovers and linkages and how these translate to actual benefits for the host economy.

A first obvious policy to promote R and D-intensive FDI is the non-discrimination of foreign-owned firms against local firms in national technology programs and R and D funding. In terms of governance, most countries have set up public agencies to distribute R and D incentives to business, and investment promotion agencies only inform foreign investors of the incentives available but lack any control over incentives themselves. However, in some countries like Ireland or Singapore investment promotion agencies may negotiate incentives directly with foreign investors in a more tailored and proactive manner.

IV) The Intellectual Property Rights Regime

From a headquarter perspective among the main drawbacks of R and D offshoring are the potential loss of control over R and D and the risk of IP theft. Therefore, another priority for governments aiming to attract R and D-intensive FDI is to develop a clear and enforceable intellectual property (IP) regime. Developing countries tend to have weaker IP regimes and judicial systems than developed countries which may act as a barrier for the attraction of certain types of MNC's R and D, as illustrated with the experience of China (Gupta and Wang, 2011).

Beyond regulatory reform, governments of developing countries should also try to ensure that an adequate skill formation in IP is available in the country, for example by sponsoring IP specific seminars and courses, and by identifying specialized law firms and consultants that can be contacted by potential foreign investors.

V) Performance Requirements

Some countries, for example India and China, have applied strict conditions and requirements to FDI in the past, such as the need to establish a joint-venture with a local firm, to engage in local sourcing or to facilitate technology transfer.

But integration into the world economy and into international institutions such as the WTO has attenuated this reliance on performance requirements.

The use of mandatory requirements related to R and D and technology transfer is not prohibited by the WTO Agreement on Trade-related Investment Measures, but it has also become increasingly restricted in international investment agreements (UNCTAD, 2005). The benefits of performance requirements related to R and D are questionable because it is unlikely that firms will establish R and D activities in the absence of a clear business case, and because they may deter firms from investing in the country in other kind of activities if forced to conduct R and D. In any case, mandatory R and D requirements appear to be rare, and it is more common to link R and D criteria to the award of public incentives (UNCTAD, 2005).

VI) After-Care Services and Linkage Development Programs

Typically, investment promotion agencies focus their efforts on marketing and pre-investment services to facilitate the initial investment in the country of foreign MNCs, providing tailored information and assistance in obtaining the necessary permits and applying for incentives. However, investment promotion agencies targeting R and D-intensive FDI need to place a higher emphasis on after-care services, because MNC subsidiaries generally engage in R and D activities sequentially over time rather than overnight through a completely new investment. Along these lines, investment promotion agencies need to evaluate the existing stock of foreign subsidiaries in order to identify specific opportunities for upgrading, which would be followed by enhanced dialogue and collaboration with subsidiary managers and by the offering of customized aftercare services and incentives.

Fiscal and financial incentives to MNCs should be designed in a way that increases the propensity of MNCs to collaborate with other domestic agents in innovative, high value-added activities. In other words, incentives should be linked to aftercare services and MNC-embedding policies. A widely use policy approach consists in linkage programs to support the formation of supplier networks and technology clusters around MNC subsidiaries. As discussed in Section 5, this involves not only information and brokerage services to connect firms together, but also capacity building initiatives to upgrade local firms so that they become better able to meet the requirements of MNCs. The case of Czech Republic is an example of the success of industrial policies aimed at building linkages, through initiatives such as the Supplier Development Programme launched in 1999. Another policy option is to stimulate entrepreneurship through incubation and start up support services with a focus on specific areas that could benefit from the R and D activity of established multinationals. In recent years several countries like Armenia, Chile and Ireland have launched new initiatives along those lines.

ACKNOWLEDGMENTS

This chapter is an output of the author's work as a consultant for the World Bank Institute.

However, the reliability of the data, interpretations and conclusions remains the author's sole responsibility and should not be attributed to the World Bank. Thanks are due to Natalia Agapitova, Bart Kaminski and Shahid Yusuf for useful comments to earlier drafts.

REFERENCES

Archibugi, D. and Pietrobelli, C. (2003). The globalisation of technology and its implications for developing countries: windows of opportunity or further burden?, *Technological Forecasting and Social Change,* 70(9), 861-884.

Barry, F. (2004). Export platform FDI: the Irish experience", *European Investment Bank EIB Papers,* 9(2), 8-37.

Barry, F. (2007). Foreign direct investment and institutional co-evolution in Ireland, *Scandinavian Economic History Review*, 55(3), 262-288.

Bas, C. and Sierra, C. (2002). Location versus home country advantages in R and D activities: Some further results on multinationals' location strategies, *Research Policy*, 31 (4), 589-609.

Brennan, L. and Verma, R. (2013). *Inward FDI in Ireland and its policy context*, Columbia FDI Profiles, March 27, 2013.

Bruche, G. (2009). The emergence of China and India as new competitors in MNCs innovation networks, *Competition and Change*, 13(3), pp. 267-288.

Cantwell, J. and Piscitello, L. (2000). Accumulating technological competence: Its changing impact on corporate diversification and internationalization, *Industrial and Corporate Change,* 9(1), 21-51.

Carlsson, B. (2006). Internationalization of innovation systems: A survey of the literature, *Research Policy*, 35(1), 56-67.

Chaminade, C. and Vang, J. (2008). Globalisation of knowledge production and regional innovation policy: Supporting specialized hubs in the Bangalore software industry, *Research Policy*, 37(10), 1684-1696.

Chen, Y.-C. (2008). Why Do Multinational Corporations Locate Their Advanced R and D Centres in Beijing?, *Journal of Development Studies*, 44(5), pp. 622-644.

Cohen, W. and Levinthal, D. (1989) Innovation and learning: The two faces of R and D, *Economic Journal*, 99(3), 569-596.

D'Costa, A. P. (2006). Exports, University-Industry Linkages, and Innovation Challenges in Bangalore, India. *World Bank Policy Research Working Paper* 3887.

Dorgan, S. (2006). *How Ireland became the Celtic Tiger, The Heritage Foundation*, Backgrounder No. 1945.

Dunning, J. H. (1981). Explaining the international direct investment position of countries: Towards a dynamic or developmental approach, *Weltwirtschaftliches Archiv* 119, 30–64.

Dunning, J. H. and Narula, R. (1996) (Eds.). *Foreign Direct Investment and Governments: Catalysts for Economic Restructuring*, London: Routledge.

Edler, J. (2008). Creative internationalization: widening the perspectives on analysis and policy regarding international R and D activities, *The Journal of Technology Transfer* 33 (4), 337-352.

Eyring, M., Johnson, M. W. and Nair, H. (2011). *New business models in emerging markets*, Harvard Business Review, January-February 2011.

Farole, T. and Winkler, D. (2012). Foreign firm characteristics, absorptive capacity and the institutional framework: The role of mediating factors for FDI spillovers in low- and middle-income countries, *World Bank Policy Research Working Paper 6265*

Florida, R., (1997). The globalization of R and D: results of a survey of foreign-affiliated R and D laboratories in the US, *Research Policy*, 26(1), 85-103.

Fosfuri, A., Motta, M. and Ronde, T. (2001). Foreign direct investment and spillovers from workers mobility, *Journal of International Economics* 53, 205-222.

Görg, H. and Strobl, E. (2001). Multinational companies and productivity spillovers: a meta-analysis, *The Economic Journal*, 111(475), 723–739.

Guimón, J. (2009). Government strategies to attract R and D-intensive FDI, *The Journal of Technology Transfer*, 34(4), pp. 364-379.

Guimón, J. and Filippov, S. (2012). Competing for high-quality FDI: Management challenges for investment promotion agencies, *Institutions and Economies*, 4(2), 25-44.

Gupta, A. K. and Wang, H. (2011). Safeguarding your intellectual property in China, *Business Week*, May 20, 2011.

Huggins, R., Demirbag, M. and Ratcheva, V. I. (2007) Global knowledge and R and D foreign direct investment flows: Recent patterns in Asia Pacific, Europe, and North America, *International Review of Applied Economic*, 21(3), 437-451.

Jaruzelski, B. and Dehoff, K. (2008). *Beyond Borders: the Global Innovation 1000*, Strategy +Business, Issue 54.

Kuemmerle, W. (1999). Foreign direct investment in industrial research in the pharmaceutical and electronics industries: Results from a survey of multinational firms, *Research Policy*, 28(2-3), 179-183.

Manning, S., Massini, S. and Lewin, A. Y. (2008). A dynamic perspective on next-generation offshoring: The global sourcing of science and engineering skills, *Academy of Management Perspectives*, 22(3), 35–54.

Medcof, J. W. (2007). Subsidiary technology upgrading and international technology transfer, with reference to China, *Asia Pacific Business Review* 13(3), 451–470.

Meyer, K. E., Mudambi, R. and Narula, R. (2011). Multinational enterprises and local contexts: the opportunities and challenges of multiple-embeddedness, *Journal of Management Studies,* 48(2), 235-252.

Mortimore, M. and Vergara, S. (2004). Targeting winners: can FDI policy help developing countries industrialize?, *European Journal of Development Research*, 16(3), 499–530.

Narula, R. and Dunning, J. H. (2010). Multinational enterprises, development and globalisation: Some clarifications and a research agenda, *Oxford Development Studies*, 38 (3), 263-287.

Narula, R. and Jormanainen, I. (2008). When a good science base is not enough to create competitive industries: Lock-in and inertia in Russian systems of innovation, *MERIT-UNU Working Papers, 59*.

Nicholson, B. and Sahay, S. (2007). Software Exports Development in Costa Rica: Contradictions and the Potential for Change, *Proceedings of the 9th International Conference on Social Implications of Computers in Developing Countries*, São Paulo.

OECD (2011). Location factors for international investment in innovation: attractiveness for innovation, Paris: Organization for Economic Cooperation and Development.

OECD (2012). Attracting knowledge-intensive FDI to Costa Rica: challenges and policy options, Paris: Organization for Economic Cooperation and Development.
Paus, E. A. and Gallagher, K. P. (2008). Missing Links: Foreign Investment and Industrial Development in Costa Rica and Mexico, *Studies in Comparative International Development*, 43, 53-80.
PROCOMER (2011). *Informe de Balance de las Zonas Francas 2011*, San José: The Foreign Trade Corporation of Costa Rica (PROCOMER).
Puga, D. and Trefler, D. (2010). Wake up and smell the ginseng: International trade and the rise of incremental innovation in low-wage countries, *Journal of Development Economics*, 91, 64-76.
Rasiah, R. (2002). Systemic coordination and the knowledge economy: Human capital development in Malaysia's MNC-driven electronics clusters", *Transnational Corporations*, 11(3), 89-129.
Ruane, F. and Buckley, P. (2006). Foreign direct investment in Ireland: Policy implications for emerging economies, *The World Economy*, 29(11), 1611-1628.
Sachwald, F. (2008). Location choices within global innovation networks: the case of Europe, *Journal of Technology Transfer*, 33(4), 364-378.
Sanchez-Ancochea, D. (2006). Development trajectories and new comparative advantages: Costa Rica and the Dominican Republic under globalization, *World Development* 34(6), 996-1015.
Santangelo, G. (ed.) (2005). Technological change and economic catch-up. *The role of science and multinationals*. Cheltenham: Edward Elgar.
Schmitz, H. and Strambach, S. (2009). The organizational decomposition of innovation and global distribution of innovative activities: insights and research agenda, *International Journal of Technological Learning, Innovation and Development*, 2(4), 231-247.
Smith, K. (2000). Innovation as a systemic phenomenon: Rethinking the role of policy, *Enterprise and Innovation Management Studies*, 1(1), 73-102.
Thursby, J. and Thursby, M. (2006). Where is the new science in corporate R and D?, *Science*, 314(8), 1547-1548.
UNCTAD (2005). Globalization of R and D and developing countries, *Proceedings of the Expert Meeting in Geneva of 24-26 January 2005*, United Nations Conference on Trade and Development: Geneva.
Vargas, T., Céspedes, O., Gonzalez, C., and Ramirez, F. (2010). Evaluación de impacto del proyecto para desarrollar suplidores para empresas multinacionales de alta tecnología en Costa Rica, Multilateral Investment Fund, Inter-American Development Bank
World Bank (2010). Innovation policy: a guide for developing countries, Washington D.C.: The World Bank Institute.
Yusuf, S. (2012). The Changing Geography of Innovation, the Current Crisis, and Implications for Economic Growth, *The Growth Dialogue, Policy Brief* No. 3-2012

In: Foreign Direct Investment (FDI)
Editors: Enzo Guillon and Lucas Chauvet

ISBN: 978-1-62808-403-0
© 2013 Nova Science Publishers, Inc.

Chapter 7

THE IMPACT OF CORRUPTION ON THE TIMING AND MODE OF ENTRY BY U.S. FIRMS IN CHINA

Rossitza B. Wooster[*] *and Jacob Billings*
Department of Economics, Portland State University,
Portland, Oregon, US

ABSTRACT

This chapter investigates the factors that determine U.S. firms' expansion strategies with respect to the timing and resource commitment in China between 1980 and 2005. We collect a new firm-level, cross-industry sample to document when and how firms invest. We find that earlier entry is undertaken by firms with larger advertising expendituresand ones that are more labor intensive. Additionally, investments by firms with high RandD expenditures occur in the later years.We analyze the role of corruption using three popular indexes: The World Bank's Worldwide Governance Indicators Project (1996-2005), Transparency International's corruption perceptions index (1980-2005), and Political Risk Services Group's quality of government index (1984-2005). We find evidence to support the hypothesis that higher corruption levels delay firms' entry and discourage high-equity commitment.

Keywords: Foreign Direct Investment; China;

I. INTRODUCTION

The speed and scope of globalization in the past two decades has generated increased public interest in the foreign direct investment (FDI) decisions of multinational firms. The

---

[*] Contact Author.We are deeply grateful for assistance from Donna L. Paul with obtaining firm-level financial data for the sample constructed and used in this chapter. We also thank Jordan C. Perry and Silvia Tanner for excellent research assistance. Wooster acknowledges financial support through the Faculty Enhancement Program with the Office of the Provost for Research and Sponsored Projects at PortlandStateUniversity. E-mail: wooster@pdx.edu, PH: 503.725.3944

importance of multinationalinvestment activity to the world economy is evident in its contribution to economic growth. According to the United Nations Commission on Trade and Development, gross product attributed to an estimated 79,000 multinational firms worldwide and their 790,000 foreign affiliates accounted for 11% of global GDP in 2007 (UNCTAD, 2008). In addition, through their operations in foreign host countries, MNEs often serve as powerful agents of technological, institutional, and political change (Dicken, 1998; Agmon, 2003). In light of this, it is not surprising that there is a voluminous body of theoretical and empirical literature on the determinants, magnitude, and effects of FDI. However, much of the empirical research relies on aggregate country and industry data and applies these within a partial or general equilibrium framework to analyze FDI activity.[1] In contrast to the expansive literature on aggregate determinants of FDI, empirical evidence on the firm characteristics affecting the timing and level of equity commitment decisions of firms investing in foreign markets is relatively sparse. This is due primarily to the lack of cross-industry, firm-level, data that document where, when, and how firms expand into foreign markets. Where available, such data are often proprietary or not comprehensive enough to analyze all aspects of firms' expansion strategies. As a result, there is a dearth of empirical analyses of companies' expansion strategies in China. Our contribution is to fill this gap in the empirical literature byproviding evidence on: (i) investment patterns of U.S. firms in China between 1980 and 2005; and (ii) the role corruption plays in determining the timing of investments and the level of equity commitment. Regarding the patterns of entry, we document when and how U.S.publicly traded companies have made capital investments in Chinaby hand-collecting announcements of such investments from 1980 through 2005. We then use this sample totest hypotheses for the firm- and country-level characteristics that affect the timing of investment and choice of entry-mode by U.S. firms in Chinaover this time period. The results show that both firm- and province-level factors influence the timing of entry into China and the level of equity commitment by U.S. companies. Firms with greater advertising intensity invest in China earlier in time, consistent with the aggressive pursuit of market share as a motive for early entry. Thus, early entry can be viewed as a response to intra-industry rivalry. Additionally, and consistent with anecdotal evidence, firms that are more labor intensive moved into China earlier in the sample period whereas investments by firms with high RandD expenditures tend to occur in the later years. With respect to the role of corruption, our results support the hypothesis that a perception of higher corruption acts as a deterrent to entry as well as an incentive to initially expand through representative offices (low-equity) as opposed to acquisitions, new plants, and wholly owned operations that entail a high levels of equity commitment. The rest of this chapter is structured as follows. Section II reviews the literature and develops testable hypotheses. Section III describes the sample and provides a univariate analysis of entry patterns. Section IV presents the empirical framework while section V documents the results. Section VI concludes and discusses future research.

II. BACKGROUND AND TESTABLE HYPOTHESES

In recent years, the emergence of China as a major trading power in the world economy has placed an increased interest in country-specific analyses of foreign direct investment

---

[1] For a good review of recent literature see Blonigen (2005)

(FDI) choices in China. FDI patterns in Chinaprovide a natural context within which to analyze foreign location strategies of multinational firms. Specifically, the economic liberalization reforms that began with China's "open door" policy in 1979allowed many western investors to expand eastward through joint ventures and acquisitions or wholly owned subsidiaries. Such forms of FDI allowed multinational firms to access new markets, natural resources and, most importantly, reduce production costs. However, the political and economic uncertainty associated with market-oriented policies in China also created an investment environment characterized by uncertainty with respect to the viability and profitability of investments. We therefore investigate the timing and equity commitment decisions by U.S. firms in China accounting for both the characteristics of the firms and the characteristics of the location where firms set up their operations.

A. Firm-Level Characteristics as Determinants of Investment Patterns in China

Empirical studies of Chinese aggregate FDI flows are numerous but shed little light on firm-level investment choices. An exception perhaps is Shapiro *et al.* (2007) who create a firm-level dataset using various Chinese sources and agencies to gather information on foreign investments over the period 1989-1999. In general, however, the literature offers several hypotheses about what motivates firms to expand operations abroad. For many firms, the decision to be the first to enter a new emerging market can be influenced by the need to secure market share. The exploitation of global markets creates opportunities to develop dynamic core competences, expand product life cycles, and earn greater returns on innovations (Hitt*et al.*, 1998). Global markets can thus be seen as an extension of domestic markets and consequently, competition for market share abroad becomes an important aspect of firm strategy. In an analysis of U.S. affiliates in Asia, Lipsey (1999) argues that market share considerations are an important motive for expansion in the region, and in particular, China. The specific testable hypothesis regarding the timing of entry in China therefore reflects the expectation that for U.S. companies, competition for market share would emerge as a central expansion motive. Anecdotal evidence suggests that old industry arch-rivals such as The Coca-Cola Company and PepsiCo Inc. view expansion into China as a race for market share(The Washington Post, December 20, 1978). Such strategic rivalry is not unlike recent wars for domination of the Internet in China by rival companies such as Microsoft, Google, and Yahoo (The New York Post, July 20, 2005). From an industrial organization perspective, firms in highly concentrated industries are more likely to expand and compete for market share in international markets (Knickerbocker, 1973). For example, Kogut and Chang (1991) and Yu and Ito (1988) conclude that expansion into foreign markets by Japanese firms is positively related to seller concentration in the home country. Thus, we expect firms with greater advertising intensityto compete more aggressively to secure, maintain, and grow their market share.

H1: *U.S. firms withhigher recent sales growth and greater advertising intensity are likely to expand operations into China earlier in time.*

While early entry may allow firms to capture first mover advantages in relation to their domestic rivals, it is not without cost. Being a first mover implies higher transaction costs as industry leaders in foreign markets encounter greater informational uncertainty. For this reason, some firms might chose to take a "wait-and-see" approach there are significant costs associated with developing capabilities in markets with unfamiliar cultural, linguistic, and demand characteristics (Tihanyi et al., 2005). In this context, Rivoli and Salorio (1996) develop a theoretical framework that shows how ownership and internalization advantages cause firms to delay or even abandon investments in high-risk environments. Since firms with intangible assets are more likely to make irreversible investments, it is reasonable to hypothesize that they would also be more likely to delay entry in China. Using RandD intensity and MTB as proxies for firm-specific assess, the second hypothesis related how firm characteristics determine the timing of entry is:

H2: *U.S. firms with higher RandD intensity and higher MTB are likely to expand operations into China later in time.*

B. Provincial Characteristics as Determinants of Investment Patterns in China

Regarding the general determinants of FDI in China, the literature outlines a number of important variables that influence the timing and choice of equity commitment. For example, Sun et al (2002) find wages, infrastructure, market demand and size, labor quality and cost, political risk, openness to outside trade, and under particular time ranges, GDP, to be important variables, while Quazi (2007) agrees generally, except that significance was not found for human capital (analog to labor quality) or infrastructure. In particular, Quazi found that economic freedom has a large impact on FDI inflows to East Asian countries. Another factor that doesn't seem obvious is the finding by Liu (2008) that Chinese FDI inflow is greater from countries that are not members of the Asia-Pacific Economic Cooperation. Findings for determinants of entry-mode choice are somewhat sparse. Chen (2006) found that firms are more likely to choose greenfield investment when they have a lot of firm-specific assets (such as knowledge) that may be difficult to transfer to an operation already running. Shapiro et al (2007) investigates this question from a slightly different angle, focusing on whether location determinants differ by entry mode. Results show that location choice for equity joint ventures is significantly determined by wage, FDI stock, education, and presence of special economic zones. At the same time, cooperative joint ventures are only significantly determined by economic zones, while for wholly owned enterprises FDI stock is the only significant determinant. Related to the study of locational determinants of FDI into China, a number of papers document findings on important variables such as: proximity to markets and suppliers (Amiti and Javorcki, 2005), governance quality and corruption (Cole et al, 2009), labor quality, economic zones, and distance (Gao, 2005), patent certification volume, share of state-owned business, GDP, wage, and road density (Kawai, 2009). While significance for these variables does not uniformly obtain across studies, expected signs are usually the same.Research on investment timing, at least in China, is even sparserthan that for mode choice. However, one paper by Raff and Ryan (2008) finds various firm characteristics that affect investment timing – size, productivity, and RandD intensity were found to be correlated with a greater eagerness to invest more quickly, while a lack of diversity in a firms product line is associated with a more conservative approach. Overall, we expect that, consistent with market-seeking as a motive for expansion, firms will invest earlier in time and with higher equity commitment in locations where the market size (as measured by GDP per capita) is relatively larger and wages are relatively lower:

H3: *U.S. firms expanding into provinces with relatively higher GDP per capita and relatively higher and relatively lower wages are likely to do so earlier in time and with higher equity commitment.*

C. Corruption as a Determinant of Expansion Patterns in China

Institutional characteristics of host countries are of particular interest in understanding the determinants of FDI. Aizenman and Spiegel (2002) analyze an expert survey-based measure of "institutional efficiency" and its effect on investment composition, and find that the ratio of FDI to domestic investment rises with greater efficiency. Similarly, Benassy-Quere*et al.* (2007) find that "quality of bureaucracy," is an important factor in FDI inflow. More specific research includes the finding by Fung *et al.* (2005) that market reforms, as proxied by proportion of state-owned enterprises in the various Chinese provinces, is a more important determinant, at least in China, of FDI inflow. Hong (2008) finds that accession into the World Trade Organization fundamentally changed the way FDI inflows to China were determined – from high reliance on GDP, university count, and road density, to wage level and agglomeration. One interesting paper by Havrylchyk and Poncet (2007) posits that distortions caused by Chinese policies, in particular state restrictions on credit access and proportion of state-owned banking, can increase FDI inflow, as such institutions can hamper domestic competition more severely than foreign competition. With respect to corruption, there is an almost unanimous agreement in the literature that, in the broadest sense, corruption is a deterrent to foreign investment. Egger and Winner (2006) proposed two opposing forces of corruption, referred to as "grabbing hand" and "helping hand," which deter and encourage investment, respectively. Their finding was that the "grabbing hand" overpowered the "helping hand" and realized an overall deterrence. This general result is obtains in most studies (e.g. Globerman and Shapiro, 2003) that employ corruption measures as an independent variable. Furthermore, Cuervo-Cazurra (2006) finds that not only is corruption in general important, but also the differential in the corruption level between investor country and host country. Interestingly, it turns out that countries which themselves have high levels of corruption send relatively more FDI to high-corruption hosts. Habib and Zurawicki (2002) provide evidence to support this result. In a finer examination specifically on corruption in China, Cole *et al.* (2009) use the number of corruption investigations per capita as a proxy for anti-corruption efforts in the various provinces of China. The authors find a positive correlation between anti-corruption efforts and FDI levels. While corruption investigations may be an unsatisfactory proxy for corruption level, it could easily be argued that it is the *perception* of corruption that affects a firm's willingness to invest, and corruption investigations may have a significant effect on those perceptions. Straub (2008) attempts to find the difference in effect on FDI between bureaucratic and political corruption, vis-à-vis their impact on investment through FDI vs. "arm's length" investment (that is, investment with looser control rights endowed to the investor, like license agreements). The author finds that bureaucratic corruption favors non-FDI investment, but at a magnitude that falls off as the level of corruption increases. Meanwhile, political corruption also favors non-FDI investment, but only very weakly unless interacted with a political risk measure.

Globerman and Shapiro (2003) provide an analysis of how governance and infrastructure affect FDI.This approach takes a broader view, in that it addresses not just corruption, but economic openness, government effectiveness, contract enforcement, and even origin of legal system in FDI host country. The authors use a panel of several countries (instead of just China) and a two stage model; a probit for likelihood of receiving FDI, followed by a regression estimating determinants on amount of FDI received. The general finding is that there is a certain threshold of governance quality below which a host country is unlikely to receive any FDI at all, whereas countries which have received FDI are more likely to see a greater volume accompanying greater economic openness and government effectiveness, and lower corruption. We incorporate these insights in formulating our testable hypothesis related to the effect of corruption on timing and entry-mode decisions:

H4: *Lower levels of corruption are likely to encourage U.S. firms to expand operations into China earlier in time and commit higher level of equity.*

D. What Measure of Corruption?

While it must be agreed that corruption, however defined, is likely to have some effect on economic behavior, deciding to use it as a statistical variable begs the question: how do we measure it? It seems that there are two options facing the researcher. One is to use a proxy variable, as in Cole *et al.*(2009). Their particular method of using number of corruption cases per capita by province is appealing, but presents both theoretical and practical problems. Theoretically, there is the problem of whether to consider a high number of cases a sign of rampant corruption or of a low tolerance of corruption (the paper in question treats it as the latter).

The other option available is a corruption index. There are at least three such indices available, all three of which were utilized during this experiment. The three are as follows: The World Bank's Worldwide Governance Indicators Project (1996-2005), which includes an index measuring "control of corruption," Transparency International's corruption perceptions index (1980-2005), and Political Risk Services Group's quality of government index (1984-2005), which incorporates a corruption measure. It is important to note that all three of these indices are based on surveys given to various experts in economics, politics, and industry, and are thus based on subjective perceptions of corruption rather than direct, tangible measurements. However, if they do accurately measure perceptions of corruption, then they can still be considered useful, as it could be argued that perceptions of corruption are what drive the behavior of firms considering investing, rather than the corruption level itself.

III. SAMPLE CONSTRUCTION, ENTRY PATTERNS, AND DESCRIPTIVE STATISTICS.

A. Sample Construction

Sample construction for this study involved several steps. We begin sample selection by searching the "Directory of American Firms Operating in Foreign Countries," Uniworld Business Publications, Inc. Names of firms with business operations in Chinafrom 1980 to 2005 were obtained from the various editions of the Directories. We search the names of firms in this initial sample to determine which of them are publicly traded, and delete all non-publicly traded firms. We then delete all financial firms, because systematic differences in the nature of their assets render cross-sectional comparisons with industrial firms inappropriate for our study. Finally, we delete firms with missing book value of assets on Compustat, leaving a usable sample of 404 firms. We continue sample construction by searching the *Lexis-Nexis Academic Universe* database for specific announcements of these firm's activities in China from 1980-2005. Specifically, we search for all announcements of unique investments in China by each sample firm. We classify these investments according to their type, that is, whether they are a joint venture, wholly owned subsidiary, acquisition of an existing company, representative office, or large sales/service contract.

B. Entry Patterns

Figure 1 shows the distribution of entry by industry. The manufacturing sector is the most widely represented segment of U.S. publicly traded companies comprising 73% of the sample. The second largest sector is services but it is interesting to note that this sector, while present in China since the early 1980s, did not excel in terms of frequency of observations until after the Asian financial crisis. In our sample, the prevalence of service-sector companies expanding operations in China begins in 1998, possibly encouraged by China's preparations toward WTO accession in 2001, and remains consistently high thereafter. Figure 2 shows the frequency of entry by year. Specifically, since some firms make multiple investments (of various types), the number of observations in each year exceeds the number of unique firms announcing expansion.

Figure 2indicates that while the frequency of entries in the 1980s was relatively low compared to the 1990s, there are a couple of noticeable patterns. First, the frequency of entry declined in the period 1989-1991. This coincided not only with the political instability surrounding the Tiananmen Square incident but also the fall of the Berlin Wall in the former Soviet bloc. The immediate suggestion is that expansion of operations in China during this period may have been, on average, less appealing to U.S. firms given the expansion opportunities made possible in Central and Eastern Europe and the countries of the former Soviet Union. The second noticeable trend in Figure 2 is that the frequency of entry, which peaked in 1995, significantly declined between 1996 and 1999 which coincides with a period of macroeconomic instability in China. In 1995, amid rising inflation, Chinese policymakers engaged in efforts to cool down economic activity which included measures such as restricting lending (New York Times, April 24, 1995).

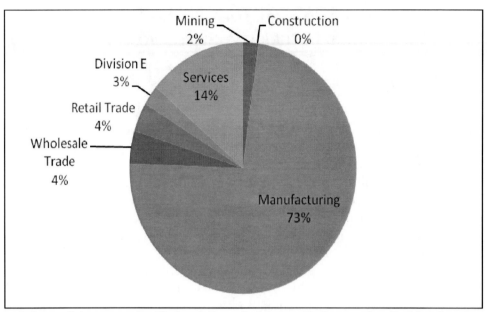

Note: Industry divisions are classified as follows. B: Mining; C: Construction; D: Manufacturing; E: Transportation, Communications and Utilities; F: Wholesale Trade; G: Retail Trade; I: Services.

Figure 1. Industry Distribution of U.S. Firms in China: 1980-2005.

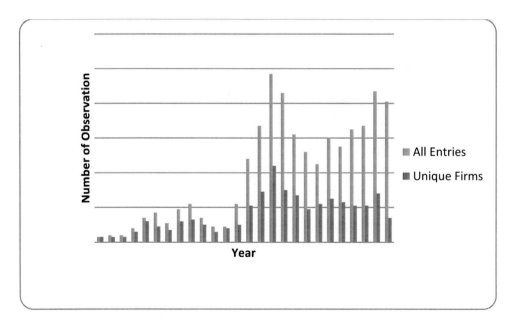

Figure 2. Frequency of Entry by U.S. Firms in China: 1980-2005.

In addition, an important and likely influential event is the 1997 Asian financial crisis. Once again, it is interesting to note that expansion by U.S. companies in transition economies peaked in 1997 for the first time since the euphoria of the early 1990s (see Wooster, 1996).

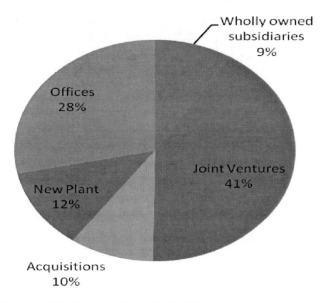

Figure 3. Mode of Entry by U.S. Firms in China: 1980-2005.

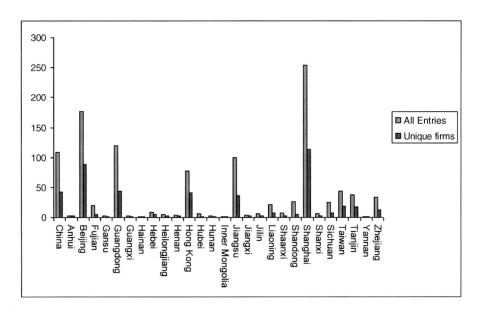

Figure 4. Expansion by U.S. Firms in China by Location: 1980-2005.

Figure 3 documents the mode-of-entry patterns for U.S. firms over the period 1980-2005. Our sample of investment observations contains data on which of five types of investment occurred: wholly owned subsidiary, joint venture, new plant, acquisition, or sales office. An significant portion of investments are made through joint ventures (41%). The People's Republic of China promulgated the Law on Sino-Foreign Joint Ventures in 1979, allowing "foreign companies,other economic entities, or individuals to … [form] joint ventures with Chinese companies or othereconomic entities" (He, 2003). Since the law was enacted in 1983, the number of direct investmentby publically traded U.S. companies has had an overall tendency to increase. The second largest category in terms of entry mode is held by "representative offices" which constitute 28% of the sample. In general, this mode of entry allows companies to set up a "toe-hold" presence and explore the investment environment for further opportunities. High-equity modes other than joint ventures, such as acquisitions, wholly owned subsidiaries, and new plant investments, together comprise 31 % of our sample. Finally, Figure 4 provides a glimpse at the regional distribution of expansion by U.S. firms in our sample. Not surprisingly, the most favored areas are the (administrative) municipalities of Beijing and Shanghai followed by the province of Guangdong which is host toa considerable amount of manufacturing production due to its proximity to Hong Kong (another high frequency destination in our sample). The province of Jiangsu which surrounds the municipality of Beijing is a popular destination due to its proximity to the nation's capitol. In addition, the category "China" captures much of the investment activity that takes the form of large service or sales contacts that constitute nation-wide operations.

C. Descriptive Statistics

All firm-level data is obtained through the Standard and PoorsCompustat database. All province level data is obtained from the China Data Online database which is the online version of the China Statistical Yearbook. The exception to the latter is the information used to construct the special economic zone variable (SEZ), which was sourced from various internet sties. Corruption measures are alternatively from the World Bank Governance Indicators Project, Transparency International, and Political Risk Services Group. Figure 5 provides a comparison of our three corruption measures. It appears at first glance that the three indices exhibit significantly different trends. PRSG essentially has no trend, while the World Bank index has a gentle downward trend, and Transparency International has a slow downward trend until the mid-90s, when it experiences a sharp dropoff, followed by somewhat chaotic swings through to the 2000s. Table 1 provides simple pair-wise correlation coefficients between these measures.

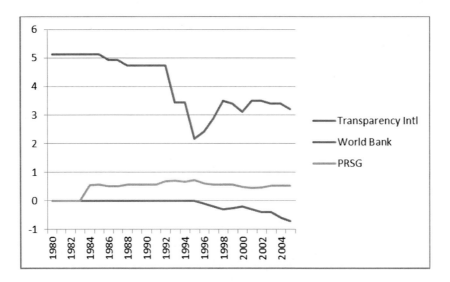

Figure 5. Comparison of Corruption Measures for China: 1980-2004.

Table 1. Correlation Coefficients Corruption Indices: 1980-2004

	TI	PRS	WB
TI	1.0		
PRS	0.2391	1.0	
WB	-0.7274	0.4294	1.0

Table 2. Descriptive Statistics

Variable	Obs.	Mean	Std. Dev.	Min.	Max.
Firm-Level Variables					
Size	423	7.00	1.718	1.447	12.575
Debt	423	0.165	0.163	0	1.159
Market-to-Book	423	2.248	2.589	0.132	34.321
Sales Growth	380	0.176	1.183	-0.977	19.460
RandD	423	0.067	0.108	0	0.880
Advertising	423	0.011	0.026	1.80E-9	0.192
Employees	423	0.007	0.006	9.37E-8	0.049
Province-Level Variables					
Highway Density(de-trended)	331	3.858	1.352	0.348	5.931
Secondary School Enrollment	331	171.193	152.314	2.08	633.96
Rural Electricity Consumption	331	90.898	104.219	7.68	714.25
Wage (de-trended)	331	1.372	0.360	0.030	1.975
GDP per Capita (de-trended)	331	2.591	1.202	0.500	5.72
Corruption Measures					
Corruption Index: World Bank	182	-2.954	0.126	-0.58	-0.1
Corruption Index: PRSG	346	0.578	0.083	0.444	0.722
Corruption Index: Transparency International	297	3.768	0.845	2.43	5.13

Notes: ASSETS is the book value of assets. DEBT is long-term debt scaled by book value of assets. MTB is market value of assets scaled by book value of assets. SALESGROWTH is the growth rate in sales for the prior two years. RandD is research and development expenditure scaled by sales. ADV is advertising expenditure scaled by sales. EMPLOYEES is number of employees scaled by sales.

As can be seen, and noting that all three indices assign a higher score to "better" corruption levels, the three indices that purport to measure roughly the same thing have poor to strikingly bad (i.e. incorrectly signed) correlation. At best this means that only one of them is worth considering, and at worst it means that all three are essentially inappropriate to use, at least without more observations. Furthermore, in the analysis of equity commitment below, we found that both the World Bank's and Political Risk Services Group's indices suffered severe multicollinearity in the probit model, and so had to be dropped in favor of Transparency International's Index.

In the timing of entry regression below, results for all three indices will be presented. Finally, Table 2 provides a summary of descriptive statistics for the remaining variables in our analysis related to firm- and province-level characteristics.

IV. EMPIRICAL FRAMEWORK

We develop two specifications related to the timing-of-entry and likelihood of higher equity commitment. We present these two models below, followed by a discussion of the explanatory variables and their expected signs. The first model is a standard Ordinary Least Squares regression that aims to investigate the effect of national-level corruption in Chinaon the timing of investments in the various Chinese provinces by U.S. firms.

$$ToE = \beta_0 + \beta_1 CORR + \beta_2 SIZE + \beta_3 DEBT + \beta_4 MTB + \beta_5 SALESGR$$
$$+ \beta_6 R\&D + \beta_7 ADV + \beta_8 EMPL + \beta_9 MFG + \beta_{10} WAGE$$
$$+ \beta_{11} GDPCAP + \beta_{12} HIGHWAY + \sum_j \gamma_j (regional\ dummies) + \varepsilon \quad (1)$$

The dependent variable in Equation (1) is the natural logarithm of the number of days that elapsed between January 1, 1980 (our proxy date for when China first opened to foreign investment), and the first investment observed by a sample company in China.

$$MoE = \beta_0 + \beta_1 CORR + \beta_2 SIZE + \beta_3 DEBT + \beta_4 MTB + \beta_5 SALESGR$$
$$+ \beta_6 R\&D + \beta_7 ADV + \beta_8 EMPL + \beta_9 ENROLL + \beta_{10} WAGE$$
$$+ \beta_{11} GDPCAP + \beta_{12} HIGHWAY + \beta_{13} RURALELEC + \beta_{14} SEZ$$
$$+ \sum_j \gamma_j (regional\ dummies) + \sum_k \delta_k (year\ dummies) + \varepsilon \quad (2)$$

The dependent variable in the probit model in Equation (2) takes on the value of 1 if a sample firm is observed making a "high-equity" investment and zero otherwise. The high equity entry modes are as follows: new plants, acquisitions, joint ventures, and wholly-owned subsidiaries. Regional representative offices are regarded as low-equity investments. The first independent variable in Equations (1) and (2), CORR, is a measure of corruption. We separately estimate Equation (1) with the World Bank's Control of Corruption index (from the Worldwide Governance Indicators Project), Transparency International's corruption perceptions index, and Political Risk Services Group's quality of government index which incorporates a corruption measure. We expect an inverse relationship between CORR and the timing of entry as a higher score in all three corruption indexes indicates less corrupt environment which would be predicted to encourage firms to enter earlier in time (lower value for TOE). We also expect that lower corruption would correlate with higher level of equity commitment so that the predicted sign of CORR in Equation (2) is positive. CORR is also our main testing variable for hypothesis H4. The next set of variables capture firm-level characteristics. SIZE is the natural log of book value of assets. DEBT is long-term debt scaled by book value of assets. MTB is market value of assets scaled by book value of assets. Market value of assets is book value of assets minus book value of equity plus the product of closing share price and number of shares outstanding. SALESGR is the growth rate in sales for the prior two years. RandD is research and development expenditure scaled by sales. ADV is advertising expenditure scaled by sales. EMPL is number of employees scaled by sales. The testing variables for hypothesis H1 are sales growth (SALESGR) and advertising intensity (ADV). We expect negative signs on these variables, denoting that higher values are associated with earlier entry.In the context of China, low-cost sourcing as a motive for expansion is also likely to be important, especially for labor-intensive firms. Equation (1) includes employee intensity (EMPL) to capture the extent to which entry motives are efficiency-seeking in addition to market-seeking (Lipsey, 1999; Altomonte, 2000). We also predict a negative sign on the EMPL variable.The test variables for H2are RandD and MTB.We expect positive coefficients on these variables, indicating that firms with greater intangible assets delay entry into an uncertain new business environment. DEBT serves as a control for financial constraints faced by firms at the time they initiate expansion into China. Finally, we include a manufacturing dummy in Equation (1), MFG, to control for whether a firm's operations in China include manufacturing. This dummy takes on the value of 1 if a sample firm undertakes a manufacturing-related investment, and zero otherwise.

Province-level control variables in Equations (1) and (2) include the following. *SEZ*in Equation (2) is a dummy that takes on the value of 1 if at least one Special Economic Zone (SEZ) was present in the province at the time of investment. We expect that SEZ presence will encourage firms to make more high-equity investments as such zones were first established in the 1980s to encourage manufacturing (export-oriented) FDI. Thus the expected sign of this variable's coefficient is positive.[2] In much of previous research, it is standard to include a variable measuring the presence, or number, of Special Economic Zones (which in this chapter refer also to open coastal cities and free trade zones) as a proxy for economic openness of a Chinese province. For example, Fung *et al.* (2005) found that number of such zones is positively correlated to amount of FDI flowing into a province. Enrollment levels in secondary schools, ENROLL, is a standard proxy of human capital and is expected to increase the probability of high-equity investment in Equation (2). In previous literature this measure has been found to have a positive relationship with FDI inflows in general (see for example, Gao, 2005). Highway densityis also a standard control variable, which can serve as a proxy for both infrastructure and ease of commerce. Almost all studies investigating the determinants of FDI include highway density or a similar measure (e.g. rail density) as a control. We expect that highway density will have a negative correlation with timing, and a positive correlation with high equity investment. Note that this variable is de-trended for use in the timing model. RURALELEC measures consumption of electricity in rural areas of the provinces and is used as a proxy for infrastructure. To the best of our knowledge, this variable has not been used in previous literature on FDI determinants in China. We expect that higher values of RURALELEC will increase the likelihood of and high-equity investment in Equation (2). Our testing variables for hypothesis H3 are GDP per capita and WAGES. The former is theoretically linked to greater FDI inflows since this is a widely used measure to proxy for market size. We expect that a relatively GDP per capita will be negatively correlated with timing of entry, and positively correlated with the probability of high-equity investment. Note that the variable is de-trended for use in the timing model. Likewise, WAGES, is an intensity variable which measures the relative wage in a province (calculated as the ration of provincial average for a given year to overall national average). For firms whose expansion into China is motivated by low-cost sourcing, higher relative wages are

---

[2] Throughout the 1990s and especially in the last half of the decade, the Chinese government used the establishment of SEZs to encourage hi-tech, R&D-intensive FDI. This presents a competing hypothesis which would predict that we obtain a negative estimated sign if this effect dominates in our sample.

expected to deter investment and thus the expected sign of this variable in the timing model is positive. Correlation with equity type is a little more difficult to discern. It may be the case that higher wages (and thus greater disposable income) could attract more sales offices, while high-equity export oriented firms may be drawn to low-wage areas. However, consistent with the low-cost sourcing motive for expansion, we predict that that relative wages will be negatively correlated with high-equity investment. Note again that the variable is de-trended for use in the timing model. Last but not least, both models include regional dummies and the equity model includes year dummies to capture unaccounted for macro-economic effects.

V. RESULTS

Table 3 contains OLS regression coefficients for the timing of entry model. Given that the dependent variable is the natural log of the number of days between the firm's first announced entry into China and January 1, 1980, positive (negative) signs on the coefficient estimates indicate later (earlier) entry.The first hypothesis is that early entry is motivated by market seeking motives. Our test variables for market seeking are advertising and sales growth. Table 3 shows a negative and significant coefficient on the advertising intensity variable (ADV). This supports the market seeking hypothesis in that firms with greater advertising invest in China earlier in time. The sign on the sales growth variable (SALESGR), however, is inconsistent with expectations. The positive and significant coefficient suggests that firms with high recent sales growth delay entry into China. While this result is unexpected, one possible explanation may be that firms with higher growth in existing markets are less likely to rush for new investments in China and incur the risk of operating in an uncertain new business environment. The second hypothesis is that the nature of a firm's assets will influence the timing of entry. Specifically, we hypothesize that firms with intangible assets are more likely to make irreversible investments, and thus, will delay their investment in a high-risk environment, waiting until some uncertainties are resolved. The test variables for intangible assets are research and development (RandD) and market to book value of assets (MTB), and we expect positive signs on these coefficients. The coefficient on RandD is positive and significant in models (1) - (3) and the coefficient on the MTB variable is positive but not significant in these models. In the last model which includes the TI corruption measure RandD loses significance and the coefficient on MTB becomes negative. The latter may be partly due to the fact that the TI index is missing observations for 1995-1997 which is the period in our sample in which companies invested with the highest frequency.

Thus, the results lend support for H3 but further investigation is warranted. We also find that the coefficient on the employee variable (EMPL) is negative and significant in models (1) - (3), suggesting cost-cutting motives for entry into China. Indeed, this evidence in consistent with the availability of relatively cheaplabor in China, and the results suggest that labor intensive firms (i.e., firms with high employee intensity) will enter China earlier in time to benefit from relatively lower production costs. The coefficient on financial leverage (DEBT) is positive and significant (although weakly so) in models (10 and (2), indicating that firms with a heavy debt burden are likely to delay entry into a risky investment environment. This significance disappears in models (3) and (4). It can be seen that the addition of any of the corruption variables improves theoverall fit of the models, and all but PRSG are highly significant as predictors, in the expected negative sign (lower corruption correlates with less waiting to invest). The PRSG index, while just outside 10% significance, edges out the others in stability, with no sign changes for significant variables, and all significant variables staying significant. In contrast, the introduction of World Bank's index causes the coefficient of SALESGR to switch from positive and significant to negative and significant. Transparency

Table 3. Timing of Entry into China

	(1) No Corruption	(2) PRSG	(3) World Bank	(4) Transparency Intl.
Intercept	7.821*** (0.239)	8.155*** (0.292)	8.698*** (0.048)	9.662*** (0.660)
CORR	N/A	-0.382 (0.234)	-0.808*** (0.038)	-0.434*** (0.066)
SIZE	-0.006 (0.013)	0.003 (0.009)	0.002 (0.003)	0.019 (0.013)
DEBT	0.199* (0.108)	0.153* (0.088)	0.005 (0.024)	0.012 (0.111)
MTB	0.011 (0.007)	0.006 (0.005)	5.6E-4 (0.001)	-0.002 (0.003)
SALESGR	0.020*** (0.005)	0.017*** (0.004)	-0.003*** (0.001)	0.009 (0.006)
RandD	0.588** (0.237)	0.386*** (0.148)	0.072* (0.037)	0.195 (0.163)
ADV	-3.75*** (1.416)	-2.328*** (0.867)	0.033 (0.189)	-1.585 (1.318)
EMPL	-10.665** (4.394)	-11.236*** (4.031)	-1.337* (0.762)	-3.172 (4.217)
HIGHWAY	0.015 (0.036)	-0.002 (0.030)	-5.27E-5 (0.009)	-0.003 (0.035)
GDP CAP	-0.211** (0.089)	-0.153** (0.076)	-0.004 (0.011)	-0.078 (0.080)
WAGE	0.935*** (0.194)	0.782*** (0.160)	0.013 (0.039)	0.378* (0.215)
MFG	-0.046 (0.048)	-0.034 (0.035)	-0.028** (0.013)	-0.121** (0.049)
N	293	277	144	206
R^2	0.4827	0.4997	0.7915	0.6993
Model P-Value	<0.0001	<0.0001	<0.0001	<0.0001

OLS regression coefficients for timing of first investment in China: model (1) serves as benchmark and excludes corruption measure; model (2) includes PRSG corruption index; model (3) includes World Bank corruption index;model (4) includes Transparency International's corruption index. The dependent variable in all models equals the natural log of the number of days between the first investment and January 1, 1980. Standard errors are given in parentheses below the coefficient estimates.

Table 4. Likelihood of High-Equity Commitment

	(1) No Corruption	(2) Transparency Intl.
Intercept	-1.706 (.)	-4.970747*** (1.974194)
CORR	N/A	1.310884*** (0.4606846)
SIZE	0.1696185*** (0.0623969)	0.132951* (0.0735474)
DEBT	-1.039365* (0.5640707)	-0.951253 (0.5945325)
MTB	-0.0164936 (0.0266875)	-0.0169897 (0.0273052)
SALESGR	0.008426 (0.0589596)	0.007944 (0.0585998)
RandD	-1.066818 (0.828705)	-1.20237 (0.8913863)
ADV	-11.18272*** (4.112753)	-16.42197*** (5.429204)
EMPL	3.805499 (17.88422)	3.87512 (19.2791)
SEZ	1.199181** (0.5695942)	1.301215** (0.6147238)
ENROLL	0.0071481*** (0.0024579)	0.0082351** (0.0033538)
HIGHWAY	8.32e-06 (7.16e-06)	0.00002** (9.24e-06)
RURAL ELEC	-0.0036409* (0.0019674)	-0.0050725** (0.0022724)
GDP CAP	0.0001187** (0.0000595)	0.0002054*** (0.000074)
WAGE	-0.0001711 (0.0001108)	-0.0002739** (0.000142)
N	271	196
Psuedo-R^2	0.2810	0.2893
Model P-Value	<0.0001	0.0003

Probit model for likelihood of high- vs. low-equity commitment by U.S. firms expanding into China between 1980 and 2005. Model (1) provides benchmark estimates and excludes corruption measure; model (2) includes Transparency International's corruption index. The dependent variable in both models equals 1 if a firm undertakes expansion via a high-equity mode of entry (joint venture, acquisition, new plant, or wholly owned subsidiary), and zero otherwise (representative office or large sales/service contract). Standard errors are given in parentheses below the coefficient estimates.

International's index causes most variables to lose significance, but does not cause any significant sign switching. Overall, the warning signs outlined in the section III (C) and Figure 5 are borne out here – the inferior performance of model (3) which uses the World Bank corruption index is largely due to the fact that it cuts off the first half of our sample as this index begins in 1996. The similarly inferior performance of model (4) is largely due to the fact that the Transparency International index is missing data for the years in which our sample registers the highest frequency of entry (1995-97). For these reasons we do not see these two models as reliable. Table 4 presents the results from the probit estimation of the level of equity commitment model. In most ways, the results for this model are better than for the timing model. First, not a single variable switches signs when adding the corruption variable. This would indicate that overall our model is fairly stable. Secondly, the corruption variable is highly significant, and in the direction we would expect (i.e., less corruption encourages high equity investment). Thirdly, the addition of a corruption variable maintains other variables' significance, and enhancing it in some cases. Finally, most included variables are of expected sign, with the exception of rural electricity consumption, which is both significant and of the opposite sign as expected.

CONCLUSION

We investigate the determinants of timing and equity commitment by U.S. firms expanding operations in China between 1980 and 2005. The data in this chapter is a new firm-level, cross-industry sample which allows us to document patterns of investment by U.S. publicly traded companies over the sample period. Our empirical analysis of the timing of entry shows that early investment in China is motivated by market seeking and significantly determined by the nature of firms' assets. Specifically, we find that firms with high advertising intensity enter China earlier in time, suggesting an aggressive pursuit of market share. On the other hand, firms with intangible assets enter China later in time. This is consistent with a cautious approach to making potentially irreversible investments. While adding corruption variables to the timing-of-entry specification resulted in a better overall fit, we also documented that these introduced instability of other variables, which were often of an unexpected sign. Transparency International's corruption index performed the worst on all counts, while PRSG and World Bank each had greater measures of success maintaining variable significance and sign stability. In the cases of World Bank and Transparency International, the corruption variable attained high statistical significance, with p-scores at or below 0.01. In the case of PRSG, results were outside conventional standards of significance, but approached 0.10.

Using a corruption measure in our equity commitment specification had somewhat better performance. While both PRSG and World Bank's indices were dropped due to multicollinearity, Transparency International's index not only found high significance in the expected sign, but kept the model stable and slightly improved significance overall for the control variables. Further, almost all variables were of their expected signs. Overall, there appears to be evidence that lower perceptions of corruption have a positive relationship with a firm's likelihood of undertaking expansion in China through a wholly-owned subsidiary, a joint venture, a new plant, or an acquisition, rather than a mere representative office. Overall, the usefulness of our corruption indices as they are now cannot be taken for granted. Some corruption measures introduce volatility in our specifications suggesting that more robust measures of corruption that are province specific may be significantly more useful in future research. Another possible venue for future work would be to investigate different subsamples over the 1980-2005 period to better account for the changing landscape in the composition of FDI into China. Specifically, while the 1980s and early 1990s were dominated by firms from the manufacturing sector, the latter part of the 1990s through 2005 is dominated by service sector firms. It is therefore likely that the relative importance of factors influencing timing and entry-mode decisions changes over the sample period as does the level of corruption.

REFERENCES

Agmon, T. (2003) 'Who Gets What: The MNE, the National State and the Distributional Effectsof Globalization,' *Journal of International Business Studies*, 34(5): 416–427.

Aizenman, Joshua and Mark M. Spiegel. " Institutional Efficiency, Monitoring Costs, and the Investment Share of FDI." *NBER Working Paper Series*. November 2002.

Altomonte, C. (2000) 'Economic Determinants and Institutional Frameworks: FDI in Economies inTransition,' *Transnational Corporations*, 9(2): 75-106.

Alvaro Cuervo-Cazurra. "Who Cares About Corruption?" Journal of *International Business Studies*. November 2006, vol.37, iss.6, pp. 807-822.

Amiti, Mary and BeataSmarzynskaJavorcki. "Trade Costs and Location of Foreign Firms in China." *International Monetary Fund Working Papers*, March 2005.

Benassy-Quere, AgnesmMaylisCoupet, and Thierry Mayer. "Institutional Determinants of Foreign Direct Investment." *World Economy*. May 2007, vol.30, iss.5, pp. 764-782.

Blonigen, B.A. (2005) 'A Review of the Empirical Literature on FDI Determinants', *AtlanticEconomic Journal*, 33(4): 383-403.

Chen, Yung-Ming. "Determinants of FDI Mode Choice: Acquisition, Brownfield, and Greenfield Entry in Foreign Markets." *Canadian Journal of Administrative Sciences*, September 2006, vol.23, iss.3, pp.202-220.

Cole, Matthew A., Robert J.R. Elliott, and Jing Zhang. " Corruption, Governance and FDI Location in China: A Province-level Analysis." *Journal of Development Studies*, October 2009, vol.45 iss.9, pp. 1494-1512.

Dicken, P. (1998) Global Shift: *Transforming the World Economy*, Paul Chapman: London.

Egger, Peter and Hannes Winner. "How Corruption Influences Foreign Direct Investment: A Panel Data Study." *Economic Development and Cultural Change*. 2006, vol.54, iss.2, pp. 459-86.

Fama, E. and French, K (1997) 'Industry Costs of Equity', *Journal of Financial Economics*, 43(2): 153-193.

Fung, K.C., Alicia Garcia-Herrero, HitomiIzaka, and Alan Siu. "Hard or Soft? Institutional Reforms and Infrastructure Spending as Determinants of Foreign Direct Investment in China." *The Japanese Economic Review, December* 2005, vol. 56, iss. 4, pp. 408-416.

Gao, Ting. "Labor Quality and the Location of Foreign Direct Investment: Evidence from China." *China Economic Review*, February 2005, vol.16, iss.3, pp. 274-292.

Globerman, Steven and Daniel Shapiro. "Governance Infrastructure and US Foreign Direct Investment." *Journal of International Business Studies,* January 2003, vol.34, iss.1, pp.19-39.

Habib, Mohsin and Leon Zurawicki. "Corruption and Foreign Direct Investment." *Journal of International Business Studies*. 2002, vol.33, iss.2, pp. 291-307.

Havrylchyk, Olena and Sandra Poncet. "Foreign Direct Investment in China: Reward or Remedy?" *The World Economy*, October 2007, vol.30, iss.11, pp. 1662-1681.

He, C. (2003) "Entry Mode and Location of Foreign Manufacturing Enterprises in China." *Eurasian Geography and Economics*, 44(1): 399-417.

Hitt, M., Keats, BW. and DeMarie, SM (1998) 'Navigating in the New Competitive Landscape:Building Strategic Flexibility and Competitive Advantage in the 21st Century', *Academy ofManagement Executive*, 12(4): 22-42.

Hong, Junjie. "Firm-specific Effects on Location Decisions of Foreign Direct Investment in China's Logistics Industry." *Regional Studies*, July 2007, vol.41, iss.5, pp. 673-683.

Hong, Junjie. "WTO Accession and foreign direct investment in China." *Journal of Chinese Economic and Foreign Trade Studies*, January 2008, vol.1, iss.2, pp. 136-147.

Kawai, Norifumi. "Locational Strategies of Foreign Investors in China: Evidence from Japanese Manufacturing Multinationals." *Global Economic Review*, June 2009, vol.38, iss.2, pp. 117-141.

Kogut, B. and Chang, S.J. (1991) 'Technological Capabilities and Japanese Foreign DirectInvestment in the United States', *Review of Economics and Statistics*, 73(3): 401-413.

Knickerbocker, F.T. (1973) *Oligopolistic Reaction and the Multinational Enterprise*, HarvardUniversity Press: Cambridge, MA.

Lipsey, R.E. (1999) "The Location and Characteristics of U.S. Affiliates in Asia," *National Bureau ofEconomic Research*, working Paper #6876.

Liu, Tianshu. "Impact of Regional Trade Agreements on Chinese Foreign Direct Investment." *The Chinese Economy*, September-October 2008, vol.41, iss.5, pp. 68-102.

Quazi, Rahim. "Economic Freedom and Foreign Direct Investment in East Asia." *Journal of the Asia Pacific Economy*, August 2007, vol.12, iss.3, pp.329-344.

Raff, Horst and Michael J. Ryan. "Firm-Specific Characteristics and the Timing of Foreign Direct Investment Projects." *Review of World Economics*, April 2008, vol.144, iss.1, pp. 1-31.

Rivoli, P., and Salorio, E. (1996) 'Foreign Direct Investment and Investment under Uncertainty', *Journal of International Business Studies*, 27(2): 335-57.

Shapiro, Daniel, Yao Tang, and Cathy Xuejing Ma. "Mode of Entry and the Regional Distribution of Foreign Direct Investment in China." *Journal of Chinese Economic and Business Studies*, 2007, vol. 5, iss. 3, pp. 261-277.

Snowdon, B. and Stonehouse, G. (2006) 'Competitiveness in a Globalised World: Michael Porteron the Microeconomic Foundations of the Competitiveness of Nations, Regions, and Firms', *Journal of International Business Studies*, 37(2): 163-175.

Straub, Stephane. "Opportunism, Corruption, and the Multinational Firm's Mode of Entry." *Journal of International Economics*. March 2008, vol.74, iss.2, pp. 245-263.

Sun, Qian, Wilson Tong, and Qiao Yu. "Determinants of Foreign Direct Investment Across China." *Jounal of International Money and Finance*, February 2002, vol.21, iss.1, pp. 79-113.

The New York Post (July 20, 2005) 'M'SFT vs. Google, Ex-Exec,' *N.Y.P. Holdings, Inc.*, p.33.

The Washington Post (December 20, 1978) 'Rival Pepsi Dealt Defeat as Chinese Decide Thingsgo better with Coke; Coca-Cola's Coup,' *The Washington Post*, section A1.

Tihanyi, L., Griffith, D.A., and Russell, C.J. (2005) 'The Effect of Cultural Distance on EntryMode Choice, International Diversification, and MNE Performance: A Meta-Analysis', *Journal of International Business Studies*, 36(3): 270-283.

United Nation Conference Trade And Development [UNCTAD] (2008) *World InvestmentReport: Transnational Corporations and the Infrastructure Challenge*, United Nations: NewYork.

Vaaler, P. and McNamara, G. (2004) 'Crisis and Competition in Expert Organizational DecisionMaking: Credit Rating Agencies and Their Response to Turbulence in EmergingEconomies', *Organization Science*, 15(6): 687-703.

Wooster, R. B. (2006) "US companies in transition economies: Wealth effects from expansion between 1987 and 1999." *Journal of International Business Studies*, 37(2): 179–195.

Yu, C-M.J. and Ito, K. (1988) 'Oligopolistic Reaction and Foreign Direct Investment: The Caseof the U.S. Tire and Textile Industries', *Journal of International Business Studies*, 19(3):449-460.

Yu, Chia-Feng, Ta-Cheng Chang, and Chinn-Ping Fan. "FDI timing: Entry cost subsidy versus tax rate reduction." *Economic Modeling*, March 2007, vol.24, iss.2, pp.262-271.

In: Foreign Direct Investment (FDI)
Editors: Enzo Guillon and Lucas Chauvet

ISBN: 978-1-62808-403-0
© 2013 Nova Science Publishers, Inc.

Chapter 8

THE PROLIFERATION OF FREE TRADE AGREEMENTS AND THEIR IMPACT ON FOREIGN DIRECT INVESTMENT: AN EMPIRICAL ANALYSIS ON PANEL DATA

Bassem Kahouli[1]* *and Samir Maktouf*[2]

[1]Faculty of Economics and Management, University of Sousse,
Sousse, Tunisia
[2]Faculty of Economics and Management, University of Tunis el Manar,
Tunis, Tunisia

ABSTRACT

In recent decades, there have been an unprecedented number of regional agreements about the crucial characteristics of the international economic relations. Many countries have begun to explore and participate in the RIA. The rise and development of capital movements and FDI are considered the primary objectives of these agreements. This article focuses on the study of the influence of regional integration, foreign direct investment in several groups over the period 1970-2009. It introduces several variables related to regional integration (trade integration index, index of financial integration and dummy variables) to test their effects on the FDI in these countries. This study examines a panel of 35 countries. The results found show the existence of a strong relationship between the factors of economic integration and the FDI in these countries.

Keywords: FTA, FDI, Regional trade block, panel data.

JEL classification: F13, F15, F23, F2, C23

---

* Corresponding author: Tel.: +216 22 758 426. E-mail addresses: kahoulibassem@yahoo.fr (K. Bassem); samir.maktouf@yahoo.fr (S. Maktouf).

INTRODUCTION

Economic integration (EI) between the countries continued to deepen over the past decade involving economic growth (Kahouli and Kadhraoui, 2012). This is particularly noticeable at the regional level, with the escalation of Regional Integration Agreements (RIAs) from free trade areas (FTAs), customs unions (CU) to full economic integration, like the EU, NAFTA, Mercosur and ASEAN. These developments have renewed interest on the subject of regional economic integration (REI). In this context, trade and foreign direct investment (FDI) are generally accepted as the two main channels of economic integration. The FDI has a significant flow of capital around the world in the recent years.

The increase in potential market size, lower production distortions and enhancing the credibility of economic and political reforms are considered results following the formation of a free trade area or other forms of integration, which can increase and develop the capital flows and the FDI. The main objectives consist mainly of the FDI to lead to a better access to markets, better forecasting of production inputs and profits due to price differences of factors when relocating production stages intensive labor to the low-wage countries. Economic integration usually results in the elimination of the customs barriers and the lowering of the transport costs for different market integrated area. This makes the region more attractive for FDI. Thus, multinational corporations (MNCs) prefer to widen the regional market as fragmented national markets. Subsequently, modernization can be achieved through access to modern technology, methods of effective management, and international trade networks.

The impact of economic integration on the foreign investment flows differs according to the objectives followed by foreign firms[1]. Moreover, one can expect that the removal of the intra-regional tariffs may lead to increased FDI flows from the rest of the world, if outside vendors lose export markets because of trade diversion. In the presence of a free trade, the locations of new FDI in the region depend on the comparative advantages of the member countries. The increase in the FDI flows is an important factor for greater competition. This encourages and forces local producers to adopt strategies to increase productivity and efficiency by rationalizing the capacity of firms and reducing the weaknesses of the production process. In this context, the FDI can be considered as the critical incentive of dynamic benefits. Moreover, transnational firms have easier access to technical progress for the host countries through the FDI that stimulates the transfer and dissemination of technology directly or through the « *spillover* » of local firms.

Therefore, this work focuses primarily on the increases in the RIA and their significance on the FDI for different parts. Thus, to understand the connections that may exist between the two variables of this research and its impact on the member countries and third countries. Similarly, an attempt to empirically test the impact of regional integration (trade and financial) on the FDI. Otherwise, we try to answer the following questions: Can regional groupings and economic relations play a fundamental role in the attractiveness of the FDI? To what extent does the strengthening of the association agreements promotes Does the location of the FMN's and stimulates the FDI?

---

[1] For example, FDI flows that are aimed at diversion of trade barriers are likely to fall with the creation of a free trade area. However, if integration generates trade creation (increased exports and imports), while the intra-regional FDI may increase in some countries due to the change in the structure of production in the region.

This work is organized as follows. The second section reviews the theoretical and empirical literature on this subject, and pays attention to the traditional and modern theories on the FDI. In other words, it highlights the original item on the FDI theories to show how they have evolved over time. In the third section, we present the different stages of integration and determine the specificity of each phase of the integration. The presentation of our estimation model and the results of econometric tests are presented in the fourth section. In section 5, we draw the conclusions and make policy recommendations.

2. REGIONAL INTEGRATION AND FDI: A REVIEW OF THEORETICAL AND EMPIRICAL LITERATURE

2.1. Theoretical Approach

Economic theory has evolved quickly over the last decade in terms of explaining the determinants of the global capital flows, in general, and the FDI, in particular. Traditionally, the FDI decisions were analyzed using the eclectic paradigm (Dunning, 1977), which distinguishes the simultaneous presence of three benefits for Multi National Companies (MNCs) : that is to say, the specific benefits related to property « ownership-specific advantage » on location « location advantage » and internationalization « internationalization advantage » of trade.

The RIAs can cause various effects on FDI flows. According to Blomström and Kokko (1997) this impact would depend on several factors such as the characteristics of countries that now form an integrated area, the nature of the agreement, the type of the FDI and the economic policies implemented in each country before and after the agreement. In addition, Blostrom and Kokko (1997) noted that if the objective of foreign investors is the internationalization of intangible assets such as commercial or technological expertise rather than to circumvent the trade barriers, then economic integration will not create an incentive to reduce the FDI. Trade liberalization within a region may also encourage firms to seek strategic alliances or mergers with regional competitors to better face the new environment. Regionalization allows the firm to achieve a more optimal size compared to a national market. Thus, if integration seems to have a positive effect on the FDI flows to the region. It is possible that some member countries are experiencing a decline in investment to the extent that the FDI will tend to concentrate on most of the attractive countries which may explain the low share of the Maghreb countries of the FDI in the region. The impact of regional integration also depends on the origin of the FDI (FDI intra-regional and extra-regional FDI). Consider intra-regional FDI, the signing of an RIA entails the abolition of trade barriers and thus the reductions of the horizontal FDI. MNF prefers to supply the common market with exports rather than bear the costs of implementation. In this contex, Neary (2002) points out that this effect occurs when investors seek to circumvent the tariff and nontariff barriers. Nevertheless, Blomström and Kokko (1997) note that integration can foster the FDI, vertical FDI in nature between the member countries, when the MNC in search of competitive production costs, fragmentation makes the production process. In the same order of ideas, IR also affects the extra-regional FDI. The gradual reduction of internal barriers to trade and the adoption of a common external tariff level vis-à-vis non-member countries, increase outside investment whose objective is to prevent trade barriers.

In addition, Eden (2002) and Ethier (1998) emphasize that the current wave of regional integration programs has significantly reduced barriers to trade and FDI in the integrated areas. There are two main schools of thought regarding the effects of regional economic integration on the FDI: the effects of the market size and fortress. First, Buckley et al. (2001) announced that regional economic integration can motivate companies to invest outside countries in the integrated economic area as the regional economic integration increases the market size. Before integration, the market of the host country may be too small for firms to internalize their competitive advantage and serve the market through the FDI. Moreover, after integration, the market is large enough to justify the FDI to serve the local market rather than through exports. Thus, Barrell and Pain (1996) and Globerman and Shapiro (2003) showed that the market size of the host country is an important determinant of the attractiveness of a market. In the same vein, the regional integration increase opportunities to exploit a larger market of MNF appear horizontal. Market size, indicative of strong demand, encourages capital inflows.

Krugman (1981), show that the size of the domestic market promotes economic activity in the area via the existence of economies of scale. Through a different approach, Motta and Norman (1996) show, in an oligopolistic model[2] with strategic behavior, that increased the size of the market, following a regional integration promotes FDI. Through a sequential game, the authors show that the effects on the FDI of regional integration between similar countries differ depending on whether one takes in an FDI intra-or extra areas. Lower intra-zone FDI is expected once the location choice of firms is driven by a strategy of « *Tariff-jumping* ». However, an increase in the market size, due to economic integration, has a positive effect on the FDI outside the region. Significant demand on the host market, low costs of implementation and high transport costs encourage the firm to install several subsidiaries abroad instead of serving the local market by exports (Brainard, 1993). Contrary to Motta and Norman (1996), Markusen (2002) studied the location strategies of firms through two types of integration. The different choices made by the MNC depend on whether integration is South-South (MERCOSUR) or North-South (NAFTA). For the author when the DCs form a region, increasing the size of the market place, offers investment opportunities for foreign firms to develop horizontal strategies. In contrast, when countries sign a regional agreement, the MNCs companies go where production costs low and are the home countries of the FDI for re-export. In most theoretical work, the effect of the market size is a major determinant in the location strategies of the MNCs. It is even more important that, even within a region, the size of integrated market countries change strategies of the MNCs. However, as pointed out by Blomström (1997), the macroeconomic reforms undertaken by the region are more important than the market size. Secondly, regional economic integration can increase the trade barriers for non-members: the effects of the regional integration fortress. The free trade agreements (FTAs) may contain elements (eg, rules of origin under NAFTA) that create barriers to competition from non-members, which increase the incentive

---

[2] In this model, the authors study the impact of regional integration on the location strategies of firms. They are placed in the context of a model with three countries of similar size (two countries form a regional bloc) and three firms located in their respective countries of origin. They operate their choice of market penetration (exports or FDI) according to the importance of tariff barriers vis-à-vis the outside, the level of intra-regional barriers and the importance of the size of the integrated area.

for the FDI in the area of free trade. The FDI motivated by concerns for future protection are widely exposed in literature through the European example. Part of the FDI from outside Europe is indeed motivated by fears of building a «*fortress Europe*».

2.2. Empirical Approach

With the proliferation of regional agreements, several empirical studies have examined the impact of IR on FDI. Taking into account the existing literature on the FDI, these studies can be classified into two categories, according to the techniques and methodologies used: the standard models of FDI determinants. Investment is explained primarily in terms of market size when the FDI is a tool for the firm to enter a market. Dunning and Robson (1987) and Blomstrom and Kokko (1997) pointed out that the effect of the regional integration on the FDI is a priori ambiguous. On the one hand, the creation and investment diversion lead to an increase in the FDI to a Member State of an RIA. Moreover, insofar as there was an « incentive » to tariff hopping, the FDI flows into force before integration, and then there would be a reduction of the outward FDI in the partner countries where there is no fee. One way to integrate the investments in models of economic regionalism is to link the trade liberalization to changes in the relative pay factors[3]. However, the relative factor prices are a key determinant of the FDI, others include, for example, the economic dimension, the per capita income, the economic dynamism in the countries of origin and destination, the geographical distance between them, the variables related to trade policy and other factors of geographical advantage.

Several empirical studies have attempted to verify the theoretical results. In this context, Jaumotte (2004) tested the importance of South-South RIA for 71 developing countries in 1980 and 1999. He use the combined GDP of the host country of the FDI (members of an integrated area) as a proxy for the regional integration. She studies the importance of market size after regional integration. The main results show that the market size of the RIA and the size of domestic population have had a positive impact on the FDI. Nevertheless, the positive impact on the FDI is not evenly distributed among the countries of the RIA. Countries with relatively higher education and economic and financial stability tend to attract a larger share of the FDI at the expense of other members of the RIA. Beside the size of the market, other works simultaneously use different measures of the effects of the regional integration. Thus, further study of Yeyati et al. (2003) focused on the OECD countries during the period 1982-1999. The authors defined three integration variables: a dummy variable, the combined GDP of the host countries members of the integrated region (Extended Market host) and the combined GDP of the country and members of the investment in the region (Extended Market source). They concluded the existence of a positive impact on the FDI. Thus, these benefits are unlikely to be uniformly distributed.

In the same direction, the work Velde et al. (2004) that integrates two indices of investment and trading rules. Indeed, the authors attempt to explain why some regions are more successful in attracting the FDI while others fail. Therefore, they consider a traditional model of the FDI determinants for two investors (the U.S. and Britain) and respectively 68

---

[3] A relatively rich in capital would experience a net inflow of investment as rents rise relative to wages, and a relatively labor-abundant suffer the opposite effect.

and 97 host countries (developing countries). In addition, they define specific rules for investment in each region (Fahnbulleh and Velde, 2004). The authors conclude that regional integration increases the extra-regional FDI following the application of regional investment and the country's position in the region.

Indeed, for Bertrand et al. (2003), the impact of the NAFTA and MERCOSUR on the FDI appeal boils down to using a dummy variable marking the date of ratification of treaties. Similarly, De Sousa et al (2004) used several dummies to measure both the economic and monetary integration through intra-and extra-regional FDI. Regarding to the intra-European FDI, the variable equals 1 if the host country and that country of the origin of investment are in the EU. Meanwhile, other authors define indicator variables to capture the extra-regional member countries of the EU. These take the value 1 when the country is an EU member country respectively, a host and a home country of the FDI. In total, the economic and monetary integration have a positive impact on the FDI intra-and extra-regional FDI respectively and intra and extra euro area. However, the use of dummy variables must be done very carefully in a particular model range.

In the same spirit, Lesher and Miroudot (2006) are based on the North-South RTA during the period 1990-2004. They showed that the investment provisions in RIAs are positively related to both trade and investment flows. The results are more profound for the FDI than for trade flows.

3. THE CONDITIONS FOR SUCCESSFUL ECONOMIC INTEGRATION

The regional integration of countries is only possible when there are a number of economic and noneconomic (political, geographical, social or cultural) preconditions. These conditions play an important role in the success of any integration project. We note the conditions for economic and political order that will be subject to the following analysis. First, successful integration depends on the nature of the countries involved. Generally, synchronicities and economic integration agreements or cooperation are easier between countries with complementary structures between countries that have competitive specialization patterns. The integration between complementary units implies more efficient use of resources and eliminates the waste and repetition of efforts in the same projects. Second, the trade complementarities[4] are a necessary condition to promote the integration phenomenon especially among the developing countries.

Apoteker et al. (2005), describe the complementarities of trade as the existence of production structures sufficiently different between the member countries to promote trade without major risks for domestic production that loses its protection. Similarly, Cassin and Zarenda (2004) add that agreements with the greatest chance of success are probably those between countries with high levels of trade complementarities. Third, the increased flows of intra-regional investment, which covers the area's capacity to obtain foreign investment flows larger, favor the process of technology diffusion and catch-up. Apoteker et al. (2005) describe this condition as one of the main arguments in favor of integration agreements North-South,

---

[4] Complementarity is an important factor in developing the intra-regional trade through specialization based on the principle of comparative advantage that facilitates the integration of each country in the area. It also allows the efficient use of natural and human resources through a better allocation across sectors.

like the NAFTA or in the general framework of the Barcelona Agreement. In the case of regional integration South-South, the attraction of a regional market may also encourage direct investment flows and therefore the transfer of technology and know-how. This requires an appropriate regulatory framework (in terms of legal basis and conditions of exercise of rights) and homogeneous in the area. Indeed, the increased flows of the FDI are considered an important engine for economic cooperation and a means of strengthening the interdependence of the economies of a region. However, the increase in these flows can be an incentive to trade and may also appear as an incentive for the economies of the region to seek a more pronounced integration of national economic policies. The risk is, however, to see these investments from countries outside the area to concentrate geographically on some points of the integrated area, thus favoring the known problems of center/periphery in the developing countries.

Mass effects are the fourth condition which concerns the effects of mass, that is to say, a global, in terms of population, demand and production, which, when integrated commercially, helps save of scale and productivity gains[5]. Fifth, the establishment of a significant level of the stock of infrastructure such as railway, highway, and electric power generated, and the number of telephone lines, is always a catalyst for the development of such a process of economic integration. The inadequacy of these facilities or their geographical misdistribution prevents the rapid movement of people, goods and services. In the presence of deficient infrastructure services, an integration project can be deceiving. Therefore, any economic integration policy must first be based on a solid and advanced infrastructure to the various member countries. Infrastructure is needed to make up for delays in the area and provide the platform capable of reaching successful integration. Sixth, the political elements are necessary conditions that play a key role in the success of economic integration. The degree of coordination and communication network among the member countries of integration plays an important role for successful integration agreements especially where it accounts for owners of the country structures and different policies.

The member countries must fulfill the basic conditions for we success regional integration to integrate and hence justify the effort of all the member countries. Countries must rely on the planning of a prudent development policy.

4. PRESENTATION VARIABLES AND THE ECONOMETRIC MODEL

This study covers the period from 1970 to 2009 on a panel of 35 developed and developing countries[6]. In this article we will estimate in the first part of a static panel (fixed and random effect). In the second part, we integrate the dummies in our estimation to better understand the impact of integration. This empirical work is part of the studies trying to identify the effects of economic integration on the FDI. This section will focus primarily on the description of the empirical adopted methodology: it is to present the model to be

---

[5] The attraction of foreign investment and size effects) are interrelated, but to exert their effects, they involve the initial implementation of a uniform body of rules in the area, including key aspects should cover a priori minimum technical standards, non-tariff barriers to trade (anti-competitive practices in the distribution, protection of intellectual property / industrial), and security (financial and legal) transactions such as contracts.

[6] See the list of countries in the Appendix.

estimated, the sample of countries and the estimation technique. Second, we will then the interpretation of results provided by the estimation of our model.

4.1. Empirical Methodology

To answer our problem empirically, we use the following two models that address the impact of regional integration as measured by the integration of trade, the index of financial integration and the dummies. However, foreign direct investment (FDI), which is the dependent variable in the model, is explained by other control variables as defined by the classical theory, namely: human capital (HK), inflation (INF), exchange rate (ER) and domestic investment (GFCF)[7]. Since our sample includes various regional groupings, we developed a dummy variable that takes value 1 if the country is a member of the RIA and 0 if not. To do this, we will estimate the following two models:

$$FDI_{i,t} = \alpha_0 + \alpha_1 INTEG_{i,t} + \alpha_2 ITI_{i,t} + \alpha_3 FII_{i,t} + \alpha_4 GDP_{i,t} + \alpha_5 HK_{i,t} + +\alpha_6 GFCF_{i,t} + \alpha_7 INF + \alpha_8 ER_{i,t} + U_{i,t}$$

(1)

$$FDI_{i,t} = \alpha_0 + \alpha_1 INTEG_{i,t} + \alpha_2 ITI_{i,t} + \alpha_3 FII_{i,t} + \alpha_4 GDP_{i,t} + \alpha_5 HK_{i,t} + +\alpha_6 GFCF_{i,t} + \alpha_7 INF + \alpha_8 ER_{i,t} + \alpha_9 MERCOSUR_{i,t} + \alpha_{10} NAFTA_{i,t} + \alpha_{11} ASEAN_{i,t} + \alpha_{12} EU_{i,t} + \alpha_{13} EUROMED_{i,t} + U_{i,t}$$

(2)

where i denotes the country and t denotes the time (year), $FDI_{i,t}$ are the inward foreign direct investment (percentage of the GDP). The $GDP_{i,t}$ refers to the growth rate of the Gross Domestic Product, a variable that reflects the level of development of a country and represents a growth indicator. $HK_{i,t}$ is the human capital is proxy by secondary school enrollment. The $GFCF_{i,t}$ indicates the Gross Fixed Capital Formation (as a percentage of GDP). $INF_{i,t}$ represent the inflation rate measured by the GDP deflator. The $ER_{i,t}$ denotes the exchange rate (percentage of the GDP). In the same order, we integrate the regional dummies. $MERCOSUR_{i,t}$ indicates the belonging to the MERCOSUR regional grouping. $NAFTA_{i,t}$ membership to the NAFTA regional grouping. $ASEAN_{i,t}$ belonging to the ASEAN regional grouping. $EU_{i,t}$ Belonging to the EU-15 regional grouping. $EUROMED_{i,t}$ membership to the Euro-Mediterranean regional grouping. $U_{i,t}$ is the error term.

Another important question concerns the integration variable calculation. The existing literature on the subject produces integration measures that are based on the FDI, trade flows and private capital (Ismihan and al. 1998). The INTEG variable consists of an index calculated as the average of two elements. The first element is an index of trade integration (CII), which is calculated as follows:

$$ITI_{it} = \frac{Opening_{it} + Min_{Opening}}{Max_{Opening} + Min_{Opening}}$$

(3)

---

[7] See Appendix.

Whith ITI$_{it}$ representing the trade integration index for country i at time t, openness is the ratio of exports and imports to the GDP (in constant prices), Min$_{Opening}$ and Max$_{Opening}$ are respectively the values of the minimum and maximum opening in the sample (both over time and between countries). The second element is an index of financial integration, which is calculated as follows:

$$FII_{it} = \frac{FI_{it} + Min_{FI}}{Max_{FI} + Min_{FI}} \qquad (4)$$

Whith FII$_{it}$ synonymous with financial integration index for country i at time t, FI$_{it}$ the ratio of financial assets and financial liabilities to the GDP for country i at time t, and Min$_{FI}$ and Max$_{FI}$ respectively the minimum and maximum values of financial integration in the sample. Finally, variable INTEG$_{i,t}$ is calculated simply as:

$$INTEG_{i,t} = \frac{IIC_{it} + IIF_{it}}{2} \qquad (5)$$

4.2. Data and Samples

Our work includes a heterogeneous sample composed of five regional groupings of developed and developments countries. RTAs are kind of South-South, South-North and North-North. These groupings are as follows: Europe 15, the countries of MERCOSUR, NAFTA, ASEAN and other Mediterranean Southeast countries[8]. The choice of these countries s due to the fact that the group of developed countries is considered the most advanced in terms of processes of integration. Thus, those countries attempted to be inserted into international economy and benefit in terms of economic growth. The period of study spreads from 1970 to 2009 according to the data availability.

4.3. The Descriptive Statistics

Table 1 shows the average rate of the FDI inflows (as a percentage of GDP) was 5.97%. The minimum average FDI inflows are registered in Ireland (15.04%), while the maximum is in Luxembourg (564.91%). Generally, the RIA results in the elimination of the customs barriers and the reduction of the transport costs for different markets. This makes the region more attractive for FDI. In addition, integration can foster the development of the cooperation between governments and companies of the member countries, particularly in the crucial area of research and development. Regarding the index of the integration value is close to 100 plus countries are integrated and vice versa. Integration can foster technology diffusion and development of cooperation between governments and companies in the member countries.

The average economic growth rate of the sample over the studied period is 3.64%. Indonesia recorded the lowest rate (13.12%) against Algeria by recording the largest value (27.42%). The increase in the FDI flows is an important factor for accelerating economic

---

[8] See the list of countries in the Appendix.

growth. The commercial and financial integration encourage and force local producers to adopt strategies to increase productivity and efficiency by rationalizing the capacity of firms and reducing the weaknesses of the production process. The human capital proxy by the secondary school enrollment rate is quite large and equal to (77.25%). The secondary school enrollment rate is the lowest mark in Algeria (11.17%) while Belgium recorded the highest rate (160.34%).

Table 1. Descriptive statistics of data from the study of the bulk sample

Variable	average	Standard Deviation	Min	Max
FDI	5.977	35.400	-15.048	564.916
INTEG	36.642	27.292	0	100
GDP	3.648	3.773	-13.126	27.423
GFCF	3.992	11.066	-44.323	100.647
INF	24.989	157.217	-9.423	3057.629
ER	230.901	959.932	1.80e-12	10400
HK	77.255	28.864	11.178	160.346

Table 2. Correlations between variables

	1	2	3	4	5	6	7
1 FDI	1						
2 GDP	0.0363	1					
3 GFCF	0.0181	0.7099*	1				
4 INF	-0.0205	-0.1076*	-0.0771*	1			
5 HK	0.0810*	-0.2745*	-0.1465*	-0.0966*	1		
6 ER	-0.0306	-0.0114	-0.0140	-0.0211	-0.0739*	1	
7 INTEG	0.0592*	0.0042	0.0414	-0.0445	0.2499*	0.0836*	1

*Significant at 5%.

Regarding the correlation between the variables (see Appendix); two observations deserve to be made. First, there is a positive and significant coefficient at the 5% between the explanatory variable of integration, human capital proxy for the secondary school enrollment rates and FDI. However, the GFCF growth rate of the GDP, the exchange rate and inflation are not significant. Arguably, then, the anticipated results will be in the same direction that is to say they have a positive effect of integration on foreign direct investment.

The analysis is devoted firstly to empirically assess the impact of the regional integration on the FDI. To do this, a panel analysis is performed to draw long-term conclusions.

4.4. Estimation Method

Using panel estimation, the techniques allow the consideration of temporal specificity a cross these samples. The panel estimation with fixed effects introduces several advantages, particularly related to the inclusion of unobservable and stable characteristics over time[9]. To validate the use of this specification, it is necessary to both confirm the presence of specific effects by testing the Lagrange multiplier (LM) Breusch-Pagan and determine their independence vis-à-vis the explanatory variables by the Hausman test.

We use Hausman test to choose between fixed and random effects. The results show that in most of the regressions, the fixed effects model is the most relevant. Then, we incorporate the dummy variables in our model to better address the phenomenon of economic integration and economic growth.

4.5. Estimates, Results and Interpretations

The development below shows our econometric results and their statistical and economic interpretations. The model results are estimated in the following tables:

Table 3. Results from the model estimated for the selected sample

Dependent variable FDI inflows as a percentage of GDP, period 1970-2009					
Explanatory variables	(1)	(2)	(3)	(4)
Constant	-18.066 (-2.86)	-20.811 (-3.25)*	-19.652 (-3.01)**	-22.127 (-3.92)*
INTEG	.181 (4.04)*			
ITI		.159 (3.81)*		.149 (2.71)***
FII			.110 (2.72)**	.011 (0.20)
GDP	.880 (2.24)**	.863 (2.19)**	.902 (2.29)***	.859 (2.17)**
GFCF	-.088 (-0.72)	-.115 (-0.94)	-.066 (-0.54)	-.112 (-0.90)
HK	.176 (2.48)**	.243 (3.32)**	.237 (3.32)**	.237 (2.94)**
INF	.007 (0.59)	.008 (0.62)	.006 (0.50)	.008 (0.66)
ER	-.001 (-1.27)	-.001 (-1.29)	-.001 (-1.16)	-.001 (-1.39)
N	1076	1076	1076	1076
Hausman Test	0,001	0.118	0.053	0.000
Breusch-pagan Test	0.000	0.000	0.000	0.000
F test	58.67	57.51	49.85	8.58
R^2	0.056	0.054	0.048	0.051

Notes: Values in parentheses are the t-statistics.
* Significant at 1%. ** Significant at 5%. *** Significant at 10% : For the Hausman test, what are the odds that are reported.

---

[9] First, this technique produces more variability, more degrees of freedom, and more efficiency and minimizes the risk of multicolinearity between the explanatory variables. Second, it treats the problem of potential correlation between some explanatory variables and the error term that does not vary over time. Third, the fixed effects model exploits the temporal dimension of data and allows taking into account the dynamics of adjustment. Fourth, control heterogeneity by the inclusion of time-invariant characteristics and / or space.

Table 4. Results from the model estimated for the selected sample with dummies

Dependent variable FDI inflows as a percentage of GDP, period 1970-2009						
Explanatory variables	(1)	(2)	(3)	(4)	(5)	(6)
Constant	-21.233 (-3.79)*	-18.748 (-3.31)**	-19.153 (-3.48)**	-18.794 (-3.42)**	-12.392 (-2.08)**	-12.285 (-1.94)**
INTEG	.185 (3.91)*	.184 (3.86)*	.200 (4.11)*	.204 (4.25)*	.134 (2.69)*	.183 (3.45)**
GDP	.894 (2.27)**	.869 (2.20)**	.865 (2.19)**	.855 (2.17)**	.812 (2.06)**	.772 (1.97)**
GFCF	-.088 (-0.72)	-.089 (-0.72)	-.085 (-0.69)	-.071 (-0.58)	-.107 (-0.87)	-.077 (-0.63)
HK	.223 (2.75)**	.193 (2.42)**	.188 (2.37)**	.229 (2.84)**	.108 (1.29)	.172 (1.96)**
INF	.002 (0.20)	.008 (0.63)	.008 (0.62)	.008 (0.68)	.006 (0.53)	.002 (0.21)
ER	-.001 (-0.95)	-.001 (-1.37)	-.001 (-1.42)	-.002 (-1.55)	-.001 (-0.93)	-.001 (-0.91)
MERCOSUR	-10.352 (-1.82)***					-8.846 (-1.49)
ASEAN		-4.300 (-0.38)				-4.331 (-0.39)
NAFTA		-9.881 (-1.56)				-8.965 (-1.39)
EU-15				-11.093 (-2.50)**		-16.388 (-3.57)*
Euro-Med					9.294 (2.96)**	10.023 (2.94)**
N	1076	1076	1076	1076	1076	1076
F test	9.31	8.83	9.18	9.75	10.13	7.91
R^2	0.059	0.056	0.058	0.061	0.064	0.077

Notes: Values in parentheses are the t-statistics.
* Significant at 1%. ** Significant at 5%. *** Significant at 10%

Empirical estimates show a positive effect of the variables of integration, trade integration index and the index of financial integration on foreign direct investment in the member countries. The coefficients of the explanatory variables (IIC, IIF, economic growth and KH approximated by the secondary school enrollment) are positive and significant in almost all the table columns (5 and 6). This implies that integration has a positive and significant effect on the FDI. However, this positive effect is relatively diminished by introducing these variables simultaneously. In this context, our results confirm those of other studies which confirmed the positive effect of integration on the FDI. Another example is the work of Darrat et al. (2005) that illustrates this approach. These authors tested the effects of the regional integration on the FDI. Their work covers a sample of 23 countries in the CEE and the MENA zone during the period (1979-2002). The main result of this study is that the FDI stimulates economic growth only in the EU candidate countries (Kahouli and Kadhraoui, 2012). The explanation is that the two authors join the EU there is a wider application and more effective reforms, which would have helped create a positive impact of FDI flows.

These results suggest the crucial role played by economic integration in the increased flows of the FDI.

This means that the two variables (FDI and integration) act simultaneously on economic growth. This result supports the idea that integration through the abolition of trade barriers and free movement of capital flows is a source of the FDI attractiveness. The entry of other variables in the regression has no effect on the significance of growth. The introduction of these variables slightly reduces the significance of the FDI. Several empirical studies, which examined the effects of the FDI, have affirmed the existence of positive impact of the FDI on growth. In this context, Bengoa and Sanchez-Robles (2003) studied the link between economic integration (opening rate) on FDI using panel data for a sample of 18 Latin American countries for the period 1970 to 1999. Their results show that economic integration of countries is a precondition for attracting the FDI and consequently improving economic growth.

Regarding the control variables, the coefficients of KH are highly significant and positive in the two tables. Some researches, like those of Coe, Helpman and Hoffmaister (1997), Edwards (1998), suggest that, to take advantage of RIA, countries must have a skilled workforce, that is to say a human capital capable of assimilating foreign technology. Along the same lines, it has been recognized for the work of Findaly (1978) and Lucas (1988), that the KH plays an important role in attracting FDI. When the KH level is high, it allows domestic companies to easily understand the technical configurations of technologies adopted by foreign companies and thereby facilitates the process of initiation and learning. In addition, it allows the host countries to benefit from the labor mobility from foreign firms to domestic firms.

In the same order, the coefficients of GFCF in the two tables are not significant. This could be explained by the absence of significant spillover effects generated by foreign companies in the territory of the developing countries (Kahouli and Kadhraoui, 2012). Generally, FDI and regional integration imply increased competition between domestic and foreign firms. However, the MNCs can also push domestic firms to improve their management or adopt certain marketing techniques employed by multinationals, either on the locally or internationally.

In conclusion, in this section, we empirically tested the impact of the different indicators of integration (the degree of openness, FDI and R&D and the dummy variables) on economic growth. Our work is based on a sample of 40 countries (20 emerging countries and 20 OECD countries) for the periods 1970-2009. As a result, we presented the econometric methodology adopted to estimate our model. The main results are as follows: the coefficients attached to the variables representing openness are in most cases positive and significant in both tables. Similarly, there is a significant positive effect of FDI and R&D on economic growth of the member countries of both samples. These results confirm the hypothesis that economic integration helps different parties' access knowledge and foreign knowledge. Concerning inflation and the exchange rates, the coefficients of this variable are also negative and insignificant. The negative relationship between the level of inflation and FDI depends on the capacity of the economy and the degree of substitutability between domestic and foreign products. Several studies found a negative relationship between the level of inflation, the integration Lane (1997) and Temple (2002). Regarding the used dummy variables, the fact of belonging to Europe and 15 Euro-Mediterranean implies the presence of significant and positive coefficients. The integration process in Europe is more profound and successful as the other experiments. However, the coefficients of being a member in the RIA are not significant for all the MERCOSUR, NAFTA and ASEAN. It is quite logical because a successful RIA's depends essentially on the integrated nature of the country. Thus, over the integration process forward, more member countries developed their growth levels. In this context, it is obvious to encourage policies and trade liberalization with a well-structured integration process.

Conclusion

Empirically, the aim of this work is to study how and to what extent regional economic integration affects the FDI. For this purpose, we used panel data on a sample of 35 countries during the period 1970-2009. The main results and the consequent recommendations are: The RIAs are not simply a question of earnings and balance between the benefits and costs. They involve national economic strategies that have ramifications.

In general, we concluded that the implementation of an integration process must be at the heart of public intervention to promote the FDI inflows. At this point, the biggest achievements in regional integration have been achieved by the EU, mainly because integration is both deeper and wider in this region. Individual countries need to learn, adopt and incorporate the lessons of trade reforms in the country's industry in order to reap the benefits of integration and liberalization process. However, this does not mean that these countries should adopt the European model as a template. Countries must take the initiative to set priorities for an economic agenda. The main priorities should be the elimination of tariff and nontariff barriers and harmonization of markets between the different members. These priorities will help to focus on concrete and achievable the agenda of the RTA.

Finally, it should be noted that this work is a modest contribution that could be improved in several directions. The results obviously depend on the methodology and the data used. However, other variables may better help understand the importance of the openness and integration on economic growth. These variables include political stability, distance, property rights, taxation, corruption, etc. A more detailed study would require the consideration of these variables.

Appendix 1: Sample of Countries

Sample	Countries
EU	Austria, Belgium, Luxembourg, France, Germany, Italy, Netherlands, United Kingdom, Ireland, Spain, Finland, Denmark, Greece, Portugal and Sweden
NAFTA	USA, Canada and Mexico
MERCOSUR	Argentina, Brazil, Paraguay, Uruguay, Venezuela
ASEAN	Japan, Singapore, Thailand, Philippine, Indonesia, Korea and Malaysia
Others	Algeria, Tunisia, Egypt, Turkey and Morocco

APPENDIX 2: NAME AND SOURCES OF VARIABLES USED

	Variables	Definition	Source
Dependent variables	FDI	Incoming foreign direct investment (percentage of GDP).	Global Development Finance (2009)
Explanatory variables	INTEG	The integration approximated by the ratio $$INTEG_{i,t} = \frac{IIC_{it} + IIF_{it}}{2}$$	World Development Indicators (2009)
	ITI	Index of trade integration $$ITI_{it} = \frac{Opening_{it} + Min_{Opening}}{Max_{Opening} + Min_{Opening}}$$ With opening: (Exports + Imports) / GDP	Calculation of author
	FII	Index of financial integration $$FII_{it} = \frac{FI_{it} + Min_{FI}}{Max_{FI} + Min_{FI}}$$ With FI_{it} is the ratio of financial assets and financial liabilities to GDP.	Calculation of author
	INFL	Annual inflation rate	World Development Indicators (2009)
	HK	Gross enrollment ratio at secondary level	WDI (2009), UNESCO Statistical Yearbooks
	GFCF	Gross fixed capital formation as percentage of GDP	World Development Indicators (2009)
	ER	Exchange rate	World Development Indicators (2009)
	GDP	Growth rate of GDP	World Development Indicators (2009)

REFERENCES

Apoteker T, Lohézic M and Crozet E (2005) L'intégration économique régionale au Moyen-Orient: conditions requises et possibilités futures, Colloque International : Les nouvelles Frontières de l'Union Européenne. Marrakech.

Barrell R and Pain N (1996) An Econometric Analysis of U.S. *Foreign Direct Investment, Review of Economics and Statistics*, 28, 2, 1996, pp. 200-207.

Bengoa M and Sánchez B (2003) Foreign Direct Investment, Economic Freedom and Growth: New Evidence for Latin America. *European Journal of Political Economy* Vol. 19, pp. 529-545.

Bertrand O and Madariaga A (2003) Choix de localisation des entreprises, mode d'entrée et intégration économique : une étude macroéconomique appliquée à l'IDE américain au sein de l'ALENA et du MERCOSUR, Région et Développement, N°18.

Blomstrom M and Kokko Ari (1997). Regional integration and foreign direct investment: a conceptual framework and three cases, *Policy Research Working Paper Series* 1750, The World Bank.

BRAINARD SL (1993) A Simple Theory of Multinational Corporations and Trade with a Trade-off between Proximity and Concentration, *NBER Working Paper*, 4269.

Buckley P J, Clegg J, Forsans N and Reilly K.T (2001) Increasing the Size of Country: Regional Economic Integration and Foreign Direct Investment in a Globalized World Economy, *Management International Review*, 41, 3, 2001, pp. 251-274.

Cassim R and Zarenda H (2004) South Africa's Trade Policy Paradigm-Evolution or involution in Sidiropoulos E (ed), *South Africa's Foreign Policy- 1994-2004*, SAIIA, Wits University.

Coe David T, Helpman E and Hoffmaister A (1997) North South R&D Spillovers, the *Economic Journal* 107 pp 134-149.

Darrat et al., (2005) FDI and Economic Growth in CEE and MENA Countries: A Tale of Two Regions, *Economic Research Forum, 12th Annual Conference,* 19th-21st December 2005, Cairo, Egypt.

De Sousa J and Lochard J (2004) Investissements directs étrangers et intégration : quels enseignements pour les PECO? *Économie et Prévision*, 163(2), pp 87-100.

Dunning J H. (1977) Trade, Location of Economic Activity, and the MNE: a Search for an Eclectic approach, in The International Allocation of Economic Activity ed. by B. Ohlin, P. O. Hesselborn, and P. M. Wijkman, *Proceedings of a Nobel Symposium held in Stockholm*, 395-418.

Dunning J H and Robson P (1987), Multinational Corporate Integration and regional economic integration. *Journal of Common Market Studies*, XXVI, pp. 103-126.

Eden L (2002) Regional Integration and Foreign Direct Investment: Theory and Lessons from NAFTA, in Kotabe, M./Aulakh, R (eds.), *Emerging Issues in International Business Research,* Cheltenham, United Kingdom: Edward Elgar 2002, pp. 15-36.

Edwards S (1998) Openness, Productivity and Growth : What do we Really Know? *Economic Journal*, vol. 18, 1998, pp 383-398.

Ethier W J (1998) The New Regionalism, *Economic Journal*, 108, 449, 1998, pp. 1149-1161.

Findlay R (1978) Relative Backwardness, Direct Foreign Investment and the Transfer of Technology : A simple Dynamic Model, *Quarterly Journal of Economic* 8 pp 373-396.

Globerman S and Shapiro D M (2003), Governance Infrastructure and US Foreign Direct Investment, *Journal of International Business Studies*, 34, 1, , pp. 19-39.

Ismihan M, Olgun H and Utku F M (1998). A Proposed Index for Measuring 'Globalization' of National Economies. METU Economic Research Center (ERC) *Working Papers in Economics,* No.98/5.

Jaumotte F (2004) Foreign Direct Investment and Regional Trade Agreements: The Market Size Effect Revisited", *IMF Working Paper*, International Monetary Fund.

Kahouli B and Kadhraoui N (2012) Consolidation of Regional Groupings and Economic Growth: Empirical Investigation by Panel Data, *International Journal of Euro-Mediterranean Studies,* Springer.

Krugman P (1981) International Trade and Income Distribution: A Reconsideration, *NBER Working Papers* 0356, National Bureau of Economic Research, Inc.

Lane P (1997) Inflation in open economies. *Journal of International Economics*, 42, 327-347.

Lesher, Molly and Sébastien Miroudot (2006) Analysis of the Economic Impact of Investment Provisions in Regional Trade Agreements, *OECD Trade Policy Working Papers* No. 36.

Levy Y E, Stein E and Daude C (2003) Regional integration and the location of FDI. Working Paper No. 492. Retrieved from Inter-American Development Bank Research.

Lucas R (1988) On the Mechanics of Economic Development, *Journal of Monetary Economics,* 22 pp 3-42.

Markusen J R (2002) *Multinational Firms and the Theory of International Trade*. Cambridge and London: MIT Press.

Motta M and Norman G (1996) Does Economic Integration Cause Foreign Direct Investment? *International Economic Review*, vol.37, n°4, pp.757-783

Neary J P (2002) Foreign Direct Investment and the Single Market, CEPR Discussion Papers 3419, *C.E.P.R. Discussion Papers*.

Temple J (2002) Openness, inflation and the Phillips curve: a puzzle. *Journal of Money, Credit, and Banking*, 34(2), May, 450-468.

Velde DW and Bezemer D (2004), Regional Integration and Foreign Direct Investment, in Regional Integration and Poverty, *The UK Department for International economic Development* (DFID).

Velde DW and Fahnbulleh M (2004) *Investment-related Provisions in Regional Trade Agreements.*

In: Foreign Direct Investment (FDI)
Editors: Enzo Guillon and Lucas Chauvet

ISBN: 978-1-62808-403-0
© 2013 Nova Science Publishers, Inc.

Chapter 9

UNION STRUCTURE AND INWARD FDI

Minas Vlassis and Stefanos Mamakis*
Department of Economics, University of Crete, University Campus
at "Gallos",
Rethymno, Crete, Greece

ABSTRACT

In a union-duopoly strategic context we explore the endogenous determination and the effects of the unionization structure in a market facing the possibility of inward foreign direct investments (FDI). Our findings suggest that, if the foreign firm's unit cost under exports-x is lower than its unit cost under FDI-c, then the domestic unionization structure is irrelevant with FDI decisions. If on the other hand c is lower than x, yet high enough, inward FDI will be − optimally in terms of social welfare − deterred in the equilibrium, so long as the domestic labour market is left to auto-regulate to a centralized union structure, hence, to a centralized wage bargaining regime. If however c is low enough, then a benevolent social planner will have to enforce decentralized union structure and wage bargaining − optimally inducing or accommodating inward FDI − in contrast to the domestic union's best interest which would have otherwise − sub-optimally led to a centralized union structure/wage bargaining regime.

1. INTRODUCTION

Foreign direct investments (FDI) and unionization in the labour market, each one separately, is a multi-dimensional field of research in economics. The interaction between them is more complicated, yet quite promising for generating findings furnishing interesting policy implications.

Focusing on the economic analysis of FDI, it appears that there are three different types of models which have been widely used to explain the nature and impact of (inward-outward)

---

* Corresponding Author: Department of Economics, University of Crete, University Campus at "Gallos", 74100 Rethymno, Crete, Greece. Tel:. ++2831077396, Fax: ++2831077404, E-mail: vlassism@uoc.gr.

foreign direct investments: (a) real capital arbitrage models (b) market power / industrial organization models and (c) firm-theoretic models. Hymer (1960) has been the first to argue that real capital arbitrage models have basic shortages, and that a multinational company should rather possess a competitive advantage (e.g. higher productivity than local firms) in order to serve a foreign market[1]. Regarding market structure, on the other hand, though earlier contributions have been mainly dealing with international monopolistic markets, most contemporary researchers focus their analysis on oligopolistic markets. Whilst, based on the works of Coase (1937), Arrow (1964) and Williamson (1975), and infused with ideas and surveys of internalization and endogenous approach, a multinational firm-theoretic paradigm has already been established.

As in particular regards the impact of FDI on labour market(s), and vice versa, Gaston and Nelson (2001) argue that FDI have negative effects on immigration, while the same authors (2000) claim that the most reasonable conclusion to draw is that the actual impact of FDI on the developed countries' labour markets is negligible. Furthermore, there is a growing interest on the unionization and/or the wage bargaining structure as important factors for firms, and social planners, regarding FDI decisions, and relevant policies, respectively [see e.g., Brander and Spencer (1988), Mezzetti and Dinopoulos (1991), Ishiguro and Shirai (1998)].

One of the most interesting folds of the latter issue is the manipulation of the labour market institutional set-up in order to induce or deter FDI. Contributions to this framework mainly come from Naylor and Santoni (2003), who proposed that the greater is unions' bargaining power the less likely is FDI to emerge, and Vlassis (2009) who stressed out that if the FDI-associated unit costs are not high enough, then employment-neutral inward FDI will emerge if the domestic wage setting is credibly centralized (so that the foreign and the domestic firms to pay equal wages) and the unemployment benefit is sufficiently high.

Along similar lines of research, in the present paper we consider two firms (home and abroad) which compete *a la Cournot* in a host country. The foreign firm has two options, either to build a plant abroad and serve the host country via exports, or to invest in the host country and thus serve the local market via FDI. Each choice is considered to be credible due to the sunk cost of building a plant for serving the host market. Following Hymer (1960), we consider that the foreign firm possesses higher productivity than the home firm. Given the possibility of FDI, as above, two different unionization structures may then arise in the host country, centralized and decentralized, giving rise to centralized or decentralized wage bargaining, respectively, as follows: Under the centralized union structure/wage bargaining, the home union bargains with both the home and the foreign firm about firm-specific wages considering that, in the event of a failure in any of those firm-specific negotiations, all union members will be employed by only the other firm (which will then become a monopolist). Under the decentralized union structure/wage bargaining, on the other hand, the home union splits in two different firm-specific unions which, independently and separately, bargain with the home and the foreign firm over firm-specific wages.

In the above context, the sequence of events is as follows: Stage 1: A benevolent social planner – if needed – establishes and legally enforces the unionization structure in the home country. Stage 2: The foreign firm chooses to serve the local market either via exports or via FDI. Stage 3: Depending on the outcome of the previous events, the foreign firm's as well as

---

[1] See also Kindleberger (1969) and Caves (1971).

the home firm's employees' wages are determined via centralized or decentralized firm-union wage bargains. Stage 4: The foreign firm and the home firm compete in the home market by adjusting their quantities.

Our analysis illustrates the conflicts arising among the agents' optimal strategies and shows that inward FDI are not axiomatically social welfare optimizing. Our findings suggest that, under certain circumstances, the unionization structure is an effective policy tool to induce or deter FDI. Otherwise, it is useless, since it cannot affect the (FDI inducing vs. FDI deterring) state of the equilibrium. Last but not least, in some cases the unionization structure must be used as a policy tool, to maximize social welfare, within an option of two different equilibrium states.

The rest of the paper is organized as follows. In Section 2 we illustrate our structural model and the game arising in its context. Solving this game in Section 3, we derive, explain, and evaluate – in terms of social welfare – the emerging equilibria. In Section 4 we summarize our major results and propose directions for further research. All proofs are relegated to the Appendix (Section 5).

2. The Model

Consider a homogenous good sector where two firms, one home firm (*h-firm*) and one foreign firm (*f-firm*), are competing in the home market by adjusting their quantities. The *f-firm* may either produce its quantity abroad and serve the home market via international trade or produce and sell in the host country via FDI. If the *f-firm* chooses international trade (FDI) it faces a unit cost x $(c)^2$. In either case, the *f-firm* will face a sunk cost (say F) made up of building a plant to serve the home market, which for simplicity is normalized to zero.[3] Production everywhere exhibits constant returns to scale and both firms possess *Leontief* technology. Therefore, provided that its capital stock is sufficient to produce the good, each firm effectively needs to adjust only its labour input in order to adjust its output. Following Hymer (1960), it is moreover assumed that the *f-firm* enjoys a technological advantage over the *h-firm*, hence, the production function of the *h-firm* (*f-firm*) is of the form: $Q_h = L_h$ ($Q_h = kL_h$; $k > 1$), where Q_i (L_i) denotes output (employment) of i firm. Whilst, keeping things as simple as possible, the inverse market demand is defined to be of the simple linear form, $P(Q) = 1 - Q$, where Q stands for the aggregate output ($Q = Q_h + Q_f$).

Consider next that the labour market is unionized both at home and abroad: *Ex-ante*, there is one union in the host country (the home union) and one abroad (the foreign union). Given risk-neutral fixed membership and immobile labour in both markets, and assuming utilitarian behavior under zero reservation wages, each union aims to maximize $U_i(w_i, L_i) = w_i \cdot L_i$, where w is the wage argument and L stands for employment with the i firm ($i=h, f$). We also assume that unions possess a bargaining power of one (zero) during the negotiations

---

[2] According to Vlassis' (2000) terminology, "c formally represents coordination and control costs, assumed to be constant per unit of production, which are incurred when the f-firm runs local production. These costs arise from cross-border differences in (other than the labour market's) legislation, taxation, language, work ethics, personnel procedures etc. Respectively, x represents (constant) export marketing costs per unit of sales, made up of transport, packaging, insurance, tariffs, etc".

[3] We assume a symmetric F in both cases (a plant for exports or a plant for FDI), therefore the normalization of F to zero will not affect the equilibrium.

over the wage (employment), acting as quasi-monopoly unions. *Ex-post*, and given the possibility of inward FDI, it then follows that, if the *f-firm* decides to serve the home market via exports, then the home firm-union pair and the foreign firm-union pair will naturally negotiate over firm/country-specific wages hence, the unionization structure and the wage bargaining regime would both be *de facto* decentralized across countries/firms. In case, however, the *f-firm* via FDI locates its production in the home country, then – in the absence of any legal/institutional constraint, and given the irreversibility of the *f-firm*'s decision (due to the FDI sunk cost) – the home workers/prospective employees in the *h-firm* and/or the *f-firm* will have two options: Either to remain members of one (i.e., of the existing home) union, and jointly negotiate wages with both the *h-firm* and the *f-firm* (centralized union structure/wage bargaining), or to split in two separate unions that will enter into wage negotiations independently with the *f-firm* and the *h-firm* (decentralized union structure/wage bargaining). As we show later on, this speculative possibility on the part of the home union of an *ex-post* adjustment of the unionization structure and wage bargaining may in turn raise the need for active institutional intervention in the labour market: In its absence, the *f-firm* may, sub-optimally for social welfare, yet at the home union's best interest, be deterred to settle production in the home market. Whilst, by enforcing the necessary unionization/wage bargaining structure, a benevolent social planner may optimally induce inward FDI, even if that proves to be sub-optimal for the home union.

The sequence of the events unravels as follows:

Stage 1: A benevolent social planner – if needed – establishes (or reforms) the unionization/wage bargaining structure at home so that to maximize social welfare. The social planner's decision may be in accordance or in contrast with the home union's goals, given that the latter do not always coincide with the socially optimal strategies. Therefore, using the unionization structure as a policy tool, the social planner may sometimes leave the labour market to optimally auto-regulate, whilst under different circumstances she/he must issue labour market legislation and enforce a particular unionization structure. Also, in some cases she/he may have to accept the second best regarding social welfare, while in other cases she/he may be unable to induce or deter FDI, and she/he will consequently be bound to find an alternative policy tool. In any instance, the social planner's criterion is as follows:

$$Max\ SW\ \{= pr_h + U_h + U_f + CS\} \qquad (1)$$

Where, SW stands for social welfare, pr_h stands for the profits of *h*-firm, U_i stands for the utility of (sub) union i (i.e., the utility of the home union's members who would respectively be employed by firm $i=h$-, f-) and CS stands for consumer surplus. Note that U_h and U_f are separately considered into the calculations only if the *f-firm* chooses to settle in the host market via FDI.

Stage 2: Given the labour market institutional resolutions in the host country, the *f-firm* decides to serve the home market via either exports or FDI, its goal being to maximize its profits, defined as follows:

$$Max\{pr_f = P \cdot q_f - w_f \cdot \frac{q_f}{k} - x \cdot q_f = \left(P - \frac{w_f}{k} - x\right) \cdot q_f\ \} \qquad (2)$$

Where, pr_f stands for f-firm's profit, q_f stands for *f-firm's* quantity and w_f is the *f-firm*-specific wage bargain.

Stage 3: Given the labour market institutional resolutions, and the *f-firm*'s irreversible decision to settle (or not) its production plant in the host market, firm(s) and union(s) bargain over wages. The optimal wages in all candidate equilibria are defined as follows:

i) Exports Case:

$$arg\,max\,\{w_{he} \cdot q_{he}\} \xrightarrow{optimal} w_{he} \qquad (3)$$

$$arg\,max\,\left\{w_{fe} \cdot \frac{q_{fe}}{k}\right\} \xrightarrow{optimal} w_{fe} \qquad (4)$$

Where, $w_{he\,(fe)}$ stand for the home (the foreign) union's bargained wages, and $q_{he\,(fe)}$ is the home (the foreign) firm's output.

ii) FDI under Decentralized Union Structure/Wage Bargaining Case:

$$arg\,max\,\{w_{hdb} \cdot q_{hdb}\} \xrightarrow{optimal} w_{hdb} \qquad (5)$$

$$arg\,max\,\left\{w_{fdb} \cdot \frac{q_{fdb}}{k}\right\} \xrightarrow{optimal} w_{fdb} \qquad (6)$$

Where, $w_{hdb\,(fdb)}$ is the wage bargain for the domestic (sub) union of workers who find employment with the home (the foreign) firm, and $q_{hdb\,(fdb)}$ is the output of the home (the foreign) firm, under FDI and a decentralized union structure/ wage bargaining regime.

FDI under Centralized Union Structure/Wage Bargaining Case:

$$arg\,max\,\left\{w_{hcb} \cdot q_{hcb} + w_{fcb} \cdot \frac{q_{fcb}}{k} - U^{fmon}\right\} \xrightarrow{optimal} w_{hcb} \qquad (7)$$

$$arg\,max\,\left\{w_{hcb} \cdot q_{hcb} + w_{fcb} \cdot \frac{q_{fcb}}{k} - U^{hmon}\right\} \xrightarrow{optimal} w_{fcb} \qquad (8)$$

Where, $w_{hcb\,(fcb)}$ is the wage bargain for the domestic union workers who find employment with the home (the foreign) firm, $q_{hcb\,(fcb)}$ is the home (the foreign) firm's output, and $U^{fmon(hmon)}$ stands for the domestic union's (reservation) utility, in case that the negotiations with the home (the foreign) firm fail, under the centralized union structure/wage employment regime.[4]

---

[4] Following Milliou and Petrakis (2007), yet in a quite different context of analysis, the union must in this case take into account the possibility of a failure in the negotiations with either the *h-firm* or the *f-firm*, any of those instances implying that union members would then prospect to be employed by a monopolist (to be either the *h-firm* or the *f-firm*) in the product market.

Stage 4: Firms compete *a la Cournot* in the home product market. That is, for any output level of its rival firm, each firm independently adjusts its output so that to maximize its own profits:

$$Max\{pr_h = P(Q) \cdot q_h - C_h(q_h) \} \qquad (9)$$

$$Max\{pr_f = P(Q) \cdot q_f - C_f(q_f) \} \qquad (10)$$

Where, the cost functions $C_{h(f)}$ are later on explicitly defined according to the outcomes of the previous stages.

3. UNIONIZATION STRUCTURE AND WAGE BARGAINING, INTERNATIONAL TRADE AND FDI

In this section, we examine whether, under the possibility of inward FDI, the domestic unionization/wage bargaining structure can be effectively used as a policy tool in order to maximize social welfare. Using backwards induction (to ensure subgame perfection), we first obtain the considered *(i)-(iii)* candidate equilibria, and figure out in each the range of values for all structural parameters that ensures consistent (internal) solutions for all endogenous arguments. We subsequently explore all possible Nash equilibria, by investigating if there is any motivation, on the part of any of the involved agents, to deviate from the (considered) candidate equilibrium.

3.1. Solving the Model

Starting from the (last) *Stage 4*, where Cournot competition takes place, using the (simultaneous and independent profit maximization) first order conditions, we derive the rival (*h* and *f*) firms' reaction functions and, by those, their optimal outputs and profits, in each instance[5].

Note that, if wages are equal ($w_{he} = w_{fe}$), in the exports case, then the *f-firm* will enjoy greater market share and profits only if $exp(A1) - exp(A2) = q_{he} - q_{fe} > 0 \leftrightarrow x > \frac{k-1}{k}w$. Hence, if the *f-firm* possesses no greater productivity than the *h-firm* (k=1), then the *h-firm* will always enjoy greater market share and profits than the *f-firm*, due to the latter firm's (extra) unit cost *x*. While, if the *f-firm's* relative technological advantage (k) over the *h-firm* is high enough, then it can render the *f-firm* dominant in the home market, despite the fact that *f-firm* always faces the (extra) unit cost x to serve this market. A similar analysis applies to the FDI case.

Proceeding (backwards), at *Stage 3*, unions set firm-specific wages so that to maximize the home union's (or the home sub-unions') relevant utility (utilities) in any instance. Thus, from the first order conditions of (3) - (8), we obtain optimal wages, for each instance, and

---

[5] The analytical results of each stage are listed in Appendix 5.1.

substituting them back we derive the firms' outputs and profits, as well as the home union's (or the home sub-unions') utility (utilities'), for all candidate equilibria. At this point, it must be stressed out that the domestic labour union may (at *Stage 3*) – prior to wage bargaining and without delay – decide to split into two sub-unions, who will separately and independently bargain the wages of those workers who (will) find employment with the *f-firm* and the *h-firm*. This case of course applies only in the event of inward FDI, since in the exports case the *f-firm* will only deal with the foreign union abroad. For such a split to emerge, nonetheless, the home unions' utility [which is always (i.e., under any unionization structure) comprised by the sum of sub-utilities of workers who find employment with the foreign and the home firm] must be strictly grater than under the centralized union structure/wage bargaining regime.[6]

At *Stage 2*, the *f-firm* decides whether to settle its (new) production (plant) in the host country, or abroad, and materializes its choice. At this stage, neither unions nor the social planner can do something in order to alter the *f-firm's* decision: If, for instance, given the host labour market's institutional set-up, the *f-firm's* profits under exports are (predicted to be) less than under FDI, then the *f-firm* will choose and materialize inward FDI in the (sub-game perfect) equilibrium. Therefore, if social welfare is optimized under this – inward FDI – state of the equilibrium, the social planner (if needed) must, at *Stage 1*, institutionalize and enforce the contingent unionization structure/wage bargaining regime.

To assure that our model retains consistency, with non trivial internal solutions, the following restrictions apply: $0 < x < \frac{5}{7}, 0 < c < \frac{1}{2}; k > 1$.[7]

3.2. Equilibrium Analysis

Given the above findings, we may now proceed to the determination of the Nash equilibria.

1st Case: High Values of C – Exports Equilibrium

If the *f-firm's* profits under exports are greater than the respective ones in all FDI cases (i.e., under decentralized or centralized union structure/wage bargaining), then the *f-firm's* choice will be to serve the local market via exports. It proves[8] that this optimal strategy occurs if $c > x(= c_{cr1})$, since then, $pr_{fe} > pr_{fdb} > pr_{fcb}$. Note that, since the choice of the *f-firm* is independent of the unionization/wage bargaining structure in the host labour market, the social planner cannot, in this case, effectively manipulate/enforce the unionization structure in order to induce FDI. Proposition 1 summarizes.

---

[6] Since the home union's members are identical, and treated identically, any decision to split, or not, requires the consent of everyone. Such a unanimous consensus is in turn expected to occur only if the average member's (expected) utility is maximized under the considered unionization structure.

[7] The relevant calculations are listed in the Appendix 5.2.

[8] The relevant calculations are listed in the Appendix 5.3.

Proposition 1

If the f-firm's FDI-associated unit cost (c) is greater than its export-associated unit cost (x), then exports will always emerge in the equilibrium. Hence, neither the social planner nor the home union can use the unionization/wage bargaining structure as an effective tool to alter the f-firm's optimal strategy and induce FDI.

An interesting point to note here is the absence of the productivity element ($k>1$) from the *f-firm's* exports choice criterion ($c > x$). Seemingly, therefore, the *f-firm's* higher relative productivity is not taken into account in choosing between international trade and FDI. This is not literally true however. What in the background happens is that, whenever wage bargaining is effectively decentralized across (the *h* and *f*) firms, for the *f-firm* to engage in cross-border rivalry via either exports or FDI, its – lower unit cost of production – advantage over the *h-firm* must be sufficient to over-compensate its extra unit cost (*x* or *c*) to serve the home market with either strategy. Therefore, the *f-firm* will definitely choose exports if the extra unit cost of exports (*x*) is lower than the extra unit cost of FDI (*c*). Yet, as it will become evident later on, under a centralized union structure/wage bargaining in the host market, the opposite (i.e., $x > c$) is not sufficient for FDI to be the *f-firm's* optimal strategy to serve the home market.

$2^{nd} - 3^{rd}$ Case(s): Intermediate values of c – FDI/Decentralized Union Structure and Exports/Centralized Union Structure equilibria

If $c_{cr2} = \frac{-5+28x}{30} < c < x$, then the profits of *f-firm* under FDI will be greater than its profits under exports, only if the *f-firm's* employment/production plans in the host market are implemented under a decentralized wage bargaining regime. However, given the *f-firm's* (irreversible) choice to locate production in the host country, it proves[9] that the home union will always $\left(0 < c < \frac{1}{2}\right)$ choose the centralized wage bargaining regime, thus deterring inward FDI. The reason is that the sum of the sub-unions' utilities is always greater under the centralized, than under the decentralized, wage bargaining setup, hence, there is no motivation for the home union to split in two sub-unions, each one setting independently the (*h* and *f*) firm-specific wages. As a consequence, in the absence of any legislation restricting the unionization/wage bargaining structure to the decentralized regime, the *f-firm* will never choose the FDI strategy to serve the home market.

Therefore, the social planner will effectively face two options to evaluate in terms of social welfare: Exports vs. FDI under a decentralized union structure/wage bargaining setup. It proves that,[10] if $c < c_{cr3} = \frac{1}{64}\left(35 - \sqrt{15}\sqrt{-25 + 64x^2}\right)$, then $SW_{db} > SW_e$, hence, in order to induce FDI, and thus maximize social welfare, the social planner will have to establish a decentralized union structure, assuring decentralized wage bargaining, in the labour market, in contrast to home union's optimal choice. If, on the other hand, $c > c_{cr3} = \frac{1}{64}\left(35 - \sqrt{15}\sqrt{-25 + 64x^2}\right)$, then $SW_{db} < SW_e$. In this case the social planner's choice will line up with the home union's one and he/she must simply leave the labour market to auto-regulate to the centralized union structure/wage bargaining regime, deterring inward FDI. Proposition 2 summarizes.

---

[9] The relevant calculations are listed in the Appendix 5.4.
[10] The relevant calculations are listed in the Appendix 5.5.

Proposition 2

(a). If $c_{cr2} = \frac{-5+28x}{30} < c < c_{cr3} = \frac{1}{64}\left(35 - \sqrt{15}\sqrt{-25 + 64x^2}\right) < x$, then the social planner must impose a decentralized union structure/wage bargaining regime, thus inducing inward FDI and maximizing social welfare in the equilibrium.

(b). If $c_{cr3} < c < x$, then the social planner must leave the home labour market to auto-regulate to the centralized union structure/wage bargaining, thus deterring inward FDI and maximizing social welfare in the equilibrium.

4th Case: Low values of c – FDI/Decentralized Union Structure Equilibrium

If c is low enough $\left(0 < c < c_{cr2} = \frac{-5+28x}{30}\right)$, then the *f-firm's* profits under exports are less than its profits in both instances of FDI (i.e., under a centralized or a decentralized unionization structure in the host labour market)[11]. It is then clear that inward FDI will definitely emerge, since the *f-firm* will gain fewer profits under the exports strategy, anyway. Nonetheless, the domestic unionization structure may still remain a worthy policy tool, the question here being: given that inward FDI will emerge, which regime is welfare maximizing, the centralized or the decentralized one?

As far it regards the home union, we have already shown that in the FDI context it maximizes utility (and/or the sum of utilities of the constituent sub-unions) under the centralized regime (for any $c \in [0, 0.5]$). However, what is best for the home union is not necessary social welfare optimizing. It in fact proves that,[12] within the above range of (low) c values, social welfare is greater under the decentralized, than under the centralized, wage bargaining regime in the FDI equilibrium. Thus, also in this case, the social planner must actively intervene in the home labour market and enforce the decentralized union structure in contrast to the home union's best interest. Proposition 3 summarizes.

Proposition 3

If c is low enough $\left(i.e., 0 < c < c_{cr2} = \frac{-5+28x}{30}\right)$, then inward FDI will always emerge. However, the social planner– in contrast to the home union's best interest –must enforce the decentralized union structure/wage bargaining regime, in order to achieve social welfare maximization in the equilibrium.

The outcomes of the above analysis can be briefly illustrated at the following table.

Critical values of c	0 c_{cr2}	c_{cr3}	x	0.5
f-firm's optimal strategy	FDI	FDI	Exports	Exports
home union's optimal strategy	Centralized union Structure/Wage bargaining (C.B.)	C.B.	C.B.	Indifferent
Social Planner's Choice	Enforces Decentralized Union Structure/Wage Bargaining (D.B.) (In contrast to the home union's best interest)	Enforces D.B. (In contrast to the home union's best interest)	Allows C.B. (allows labour market to auto-regulate)	Indifferent
Equilibrium	FDI under the D.B. regime	FDI under the D.B. regime	Exports under the C.B. regime	Exports under the C.B. regime

---

[11] The relevant calculations are listed in the Appendix 5.3.
[12] The relevant calculations are listed in the Appendix 5.5.

CONCLUSION

In this paper we have examined whether enforcing a particular unionization structure in the host labour market is an effective policy tool in order to induce or deter inward FDI. Our analysis diverts from previous works [see, e.g., Vlassis (2009) and the references therein] in two major aspects. First, we have addressed the home union's structure as a strategy (rather than as a given institutional factor) to deter or accommodate inward FDI at the union's best interest, and confronted it against the society's best interest. In terms of methodology, moreover, we have inbuilt to our model the concept of the home union's reservation utility under the possibility of inward FDI, thus addressing the centralized structure of wage bargaining in the event of inward FDI.

By these means new interesting findings are brought regarding the status and treatment of a host labour market's institutions under the possibility of inward FDI. Appealing for further/empirical investigation, it seems that the centralized union/wage bargaining setup is a factor deterring inward FDI (thus, accommodating exports), while its decentralized counterpart seems to be associated with FDI accommodation. Most important, yet quite challenging (and even heretic) for conventional wisdom, we hereby propose that a policy maker may sometimes need to intervene against the unions' choice regarding their structure and organization, in order to serve the society's best interest.

Two possible extensions of the present model are left open for further research. The first is to address in the analysis the union bargaining power to be less than one, and also consider reservation wages. The second, and most ambitious one, is to conduct analysis on the critical scope of the labour market institutions regarding FDI.

5. APPENDIX

5.1. Results per Stage

4th stage: Cournot Competition

Exports case:

$$q_{he} = \frac{k + w_{fe} - 2k w_{he} + kx}{3k} \tag{A1}$$

$$q_{fe} = \frac{k - 2w_{fe} + k w_{he} - 2kx}{3k} \tag{A2}$$

$$pr_{he} = \frac{\left(w_{fe} + k(1 - 2w_{he} + x)\right)^2}{9k^2} \tag{A3}$$

$$pr_{fe} = \frac{\left(-2w_{fe} + k(1 + w_{he} - 2x)\right)^2}{9k^2} \tag{A4}$$

$$P_e = \frac{w_{fe} + k(1 + w_{he} + x)}{3k} \tag{A5}$$

FDI case:

Union Structure and Inward FDI

$$q_{hf} = \frac{(1+c)\,k + w_{ff} - 2\,k\,w_{hf}}{3\,k} \tag{A6}$$

$$q_{ff} = \frac{(1-2c)\,k - 2\,w_{ff} + k\,w_{hf}}{3\,k} \tag{A7}$$

$$pr_{hf} = \frac{\left(w_{ff} + k\,(1+c-2\,w_{hf})\right)^2}{9\,k^2} \tag{A8}$$

$$pr_{ff} = \frac{\left(-2\,w_{ff} + k\,(1-2c+w_{hf})\right)^2}{9\,k^2} \tag{A9}$$

$$P_f = \frac{w_{ff} + k\,(1+c+w_{hf})}{3\,k} \tag{A10}$$

3rd stage: Wage Bargaining

Exports case:

$$w_{he} = \frac{5+2x}{15} \tag{A11}$$

$$w_{fe} = \frac{5-7x}{15}\,k \tag{A12}$$

$$q_{he} = \frac{2\,(5+2x)}{45} \tag{A13}$$

$$q_{fe} = \frac{2\,(5-7x)}{45} \tag{A14}$$

$$pr_{he} = \frac{4\,(5+2x)^2}{2025} \tag{A15}$$

$$pr_{fe} = \frac{4\,(5-7x)^2}{2025} \tag{A16}$$

$$p_e = \frac{5+2x}{9} \tag{A17}$$

FDI under decentralized wage bargaining case:

$$w_{hdb} = \frac{5+2c}{15} \tag{A18}$$

$$w_{fdb} = \frac{5-7c}{15}\,k \tag{A19}$$

$$q_{hdb} = \frac{2\,(5+2c)}{45} \tag{A20}$$

$$q_{fdb} = \frac{2\,(5-7c)}{45} \tag{A21}$$

$$pr_{hdb} = \frac{4\,(5+2c)^2}{2025} \tag{A22}$$

$$pr_{fdb} = \frac{4\,(5-7c)^2}{2025} \tag{A23}$$

$$p_{db} = \frac{5+2c}{9} \tag{A24}$$

FDI under centralized wage bargaining case:

$$w_{hcb} = \frac{1}{2} \tag{A18}$$

$$w_{fcb} = \frac{1-c}{2}\cdot k \tag{A19}$$

$$q_{hcb} = \frac{1+c}{6} \tag{A20}$$

$$q_{fcb} = \frac{1-2c}{6} \tag{A21}$$

$$pr_{hcb} = \frac{(1+c)^2}{36} \tag{A22}$$
$$pr_{fcb} = \frac{(1-2c)^2}{36} \tag{A23}$$
$$p_{cb} = \frac{4+c}{6} \tag{A24}$$

2nd stage: f-firm's choice (Exports vs. FDI)

See in 3rd stage for the relevant profit outcomes in each instance

1st stage: Social Planner

Exports case:

$$U_{he} = \frac{2(5+2x)^2}{675} \tag{A25}$$
$$U_{fe} = \frac{2(5-7x)^2}{675} \tag{A26}$$
$$CS_e = \frac{2(-2+x)^2}{81} \tag{A27}$$
$$SW_e = \frac{2(5+x^2)}{45} \tag{A28}$$

FDI under decentralized wage bargaining case:

$$U_{hdb} = \frac{2(5+2c)^2}{675} \tag{A29}$$
$$U_{fdb} = \frac{2(5-7c)^2}{675} \tag{A30}$$
$$CS_{db} = \frac{2(-2+c)^2}{81} \tag{A31}$$
$$SW_{db} = \frac{4(50+c(-35+32c))}{675} \tag{A32}$$

FDI under centralized wage bargaining case:

$$U_{hcb} = \frac{1+c}{12} \tag{A33}$$
$$U_{fcb} = \frac{(1-c)(1-2c)}{12} \tag{A34}$$
$$CS_{cb} = \frac{(-2+c)^2}{72} \tag{A35}$$
$$SW_{cb} = \frac{(6+c(-4+5c))}{24} \tag{A36}$$

5.2. Parameter Restrictions

We have checked for the sufficient restrictions of the parameter values so that the model to be consistent and entailing non-trivial interior solutions for all endogenous variables. We conclude that $w_{he}, q_{he}, pr_{he}, pr_{fe}, p_e$ are all positive for any $x \in (0,1)$. However, $w_{fe} = \frac{5-7x}{15} \cdot k > 0 \leftrightarrow 5 - 7x > 0 \leftrightarrow x < \frac{5}{7}$. The same restriction applies for $q_{fe} > 0$.

For the FDI under decentralized bargaining case, it can be easily checked that $w_{hdb}, q_{hdb}, pr_{hdb}, pr_{fdb}, p_{db}$ are all positive for any $c \in (0,1)$. However, $w_{fdb} = \frac{5-7c}{15} k > 0 \leftrightarrow 5 - 7c > 0 \leftrightarrow c < \frac{5}{7}$. The same restriction applies for $q_{fdb} > 0$.

For the FDI under centralized bargaining case, all results are positive for any $c \in (0,1)$, exept for $q_{fcb} = \frac{1-2c}{6} > 0 \leftrightarrow c < \frac{1}{2}$.

No special analysis is needed to find out that $U_{he}, U_{fe}, CS_e, SW_e$ are all positive for any $x \in (0,1)$. The same findings also apply for $U_{hdb}, U_{fdb}, CS_{db}, U_{hcb}, CS_{cb}$ which are all positive for any $c \in (0,1)$. Moreover, it can be checked that:

- $SW_{db} = \frac{4(50 + c(-35+32c))}{675} > 0 (50 + c(-35 + 32c)) > 0$, which is valid for any $0 < c < \frac{1}{2}$.
- $U_{fcb} = \frac{(1-c)(1-2c)}{12} > 0 \leftrightarrow (1-c)(1-2c) > 0$, which is valid for any $0 < c < \frac{1}{2}$.
- $SW_{cb} = \frac{(6+c(-4+5c))}{24} > 0 \leftrightarrow 6 + c(-4+5c) > 0$, which is valid for any $0 < c < \frac{1}{2}$.

Summarizing the above, the following restrictions apply:
$0 < x < \frac{5}{7}, 0 < c < \frac{1}{2}$ and $k > 1$.

5.3. *f*-firm's choice

The following critical profit differentials arise.

- $pr_{fcb} - pr_{fdb} = \frac{(5+2c)(-35+58c)}{8.100}$

  Hence, $0 < c < \frac{1}{2} \rightarrow pr_{fcb} < pr_{fdb}$.

- $pr_{fe} - pr_{fdb} = -\frac{28(c-x)(-10+7c+7x)}{2025}$. The term $-\frac{28(-10+7c+7x)}{2025}$ is always positive, hence, if $c > x \rightarrow pr_{fe} > pr_{fdb}$, while, if $c < x \rightarrow pr_{fe} < pr_{fdb}$.

- $pr_{fe} - pr_{fcb} = -\frac{1}{36}(1-2c)^2 + \frac{4(5-7x)^2}{2025}$. The roots of this expression are $c_1 = -\frac{7}{30}(-5+4x)$ and $c_2 = \frac{1}{30}(-5+28x)$. For $0 < x < \frac{5}{7}$, $c_1 < 0$, so we reject it. Furthermore, it can be checked that if $0.5 > c > c_2 =$

$\frac{1}{30}(-5+28x) \to pr_{fe} > pr_{fcb}$, while if $0 < c < c_2 = \frac{1}{30}(-5+28x) \to pr_{fe} < pr_{fcb}$.

Hence, there are two critical values of c, $c_{cr1} = x$, and $c_{cr2} = \frac{-5+28x}{30}$. Since $c_{cr2} - c_{cr1} = \frac{-5+28x}{30} - x = -\frac{5+2x}{30} < 0 \to c_{cr2} < c_{cr1}$, we can subsequently sort the profits of the f-firm against these c-critical values, as in the following table (profits in row 1 > profits in row 2 > profits in row 3).

0		$c_{cr2} = \frac{-5+28x}{30}$		$c_{cr1} = x$		0.5
row1 $\longrightarrow$		pr_{fdb}		pr_{fdb}		pr_{fe}
row2 $\longrightarrow$		pr_{fcb}		pr_{fe}		pr_{fdb}
row3 $\longrightarrow$		pr_{fe}		pr_{fcb}		pr_{fcb}

5.4. Home Union's Choice

The sum of the sub-unions' utilities under the centralized union/wage bargaining structure is,

$$\text{Exp(A33)} + \text{Exp(A34)} = U_{hcb} + U_{fcb} = \frac{1+c}{12} + \frac{(1-c)(1-2c)}{12} = \frac{1}{6}(1+(-1+c)c)$$

While, the sum of the sub-unions' utilities under the decentralized union/ wage bargaining structure is,

$$\text{Exp(A29)} + \text{Exp(A30)} = U_{hdb} + U_{fdb} = \frac{2(5+2c)^2}{675} + \frac{2(5-7c)^2}{675}$$
$$= \frac{2}{675}(50 + c(-50 + 53c))$$

Subtracting – the first minus the second expression– we subsequently get,

$$\left(\frac{1}{6}(1+(-1+c)c)\right) - \left(\frac{2}{675}(50 + c(-50+53c))\right) = \frac{25+c(-25+13c)}{1350},$$

The latter expression is positive for any $c \in [0,0.5]$. Thus, the home union's utility in the FDI case(s) is greater under the centralized, than under the decentralized, regime.

5.5. Social Welfare

The following social welfare differentials arise.

- $SW_{cb} - SW_{db} = \frac{-250+c(220+101c)}{5400} < 0$ for $0 < c < 0.5 \to SW_{cb} < SW_{db}$
- $SW_{db} - SW_e = \frac{2}{675}(25 - 70c + 64c^2 - 15x^2)$.
- If $0 < c < \frac{1}{64}\left(35 - \sqrt{15}\sqrt{-25 + 64x^2}\right) = c_{cr3} \to \frac{2}{675}(25 - 70c + 64c^2 - 15x^2) > 0 \to SW_{db} > SW_e$,
- else, if $\frac{1}{64}\left(35 - \sqrt{15}\sqrt{-25 + 64x^2}\right) = c_{cr3} < c < 0.5 \to \frac{2}{675}(25 - 70c + 64c^2 - 15x^2) < 0 \to SW_{db} < SW_e$.

REFERENCES

Arrow, K, 1964, Control in Large Organisations, *Management Science*; V.10-#4, pp. 397-408.

Brander, J., Spencer, B., 1988, Unionised Oligopoly and International Trade Policy, *Journal of International Economics*; V.24-#3/4, pp. 217-234.

Caves, R., 1971, International Corporations: The Industrial Economics of Foreign Investment, *Economica*; V.38-#149, pp. 1-27.

Coase, R., 1937, The Nature of the Firm, *Economica*; V.4, pp. 386-405.

Gaston, N., Nelson, D., 2000, The Wage and Employment Effects of Immigration: Trade and Labour Economics Perspectives, ms: *Centre for Research on Globalisation and Labour Markets*.

Gaston, N., Nelson, D., 2001, Multinational Location Decisions And The Impact On Labour Markets, *Discussion Papers 18747, University of Bonn, Center for Development Research (ZEF)*.

Greenaway, D., Nelson, D., 2001, Globalisation and Labour Markets: Literature Review and Synthesis, *Globalisation and Labour Markets*, Vols. 1 and 2, p.1,068 (Edward Elgar).

Horn, H., Wolinsky, A., 1988, Bilateral Monopolies and Incentives for Merger, *Rand Journal of Economics* 19, 408–419.

Hymer, S., 1960, The International Operations of National Firms: A Study Of Direct Foreign Investment, *Cambridge: MIT Press*.

Ishiguro, S., Shirai, Y., 1998, Entry Deterrence in Unionized Oligopoly, *The Japanese Economic Review*, 49.

Kindleberger, C., 1969, American Business Abroad, *New Haven: Yale University Press*.

Mezzetti, C., Dinopoulos E., 1991, Domestic Unionisation and Import Competition, *Journal of International Economics*; V.31-#1/2, pp. 79-100.

Milliou, C., Petrakis, E., 2007, Upstream Horizontal Mergers, Vertical Contracts, and Bargaining, *International Journal of Industrial Organization* 25, 963-987.

Naylor, R., Santoni, M., 2003, Foreign direct investment and wage bargaining, *Journal of International Trade and Economic Development*, Taylor and Francis Journals, vol. 12(1), pages 1-18.

Petrakis, E., Vlassis, M., 2000, Endogenous Scope of Bargaining in a Union-Oligopoly Model: when will firms and unions bargain about employment?, *Labour Economics*, 7(3), pp. 261-281.

Vlassis, M., 2009, Employment-Protecting Labour Market Institutions and Inward Foreign Direct Investments, *Labour*, 23(4), pp. 667-696.

Williamson, O., 1975, Markets and Hierarchies: Analysis and Anti-Trust Implications, *New York: Free Press*.

In: Foreign Direct Investment (FDI)
Editors: Enzo Guillon and Lucas Chauvet

ISBN: 978-1-62808-403-0
© 2013 Nova Science Publishers, Inc.

Chapter 10

INWARD FDI PERFORMANCE AND DETERMINANTS OF FDI REGIONAL DISPARITY IN CHINA

Lucy Zheng[*]
Westminster Business School, University of Westminster, London, UK

ABSTRACT

This study investigates China's inward FDI performance and determinants of FDI regional disparities among the three macro-regions of China. A panel dataset at provincial level and the GLS statistics model are used to identify the factors of FDI regional disparities by considering provincial and regional characteristics. The empirical results indicate that variations in economic openness and industrial and economic development are the prime causes of the unbalance regional distribution of China's inward FDI. The study further discusses the impact of FDI regional disparities on China's economy and finally, the policy implications are provided to reduce the degree of FDI regional disparity.

CHINA INWARD FDI PERFORMANCE

As the largest emerging economy, China has received remarkably high levels of foreign direct investment (FDI) inflows and achieved high economic growth rates since 1984. China has received inward FDI from over 150 countries and regions worldwide and has been the largest recipient of FDI among developing countries and regions since 1993. China has maintained its position as the most attractive FDI destination in the world since 2002 (Kearney, 2010). Chinese inward FDI stock amounted to US$711 billion in 2011 increased from US$306 billion in 1999 and its annual FDI inflows reached to US$124 billion in 2011

increased from US$40 billion in 1999 and US$11 billion in 1992. The Chinese economy has grown strongly at an annual average rate of over 9 percent in the last three decades, ranking

---

[*] Corresponding author: Tel: +44 (0)20 350 66598, Fax: +44 (0)20 7911 5723, E-mail: zhengp@wmin.ac.uk.

China among the fastest growing economies in the world. China is now the second largest economy in the world, behind only the USA, replaced Japan in 2010. An important driving force for this remarkable growth and development has been inward FDI (Buckley, et al., 2002; Zheng, et al., 2006).

The geographical distribution of FDI in China is highly concentrated in the eastern coastal region, which is considered more developed than the rest of China. About 88 percent of inward FDI was accounted for by the eastern coastal region, which comprises nine provinces (including three central municipalities). The remaining 12 percent is spread across in the vast inland regions of China, 9 percent in the central region and 3 percent in the western region (Zheng et. al., 2004). If FDI is to continue to contribute to China's growth and further its economic development, the skewed spatial distribution of investment and economic activity must be addressed. For this reason, a leading task of the current Five-Year Plan of the Chinese government has been to develop the western region, an area covering 56 percent of the country's total land and 23 percent of the population, which is considerably less developed and much poorer than the eastern region. Regional disparity along with corruption and pollution has been the major problems in China over the last three decades. The Chinese government aims to eliminate poverty in the western provinces and significantly reduce the regional development disparity by the middle of this century.

A number of studies have explored the determinants of Chinese inward FDI. These studies, however, do not investigate the reasons behind China's inward FDI locational disparity among the three macro regions. Using varying data sets and methodologies, these previous studies inevitably produce diverse results. The present study differs from the previous studies in three ways. First, it develops the literature by identifying and analysing the factors causing disparities in inward FDI flows to the three macro-regions. Second, the investigation extends the previous studies by using a longer and more recent data set covering 24 years (1984-2007). Third, the research methodology is more robust as it introduces a structural break framework to obtain robust estimates for the three macro regions. The data are divided into two time periods, i.e. 1984-1992 and 1993-2007 to investigate any variation in determinants between the sub-periods. The findings generated from this study provide important implications for both the Chinese government and business practitioners.

The rest of the chapter is organised as follows. Section 2 discusses FDI regional disparity determinants. Section 3 discusses the model and research methodology. Section 4 presents the findings, while the last section summarises the key conclusions and offers policy implications.

FDI REGIONAL DISPARITY DETERMINANTS

According to the previous studies, the main FDI determinants include market size, labour cost, infrastructure, human capital and agglomeration economies (Guimaraes et al., 2000; Cheng and Kwan, 2000; Wei et al., 1999; de Mello, 1997). FDI is assumed to be a function of the size of the regional market because market size affects the expected return on investment.

In fact, an important motivation of FDI is market-seeking to develop new markets for existing products. The larger the market size of a particular province, *ceteris paribus*, the more market-seeking FDI the province should attract. Thus, market size is expected to positively influence FDI inflows at a provincial level.

The efficiency-seeking FDI aim to take advantage of host countries' cheaper factor inputs such as labour cost (Dunning, 1988, 1993, 1998), which should, therefore, be negatively related to FDI inflows (Culem, 1988). However, if higher labour cost is also related to higher labour quality (and so to higher productivity) then higher labour cost might attract more FDI. Wang and Swain (1995) point out that nominal wage differences may not induce FDI if labour productivity is very low. Countries or regions with low labour productivity coupled with relatively cheap labour may attract less FDI than those with high labour productivity and more costly labour even when FDI is motivated by efficiency-seeking. Therefore the empirical relationship between labour cost and FDI inflows is ambiguous.

The labour quality of a region also influences FDI location decisions. Regions with highly skilled workers measured by educational levels, *ceteris paribus*, would be expected to be more attractive to FDI especially those for resource-seeking purpose. Therefore, this variable, unlike labour cost, is expected to have a positive effect on FDI inflows.

The infrastructure development of a region is an important factor to be considered when foreign investors make investment locational choice. This variable is expected to be positively related to FDI inflows especially to those efficiency-seeking FDI. Porter (1998) notes that Agglomeration (or clusters) means that groups of interconnected firms, suppliers, related industries and specialised institutions in particular fields are simultaneously present in particular locations. New growth theory argues that knowledge spillovers, diffusion, and externalities can reduce the costs of firms that are co-located (Griliches, 1979). Braunerhjelm and Svensson (1996) pointed out that if it is important for firms' competitiveness to gain knowledge spillovers and pecuniary externalities, we should expect agglomeration effect to influence firms' locational decisions. A region, in which there is substantial clustering of industrial activities, is likely to enjoy relatively lower costs than a region with a dispersed manufacturing sector. Porter (1998, p. xii) further argued that agglomeration effect "not only reduce transaction costs and boost efficiency, but also improve incentives for investment and create collective assets in the form of information, specialised institutions and reputation effects". Agglomeration effect is conducive to innovation, speed productivity growth and also ease the formation of new business. This variable is therefore expected to be positively related to FDI inflows.

It has been proposed that FDI inflows might depend on the existing capital stock in a location, particularly the existing FDI stock. The argument here is that adding to existing stock in a particular location is less risky and less costly for subsequent investors (Billington, 1999). Head et al. (1995) estimated the location choices of 751 Japanese manufacturing plants built in the USA since 1980 and found that initial investments by Japanese firms encourage subsequent investors in the same industry to select the same states. Foreign firms face greater uncertainties than domestic firms in a host country, therefore, they have a strong incentive to follow previous investors, signal as to the reliability of a particular location (Krugman, 1997; Barry, et al, 2003). Furthermore, existing investors in a location offer opportunities for subsequent investors to develop forward and backward linkages with them, increasing the attractiveness of the location in question. Existing investors may also make sequential investments, either in the form of new FDI projects or by re-investing earnings locally. In order to take account of the dynamic process of FDI inflows, one year-lagged inward FDI inflows will be included as an explanatory variable. In view of the above discussion, this is expected to be positively related to FDI inflows.

As mentioned earlier, the coastal provinces attract much more FDI than inland provinces due to their superior natural, social, and economic conditions. China is often visualized as a three-step "staircase" from the plateau and desert in the western region down to the highlands and basins in the central region, and further down to the hills and plains in the eastern coastal region. The natural geographic conditions in the inland areas are unfavourable for economic development because of the inferior transport facilities and infrastructure and the high costs of transportation. In contrast, the eastern region has advantages in production, transportation, trade, and economic development. As a result, the country's population and industrial base are concentrated in the eastern area. According to the Growth Pole Theory (Perroux, 1950, 1970, 1988), a concentration of population and industry is conducive to economic growth and development. Song, et al, (2000) argue that regional inequality is a direct consequence of the growth pole process in which the more populated regions grow faster and achieve higher income and economic development levels than other regions. Another major advantage for the coast regions compared to the inland regions is the familial connections with overseas Chinese (in Hong Kong, Macao and Taiwan particularly), who have been a major contributor for Chinese inward FDI (Zheng, 2009). This inward FDI has preferentially flowed to China's coastal region, following family links. Therefore, the economy in the eastern region has grown fastest, increasing regional disparities within China. The Chinese economy was a highly centrally planned economy, following the Soviet Union model, before the economic reforms of 1978. Since this time, the Chinese government has continued to play a crucial role in the economy. Many preferential policies were offered to foreign investors in the Special Economic Zones, open coastal cities, economic and technological development zones, and special economic deltas established in the eastern coastal region by the Chinese government. The coastal provinces also provide export-oriented FDI with proximity to major international markets. Therefore, the geographical location of a province is thought to be an important determinant of the distribution of FDI in China. In order to include these factors into the estimation, a dummy variable combining provincial geographical location and preferential policy (which assume the same values) is included in the estimated model.

Finally, a time dummy variable is entered into the model to test whether the Tiananmen Square Incident of 1989 affected FDI inflows. It would be expected this variable to have a negative effect on FDI inflows. A brief summary of the variables, the proxies, the expected signs and the data sources is given in Table 1.

MODEL AND METHODOLOGY

The above discussion suggests the following model:

$$FDI = f\ (FDI_{(t-1)}, \text{market size, labour cost, human capital, infrastructure, agglomeration, dummy location/policy, dummy89-91}) \qquad (1)$$

Table 1. The determinants of disparity in inward FDI in China

Determinant	Proxy	Expected Sign	Data Source
Previous year's FDI (FDI $_{t-1}$)	One year-lagged FDI	+	*Almanac of China's Foreign Economic Relations and Trade*
Market size (GDP)	Real GDP (1995 prices)	+	*China Statistical Yearbook*
Labour cost (WAGE)	Annual average of staff and workers wage at 1995 prices	?	*China Statistical Yearbook*
Human capital (EDU)	Ratio of higher education enrolment to population	+	*China Statistical Yearbook*
Agglomeration (AGG)	Ratio of employee numbers to land area	+	*China Statistical Yearbook*
Infrastructure (INFR)	Ratio of total length of highways, railways and waterways to land area	+	*China Statistical Yearbook*
Location and policy (DLP)	Coastal region location Coastal provinces=1, others=0	+	
Time dummy variable (DTM)	The period 1989-91 following the Tiananmen Square Incident, 1989-91=1, others=0	-	

To test the model, a panel data set is employed of pooled cross-section and time-series data for 29 provinces over 24 years from 1984 to 2007. The dependent variable employed in the model is annual realized FDI in real terms (at 1995 prices) in each province of China. To measure the impact of the explanatory variables on the dependent variable (FDI) in terms of elasticity, the log-linear model is to be used. Thus, equation (1) in logarithmic form is:

$$LFDI_{it} = \alpha + \beta_0 LFDI_{it-1} + \beta_1 LGDP_{it} + \beta_2 LWAGE_{it} + \beta_3 LEDU_{it} + \beta_4 LINFR_{it} + \beta_5 LAGG_{it} + \beta_6 DLP + \beta_7 DTM + \varepsilon_{it} \quad (2)$$

Three statistical models are commonly used in panel data set estimation: pooled ordinary least squares (POLS), fixed effects (FEs), and random effects (REs). In this study, we employ only the POLS model. This is because the equation (2) includes two dummy variables in which case the application of a FEs model would generate perfect multicollinearity. The third model, REs, is not used because the number of parameters exceeded the number of cross-sections in the western regions. A final reason why both the FEs and REs models can not be used here is because equation (2) also includes the lagged dependent variable (LFDI$_{t-1}$). If an equation includes a lagged dependent variable, as Greene (2003) points out, there are difficulties in both the FEs and REs models, specifically that the lagged dependent variable becomes correlated with the disturbance term, even though it is assumed that $\square_{it}$ is not itself autocorrelated. A structural break framework is conducted to obtain robust estimates for the three macro regions. The data are divided into two time periods, i.e. 1984-1992 and 1993-2007. The break point chosen captures Deng's South China Tour in 1992 and the government policy re-orientation, which began in 1992. This approach is developed to investigate any variation in determinants between the sub-periods.

FINDINGS AND DISCUSSIONS

The empirical results obtained from the POLS model are summarised in Table 2. The high values of adjusted R-squared indicate that the explanatory variables in the models explain most of the variation in the dependent variables, i.e. the equations are capturing the major determinants of aggregate FDI location in China.

As can be seen from column (1), when equation 2 is estimated for the whole sample, all the explanatory variables are significant with the expected signs. The variables for FDI in the previous year (LFDI $_{t-1}$), market size (LGDP), human capital (LEDU), agglomeration (LAGG), infrastructure (LINFR), geographical location/preferential policy (DLP) and the Tiananmen Square Incident (DTM) are statistically significant at the 1 percent high level while the labour cost variable (LWAGE) is significant at 10 percent level with negative sign. LFDI $_{(t-1)}$ appears to have positive influence on current inflows of FDI, suggesting a self-reinforcing effect of FDI. This result is consistent with that of Cheng and Kwan (2000) using a different estimation methodology. It can be expected that more previous FDI received by the costal region will bring further greater FDI inflows into the region compared to the inland areas, which further widen the FDI disparity between the regions. The large coefficient on market size (LGDP) indicates that market size is the most important determinant of FDI. This illustrates the fact that the most important motive for investing in China is market-seeking, aimed at taking advantage of the vast Chinese domestic market. It could be expected that the coastal region, with much larger market size, will attract more FDI than the inland regions.

Table 2. Empirical results

	1984-2007 (1)	1984-1992 (2)	1993-2007 (3)	Coastal region (4)	Central region (5)	Western region (6)
LFDI$_{(t-1)}$	0.25 (0.03)***	0.08 (0.05)*	0.15 (0.06)**	0.19 (0.04)***	0.65 (0.17)***	0.21 (0.09)**
LGDP	1.70 (0.27)***	1.26 (0.12)***	1.01 (0.05)***	0.87 (0.14)***	2.79 (0.20)***	1.25 (0.13)***
LWAGE	-0.35 (0.23)*	1.77 (0.60)***	-1.54 (0.16)***	-1.23 (0.39)***	-0.87 (0.46)*	-1.05 (0.56)*
LEDU	0.55 (0.16)***	0.37 (0.16)**	0.37 (0.07)***	1.09 (0.15)***	0.25 (0.29)	1.34 (0.27)***
LAGG	0.78 (0.16)***	0.85 (0.23)***	0.28 (0.12)**	1.25 (0.21)***	1.48 (0.35)***	-0.18 (0.39)
LINFR	0.48 (0.09)***	0.64 (0.11)***	0.61 (0.07)***	1.80 (0.35)***	-0.20 (0.24)	0.25 (0.13)*
DTM	-0.65 (0.16)***	–	–	-0.05 (0.21)	-0.86 (0.15)***	-1.19 (0.21)***
DLP	1.48 (0.12)***	1.59 (0.31)***	1.62 (0.19)***	–	–	–
NT	696	261	435	288	216	192
$\bar{R}^2$	0.80	0.69	0.82	0.72	0.78	0.75

Notes: 1. Standard errors are in parentheses.
2. ***, ** and * indicate that the coefficient is significant at the 1%, 5% and 10% levels, respectively.

Human capital (LEDU) appears to exert a positive influence on FDI inflows. This is different from the result obtained by Cheng and Kwan (2000), who found that the effect of education was not statistically significant. The agglomeration effect (LAGG) and infrastructure (LINFR) are also important considerations in FDI location within China. The interpretation of the results is that regional transportation infrastructure, the size and the depth of industrial and economic activity and capacity are important determinants of subsequent FDI inflows. The coastal region possesses a higher level of educated human capital, better infrastructure and higher agglomeration should attract more FDI than the inland regions, further widen the disparity in inward FDI flows to the three macro-regions of China.

The significant coefficients for the two dummy variables, capturing the effects of geographical location/preferential policy (DLP) and the Tiananmen Square Incident (DTM) reveal that FDI responded strongly to policy incentives, and negatively to the political risk. The coastal region with superior geographic location and preferential FDI policies attracts greater FDI inflows than the inland regions.

Columns (2) and (3) present the results for the two time periods, i.e., 1984-1992 and 1993-2007. All variables are significant at different levels. There is no significant difference between the two columns except for the variable of LWAGE, positive in the first period and negative in the second period, which is consistent with the results identified by Sun et al., (2002). This finding might be a result of the fact that wage levels in China before the 1990s were very low - much lower than that in developed countries and even lower than most developing countries due to China's legacy of central control and planning. As argued earlier, relatively higher wages between the regions might attract more FDI if higher labour cost is linked to higher labour productivity. However, the situation has been changing and wage levels have been rising fast since the beginning of the 1990s. Eventually, higher wages may deter rather than attract particular efficiency-seeking FDI inflows, when more cost efficient locations are available. In other words, lower labour cost attracts more FDI. The large coefficient on LWAGE for the later stage (1993-2007) indicates that labour cost is another most important determinant along with Chinese market size. This might suggest that efficiency-seeking and market-seeking are the most important motives for FDI flows into China, taking advantage of Chinese large market and its low cost labour.

Results in column (4), for the coastal region, show slight different with column (1) with all variables remain significant except the DTM variable, which turns into insignificant. The relative high coefficients on LINFR, LAGG, LGDP, LEDU and LWAGE indicate that infrastructure, agglomeration, market size, human capital and labour cost are the important determinants for FDI located in the coastal region and attract FDI for market-seeking, efficiency-seeking and resource-seeking purposes. As noted above, the coastal region possesses a much better infrastructural network, higher level of agglomeration, bigger market size and higher level of educated human capital, attracts more FDI than the inland regions.

The Tiananmen Square Incident variable, DTM, is correctly signed but insignificant which is different from the result in Column (1). This suggests that the influence of this event, and the political upheavals that followed, had no significant effect on inward FDI to the coastal region, in comparison to the effect on FDI to the central and western regions.

The evidence from column (5), for the central region, indicates that LWAGE, LGDP are the important variables and the main types of FDI in the region are efficiency and market seeking, motivated by cheap labour cost and the market in the central area. LAGG is also a very important variable, a 1 percent increase in LAGG results in a 1.48 percent increase in

FDI inflows. LFDI $_{(t-1)}$ play positive roles in attracting inward FDI. However, LEDU and LINFR are not significant, which might imply that FDI flows to the area are not for skilled workers or good infrastructure these resource-seeking purposes. As expected, DTM has a negative influence on inward FDI in this region.

In column (6), the results for the western region, LGDP, LEDU and LINFR are positive and significant while LWAGE and DTM are negative and significant at different levels. LGDP, LWAGE and LEDU are the most important determinants for inward FDI as indicated by the size of its coefficient, which may suggest that the main types of FDI in this region are market, efficiency and resource seeking FDI. A comparison of the coefficients for Tiananmen incident variable (DTM) in the three macro-regions shows that the aftermath of the Tiananmen Incident had a greatest effect on FDI inflows in the western region. This finding raises an interesting question about the internal homogeneity of China regarding foreign investors' perceptions of risk.

CONCLUSION AND POLICY IMPLICATIONS

The purpose of this study has been to investigate the determinants of the skewed spatial pattern of FDI in China. A larger panel data set has been employed with longer and more recent data. The findings from the study have developed our knowledge and understanding on the factors that cause disparities in Chinese inward FDI between the three macro regions and what the Chinese government should do to reduce these disparities in FDI inflows.

The findings suggest that previous inflows of FDI, market size, preferential policies towards FDI and geographical location, agglomeration effects, human capital and infrastructure exercise important positive influences upon inflows of FDI to China. The causes of the skewed spatial pattern of FDI in China and its high concentration in the coastal region have been identified as the results of preferential government policies offered to the coastal region, superiority in industrial and economic development in terms of larger market size, better infrastructure, more human capital and higher agglomeration in the coastal region, and geographical proximity of the region to Hong Kong, Macao and Taiwan.

The important determinants of FDI in the central region are labour cost, market size, agglomeration and political risk. To attract greater FDI flows into the area, the central and local governments should keep inflation, especially labour cost, under control. Efforts should be made to increase the local market size and agglomeration effects by increasing investments from both the central and local governments.

The important determinants of inward FDI in the western region are market size, political risk, labour cost, education and infrastructure. To attract significant FDI flows into the region, both central and local governments should make efforts to achieve political and social stability in the area. Endeavours should also be made to enlarge the local market, offer more extensive preferential policies and improve education and infrastructure in the area.

Regional disparities are now one of the major national policy issues in China and the Chinese government faces the challenge of reducing the growth in regional disparities. It is recognised that the widening of regional disparities could cause social conflicts and political problems which further threaten the country's prosperity. As mentioned earlier, a leading task of the current Five-Year Plans is to develop the western region of China. Previous studies

(Buckley, et al., 2002; Zheng, et al., 2006) have shown that inward FDI is one of the most important engines for regional economic growth in both central and western regions. To develop inland regions, the Chinese government must expedite the improvement of the regional investment environment and must encourage both domestic and foreign investments into the western region especially in the encouraged industries such as energy, transportation, resources, high and new technology by offering more extensive preferential policies. Local governments should also offer their own incentives in their economic and high-tech development zones.

Inland regions especially the western areas have abundant natural materials and tourism resources. Government preferential policies should be offered to attract large scale resource-seeking FDI in mining and raw materials industries and chemical industry into the inland regions by mergers and acquisitions (M&A) of existing large state-owned enterprises (SOEs). This will also help to speed up SOEs reforms in the area.

The coastal region has been very successful in attracting export-oriented FDI to promote the regional export performance and economic growth. Previous research found that export in the western region is one of the most important factors promoting regional economic growth. The western area, therefore, should also attract export-oriented FDI, using local cheap labour and materials inputs, exporting final products to the neighbour countries, e.g. Russia, south and central Asian countries, thus achieving regional export-led growth.

The Chinese government should encourage immigration from the coastal to the western region to increase population, labour force and educated human capital in the area. New secondary schools, colleges and universities should also be created to raise education levels and improve the quality of human resources in long-run. Further efforts should be made to increase government investment in energy (e.g. oil and natural gas), steel and auto industries and infrastructure especially waterways and new airports construction in the area. The inland regions have their own advantages compared with the coastal region: much cheaper production inputs in terms of land and abundant natural resources/ materials. As an important driving force for economic growth, FDI will help to reduce poverty in the inland area and further eliminate uneven economic development across China.

ACKNOWLEDGMENT

this is a modified version of the published article entitled "The determinants of disparities in inward FDI flows to the three macro-regions of China", published in the journal of *Post-Communist Economics*, 2011, 23(2), 257-270

REFERENCES

Barry, F. Gorg, H. & Strobl, E. (2003). Foreign direct investment, agglomerations, and demonstration effects: An empirical investigation. *Review of World Economics*, *139*(4), 583-600.

Billington, N. (1999). The location of foreign direct investment: an empirical analysis. *Applied Economics*, *31*(1), 65-76.

Braunerhjelm,P. & Svensson, R. (1996). Host country characteristics and agglomeration in foreign direct investment. *Applied Economics, 28*, 833-840.

Buckley, P. J., Clegg, J., Wang, C. & Cross, A. (2002). FDI, regional differences and economic growth: panel data evidence from China. *Transnational Corporations, 11*(1), 1-28.

Cheng,L. K. & Kwan, Y. K. (2000). What are the determinants of the location of foreign direct investment? The Chinese experience. *Journal of International Economics, 51*, 379-400.

Culem, C. G. (1988). The locational determinants of direct investments among industrialized countries. *European Economic Review, 32*, 885-904.

De Mello, L. R. (1997). Foreign direct investment in developing countries and growth: a selective survey. *The Journal of Development Studies, 34*(1), 1-34.

Dunning, J. H. (1988). *Multinationals, Technology and Competitiveness.* London: Unwin Hyman.

Dunning, J. H. (1993). *Multinational Enterprises and the Global Economy.* Wokingham, England : Addison-Wesley.

Dunning, J. H. (1998). Location and the multinational enterprises: a neglected factor? *Journal of International Business Studies, 29*(1), 45-66.

Greene,W. (2003). *Econometric Analysis,* 5th, NJ: Prentice Hall.

Griliches, Z. (1979). Issues in assessing the contribution of research and development to productivity growth. *Bell Journal of Economics, 10,* 92-116

Guimaraes, P., Figueiredo, O. & Woodward, D. (2000). Agglomeration and the location of foreign direct investment in Portugal. *Journal of Urban Economics, 47*(1), 115-135.

Head, K., Ries, J. & Swenson, D. (1995). Agglomeration benefits and location choice: evidence from Japanese manufacturing investments in the United States. *Journal of International Economics, 38,* 223-247

Kearney, A. T. (2010). *Investing in a Rebound, FDI Confidence Index,* 2010.

Krugman, P. R. (1997). Good news from Ireland: a geographic perspective. In A. W. Gray (ed.), *International Perspectives in the Irish Economy.* Dublin: Indecon.

Perroux, F. (1950). Economic space: theory and applications. *Quarterly Journal of Economics, 64,* 89-104.

Perroux, F. (1970). Notes on the concept of growth poles. in D. McKee et al. (eds.) *Regional Economics: Theory and Practice.* The Free Press, New York, 93-104.

Perroux, F. (1988). The pole of development's new place in a general theory of economic activity. In B, Higgins and D. Savoie (eds.) Regional Economic Development, Essays in Honour of Francis Perroux. Unwin Hyman, London, 48-87.

Porter, M. (1998). *The Competitive Advantage of Nations.* London: Macmillan Press 1998.

Przybylska, K. & Malina, A. (2000). The determinants of foreign direct investment in transforming economies: empirical evidence from Poland. *Statistics in Transition, 4*(5), 883-899.

Song, S., Chu, G. & Chao, R. (2000). Intercity regional disparity in China. *China Economic Review, 11*(3), 246-261.

Wang, Z. & Swain, N. (1995). The determinants of foreign direct investment in transforming economies: Empirical evidence from Hungary and China. *Weltwirtschaftliches Archiv, 131,* 359-382.

Wei, Y., Liu, X., Parker, D., Vaidya, K. (1999). The regional distribution of foreign direct investment in China. *Regional Studies*, *33*(9), 857-867.

Zheng, P., Siler, P. & Giorgioni, G. (2004). FDI and the export performance of Chinese indigenous firms: a regional approach. *Journal of Chinese Economic and Business Studies*, *2*(1), 55-71.

Zheng, P., Siler, P. & Giorgioni, G. (2006). Sustaining growth in China's regions through FDI. *World Review of Entrepreneurship, Management and Sustainable Development*, *2*(1/2), 4-22.

Zheng, P. (2009). A comparison of FDI determinants in China and India, *Thunderbird International Business Review*, *51*(3), 263-279.

In: Foreign Direct Investment (FDI)
Editors: Enzo Guillon and Lucas Chauvet

ISBN: 978-1-62808-403-0
© 2013 Nova Science Publishers, Inc.

Chapter 11

TRADE, FDI, EXCHANGE RATE, AND THE EFFECT OF CORPORATE TAX REDUCTION POLICY

Hiroyuki Nishiyama[*]
School of Economics, University of Hyogo, Kobe, Japan

ABSTRACT

This chapter investigates the policy effect of decreasing the corporate tax rate on the economy and welfare of a home country and a foreign country using a two-country model with international trade, foreign direct investment (FDI), and an exchange rate. Decreasing the corporate tax rate leads to an appreciation of the domestic currency and increases the FDI inflows. If the corporate tax rate in the home country is higher than that in the foreign country (Case 1), the tax reduction policy increases the real national income and improves welfare in the home country via a decrease in home prices, but it can either increase or decrease the income and welfare in the foreign country, because the effect of this policy on foreign prices is ambiguous. That is, in Case 1, this policy can be either a prosper-thy-neighbor or a beggar-thy-neighbor policy, depending on conditions. On the other hand, if the corporate tax rate in the home country is lower than that in the foreign country (Case 2), the policy can either increase or decrease the home country's income and welfare, but it certainly decreases the foreign country's income and welfare. Therefore, this policy can be either a beggar-thyself or a beggar-thy-neighbor policy in Case 2. The basic cause of the ambiguity of the policy effects on the foreign (the home) income and welfare in Case 1 (Case 2) depends on the production relocation according to FDI by multinational enterprises responding to the policy change. In conclusion, contrary to the conventional wisdom, in an era of globalization, it's not always true that the corporate tax reduction policy leads an economic expansion and a welfare improvement. This analytical result can be a theoretical rationale for reviewing the current trend of corporate tax reduction in the world.

Keywords: Corporate tax; exchange rate; foreign direct investment; international trade; terms of trade; welfare

---

[*] Corresponding author: School of Economics, University of Hyogo, 8-2-1, Nishi-Ku, Kobe, 651-2197, Japan. Email: nisiyama@econ.u-hyogo.ac.jp (H. Nishiyama).

JEL classifications: F2; F4; H2

1. INTRODUCTION

In recent years, many governments have continuously reduced their corporate tax rate. For example, the Singapore government has reduced this rate repeatedly (by 40% in 1965, 30% in 1993, 20% in 2005, and 17% in 2011), and the rate will be further reduced, as the Singapore government aims to reduce the rate to the level in Hong Kong. Similarly, many other governments (of course, including Japan) also aim to put their corporate tax rate on a par with international standards. Some of the most important motivations for this policy are to strengthen the international competition power of firms and to invite foreign direct investment (FDI) to vitalize the domestic economy.[1] However, economic expansion tends to lead to inflation and appreciation of the domestic currency, which can contribute to recession.[2] The questions, from the viewpoint of the national economy, are the following: Is the policy of decreasing the corporate tax rate really beneficial? And are there any theoretical rationales for the policy target of reducing the level of a country's corporate tax rate to match the international standard? To answer these queries, it is important to conduct a policy analysis within the open macroeconomic framework, because, in an era of economic openness, the economic policy of a country can affect and can be strongly influenced by variations in trade, FDI, and exchange rate (or terms of trade: TOT).

Despite the importance of examining the tax reduction policy, there are few theoretical works that analyze the effect of a decrease in the corporation tax rate within the open macroeconomic framework with FDI. The study of [Johdo and Hashimoto (2005)] is one of the few works that looks at the impact of a rise in corporate tax on the spatial distribution of firms, real exchange rate, and welfare theoretically, but they did not examine the influence of a difference in corporate tax rates between two countries. [Botman et al. (2006)] investigated the effect of a cut in corporate income tax using the New Open Economy Macroeconomic (NOEM) model. Their analysis includes many suggestions, but they examine the policy impact in the calibration of this model, so it is difficult to understand the linkage among variables. Additionally, there is no FDI in their model.

In this chapter, we develop a simple static NOEM model based on [Nishiyama (2005)], which introduces endogenous FDI into the framework of [Obstfeld and Rogoff (1995)], and investigate the effect of the home country's tax reduction policy by using this model. Our result suggests that this policy accelerates FDI inflow and leads to an appreciation of

---

[1] [Haufler (2001)] suggests that understanding the difference between FDI and other types of international capital movement is important in the study of the effect of tax reduction policy, because "there are taxes which do affect the location of firms, but not the location on capital." For example, [Pethig and Wagener (2007)] introduce the behavior of multinational enterprises into the theoretical analysis of corporate income tax competition. A number of studies examine the linkage between tax and FDI (see, for instance, [Bellak and Leibrecht, 2009]; [Benassy et al., 2005]; [de Mooij and Ederveen, 2003, 2006]; [Devereux and Griffith, 1999, 2002]).

[2] Actually, recent economic growth in Singapore mainly caused by an expansion in trade and FDI seems to create the causes for worry about limiting growth such as persistent inflation and appreciation of the Singapore dollar. The inflation rate of the Consumer Price Index in Singapore was 1.0%, 2.1%, 6.6%, 0.6%, 2.8%, and 5.2% in 2006-2011, and the market rate of Singapore dollar per US dollar (End of period) was 1.73, 1.66, and 1.28 in 2000, 2005, and 2010, respectively. Source: Statistics, Department of Statistics Singapore [Online]. http://www.singstat.gov.sg/stats/stats.html

domestic currency. We also investigate the policy effects on prices, income, and welfare in two different cases: One is the case in which the corporate tax rate in the home country is higher than that in the foreign country (Case 1), and the other is the case in which the home country tax rate is lower than that in the foreign country (Case 2). In Case 1, the home tax reduction policy increases domestic income via falling prices, and therefore domestic welfare also improves. However, the foreign country's income and welfare can either increase or decrease. This result implies that the policy of reducing the domestic corporate tax rate to the international standard level could be effective from the viewpoint of an increase in domestic economy and welfare, but it may be a beggar-thy-neighbor policy in some situations. In Case 2, this policy can either increase or decrease the home country's income and welfare, and it strictly worsens the foreign country's economy and welfare via a rise in foreign prices. That is, if the home country is the lower tax country, the home country's tax reduction policy can be either a beggar-thyself or a beggar-thy-neighbor policy. Therefore, in the era of economic openness, the government should implement this policy carefully depending on the situation.

The remainder of this chapter is organized into four sections. Section 2 presents a static version of the NOEM model with FDI. Section 3 analyzes the policy effect of decreasing the corporation tax rate. Section 4 presents our conclusions.

2. Model

2.1. Household

There are two countries in the world: the home country and the foreign country. The home country's representative household determines the money demand, L, and the consumption demand to maximize the utility, U, as follows:

$$U = \alpha \ln L + (1 - \alpha) \ln C \ (0 < \alpha < 1), \tag{1}$$

subject to the budget constraint

$$L + C = [wN + (1 - t)\Pi + TR + \bar{M}]/P, \tag{2}$$

where $C = \left(\int_0^1 c_i^\rho di\right)^{\frac{1}{\rho}}$ ($0 < \rho < 1$) is the aggregate consumption of individual consumption demand c_i, wN is the labor income, t ($0 < t < 1$) is the corporate tax rate, Π is the aggregate profit of the firms operating in the home country, TR is the transfer from the government, $\bar{M}$ is the money holding at the beginning of a period, and $P = \left(\int_0^1 p_i^{\frac{\rho}{\rho-1}} di\right)^{\frac{\rho-1}{\rho}}$ is the price index of goods price p_i. The government budget constraint is shown as follows:

$$TR = M - \bar{M} + t\Pi, \tag{3}$$

where M is the nominal money stock, which is exogenously given. From the utility maximization, we have the following demand functions:

$$L = \alpha\left(\frac{M}{P} + y\right), \tag{4}$$

$$C = (1-\alpha)\left(\frac{M}{P} + y\right), \tag{5}$$

$$c_i = \left(\frac{p_i}{P}\right)^{\frac{1}{\rho-1}} C, \tag{6}$$

where y is the real national income and $y = (wN + \Pi)/P$. The behavior of the representative foreign household is the same as that of the home representative household.

2.2. Firm

The ith differentiated goods are produced by the monopolistic competition firm by using labor n_i ($i \in [0,1]$). Each firm sells its produced goods in a domestic market and exports goods to the other country. The goods indexed by an interval of $i \in [0,v]$ are produced in the home country, and the rest, i.e., $i \in [v,1]$, are produced in the foreign country. Each firm takes wage rate w as a given, choosing prices to maximize the after-tax profit $(1-t)\pi_i \leftrightarrow (1-t)(p_i c_i + ep_i^* c_i^* - wn_i)$ subject to Eq. (6) and its foreign counterpart, and $n_i = c_i + c_i^*$, where e is the nominal exchange rate. The asterisk shows the foreign variable. For simplicity, we assume that there is no transport cost and no profit remittance in our analysis. The after-tax profit of the firm, which operates in the foreign country, is shown as $(1-t^*)\pi_i^* \leftrightarrow (1-t^*)(e^{-1}p_i c_i + p_i^* c_i^* - w^* n_i^*)$, where $n_i^* = c_i + c_i^*$. Then, we have the following:

$$p_i = \frac{w}{\rho}, \quad p_i^* = \frac{w}{e\rho} \text{ (for } i \in [0,v]\text{)}, \tag{7, 8}$$

$$p_i = \frac{ew^*}{\rho}, \quad p_i^* = \frac{w^*}{\rho} \text{ (for } i \in [v,1]\text{)}. \tag{9, 10}$$

Substituting Eqs. (7)-(10) into the definitions of price indexes, we have

$$p = \left[v + (1-v)\varepsilon^{\frac{\rho}{\rho-1}}\right]^{\frac{\rho-1}{\rho}}, \tag{11}$$

$$p^* = \left[v\left(\frac{1}{\varepsilon}\right)^{\frac{\rho}{\rho-1}} + (1-v)\right]^{\frac{\rho-1}{\rho}}, \tag{12}$$

where $p \equiv P/p_H$, $p^* \equiv P^*/p_F^*$, $p_H \equiv w/\rho$, $p_F^* \equiv w^*/\rho$, and $\varepsilon \equiv ep_F^*/p_H = ew^*/w$, which is the real exchange rate or the inverse of TOT. From Eqs. (11) and (12), we find that $p = \varepsilon p^*$, and therefore $P = eP^*$, which describes the expression of purchasing power parity (PPP).

2.3. Location Arbitrage

Besides optimal pricing, each firm also chooses its optimal production location. Location arbitrage ensures $(1-t)\pi_i = (1-t^*)e\pi_i^*$. Using this arbitrage condition and Eqs. (6)-(12), we have the following condition:

$$(1-t)p^{\frac{\rho}{1-\rho}} = (1-t^*)p^{*\frac{\rho}{1-\rho}}. \tag{13}$$

2.4. Money Market Equilibrium and National Income

The money market equilibrium and the real national income in the home country are shown as $M/P = L$ and $y = [wN + (1-t)\Pi + t\Pi]/P$, respectively, where $\Pi \equiv \int_0^v \pi_i di$, $N \equiv \int_0^v n_i di$. Using these equations and their foreign counterparts, and Eqs. (4)-(10), we have the following:

$$\frac{m}{p} = \left(\frac{\alpha}{1-\alpha}\right) y, \tag{14}$$

$$\frac{m^*}{p^*} = \left(\frac{\alpha}{1-\alpha}\right) y^*, \tag{15}$$

$$y = v p^{\frac{\rho}{1-\rho}} (1-\alpha) \left(\frac{m}{p} + \frac{m^*}{p^*} + y + y^*\right), \tag{16}$$

$$y^* = (1-v) p^{*\frac{\rho}{1-\rho}} (1-\alpha) \left(\frac{m}{p} + \frac{m^*}{p^*} + y + y^*\right), \tag{17}$$

where $m \equiv M/p_H$ and $m^* \equiv M^*/p_F^*$. Note that $v p^{\frac{\rho}{1-\rho}}$ and $(1-v) p^{*\frac{\rho}{1-\rho}}$ in Eqs. (16) and (17) are the propensities to spend the goods in the home country and the foreign country, respectively. Of course, $v p^{\frac{\rho}{1-\rho}} + (1-v) p^{*\frac{\rho}{1-\rho}}$ equals one.

2.5. Solution

The system of Eqs. (11)-(17) gives six unknown variables $(p, p^*, \varepsilon, v, y, \text{and } y^*)$ because one of Eqs. (14)-(17) is redundant. The equilibrium values of these variables are shown as follows:

$$\tilde{v} = \left[\left(\frac{m^*}{m}\right) \tau^{\frac{-1}{\rho}} + 1\right]^{-1}, \tag{18}$$

$$\tilde{\varepsilon} = \tau^{\frac{\rho-1}{\rho}}, \tag{19}$$

$$\tilde{p} = \left[\tilde{v} + (1-\tilde{v}) \tilde{\varepsilon}^{\frac{\rho}{\rho-1}}\right]^{\frac{\rho-1}{\rho}}, \tag{20}$$

$$\tilde{p}^* = \frac{\tilde{p}}{\tilde{\varepsilon}}, \tag{21}$$

$$\tilde{y} = \left(\frac{1-\alpha}{\alpha}\right) \left(\frac{m}{\tilde{p}}\right), \tag{22}$$

$$\tilde{y}^* = \left(\frac{1-\alpha}{\alpha}\right) \left(\frac{m^*}{\tilde{p}^*}\right), \tag{23}$$

where $\tau \equiv (1-t)/(1-t^*)$. A tilde shows the equilibrium value of the endogenous variable. From Eq. (18), we find that $0 < \tilde{v} < 1$, because $(m^*/m) \tau^{\frac{-1}{\rho}} > 0$.

3. POLICY ANALYSIS

In this section, we examine the policy effect of decreasing the home corporate tax rate, t, that is an increase in τ. A rise in τ can also be caused by a rise in t^*, but we assume that the foreign tax rate is given at a level that focuses our analysis on the effect of the home tax reduction policy.

3.1. Policy Effects on FDI and Exchange Rate

Differentiating Eqs. (18) and (19), we find that $d\tilde{v}/d\tau > 0$ and $d\tilde{\varepsilon}/d\tau < 0$. Note that $d\tilde{v}/d\tau$ suggests a variation in the number of firms operating in the home country caused by the production relocation behavior according to the international arbitrage responding to the tax reduction policy. That is, a corporate tax reduction policy (a rise in τ) increases the FDI inflow ($d\tilde{v}/d\tau > 0$) and leads to an appreciation of the domestic currency ($d\tilde{\varepsilon}/d\tau < 0$).

We can explain these results intuitively: The home country's tax reduction policy increases the relative after-tax profit of the firm operating in the home country, and therefore FDI in the home country increases. Then, the real exchange rate decreases, i.e., TOT improves, to maintain the location arbitrage condition shown as Eq. (13). These findings are summarized as Proposition 1:

Proposition 1: The corporate tax reduction policy accelerates FDI inflow and improves the terms of trade caused by an appreciation of the domestic currency (a decrease in the real exchange rate).

We should remember that the main target of the tax reduction policy is not so much accelerating FDI inflow itself as expanding the domestic economy or improving welfare via an increase in FDI. Therefore, it is important to examine the policy effect of decreasing the corporate tax rate on income and welfare. Hereafter we examine the effect of the tax reduction policy under the following two cases, because the effect varies depending on the level of τ: Case 1 is the case in which the home country's corporate tax rate is higher than that of the foreign country, i.e., $0 < t^* < t < 1 \leftrightarrow 0 < \tau < 1$. Case 2 is the case in which the home country's corporate tax rate is lower than that of the foreign country, i.e., $0 < t < t^* < 1 \leftrightarrow 1 < \tau$. In both cases, the nearer to the given level of t^* the level of t is, the nearer to 1 the level of τ is. In addition, considering Eq. (19), $\varepsilon \equiv ep_F^*/p_H = ew^*/w$, and $0 < \rho < 1$, we find that the case $0 < \tau < 1$ ($1 < \tau$) corresponds to the situation in which the price of the home country's produced goods and the home country's wages are lower (higher) than the price of the foreign country's produced goods and the foreign country's wages as expressed in the home currency.

3.2. Policy Effects on Prices, Income, and Welfare in Case 1: $0 < \tau < 1$

As examples, the central government corporate income tax rates of France, Japan, the UK, and the US in 2012 were 34.4%, 25.5%, 24.0%, and 30.0%, respectively.[3] They are in

---

[3] The combined corporate income tax rates of Japan and the US in 2012 were 37.0% and 39.1%. OECD Tax Database [Online]. http://www.oecd.org/tax/taxpolicyanalysis/oecdtaxdatabase.htm

the higher tax rate group among the Organization for Economic Co-operation and Development (OECD) countries. Case 1 corresponds to the case in which these higher tax countries are assumed to be the home country and a country with lower corporation tax rate than them is the foreign country. Therefore, in Case 1, we examine the policy effect of a reduction in the domestic corporate tax rate to its foreign level.

To understand the effect of the policy of home tax reduction on income and welfare, we examine its effect on prices first. In this model, variations in prices in response to this policy change the equilibrium values of other endogenous variables, i.e., national incomes and welfares in both countries.

Policy Effect on Prices

Using Eqs. (19) and (20), we have

$$\frac{d\tilde{p}}{d\tau} = \left(\frac{\rho-1}{\rho}\right)\tilde{p}^{\frac{1}{1-\rho}}\left[(1-\tau)\left(\frac{d\tilde{v}}{d\tau}\right) + (1-\tilde{v})\right]. \quad (24)$$

The home tax reduction policy affects the domestic prices via two paths: One is the effect via a change in the international location choice of firms (hereafter, we call this the FDI effect), and the other is the effect via the terms of trade fluctuation based on an exchange rate fluctuation (the TOT effect). The FDI effect is shown as the first term in the rightmost square bracket in Eq. (24), i.e., $(1-\tau)(d\tilde{v}/d\tau)$, which suggests the policy effect on prices via a variation in FDI, that is, the number of firms operating in each country. The TOT effect corresponds to the second term, i.e., $(1-\tilde{v})$, which suggests the effect on prices via a variation in the import prices of the foreign produced goods expressed in the domestic currency because of a change in the real exchange rate, $\tilde{\varepsilon}$. The FDI effect decreases the home price index, $\tilde{p}$, because a rise in τ increases and decreases the variety of the cheaper home-produced goods and the higher foreign-produced goods sold in the home market in Case 1, respectively. The TOT effect also decreases $\tilde{p}$, because a rise in τ reduces the price of the foreign produced goods expressed in the home currency via a decrease in the real exchange rate. Therefore, the sign of Eq. (24) becomes strictly negative in Case 1.

On the other hand, as shown in Eq. (25), a rise in τ can either increase or decrease the foreign price index, $\tilde{p}^*$.

$$\frac{d\tilde{p}^*}{d\tau} = \left(\frac{\rho-1}{\rho}\right)\tilde{p}^{*\frac{1}{1-\rho}}\tau^{-2}\left[\tau(1-\tau)\left(\frac{d\tilde{v}}{d\tau}\right) - \tilde{v}\right]. \quad (25)$$

Similar to the policy effect on the home price index, the tax reduction policy varies the foreign price index, $\tilde{p}^*$, via the FDI effect (the first term in the rightmost square bracket in Eq. (25)) and the TOT effect (the second term in the bracket).

In Case 1, the FDI effect decreases $\tilde{p}^*$, but the TOT effect increases $\tilde{p}^*$. Therefore, the sign of $d\tilde{p}^*/d\tau$ depends on which is the dominant effect, and if the FDI (TOT) effect dominates the TOT (FDI) effect, the home tax reduction policy causes foreign deflation (inflation) in Case 1.[4]

---

[4] The magnitude relation between the FDI effect and the TOT effect depends strongly on the levels of τ and ρ (see the Appendix).

Policy Effect on Income and Welfare

Using Eqs. (1), (4), and (5), and their foreign counterparts, and Eqs. (22)-(25), we have the following:

$$\frac{d\tilde{y}}{d\tau} = -\left(\frac{\tilde{y}}{\tilde{p}}\right)\left(\frac{d\tilde{p}}{d\tau}\right) > 0, \tag{26}$$

$$\frac{d\tilde{U}}{d\tau} = \left(\frac{1}{\tilde{y}}\right)\left(\frac{d\tilde{y}}{d\tau}\right) > 0, \tag{27}$$

$$\frac{d\tilde{y}^*}{d\tau} = -\left(\frac{\tilde{y}^*}{\tilde{p}^*}\right)\left(\frac{d\tilde{p}^*}{d\tau}\right) \lessgtr 0, \tag{28}$$

$$\frac{d\tilde{U}^*}{d\tau} = \left(\frac{1}{\tilde{y}^*}\right)\left(\frac{d\tilde{y}^*}{d\tau}\right) \lessgtr 0. \tag{29}$$

Eqs. (26) and (27) suggest that the home tax reduction policy increases domestic income via falling prices, and therefore domestic welfare also improves in Case 1. This welfare effect is illustrated in Figure 1. As shown in Figure 1, an increase in τ improves welfare in the range of $0 < \tau < 1$ for any level in ρ ($0 < \rho < 1$).

As shown in Eqs. (28) and (29), this policy can either increase or decrease the foreign income and welfare. This effect on the foreign income depends on the variation in $\tilde{p}^*$.

If the FDI effect is stronger than the TOT effect, that is, $d\tilde{p}^*/d\tau < 0$ (see Eq. (25)), then the tax reduction policy increases the foreign income and therefore improves welfare ($d\tilde{y}^*/d\tau > 0$, $d\tilde{U}^*/d\tau > 0$). On the other hand, if the TOT effect is the dominant effect, it decreases the foreign income and welfare ($d\tilde{y}^*/d\tau < 0$, $d\tilde{U}^*/d\tau < 0$). This effect on the foreign welfare is shown in the range of $0 < \tau < 1$ in Figure 2. We can see that an increase in τ can either increase or decrease the foreign welfare in the range of $0 < \tau < 1$ in Figure 2.

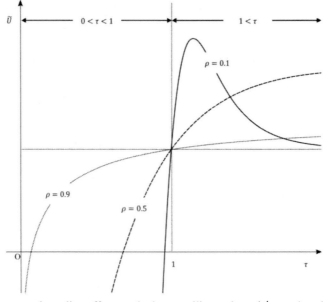

Note: Figure 1 illustrates the policy effect on the home utility under $m^*/m = 1$ and $\alpha = 0.4$.

Figure 1. Policy effect on home welfare.

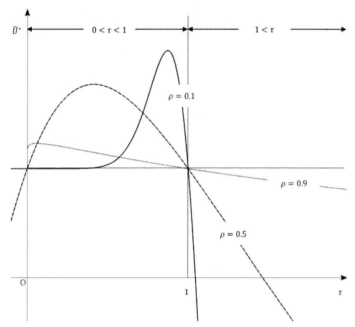

Note: Figure 2 illustrates the policy effect on the foreign utility under $m^*/m = 1$ and $\alpha = 0.4$.

Figure 2. Policy effect on foreign welfare.

The implication of these policy effects on income and welfare can be expressed as the following proposition:

Proposition 2: A reduction in the domestic corporate tax rate to its foreign level by the government of the higher tax country will be an effective policy only from the viewpoint of an increase in domestic economy and welfare. However, this government should implement this policy carefully, because it can be a beggar-thy-neighbor policy in some situations.

3.3. Policy Effects on Prices, Income, and Welfare in Case 2: $1 < \tau$

We examine the policy effect under the case in which the home tax rate is lower than that of the foreign country's tax rate, that is, the case of $1 < \tau$. For example, as is well known, the corporate tax rates in Hong Kong, Ireland, and Singapore (16.5%, 12.5%, and 17%, respectively, as of 2012) are low compared to much of the rest of the world.[5] Case 2 corresponds to the case in which these countries with lower tax rates are assumed to be the home country.

---

[5] The levels of the corporate tax rate in some countries and regions included in The List of Unco-operative Tax Havens issued by OECD, such as Bermuda, the British Virgin Islands, and the Cayman Islands, are quite low (those in some countries and regions are zero), but FDI in these countries and regions are not adequate for our analysis of production relocation in the manufacturing industry. For example, except for these countries and regions, the corporate tax rate is anywhere from 10% to 40% in most countries in the world. In this case, the level of τ will be at most 1.5 $(= (1 - 0.1)/(1 - 0.4))$ in Case 2. (See the website of OECD for more details on The List of Unco-operative Tax Havens [Online]. http://www.oecd.org/ctp/harmfultaxpractices/listofunco-operativetaxhavens.htm).

Policy Effect on Price

Under $1 < \tau$, the FDI effect and the TOT effect in Eq. (24) increases and decreases prices, respectively, and therefore the sign of Eq. (24) can be positive or negative. If the FDI (TOT) effect dominates the TOT (FDI) effect, an increase in τ leads to domestic inflation (deflation). On the other hand, from Eq. (25), we find that this policy certainly raises the foreign country's prices.

Considering the policy effect on prices (p, p^*) in both Case 1 and 2, we find the following: In both Cases 1 and 2, the policy effect via the TOT effect becomes a cause for deflation (inflation) in the home (the foreign) country, but the policy effect on prices via the FDI effect varies depending on the level of τ, i.e., the corporation tax rates t and t^*.

Policy Effect on Income and Welfare

The policy effects on national income and welfare depend on the price variation under $1 < \tau$, as occurs in Case 1 ($0 < \tau < 1$), and therefore the signs of $d\tilde{y}/d\tau$ and $d\tilde{U}/d\tau$ can be either positive or negative, because the sign of Eq. (24) isn't strictly determined. That is, the tax reduction policy implemented by the government of the country with the lower corporate tax can either increase or decrease the domestic income and welfare. This result can be confirmed in the range of $1 < \tau$ in Figure 1. On the other hand, this policy certainly reduces the national income and worsens welfare via a rise in $\tilde{p}^*$ in the foreign country ($d\tilde{y}^*/d\tau < 0$ and $d\tilde{U}^*/d\tau < 0$) in Case 2. This policy effect on foreign welfare is shown in the range of $1 < \tau$ in Figure 2. Therefore, in Case 2, a reduction in the home corporation tax rate can be a beggar-thyself or a beggar-thy-neighbor policy. This leads to the following proposition:

Proposition 3: If the home country is the lower tax country, its tax reduction policy can be either a beggar-thyself or a beggar-thy-neighbor policy.

We should note that the effect of the home corporation tax reduction policy via the TOT effect of the price variation certainly increases (decreases) in the home (the foreign) income and welfare in both Cases 1 and 2. However, this policy effect via the FDI effect varies depending on the situation. That is, the optimal behavior of the international location choice by multinational enterprises (production relocation), shown as the FDI effect in our analysis, is a basic cause of the complexity of the policy effects on national income and welfare. The nearer to the level of t^* the level of t is, i.e., the closer to 1 the level of τ is, the weaker the FDI effect becomes (see Eqs. (24) and (25)).

CONCLUSION

This chapter investigates the economic and welfare effects of the policy that decreases the corporate tax rate by using a simple NOEM model with international trade, FDI, and exchange rate. Our theoretical results suggest that the corporate tax reduction policy accelerates FDI inflow and leads to an appreciation of domestic currency. We also find that the policy effects on national income and welfare depend mainly on the price variation in response to a tax reduction, and these effects vary depending on the situation. This policy could be a beggar-thyself or a beggar-thy-neighbor policy, and therefore the government should implement such a policy carefully with due consideration to the situation. The complexity of the policy's effects on income and welfare depends largely on the optimal location decision by multinationals (production relocation), which is shown as the FDI effect in our analysis. In conclusion, contrary to the conventional wisdom, in an era of globalization accelerated by an expansion in international trade and FDI, it's not always true that the corporate tax reduction policy leads to economic expansion and welfare improvement. These results can be a theoretical rationale for reviewing the current trend of corporate tax reduction in the world.

APPENDIX

We focus here on the magnitude relation between the FDI effect and the TOT effect in Case 1 ($0 < \tau < 1$). As we noted in Section 3.2, the sign of Eq. (25), that is the policy effect on the foreign price index, $\tilde{p}^*$, depends on the magnitude relation between the FDI and TOT effects. If the FDI effect ($\tau(1-\tau)(d\tilde{v}/d\tau) > 0$ in Case 1) is the dominant effect, the sign of Eq. (25) is negative, and if the TOT effect is the dominant effect, the sign of Eq. (25) is positive. The FDI effect and the TOT effect can be rewritten as follows:

FDI effect: $\left(\frac{m^*}{m}\right)\tau^{\frac{-1}{\rho}}(1-\tau)\left(\frac{1}{\rho}\right)\left[\left(\frac{m^*}{m}\right)\tau^{\frac{-1}{\rho}}+1\right]^{-2}$,

TOT effect: $\left[\left(\frac{m^*}{m}\right)\tau^{\frac{-1}{\rho}}+1\right]^{-1}$,

and then the rightmost square bracket, i.e., $\tau(1-\tau)\left(\frac{d\tilde{v}}{d\tau}\right) - \tilde{v}$ can be shown as follows:

$$\tilde{v}^2\left[\left(\frac{m^*}{m}\right)\tau^{\frac{-1}{\rho}}\left(\frac{1}{\rho}\right)(1-\tau-\rho)-1\right].$$

Now we can see that the magnitude relation between these two effects depends strongly on the levels of τ and ρ. Of course, this relationship can also be influenced by money stock levels in both countries (m, m^*). However, the chief determinants of the sign in Eq. (25) are not the money stock levels but rather those of τ and ρ.

The same is true of the sign in Eq. (24). Therefore, even though the money stock is an important variable (especially for the examination of the effect of monetary policy) in the NOEM framework, we can assume $m^*/m = 1$ in the Appendix and in Figures 1-3 without alteration of our results.

Figure 3 illustrates the relationship between τ and ρ and $\phi \equiv \tau(1-\tau)(d\tilde{v}/d\tau) - \tilde{v}$, which corresponds to the square bracket in the right-hand side of Eq. (25) under $\tau = 0.1, 0.5$, and 0.9. As we noted above, if the FDI effect dominates the TOT effect, then $d\tilde{p}^*/d\tau < 0$ in Case 1. This situation corresponds to the case that $\phi > 0$ in Figure 3.

On the other hand, if the TOT effect dominates the FDI effect, $d\tilde{p}^*/d\tau > 0$. This situation corresponds to the case that $\phi < 0$. It is difficult to find a clear relationship between the levels of parameters τ and ρ and the level of ϕ, but roughly speaking, the higher the level of τ and/or ρ, the higher the level of ϕ tends to be, as shown in Figure 3.

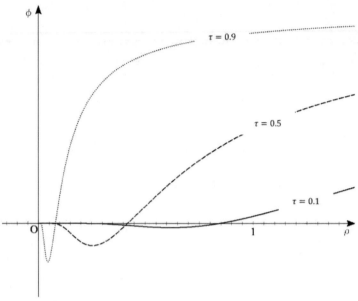

Note: We assume that $m^*/m = 1$ in Figure 3.

Figure 3. The sign of the square bracket in Eq. (25).

ACKNOWLEDGMENTS

The author is grateful to Shigeki Maeda and Kohei Shiino (staff members of JETRO Singapore) for the provision of valuable information about the Singapore economy, and to Masanori Tahira and Yasuhiro Gintani for some helpful comments and suggestions about this work. This research was supported in part by KAKENHI (22530234).

REFERENCES

Bellak, C., and Leibrecht, M. (2009). Do low corporate income tax rates attract FDI?: Evidence from Central and East European countries. *Applied Economics*, 41, 2691-2703.

Benassy-Quere, A., Fontagne, L. and Lahreche-Revil, A. (2005). How does FDI react to corporate taxation? *International Tax and Public Finance*, 12, 583-603.

de Mooij, R.A. and Ederveen, S. (2003). Taxation and foreign direct investment: A synthesis of empirical research. *International Tax and Public Finance,* 10,673-693.

de Mooij, R.A. and Ederveen, S. (2006). What a difference does it make? Understanding the empirical literature on taxation and international capital flows. *European Commission Economic Papers*, 261.

Devereux, M.P. and Griffith, R. (1999). The taxation of discrete investment choices. *IFS Working Paper Series*, W98/16.

Devereux, M.P. and Griffith, R. (2002). The impact of corporate taxation on the location of capital: A review. *Swedish Economic Policy Review*, 9, 79-102.

Haufler, A. (2001). *Taxation in a global economy*. New York: Cambridge University Press.

Johdo, W. and Hashimoto, K. (2005). International relocation, the real exchange rate and welfare. *Journal of Economic Dynamics and Control*, 29, 1449-1469.

Nishiyama, H. (2005). Production relocation and the effect of monetary policy. *Journal of Economic Integration*, 20, 93-108.

Pethig, R. and Wagener, A. (2007). Profit tax competition and formula apportionment. *International Tax and Public Finance*, 14, 631-655.

In: Foreign Direct Investment (FDI)
Editors: Enzo Guillon and Lucas Chauvet

ISBN: 978-1-62808-403-0
© 2013 Nova Science Publishers, Inc.

Chapter 12

FOREIGN DIRECT INVESTMENT AND PRODUCTIVITY SPILLOVERS: EVIDENCE FROM PLANT-LEVEL DATA

Jayjit Roy[1] and Mahmut Yasar[2]*

[1]Appalachian State University, Boone, North Carolina, US
[2]University of Texas at Arlington, Texas
and Emory University, Atlanta, Georgia, US

ABSTRACT

Foreign direct investment (FDI) is often advocated as one of the main sources of international technology diffusion and productivity enhancement in developing (host) countries. Given the policy implications, in this study, we explore whether foreign ownership is associated with spillover effects by using plant-level data from Indonesian manufacturing industries over the period 2001-2007. Our results indicate that positive spillovers to domestic firms are plausible; an increment in the foreign equity share in an industry in a province is associated with significantly higher productivity of plants. These effects, however, are more pronounced for plants with greater foreign equity share.

Keywords: Total Factor Productivity, Foreign Direct Investment, Spillovers

1. INTRODUCTION

Foreign direct investment (FDI) is often advocated to have a significant impact on less developed host countries. Apart from providing additional capital and managerial skills (Blomström and Kokko 1998; Aitken and Harrison 1999; Carr et al. 2001; Yasar and Paul 2009), multinational enterprises (MNEs) are also likely to encourage employment(e.g., Javorcik 2008). Moreover, as discussed inNavaretti and Venables(2006, p. 151), if MNEs are more productive than local firms (in the host country), FDI is likely to result in a "*compositional effect*"such that productivity in the host economyis enhanced. In addition, the

---

* Corresponding author: Email: myasar@uta.edu.

presence of multinationals may alter the scale of local firms(e.g., Aitken and Harrison 1999), enable technology transfer to domestic firms (e.g., Blomström and Kokko 1998), and lead to pecuniary externalities arising from vertical linkages (e.g., Javorcik 2004). Accordingly, it is hardly surprising that "large sums are often spent attracting FDI" (Javorcik 2008,p. 139).

A number of empirical studies have compared foreign- and domestic-owned firms along several dimensions such as productivity, wages, and environmental performance.[1] In this study, we focus on two such dimensions. While the first relates to the productivity of foreign-owned plants relative to domestic-owned plants, the second pertains to "*spillovers*" arising from technological as well as pecuniary externalities (Navaretti and Venables 2006, p. 152).[2]

Along the first dimension, MNEs have often been suggested to be more productive than local firms based on measures of labor productivity as well as total factor productivity(TFP).For example, in the context of Venezuela, Aitken and Harrison (1999) find some evidence in favor of foreign affiliates being more productive. Similarly, Blomström and Wolff (1994) and Haddad and Harrison (1993) document the superior performance of foreign firms in case of Mexico and Morocco, respectively. Nonetheless, as Harris and Robinson (2003) and Javorcik (2010) contend,relatively productive domestic firms are also more likely to be acquired by MNEs. In other words, as Navaretti and Venables (2006, p. 182) opine, foreign investors may "cherry pick the best firms." Accordingly,due to this issue of non-random selection,identifying the causal effect of foreign ownership has proven challenging.

Similarly, along the second dimension, the evidence in favor of spillover effects has been less than conclusive. For instance, empirical studies such as Blomström and Wolff (1994) in the context of Mexico and Haddad and Harrison (1993) in case of Morocco fail to detect the presence of beneficial spillover effects. However, in the context of the UK, Girma and Wakelin (2001) find evidence suggestive of spillover effects in skill-intensive industries.

It is, however, essential to compute reliable measures of TFP when examining the productive impact of foreign ownership. In this study, we use a technique developed by Wooldridge (2009) which advances the methods proposed by Olley and Pakes (1996) and Levinsohn and Petrin (2003) by incorporating the issues highlighted by Ackerberg et al. (2006). While the approach allows us to address some of the problems inherent in the estimation of production functions, to our knowledge, it is also relatively novel in the literature analyzing the effect of FDI on productiviy.

This study also contributes to the literature on foreign ownership premium by utilizing relatively recent plant-level data from Indonesia.[3] While Arnold and Javorcik (2009) and Sun (2012) use data from Indonesia up to 2001 and 2005, respectively, to examine the effect of foreign ownership on productivity, they do not analyze the role of spillover effects. However,Sjöholm (1999) uses plant-level data from 1980 to 1991 to examine whether spillovers are present and affected by the degree of competition in an industry and the technology gap between domestic and foreign establishments. Although the results in Sjöholm (1999)indicate that productivity spillovers are greater when the degree of competition in an industry is higher and the technology gap among establishments is larger,

---

[1] See Lipsey (2002) and Navaretti and Venables (2006) for surveys of the literature.

[2] Two types of spillovers have been identified and examined in the literature. The first one takes place through the interactions of plants or firms within an industry (Romer 1990; Porter 1990). The second one (referred to as Jacobian spillovers) occurs whenplants or firms in different industries learn from each other and thus transferknowledge and skills.See Glaeser et al. (1992) for details of both types of spillovers.

[3] Note that we do not distinguish between firms and plants in our analysis.

the latter is found to depend on the specification used. More recently, Negara and Adam (2012) utilize Indonesian data up to 2005 to assess both the impact of foreign ownership on productivity as well as the role of forward and backward linkages.In the context of Indonesia, the contributions by Takii (2004) and Todo and Miyamoto (2006), among others, are also worth noting especially given our findings. While Takii (2004) finds foreign-owned plants to be more productive, the foreign ownership premium is greater for plants which are wholly foreign-owned. Similarly, Todo and Miyamoto (2006) employ the Olley and Pakes (1996) approach but find the foreign ownership premium to be relevant in the context of foreign firms who engage in research and development. Again, this is relevant in the context of our findings. The current study utilizes data from 2001 to 2007 to analyze the role of foreign ownership on TFP. The presence of local spillover effects is also examined.

Strikingly, in specifications that do not control for spillovers, foreign ownership is associated with higher productivity. Moreover, the share of foreign equity is found to be associated with positive spillovers for domestic plants. An increment in the foreign equity share in an industry in a province is associated with higher productivity of plants. However, such spillover effectsare more pronounced for plants with greater foreign equity share.

2. ECONOMETRIC FRAMEWORK

In order to examine whether there are knowledge spillovers from foreign firms to plants that operate in the host country, we begin by measuring the TFP of the plants. To this end, we estimate a Cobb-Douglas production function specifying output as a function of labor, capital, material, and energy. The estimation is performed for each (two-digit) industry separately by using the Wooldridge (2009) methodology given the simultaneity issue that arises when estimating a production function.[4] This approach integrates and improves the methods proposed by Olley and Pakes (1996) and Levinsohn and Petrin (2003) by incorporating the issues highlighted by Ackerberg et al. (2006). The simultaneity issue is attributable to the fact that productivity is unobservable to the econometrician but available to firms in the formof prior beliefs (Marschak and Andrews, 1944). For example, firms with prior beliefs about positive productivity shocks are likely to utilize more inputs (Yasar et al. 2008).Accordingly, we utilize the approach suggested by Wooldridge (2009) to control for this issue and obtain consistent output elasticities with respect to each input. We use a second order polynomial series in capital and treat intermediate material as a proxy for unobserved productivity. Labor and energy are the two free variable inputs. We then obtain TFP level by using these elasticities, from $\ln \text{TFP}_{it} = \ln Y_{it} - \hat{\beta}_L \ln L_{it} - \hat{\beta}_K \ln K_{it} - \hat{\beta}_M \ln M_{it} - \hat{\beta}_E \ln E_{it}$, where i isa the plant subscript; t is the time subscript; $\ln Y$is the log of gross output; $\ln L$, $\ln K$, $\ln M$, and $\ln E$ are the log values of labor, capital, material, and energy inputs, respectively; $\hat{\beta}_L, \hat{\beta}_K, \hat{\beta}_M$, and $\hat{\beta}_E$ are the output elasticities of the inputs.

We then estimate the following baseline specification to examine whether plants that have foreign ownership, i.e.,foreign equity share amounting to at least ten percent, are more productive than domestic firms (i.e., with less than ten percent foreign share):

---

[4] We refer the reader to Olley and Pakes (1996), Levinsohn and Petrin (2003), Ackerberg et al. (2006), and Wooldridge (2009) for additional details and alternative approaches.

$$\ln \text{TFP}_{it} = \beta_0 + \beta_1 FOR_{it} + \beta_2 IMPshare_{it} + \beta_3 EXP_{it} + \beta_4 SKILLshare_{it} + \theta_t + u_{it} \quad (1)$$

where *FOR* is a dummy variable depicting foreign ownership; *IMPshare* denotes the share of imported materials in total material; *EXP* is a dummy variable representing export status; *SKILLshare* depicts the share of skilled labor in total labor; θ_t corresponds to time fixed effects which control for unobservable factors (such as business cycles) at time *t* that affect all plants; and u_{it} is the error term consisting of potentially time-varying and time-invariant unobservables.

Now, in order to control for province- and industry-specificfactors, we consider the specification given by

$$\ln \text{TFP}_{it} = \beta_0 + \beta_1 FOR_{it} + \beta_2 IMPshare_{it} + \beta_3 EXP_{it} + \beta_4 SKILLshare_{it} + \delta_{jt} + \varphi_{pt} + \upsilon_{it} \quad (2)$$

where δ_{jt} and ϕ_{pt} correspond to industry-by-time and province-by-time fixed effects, respectively. The industry-by-time dummies control for unobservables such as industry-level tariffs and demand shocks. Similarly, the province-by-time effects control for factors such as environmental regulations across provinces and local infrastructure.

However, the estimates from (2) are still susceptible to bias arising from plant-specific factors such as managerial ability. Upon including plant fixed effects to control for such factors, the specification is given by

$$\ln \text{TFP}_{it} = \beta_0 + \beta_1 FOR_{it} + \beta_2 IMPshare_{it} + \beta_3 EXP_{it} + \beta_4 SKILLshare_{it} + \delta_{jt} + \varphi_{pt} + \lambda_i + \varepsilon_{it} \quad (3)$$

where λ_i denotes plant dummies.

Our main objective is to examine whether Indonesian manufacturing plants benefit from international technology spillovers due to FDI. In order to accomplish this, for any plant *i*, we first compute the following variable denoting local spillover effects (e.g., Aitken and Harrison, 1999):

$$Spillover_{jpt} = \frac{\sum_{n \in \Omega} FORshare_{nt} * Y_{nt}}{\sum_{n \in \Omega} Y_{nt}}.$$

Here, Ω depicts the set of plants in the same province (*p*) and industry (*j*) as *i* at time *t* and *FORshare* represents the share of foreign equity. For any province and industry, it is a weighted-average of foreign equity participation. We then estimate the following specification to examine whether there are FDI-induced spillovers with respect to Indonesian manufacturing plants:

$$\ln \text{TFP}_{it} = \beta_0 + \beta_1 FORshare_{it} + \beta_2 Spillover_{jpt} + \beta_3 FORshare_{it} * Spillover_{jpt} \\ + \beta_4 IMPshare_{it} + \beta_5 EXP_{it} + \beta_6 SKILLshare_{it} + \delta_{jt} + \varphi_{pt} + \lambda_i + \varepsilon_{it} \quad (4)$$

where *FORshare*$_{it}$ represents the foreign equity share of plant *i* in year *t*. We expect the coefficients on *Spillover*$_{jpt}$ and *FORshare*$_{it}$* *Spillover*$_{jpt}$ to both be positive and statistically significant. An increase in the share of foreign equity in an industry can induce spillovers to domestic firms via technology and managerial skills.

3. DATA

The majority of the data come from *SurveiTahunan Perusahaan IndustriPengolahan*, an annual survey of manufacturing establishments in Indonesia conducted by *BadanPusatStatistik* (BPS), i.e., the Central Bureau of Statistics of Indonesia. Since the surveyhas been used in several plant level studies (e.g., Amiti and Konings 2007; Arnold and Javorcik2009), we provide only limited details. However, while most of the existing studies have relied on data up to 2001, we utilize data from 2001 to 2007.[5] Among other variables, for each year and manufacturing establishment, the survey includes information on value of goods produced, value of domestic and imported materials used, number of skilled and unskilled workers,value of capital goods, quantity and value of electricity and fuels and lubricants used, export status, and share of foreign equity. In addition, for each facility, the survey typically reports the International Standard of Industrial Classification (ISIC) code based on the product. In the analysis below, we resort to the two-digit level of classification.

From the survey, output is calculated as the valueofproductionadjusted for changes in inventories of finished goods. Labor employed is defined as the total number of workers. The value of capital utilized is obtained from the value of all capital goods such as land, buildings, machinery, and vehicles. Next, the value of materials used is simply the total value of raw materials. Moreover, the share of imports alludes to the ratio of the value of imported raw materials used to total raw materials. Energy utilized is defined as the sum of the values of electricity purchased (net of sales) and fuels and lubricants used.For any establishment in a year, export status takes the value one if it exports any of its products and zero otherwise. The foreign ownershipdummy takes the value one if the foreign equity share is at least ten percent and zero otherwise. Finally, the share of skilled labor is defined as the share of non-production workers.

Next, additional sources are relied upon to express the nominal variables in constant value (i.e., 2000 rupiahs). For instance, output and materials are deflated using *IndeksHargaPerdaganganBesar*, i.e., the wholesale price indexes (WPIs) available in *BuletinStatistikBulananIndikatorEkonomi* or the Monthly Statistical Bulletin of Economic Indicators. Since the analysis corresponds to the two-digit level of classification, the WPIs at the two-digit level are mainly obtained. In some cases, WPIs at the three-digit level are averaged to arrive at deflators corresponding to the two-digit level. In case of missing WPIs, the values from similar industries are employed.Similarly, the capital price deflators are obtained from the webpage of Bank Indonesia (the central bank of Indonesia). Finally, the real value of energy is obtained by adding the real values of electricity and fuels and lubricants. Electricity and fuels and lubricants are deflated using an index for electricity price and an average of indexes for fuel and coal price, respectively, obtained from the Handbook of Energy & Economics Statistics of Indonesia.

---

[5]Negara and Adam (2012) and Sun (2012) utilize data up to 2005.

At this juncture, a few comments on preparing the dataset are noteworthy. First, the value of capital goods for 2006 is missing and obtained by simple interpolation.[6] Second, observations with non-positive values of output, materials used, energy (i.e., the sum of fuels and lubricants and electricity) utilized are omitted from the analysis.[7] Third, missing values of electricity sales are replaced by zero.

Before moving to our estimation results, we analyze the mean characteristics of foreign-owned and domestic firms. The results are illustrated in Table 1. For example, the share of imported material in total intermediate material is 36.3% for foreign-owned plants and only 5.3% for the domestic ones. Upon testing for the statistical significance of these differences, the null hypothesis of equal means is rejected for all of the variables used in this paper (at reasonable levels of significance). For instance, the mean difference for *IMPshare* is significant at the 1% level of significance as shown by the triple asterisks (***).

4. RESULTS AND DISCUSSIONS

Our estimates for equations (1), (2), (3), and (4) are presented in Table 2, with one, two, and three asterisks indicating statistical significance at the 10, 5, and 1% significance levels, respectively. The cluster-robust standard errors are in parentheses. The estimates from the first three equations indicate that TFP is positively associated with foreign ownership. More specifically, foreign-owned plants are found to be significantly more productive with the foreign-ownership premium varying between 5 and 20%.

In case of equation (1), foreign ownership is associated with an increase in TFP amounting to about 22.4%.[8] Interestingly, upon including the industry-by-time and province-by-time fixed effects, the foreign ownership premium declines only slightly; foreign firms are now 15.5% more productive than the domestic firms.

Table 1. Comparison of Foreign-owned and Domestic Plants

	Foreign-owned Plants	Domestic Plants	Difference
Log Output (ln$Y$)	12.420	9.368	3.051***
Log Material Input (ln$M$)	11.650	8.581	3.069***
Log Energy Input (ln$E$)	8.071	5.249	2.822***
Log Capital Input (ln$K$)	11.011	8.337	2.674***
Log Total Employment (ln$L$)	5.453	4.016	1.436***
Log Total Factor Productivity (lnTFP)	2.203	1.844	0.359***
Import Share (*IMPshare*)	0.363	0.053	0.310***
Export Dummy (*EXP*)	0.675	0.189	0.486***
Share of Skilled Labor(*SKILLshare*)	0.208	0.145	0.063***

Notes: *** Mean difference is significant at the 1% level (of significance). ** Mean difference is significant at the 5% level. * Mean difference significant at the 10% level. See text for further details.

---

[6] For each firm, real capital stock (K) during year t is first obtained from $K(t) = \{(K(t_1) - K(t_0))/(t_1 - t_0)\}(t - t_0) + K(t_0)$; t_0 (t_1) corresponds to the period before (after) t for which the value is available. Then the values for 2006 are updated.

[7] Note that a few observations (from 2001) with duplicate values of plant identification numbers are omitted.

[8] exp(0.202) -1= 0.224.

Table 2. Productive Impact of Foreign Ownership

	Equation (1)	Equation (2)	Equation (3)	Equation (4)
FOR	0.202 (0.026)***	0.144 (0.013)***	0.050 (0.024)**	
IMPshare	-0.077 (0.026)***	0.059 (0.013)***	0.015 (0.031)	0.012 (0.031)
EXP	0.414 (0.009)***	0.059 (0.006)***	0.014 (0.011)	0.014 (0.011)
SKILLshare	0.310 (0.029)***	0.210 (0.019)***	0.112 (0.034)***	0.112 (0.034)
FORshare				-0.012 (0.043)
Spillover				0.072 (0.040)*
FORshare*Spillover				0.275 (0.151)*
Observations	74,366	74,366	74,366	74,366

1. *Significant at the 10% level. **Significant at the 5% level. ***Significant at the 1% level.
2. Equation (1) includes year dummies; (2) also includes province-by-year and industry-by-year dummies; (3) and (4) also control for plant fixed effects. See text for further details. The coefficients for these dummy variables are not reported here in the interest of space, but are available from the authors upon request.
3. The standard errors are heteroskedasticity-robust in (1) and (2) and adjusted for clustering within plants in (3) and (4).

As discussed in Javorcik (2010), a superior performance of foreign affiliates may arise from the fact that multinational enterprises may acquire the most efficient indigenous plants in a host country. Accordingly, while examining the role of foreign ownership on productivity, it is crucial to consider plant-specific unobservable components of efficiency such as managerial ability. Thus, in order to at least control for such unobservables that are time-invariant, we include plant fixed effects and arrive at the estimates corresponding to equation (3). Foreign-owned firms are now only 5.1% more productive than the domestic firms. However, across all specifications, the coefficient estimate of the foreign ownership dummy is always found to be statistically significant.

Before proceeding to examine spillover effects, a further comment is warranted. It is worth noting that the estimates obtained here should not be viewed as causal. While the plant dummies control for crucial time-invariant unobservables, there might still be time-varying unobservables such as managerial experience at the firm-level which may encourage foreign takeover as well as productivity. In other words, as Navaretti and Venables (2005, p. 160) state, the above results "could still be driven by other variables, which are correlated with foreign ownership and performance and ... not time invariant."

The estimates in the last column of Table 2 are obtained by estimating equation (4). The spillover effects are examined with the industry-by-time, province-by-time, as well as plant fixed effects. Our results indicate the presence of spillovers from foreign firms to domestic ones. However, these productivity spillovers are more pronounced for plants with greater foreign equity share. In other words, plants with greater foreign equity share appear to benefit more from any increase in foreign investment with respect to plants in the same industry and province.This is reasonable given the findings in Takii (2004). Both coefficients are significant at the 7% level of significance.

CONCLUDING REMARKS

Policymakers across countries devote significant amounts of resources to attract FDI. This is especially true for developing countries who consider FDI as one of the main sources of technology and managerial skills needed to boost their economic growth. According to UNCTAD (2011, p. iii), global FDI flows increased to $1.24 trillion in 2010, and "developing economies absorbed close to half of global FDI inflows."Multinational firms not only facilitate transfer of technology and managerial skills from their home countries to the host economies, but also create technology and knowledge in the latter thorough direct investment in research and development (Todo and Miyamoto 2006; UNCTAD 2011). Furthermore, FDI inflows are expected to increase competition in the host country and thus promote domestic investment over time. Domestic firms may devote resources to training and research and development, which can result in technology and skill upgradation or product and process innovations that may accelerate productivity and economic growth.

Accordingly, in this study, we utilize plant level data from Indonesia to examine whether foreign participation is associated with increased productivity. In addition, we check for the presence of international knowledge spillovers over the period 2001-2007.While most empirical studies do not find significant evidence of spillover effects, our results indicate that plants with foreign ownership are relatively more productive than domestic plants. We also find evidence in favor of knowledge spillovers. However, the productivity spillovers are more enhanced for plants that have greater foreign equity share. If the spillovers are sensitive to the absorptive capacity of plants (Yasar, 2013), then this result seems to suggest that only the plants with a sufficient foreign equity share have the necessary knowledge and skills to internalize such spillovers more effectively. This is an avenue that we plan to pursue in future work.

The results of the study have policy implications. The productivity spillover effects of foreign owned firms should be taken into consideration in any policy recommendations that seek to improve economic performance of manufacturing plants in Indonesia. The knowledge generation and spillovers associated with FDI can contribute significantly to the economic performance of plants, firms, industries, and thus the economic development of this country.

Our results, however, should be interpreted cautiously. Although we use a specification that allows us to control for time-invariant-plant-specificunobservables, the estimates should not be interpreted as showing a causal relationship. While endogeneity bias due to time-varying unobservables may be a concern, the assumption of strict exogeneity required in panel fixed effects methods is also nontrivial.

ACKNOWLEDGMENTS

We thank BanaBodri, Stefanie Christienova, Pierre van der Eng, Jap Efendi, Ida Fariana, Joel Rodrigue, and Jing Sun for helpful information or discussions about the data.

REFERENCES

Ackerberg, D. A., Caves, K. & Frazer, G. (2006). "Structural Identification of Production Functions," MPRA Paper No. 38349.

Aitken, B. J. & Harrison, A.E. (1999). "Do Domestic Firms Benefit from Direct Foreign Investment?Evidence from Venezuela," *American Economic Review*, 89, 605-618.

Amiti, M. &Konings, J. (2007). "Trade Liberalization, Intermediate Inputs & Productivity: Evidence from Indonesia," *American Economic Review*, 97, 1611-1638.

Arnold, J. M. &Javorcik, B. S. (2009)."Gifted Kids or Pushy Parents? Foreign Direct Investment and Plant Productivity in Indonesia," *Journal of International Economics*, 79, 42-53.

Blomström, M. &Kokko, A. (1998). "Multinational Corporations and Spillovers," *Journal of Economic Surveys*, 12, 247-277.

Blomström, M. & Wolff, E. N. (1994)."Multinational Corporations and Productivity Convergence in Mexico," NBER Working Papers 3141, National Bureau of Economic Research, Inc.

Carr, D. L., Markusen, J. R. &Maskus, K. E. (2001). "Estimating the Knowledge-Capital Model of the Multinational Enterprise,"*American Economic Review*, 91, 693-708.

Girma, S. & Wakelin, K. (2001). "Regional Underdevelopment: Is FDI the Solution? A Semiparametric Analysis," CEPR Discussion Paper No. 2995.

Glaeser, E., Kallal, H., Scheinkman, J. &Shleifer, A. (1992). "Growth in Cities," *Journal of Political Economy*, 100, 1126-1152.

Haddad, M. &Harrison, A. (1993). "Are there Positive Spillovers from Direct Foreign Investment?: Evidence from Panel Data for Morocco," *Journal of Development Economics*, 42, 51-74.

Harris, R. & Robinson, C. (2003). "Foreign Ownership and Productivity in the United Kingdom Estimates for U.K. Manufacturing Usingthe ARD," *Review of Industrial Organization*, 22, 207-223.

Javorcik, B. S. (2004). "Does Foreign Direct Investment Increase the Productivity of Domestic Firms?In Search of Spillovers through Backward Linkages," *American Economic Review*, 94, 605-627.

Javorcik, B. S. (2008). "Can Survey Evidence Shed Lighton Spillovers from ForeignDirect Investment?" *World Bank Research Observer*, 23, 139-159.

Javorcik, B. S. (2010). "Foreign Direct Investment and International Technology Transfer" *Encyclopedia of Financial Globalization*.

Levinsohn, J. &Petrin, A. (2003). "Estimating Production Functions using Inputs to Control for Unobservables," *Review of Economic Studies*, 70, 317-341.

Lipsey, R. E. (2002). "Home and Host Country Effects of FDI," NBER Working Paper 9293, National Bureau of Economic Research, Inc.

Marschak, J. & Andrews Jr. W. H. (1944). "Random Simultaneous Equations and the Theory of Production," *Econometrica*, 12, 143-205.

Navaretti, G. B. &Venables, A. J.. (2006). *Multinational Firms in the World Economy*, Princeton University Press.

Negara, S. D. & Adam, L. (2012). "Foreign Direct Investment and Firms' Productivity Level: Lesson Learned from Indonesia,"*ASEAN Economic Bulletin*, 29, 116-127.

Olley, S. &Pakes, A. (1996). "The Dynamics of Productivity in the Telecommunications Equipment Industry," *Econometrica, 64*, 1263-1298.

Porter, M. E. (1990). *The Competitive Advantage of Nations*, New York: Free Press.

Romer, P. M. (1990). "Endogenous Technological Change," *Journal of Political Economy, 98*, 71-101.

Sjöholm, F. (1999). "Technology Gap, Competition & Spillovers from Direct Foreign Investment: Evidence from Establishment Data," *Journal of Development Studies, 36*, 53-73.

Sun, J. (2012). "The Sensitivity of Matched Sampling Methodology in the Literature of Foreign Acquisition," *Applied Economics Letters, 19*, 1567-1570.

Takii, S. (2004). "Productivity Differentials between Local and Foreign Plants in Indonesian Manufacturing, 1995," *World Development, 32*, 1957-1969.

Todo, Y. & Miyamoto, K. (2006). "Knowledge Spillovers from Foreign Direct Investment and the Role of Local R&D Activities: Evidence from Indonesia," *Economic Development and Cultural Change, 55*, 173-200.

UNCTAD. (2011). *World Investment Report 2011*, United Nations: New York and Geneva.

Wooldridge, J. M. (2009). "On Estimating Firm-level Production Functions using Proxy Variables to Control for Unobservables," *Economics Letters, 104*, 112-114.

Yaşar, M. (2013). "Imported Capital Input, Absorptive Capacity and Firm Performance: Evidence from Firm-Level Data,"*Economic Inquiry, 51*(1), 88-100.

Yaşar, M. & Paul. C. M. (2009). "Size & Foreign Ownership Effects on Productivity and Efficiency: An Analysis of Turkish Motor Vehicle and Parts Plants," *Review of Development Economics, 13*, 576-591.

Yaşar, M., Raciborski, R. & Poi, B. (2008)."Production Function Estimation in Stata Using the Olley&Pakes Method," *Stata Journal, 8*, 221-231.

In: Foreign Direct Investment (FDI)
Editors: Enzo Guillon and Lucas Chauvet
ISBN: 978-1-62808-403-0
© 2013 Nova Science Publishers, Inc.

Chapter 13

REGIONAL FDI SPILLOVERS IN THE SWISS SERVICE/CONSTRUCTION INDUSTRY: THE ROLE OF SPILLOVER MECHANISMS AND LOCAL TECHNOLOGICAL CHARACTERISTICS

Lamia Ben Hamida
University of Applied Sciences of Western Switzerland,
La Haute Ecole de Gestion Arc, Switzerland

Abstract

This study analyzes regional spillover effects from Switzerland. It covers firms in services/construction, whereas most existing studies deal with manufacturing. We highlight the role of spillover mechanisms and the absorptive capacity of local firms in assessing regional benefits. We hypothesize that the size and the extent of regional spillovers depend largely upon the interaction between their channels and the existing technological capacities of local firms. Moreover, only local firms which have largely invested in the absorption of foreign technologies benefit from regional spillovers. The results confirm to a great extent our hypotheses.

Keywords: Regional FDI inra-industry spillovers; Demonstration effects; Competition effects; Worker mobility; Domestic absorptive capacity; Services/construction industries

JEL Classification: D21; D62; F21; F23; O33; R11

1. Introduction

MNCs are assumed to possess a countervailing advantage over the host country's firms (Hymer, 1960, 1968). They use advanced technology (production technology, technological know-how, marketing and managerial skills, international experience or reputation, etc.) which makes them more efficient than domestic counterparts (Dunning and Rugman, 1985). Knowledge can be transferred either voluntary through technology transfer agreements or involuntary through spillovers (Perez, 1998). Our paper analyzes spillover effects from MNCs to host country's firms in the services/construction industries, wherein very little attention has been paid by scholars to this aspect.

Despite the sectorial pattern of FDI shifting towards services, most discussions on spillovers from FDI focuses on manufacturing industries (among others Haddad and Harrison, 1993; Kokko, 1994; Kokko at al., 1996; Konings, 1999; Yeaple and Keller, 2003; Dimelis, 2005; Liu and Wei, 2006; Hale and Long, 2006; Svejnar et al., 2007; Buckley et al., 2007 and 2009; Castellani and Zanfei, 2007; Zhang et al., 2009; and Barbosa and Eiriz, 2009). In this paper, we aim to bring new elements into the discussions by testing the presence and the extent of intra-industry spillovers for the services/construction industry in Switzerland. According to UNCTAD (2004), the global FDI stock in the service industry more than quadrupled during the period 1990-2002. As a result of rapider growth in this sector than in the other sectors, services accounted for about 60% of the global stock of inward FDI in 2002. In Switzerland, the importance of foreign-owned investors in services has significantly increased, in particular, over the period in which we focus on, 2001 to 2004. This is mainly in transport, R&D institutions, wholesale trade, and tourism.

In addition, our paper argues that learning is highly localized and spillovers are geographically bounded. The effect of spillovers tends to be captured first by neighboring local firms, and gradually spread to other, more distant ones. The geographic dimension has been controlled by a number of scholars who used regional level and tested spillovers within and outside the region. To the best of our knowledge, except the work of Higón and Vasilakos in 2011, most of these existing empirical studies focus on the manufacturing industry (Aitken and Harrison, 1999; Liu and Wei, 2006; Sjohölm, 1999; Halpern and Muraközy, 2005, etc.). Furthermore, existing results for regional spillovers have been mixed for both developed and developing countries and evidence on regional spillovers has not yet been conclusive. It shows that regional spillover effects of FDI on host economies are not well understood.

This heterogeneity on regional spillover findings could be a result of misspecifications of these effects. Firstly, spillovers might not be observed at the aggregate level (for all firms/industries), but only in the sub-set of firms which share some common technological characteristics. We argue that domestic firms should possess a sufficient technological level to recognize valuable new knowledge; invest in training and learning to integrate the new knowledge and use it productively into its existing technological process. Doing so, local firms might be able to successfully absorb foreign knowledge. Secondly, the literature recognizes that spillovers occur through a variety of mechanisms, namely demonstration, increased competition and worker mobility. The size and the extent of spillovers depend on the type of their mechanisms and the assessment of the entire spillover effects needs to disentangle these effects according to their mechanisms. Thirdly, we assume that possible interactions between technological capacities of domestic firms and spillover mechanisms might influence spillover effects in the region. That is high technology firms which fiercely compete with foreign affiliates would not seek to absorb foreign knowledge but rather work harder to maintain their market share. However, low technology firms seem to gain a lot from other mechanisms of spillovers such as worker mobility, since these firms could benefit from personnel assistance which helps them to better understand and implement foreign technologies (Mody, 1989).

This paper attempts to empirically analyze regional intra-industry spillover effects from FDI using firm-level data from the services/construction industries in Switzerland; to the best of our knowledge, this study will be the first to explore regional effects in the Swiss services/construction industry. As stated by Blomström and Kokko (2002), the composition of inward FDI has changed, thus most FDI concerns services, rather than manufacturing. As a result, we could expect FDI to have more spillover effects in services. Unlike existing empirical studies, our paper attempts a detailed analysis in regional spillovers in the Swiss services/construction industry according to their mechanisms. It controls for the role of the existing technological capacity of domestic firms and their investment efforts in training and learning in determining regional spillovers, and suggests that the size and the extent of these effects depend on the interaction between the mechanisms by which they occur and the existing technological capacities of domestic users.

The structure of the paper is as follows; section 2 analyzes the theoretical framework underlying our hypotheses, together with a review of relevant empirical studies, section 3 discusses the Swiss services/construction data, section 4 presents the econometric model, section 5 presents the regression results, and section 6 concludes the paper.

2. FDI and Spillovers: The Framework

Recent literature suggests that learning is highly localized and requires geographic proximity (Yildizoglu and Jonard, 1999 and Narula, 2010) furthermore spillovers are geographically bounded – technological interaction among firms is deeply rooted in regional space (Driffield et al. 2010). This paper investigates the role of regional dimension on spillovers in the services/construction and argues that the size and the extent of regional spillover effects vary according to the mechanisms by which they occur and depend on the interaction between these mechanisms and the capacity of domestic firms to absorb and use foreign knowledge productively.

In the following sub-sections, we discuss the theoretical and empirical frameworks underlying these arguments. Sub-section 1 highlights the role of the regional dimension in assessing the benefits of spillovers. Sub-section 2 analyzes the different mechanisms of intra-industry spillovers and calls for a detailed analysis of these effects according to the mechanisms by which they occur. Sub-section 3 highlights the role of the absorptive capacity of domestic firms and demonstrates that the assessment of regional spillovers depends on the interaction between their mechanisms and the technological capacity of local firms.

2.1. Spillovers within Regional Boundaries

When spillover effects are measured for domestic firms in all regions (i.e. at a national level), the regional benefits might not be observed if they are too small to offset the overall negative effect across all regions (Aitken and Harrison, 1999). Spillover benefits tend to be captured first by neighboring domestic firms, and gradually spread to other, more distant firms. Firstly, MNCs tend to establish affiliates in more competitive regions (Dunning, 1992, and Dunning and Gugler, 2008). Consequently, domestic firms within the same location/region are expected to follow the same technological trajectory and are highly likely to benefit from spillovers. Secondly, knowledge is generated and easily transmitted via local proximity, since its transmission costs are assumed to increase with distance (Audretsch, 1998). Given that, the impact of spillover mechanisms, namely labor mobility and demonstration is expected to be greater in the region. Domestic firms located in the same region as foreign affiliates observe and imitate foreign knowledge more efficiently. In addition, they could easily attract domestic employees who have been trained by and/or worked at foreign firms than more distant ones. The mechanisms of technological diffusion are reinforced at regional level (Crespo et al., 2008) and spillovers are expected to be larger (Ben Hamida, 2013). However, despite these strong arguments supporting that inward foreign direct investment generate spillover benefits at regional level, this area remains under-researched.

The few existing studies have focused on manufacturing industries, except Higón and Vasilakos (2011) who tested regional spillovers for the British retail sector during the period 1997-2003 and found strong evidence of regional effects. Aitken and Harrison (1999) advanced the idea that spillovers have a regional dimension. They tested whether FDI spillovers occur at the regional level in Venezuelan manufacturing firms. They found that regional foreign investment has positive and significant effects on the productivity of Venezuelan firms, while sectorial foreign investment has negative effects. Regional evidence for spillovers was later confirmed by a few number of scholars focusing on manufacturing. For example, using sector-level data in the UK, Driffield (2004) found positive productivity spillovers from inward FDI in the same region, while these effects are negative outside the regional boundaries. Liu and Wei (2006) found evidence of regional spillovers from inward FDI in China. Spillovers across Chinese regions are negative and insignificant, which might be due to the existence of barriers in the movement of production and output factors across regions in China. Conversely, there exists studies which failed to assess the beneficial return of spillovers in the region, such as Sjohölm (1999) and Halpern and Muraközy (2005). Sjohölm found evidence of positive spillovers for Indonesian manufacturing firms at the national level, whereas regional spillovers from FDI were negative. Based on panel data for Hungarian manufacturing firms, Halpern and Muraközy also found that spillovers within or across regions were not different from each other, both were insignificant. Halpern and Muraközy explain this finding by the fact that Hungary is a homogenous country from the point of view of spillovers because of its small size.

Accordingly, we recognize that evidence on regional spillovers has yet to be conclusive. These apparently contradictory results could be explained by the fact that regional spillovers do not automatically occur, but depend on the mechanisms by which they occur. Other factors such as the level of the technological capacity of domestic firms as well as their investment and learning efforts could also influence regional effects. We debate that these arguments are fundamentals to control for when testing regional spillover effects and that scholars disregarding them may fail in assessing regional spillovers.

2.2. On the Role of Spillover Mechanisms

Regional intra-industry spillovers appear to occur through three mechanisms. The literature distinguishes between competition-related spillovers and knowledge spillovers. The first kind of effects occur when domestic firms are forced to work harder to face the increased competition that follows the entry and the presence of foreign affiliates – competition -related spillovers could be over the short term a negative sign in terms of market stealing effects. Whereas, the latter occurs when firms imitate foreign knowledge by means of demonstration or succeed in getting foreign know-how via the mobility of domestic employees trained by or previously worked in foreign affiliates. The mechanism of worker mobility is particularly interesting in services, since training and human capital development in this sector are more directly focused on strengthening the skills and know-how of employees (Blomström and Kokko, 2002). Some or all of the foreign firm's specific knowledge could be expected to move to domestic firms when domestic employees decide to leave foreign firms and join domestic ones.

Accordingly, the amount and nature of knowledge transferred from foreign to domestic firms depend largely upon the mechanism by which they are transmitted. We expect that worker mobility, for example, can lead to higher spillovers and substantial growth in the productivity of domestic firms, since this mechanism transfers not only public knowledge ("the logy" in the terminology of Nelson (1982)), but also the tacit element (the technique) that is unlikely to be transferred through direct contacts between firms.

Nelson (1982, page 467) states that *"research and development scientists from rival firms give papers at meetings of professional societies. They meet together for lunch to exchange information on the evolving frontiers of the logy, while trying to avoid disclosing details of particular techniques their firms may have under development at the time"*.

Futherrmore, as we shall see in the following sub-section, the relevance of each mechanism depends on the technological capacity of domestic firms. If knowledge accumulation is continuous in domestic firm, raising its productivity or lowering its costs along a given line of technological development, then this firm would not abandon its existing pattern of innovation and imitate foreign knowledge (Cantwell, 1999 and Silverberg and Verspagen, 1994). However, large knowledge disparities force domestic firms to introduce the new knowledge of foreign firms. Domestic users in this case would need to invest in training and learning to be able to decode foreign knowledge and use it productively.

Prior empirical studies analyzing spillovers at both national and regional levels have employed a share of foreign presence in the corresponding industry within the region/ nation – e.g. foreign employment/sales/equity shares to measure spillover effects (among others, Aitken and Harrison, 1999; Haskel et al., 2007; Karpaty and Lundberg, 2004; Buckley et al., 2007; Castellani and Zanfei, 2007; and Tian, 2007). We argue that the share of foreign presence could capture spillovers from demonstration effects but does not seem appropriate to assess the effects of both increased competition and worker mobility (Kokko, 1996 and Ben Hamida, 2007). Competition-related spillovers, for example, could not be determined by the share of foreign presence alone, but rather by the simultaneous interaction between foreign and domestic firms (Kokko, 1996 and Wang and Blomström, 1992).[1]

Based on the above statements, we argue then that a more satisfactory model of regional spillover effects providing a deeper understanding of the process according to the mechanisms by which they occur. Such modeling strategy is likely to describe the process of spilling- over more correctly and then identify with accuracy the nature and the size of the resultant effects. Then emerges the following hypothesis:

---

[1] Furthermore, scholars analyzing spillovers at national level, measured by the share of foreign presence, reported controversial results. For example, Haskel et al. (2007), Karpaty and Lundberg (2004), and Buckley et al. (2007) found positive evidence for the existence of spillover benefits from FDI for the UK, Sweden, and China, respectively. While, Castellani and Zanfei (2007), and Tian (2007) reported, however, negative and significant spillovers for Italy, and China, respectively.

Hypothesis 1. The distinction of regional spillovers according to the mechanism by which they are transmitted provides different effects in the services/construction industry.

2.3. On the Role of the Interaction between Spillover Mechanisms and Technological Capacities of Domestic Firms

It is well known in the literature on spillovers that the absorptive capacity of domestic firms is the most important determinant of spillovers. That is only domestic firms that have largely invested in the absorptive capacity benefit from spillovers (Cohen and Levinthal 1989, 1990 and Cantwell, 1989). Many scholars have employed this concept to determine significant spillover effects, particularly, at national level (Cantwell, 1989, Konings, 1999, Girma et al., 1999, Liu et al., 2000, Flôres et al., 2002, Yeaple and Keller, 2003, Narula and Marin, 2003, and Dimelis, 2005, etc.).

At the regional level, Higón and Vasilakos (2011) found that regional spillover effects increase with the absorptive capacity of local retailers, measured by the firm's total factor productivity "TFP" relative to the average of TFP of the 95th percentile most productive firms in the industry. For manufacturing, Girma and Wakelin (2002) found that sectors with high levels of competition and a low technology gap (as a proxy for absorptive capacity) experienced higher spillovers, and more-developed regions in UK gain more from spillovers than others. Girma and Görg (2007) also considered in their specification of regional spillovers the domestic absorptive capacity (proxied by the difference in TFP between the firm and the maximum TFP in the industry), which is quadratically related to the spillover effects. Using the technique of conditional quantile regression, they found a U-shaped relationship between the absorptive capacity and spillovers from FDI in the region in all quantiles, while there is an inverted U-shaped relationship for spillovers from FDI outside the region. Conversely, using the same measure of domestic absorptive capacity as Girma and Görg (2007), Girma (2003) found that the relationship between spillovers and domestic absorptive capacity is an inverted U-shape, either from FDI located in the same region as UK firms or outside the region.

This heterogeneity in results regarding the relationship between spillovers and domestic absorptive capacity at the regional level might be the fact that these studies disregarded the role of learning and investment in the firm when measuring domestic absorptive capacity and only retained its existing technological gap. Domestic firms should possess sufficient technological level to recognize valuable new knowledge (proxied by among others the firm's technological gap); invest in new equipment and human capital (for example, training their domestic employees and/or recruiting new ones) to be able to absorb foreign knowledge and successfully integrate it into its existing technological process.

In this paper we recognize the above problem and consider a thorough measurement for domestic absorptive capacity. We control for firm's investment and learning and argue that, according to its existing technological level, domestic firm does not benefit from regional spillovers in the same way. Actually, domestic firms that have high technological capacities do not look to imitate foreign knowledge, they rather attempt to work harder to reduce imperfection costs related to internalization process in order to maintain their market shares. Whereas, domestic firms that are in a position to not compete fiercely with foreign firms would prefer to introduce foreign best knowledge in their existing technological process, by means of demonstration and/or worker mobility mechanisms. Recently, Ben Hamida (2013) has analyzed regional FDI spillovers in Swiss manufacturing and controlled for the relationship between spillover channels and the diverse levels of domestic technological capacity. She found that competition-related spillovers appear to be fully absorbed by local firms with high technological capacities; worker-mobility-related spillovers are fully absorbed by low technology firms; while demonstration-related spillovers are absorbed by all groups of firms with mid technology firms experiencing the larger benefit.

Our paper tests the relationship between spillover mechanisms and domestic technological capacities for the services/construction industry and tries to draw some conclusions about the differences in results between manufacturing and services/construction in Switzerland, since the nature of the knowledge transferred between firms in services tends to be different from that in manufacturing (Giroud et al., 2009).

These discussions point to the following hypothesis:

Hypothesis 2. Different interactions between spillover mechanisms and existing domestic technological capacities provide different regional spillovers in the services/construction.

3. Data

Switzerland recorded increased inward FDI over the last years, particularly, between 2001 and 2004, which even surpassed the flows of outward investment in 2003. FDI inflows are not equally distributed across regions. According to Crevoisier and Roth (2005), the Alpes for example are not internationalized, while cantons such as Vaud, Geneva, Basel, and Zurich experienced large flows of inward FDI which are above the national average. In addition, Switzerland has achieved competitive technological levels in many service industries such as Geneva area in Banking and Swiss government is increasingly encouraging inward FDI and attracting foreign MNCs.

Switzerland is thus an interesting example to investigate regional spillovers. We believe that it is promising to investigate the key determinants of regional spillovers to give insights to policy makers, particularly, at cantonal level about how to promote inward FDI as well as leverage spillover benefits.

This study uses data derived from innovation activity surveys (2002 and 2005) of services/construction firms, with at least 5 employees, conducted at the Swiss institute for business cycle research "KOF".[2] Individual information covers the productivity and technological behaviors of 1107 firms – 127 majority-owned foreign affiliates – in 2001 and 1170 firms – 134 majority-owned foreign affiliates – in 2004.

Figures 1 to 7 report sectorial distribution of inward FDI in Swiss regions, measured by the share of foreign investment in services/construction total sales. Following the regional distribution of the KOF institute, the regions considered here are: the Lemanic region, Mittelland space, North West Switzerland, Zurich, Western Switzerland, Central Switzerland, and Ticino.[3] All these calculations are based on weighted data sets so as to give a represen-

---

[2]Questionnaires can be downloaded from www.kof.ethz.ch (Industrieökonomik).

[3]Lemanic region includes the cantons of Vaud, Valais, and Geneva. Mittelland space includes the cantons of Bern, Fribourg, Jura, Neuchâtel, Solothurn. North West Switzerland includes the cantons of Aargau, Basel-Stadt, and Basel-Landshaft. Western Switzerland includes the cantons of Appenzell Ausserrhoden, Appenzell

tative picture of Swiss economy.[4]

In 2001 figure 1 shows that foreign share in wholesale trade and computer services was preeminent in the Lemanic region. Central Switzerland also holds large foreign share in wholesale trade sectors as well as in transport and banking (figure 6). While foreign share in Mittelland space is preeminent in trading and maintenance of motor vehicles (figure 2). Zurich recognizes large shares mainly in computer services and banking (figure 4). Foreign firms dominate in R&D institutions within both North West and Western Switzerland (figures 3 and 5), while in Ticino they are rather dominant in personal services (figure 7). In 2004, the results change considerably across regions. Some sectors recognize a decrease in foreign shares, mainly, computer services in the Lemanic region and Western Switzerland; banking in Central Switzerland and Mittelland space; and insurance and retail trade in Zurich. However, an increase in foreign shares is identified within, for example, Western Switzerland in mainly R&D institutions and retail trade and wholesale trade; Zurich in other business services; and North West and Western Switzerland and Lemanic region in banking.

Whether foreign presence in Swiss regions results in spillover benefits arising from domestic learning process of foreign technologies is the focal point of our empirical analysis discussed in the next section.[5]

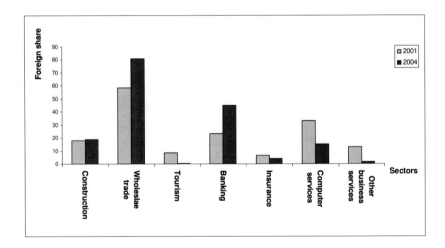

Figure 1. Percent share of foreign firms in total sales in the same sector and region "Lemanic region".

Innerrhoden, Glarus, Graubünden, Schaffhausen, St-Gallen, and Thurgau. Central Switzerland includes the cantons of Lucerne, Nidwalden, Obwalden, Schwyz, Uri, and Zug.

[4]The weights are used to correct for the selection bias resulting from "unit" non-response and for the deviations of the sample structure from that of the underlying population.

[5]The regression analysis makes use of a sample of only 226 services/construction firms because of missing data for some variables when matching the two data sets of 2002 and 2005 surveys.

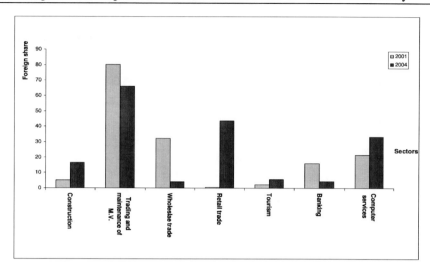

Figure 2. Percent share of foreign firms in total sales in the same sector and region "Mittelland space".

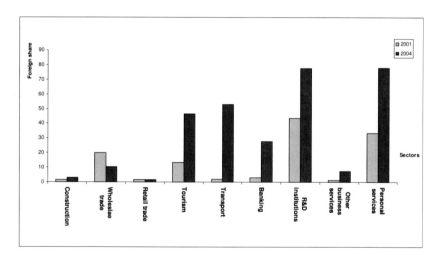

Figure 3. Percent share of foreign firms in total sales in the same sector and region "North West Switzerland".

4. Methodology

We model the effect of regional spillovers within the context of a Cobb-Douglas production function, in which the value-added Y is a function of two inputs, capital and labor. $A_{i,j,t}$ is the level of firm's productivity. The subscripts i and j denote firm and industry, respectively.

$$Y_{i,j,t} = A_{i,j,t} L_{i,j,t}^{\alpha 1} K_{i,j,t}^{\alpha 2}. \tag{1}$$

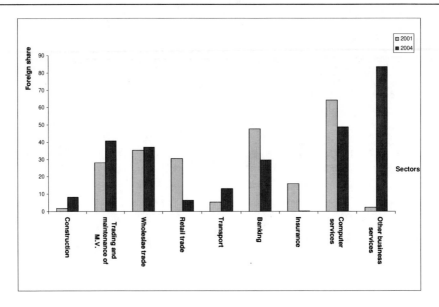

Figure 4. Percent share of foreign firms in total sales in the same sector and region "Zurich".

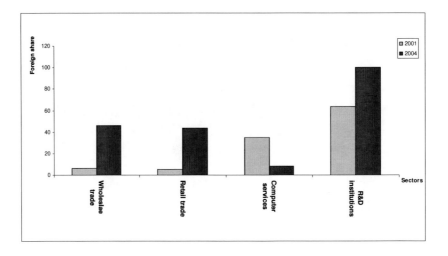

Figure 5. Percent share of foreign firms in total sales in the same sector and region "Western Switzerland".

To estimate equation (1), we take the logarithms of the variables in order to get into a linear form equation and add a stochastic disturbance term $u_{i,j,t}$ to account for variations in the productive capabilities of the i-th firm, Consequently, we rewrite the above equation for $t-3 = 2001$ and $t = 2004$ as

$$LnY_{i,j,t} = a_{i,j,t} + \alpha_1 LnL_{i,j,t} + \alpha_2 LnK_{i,j,t} + u_{i,j,t}, (a_{i,j,t} = LnA_{i,j,t}), \qquad (2)$$

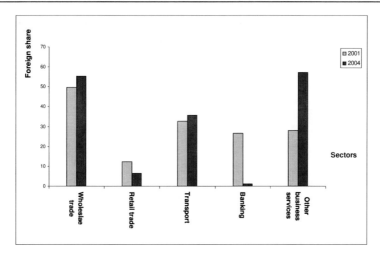

Figure 6. Percent share of foreign firms in total sales in the same sector and region "Central Switzerland".

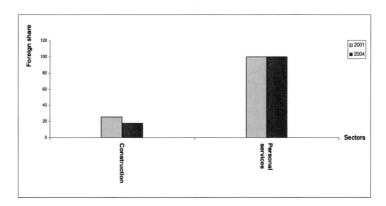

Figure 7. Percent share of foreign firms in total sales in the same sector and region "Ticino".

$$LnY_{i,j,t-3} = a_{i,j,t-3} + \alpha_1 LnL_{i,j,t-3} + \alpha_2 LnK_{i,j,t-3} + u_{i,j,t-3},$$
$$(a_{i,j,t-3} = LnA_{i,j,t-3}). \qquad (3)$$

By taking the difference (2-3), we obtain the following equation with Δ denotes the variation between 2004 and 2001.

$$\Delta LnY_{i,j} = \Delta a_{i,j} + \alpha_1 \Delta LnL_{i,j} + \alpha_2 \Delta LnK_{i,j} + \varepsilon_{i,j}. \qquad (4)$$

Based on the study of Ben Hamida (2013) for manufacturing, we distinguish between spillover mechanisms by employing different control variables. Firstly, the main effect of the share of foreign presence at level of the four-digit services/construction industry, FP, reflects spillovers from demonstration effects. Secondly, the interaction term $FP * HC$ between foreign presence and human capital is assumed to determine the effect of worker mobility related to the presence of foreign firms in the domestic market. Third, the price markup, $\Delta Comp$, is used to assess competition effects. By including these variables, we model the change in a as follows

$$\Delta a_{i,j} = \alpha_3 FP_{j,r,t-3} + \alpha_4 FP_{j,R-r,t-3} + \alpha_5 HC_{i,j,t} + \alpha_6 FP_{j,r,t-3} * HC_{i,j,t}$$
$$+ \alpha_7 FP_{j,R-r,t-3} * HC_{i,j,t} + \alpha_8 \Delta Comp_j + \alpha_9 \operatorname{Si} ze_{i,j,t} + \alpha_{10} Industry_{i,j}$$
$$+ \alpha_{11} \operatorname{Re} gion_r + \varepsilon_{i,j,r}, \quad (5)$$

Where, the change in a is also assumed to vary across sectors, the size of the domestic firms and its human capital (Griliches, 1998 and Dimelis and Louri, 2002). The subscript r denotes region.

Finally, we can rewrite equation (4) as

$$\Delta LnY_{i,j} = \alpha_0 + \alpha_1 \Delta LnK_{i,j} + \alpha_2 \Delta LnL_{i,j} + \alpha_3 FP_{j,r} + \alpha_4 FP_{j,R-r} + \alpha_5 HC_{i,j}$$
$$\alpha_6 FP_{j,r} * HC_{i,j} + \alpha_7 FP_{j,R-r} * HC_{i,j} + \alpha_8 \Delta Comp_{i,j} + \alpha_9 \operatorname{Si} ze_{i,j}$$
$$+ \alpha_{10} Industry_j + \alpha_{11} \operatorname{Re} gion_r + \varepsilon_{i,j,r}, \quad (6)$$

Where α_0 to α_{11} the parameters to be estimated. Table 1 describes the variables and their measurements. $Industry$ and $\operatorname{Re} gion$ denote, respectively, industry and region dummies.[6] The inclusion of dummies and the use of changes over time control for industry- and region- specific productivity differences – $\operatorname{Re} gion$ also correct for agglomeration effects, since some foreign firms could be attracted to regions which benefit from agglomeration economies (Aitken and Harrison, 1999). In addition, both dummies are used to correct the omission of unobservable variables that might undermine the relationship between regional spillover variables and the productivity growth of domestic firms (Aitken and Harrison, 1999 and Narula and Marin, 2003).

We employ an interaction term between foreign presence and human capital to assess spillovers from the mechanism of worker moility and we expect its sign to be positive. This implies that the effect of the entry and presence of foreign firms on the productivity growth of domestic firms is co-determined by the level of their human capital development (Borensztein et al., 1998 and Meyer and Sinani, 2002). Domestic firms that invest in upgrading the level of their human capital expect that the entry and the presence of foreign firms in their region increase their productivity growth. We argue that the heterogeneity of domestic firms according to their technological capacity impact the way of upgrading the level of their human capital. Since relatively high technology firms tend to benefit from spillovers through demonstration and/or competition effects (Mody, 1989 and Ben Hamida, 2007), they are likely to invest in learning by training their domestic employees. We expect that training activities would be sufficient to succeed in absorbing and implementing foreign knowledg by this category of firms. However, small technological firms, which are not able to benefit from foreign affiliates via demonstration effects alone, tend to recruit domestic employees previously trained by or worked in foreign affiliates by giving them better work conditions than foreign firms such as higher salaries. By doing so, these firms can benefit

---

[6]This study makes use of 19 industry dummies in the services/construction industry.

Table 1. Variable definitions

Variables	Definitions
$\Delta LnY_{i,j}$	The log change in value-added in a firm.
$\Delta LnK_{i,j}$	The log change in physical capital, measured by gross capital income – firm level.
$\Delta LnL_{i,j}$	The log change in total number of employees at the firm level.
$FP_{j,r}$	The share of total sales in an industry j within the region r accounted for by foreign firms, calculated for 2001, $r = 1...R$, with $R = 7$.
$FP_{j,R-r}$	The share of total sales in an industry j outside the region r accounted for by foreign firms, calculated for 2001.
$HC_{i,j}$	The average labor cost of the firm (in 100'000 CHF) constructed as the ratio of the firm's labor costs to the number of employees, calculated for 2004.
$\Delta Comp_{i,j}$	The change in price markup in a firm measured by the difference between firm's total sales and costs over total sales.
$Size_{ij}$	The log total sales of the firm, calculated for 2004.
$GAP_{i,j}$	The ratio of the average labour productivity of foreign-owned firms to domestic firm's own labor productivity, calculated for 2001.
$INVEST_{i,j}$	The level of investment expenditures in new equipment and training activities for product/process innovation, within the period 2002-2004.

from a technical, managerial, etc. assistance which can help them to properly decode and implement foreign knowledge – it is argued that when leaving the MNCs these employees will take with them some or all of the firm specific knowledge (Blomström and Kokko, 2002).

We use price markup or the so-called Lerner index to assess competition-related spillovers (Baye, 2006), proxied by the difference between the firm's sales and its costs over its total sales (Narula and Marin, 2003 and Chung, 2001). When markup is high, a value near 1, competition is low. When markup is low, a value near 0, competition is high. Since competition-related spillovers are associated with the increase in the level of competition, resulting from the entry and the presence of foreign firms, we use the change in markup to measure the change in the level of competition. A negative estimated coefficient of the change in markup implies that decreased markup (increased competition) increases domestic productivity growth.

The existing technological capacity of domestic firm is measured by its existing technology gap, GAP, compared to its foreign counterparts.[7] GAP is equal to one – the technological frontier of the industry – if local firms operating at the same labour productivity

---
[7] Please use table 1 for GAP definition.

as the average of their foreign counterparts. Values that are smaller than or equal to one are interpreted as signs of small productivity gaps or high existing technology capacity. Values which are higher than one but near the technological frontier of the industry are interpreted as signs of mid productivity gaps or mid existing technological capacities. Whereas, those which are far behind the technological frontier characterize high productivity gaps or low technology capacities. To test our hypothesis 2, we proceed to make various tests using equation (6) separately for local firms with high, mid, and small productivity gaps.

In addition, we control for the investment level of local firms in new equipment and training when assessing spillovers in the region and outside. To do so, we divide our full sample of firms into two sub-samples characterized by small and high $INVEST$ and proceed to make various tests using equation (6) separately for both categories of domestic firms.

We test for the equality of coefficients across sub-samples using Chow-tests. All results are robust and refer to OLS estimations of equation (6). All Standard errors are corrected for heteroskedasticity. Problem of multicollinearity between interacted variables (HC and FP) is eliminated by centering them (i.e. subtracting the full sample means). More meaningful interpretations of those estimates are then granted (Aiken and West, 1991). Simultaneity problem is reduced by the fact that all production variables are measured in differences from their logarithmic levels (Dimelis, 2005).

5. The Evidence

Column 1 of table 2 reports regression results for the full sample of services/construction. The estimated coefficients of $FP_{j,r}$ and $FP_{j,r} * HC$ are positive and significant while $FP_{j,R-r}$ and $FP_{j,R-r} * HC$ are insignificant and even significantly negative. This result demonstrates that domestic firms gain from the presence of foreign firms in their region, but loose out if the firms are located in different regions. The benefit within the region seems to occur from demonstration and worker mobility mechanisms. The estimated coefficient of $\Delta Comp$ is positive and significant, indicating that the full sample data have not demonstrated that the increase in competition contribute to productivity growth of local firms. These findings confirms hypothesis 1 in which the distinction of regional spillovers according to the mechanism by which they are transmitted provides different effects in the services/construction industry.

The estimated coefficients of HC and ΔLnL, ΔLnK, and $Size$ are positive and significant in columns 1, showing that the change in the level of human capital, employment, physical capital, and size of local firms significantly increase the productivity of domestic firms in the services/construction industry.

Columns 2-4 of table 2 reports spillover results in the region and outside according to the diverse existing technological capacities of domestic (measured by the variable GAP). We find that the size and the extent of regional spillovers according to the mechanism by which they occur depend on the level of domestic technological capacity, demonstrating the strong relationship between the mechanisms by which domestic firms benefit from spillovers and their capability to understand and potentially decode foreign knowledge. This finding confirms our hypothesis 2 in which different interactions between spillover mechanisms and

Table 2. Estimation results for services/construction: Spillovers from FDI and existing level of technology gap between foreign and domestic firms

Variables	1 Full	2 Small GAP	3 Mid GAP	4 Large GAP	5 High INVEST	6 Small INVEST
ΔLnK	0.01***	0.53***	0.36***	0.01***	0.36***	0.47***
	(0.004)	(0.05)	(0.05)	(0.002)	(0.05)	(0.1)
ΔLnL	0.69***	0.35***	0.64***	0.72***	0.54***	0.29**
	(0.03)	(0.05)	(0.05)	(0.05)	(0.1)	(0.1)
HC	0.38***	0.38***	0.41***	0.42***	0.29***	0.009
	(0.03)	(0.1)	(0.09)	(0.05)	(0.07)	(0.09)
$FP_{j,r}$	0.001***	0.0009	0.006***	0.002**	0.003***	0.002
	(0.0003)	(0.001)	(0.001)	(0.0003)	(0.001)	(0.002)
$FP_{j,R-r}$	-0.0005***	0.0002	0.0002	-0.0005	-0.0007	0.0003
	(0.0001)	(0.0004)	(0.0006)	(0.0002)	(0.0005)	(0.0004)
$FP_{j,r}*HC$	0.004***	0.017*	0.004	0.0035**	0.006*	-0.003
	(0.001)	(0.009)	(0.005)	(0.001)	(0.003)	(0.004)
$FP_{j,R-r}*HC$	-0.001***	-0.002	0.004***	-0.0033***	0.001	0.0006
	(0.0004)	(0.001)	(0.001)	(0.0004)	(0.001)	(0.001)
$\Delta Comp$	1.06***	-0.4***	-0.46	0.86***	-0.24	-0.29
	(0.08)	(0.1)	(0.2)	(0.1)	(0.2)	(0.4)
$Size$	0.02***	0.001	0.038**	0.008	0.02	-0.02
	(0.004)	(0.02)	(0.01)	(0.005)	(0.01)	(0.03)
$\bar{R}^2$	0.59	0.96	0.96	0.45	0.72	0.88
$F - Chow$			8.41		6.6	
N	226	28	64	134	52	34

Note: All estimations include industry dummies. All standard errors, in parentheses, are corrected for heteroskedasticiy.

Variables (HC and FP) used for interactions are centered by subtracting the full sample means, so that (1) multicollinearity between the variables and their product is reduced, (2) better estimates of (HC and FP) are ensured, and (3) more meaningful interpretations of those estimates are granted (Aiken and West, 1991).

*, **, and *** denote significance at the 10%, 5%, and 1% levels, respectively.

existing domestic technological capacities provide different regional spillovers in the services/construction.

The estimated coefficient of $FP_{j,r}$ remains positive and significant for mid and low technology firms, indicating that both kinds of firms benefit from regional demonstration-related spillover. In addition, it appears that domestic firms with mid technological capacities experience greater effects. This finding for the services/construction industry is consistent with that for manufacturing in Ben Hamida (2013). High technology firms in the services/construction industry do not need to absorb foreign knowledge to augment their productivity. FP outside the region "$FP_{j,R-r}$" is not significant for all the sub-samples indicating that domestic firms do not benefit from foreign presence outside their regions.

The estimated coefficients of $FP_{j,r} * HC$ are significantly positive for the high gap firms, indicating that the combined effect of these variables contribute to augment the productivity of low technology firms. The size of such interaction effect is larger than that of $FP_{j,r}$, suggesting that the influence of regional FDI on the productivity development of these firms is broadly co-determined by the level of their human capital – this could be evidence for worker mobility-related spillovers. Alike Ben Hamida (2013) for manufacturing, the direct contacts in the same region between low technology firms and foreign affiliates in the services/construction industry seem to be not sufficient for this kind of domestic firms to successfully absorb and implement foreign knowledge. In addition, these firms do not seem to benefit from foreign firms located outside their region, since $FP_{j,R-r}$ is not significantly positive.

In addition, mid technology services/construction firms succeed in reaping spillover benefits from the interaction between $FP_{j,R-r}$ and HC; this implies that these firms need to upgrade their human capital level to benefit from foreign presence outside the region– this kind of interaction does not seem to have any significantly positive effects for other groups of firms. Surprisingly, small gap services/construction firms appear to benefit from the combined effect $FP_{j,r}$ and HC. These findings do not seem to corroborate those for manufacturing.

Regarding $\Delta Comp$, its estimated coefficient becomes negative and significant for small gap firms, while remains positive for large gap firms and insignificant for mid technology firms. This indicates that only high technology firms appear to benefit from competition-related spillovers. This finding is consistent with the result for manufacturing in Ben Hamida (2013).

In columns 5 and 6 in table 2 we report the results of spillover effects in the region and outside for the sub-samples characterized by the values of the variable $INVEST$. We find that only domestic firms which have highly invested in the absorptive capacity in terms of learning and investment seem to benefit from spillovers. Such benefits occur at regional level and result from technology transfer – according to Ben Hamida (2013), manufacturing firms seem also to benefit from outside the region since $FP_{j,R-r}$ is significantly positive; however, his benefit is by far smaller than that of $FP_{j,r}$. $\Delta Comp$ is negative but insignificant, demonstrating that the increase in competition does not appear to have any positive spillover effects on the productivity increase of both sub-samples.

The Chow tests soundly support our divisions (with respect to GAP and $INVEST$) of the services/construction sample.

6. Conclusion

This paper studies regional spillover effects from services/construction firms in Switzerland, while most existing studies analyze the manufacturing industry. It particularly examines the value of inward FDI in Swiss services/construction where foreign MNCs are expanding. It highlights the role of spillover mechanisms in determining regional benefit and controls for the existing technological capacity of domestic firms and their investment efforts in training and learning. It argues that possible interaction effects between spillover mechanisms and the technological capacity of domestic firms impact regional spillovers in the services/construction industry.

Our findings show that is important to take account of diverse spillover mechanisms and their relationship with the level of technological capacity of the domestic firms when assessing regional inward FDI spillovers. Actually, alike manufacturing firms in Ben Hamida (2013), competition-related spillovers seem to be totally absorbed by local firms with high technological capacities. Worker-mobility-related spillovers are to the great extent absorbed by low technology firms, while demonstration-related regional spillovers in the services/construction industry are absorbed by both mid and low technology firms with lager effects are found in mid technology firms. Unlike Ben Hamida (2013), there are also positive and significant interaction effects for the sub-sample of firms with small GAP, implying the importance of human capital in this kind of firms to reap the benefit from foreign presence in their region.

Regarding the role of firms' investment in training and learning, our finding confirm that of Ben Hamida 2013), in which only firms with relatively high $INVEST$ level benefit from regional spillovers from demonstration and worker mobility effects.

Regarding policy prescriptions that follows our findings, we suggest actions that encourage foreign MNCs to establish affiliates near local counterparts. In addition, Swiss government, particularly at the regional and cantonal levels, has to consider that the technological behavior of domestic firms plays a crucial role in determining whether they benefit from FDI regional spillovers. Firms do not benefit from regional spillovers using the same mechanism and that the level of their existing technological capacity guides the way they benefit from these effects. Furthermore, regional spillovers require sufficient level of human capital, especially for low technology firms, to be capable of decoding and implementing foreign best knowledge in their existing technological process. Thus, actions to support learning and investment in this kind of domestic firms and upgrade the level of their human capital are in our view necessary ingredients in a policy package to maximize regional FDI spillovers.

References

Aiken, L. and West, S. (1991), *Multiple regression: Testing and interpreting interactions*, Sage Publications, Newbury Park, London.

Aitken, B. J. and Harrison, A. E. (1999), Do Domestic Firms Benefit from Direct Foreign Investment? Evidence from Venezuela, *American Economic Review*, 89, 605-618.

Audretsch, D. B. (1998), Agglomeration and the Location of Innovative activity, *Oxford Review of Economic Policy*, 14, 18-29.

Baye, Michael R. (2006), *Managerial Economics and Business Strategy*, 5th Edition, McGraw-Hill.

Ben Hamida, L. and Gugler, P. (2009), Are There Demonstration-Related Spillovers From FDI? Evidence From Switzerland, *International Business Review*, 18, 494-508.

Ben Hamida, L. (2007), *Inward Foreign Direct Investment and Intra-Industry Spillovers: The Swiss Case*, Ph.D dissertation, University of Fribourg, Switzerland.

Ben Hamida, L. (2013), Are There Regional Spillovers from FDI in the Swiss Manufacturing Industry?, *International Business Review*, in Press.

Blomström, M. and Kokko, A. (2002),FDI and Human Capital: A Research Agenda", *OECD Working Paper*, No. 195, Paris.

Borensztein, E., De Gregorio, J. and J-W. Lee. (1998), How does foreign direct investment affect economic growth?, *Journal of International Economics*, 45, 115-135.

Buckley, P. J., Clegg, J., and Wang, C. (2007), The impact of foreign ownership, local ownership and industry characteristics on spillover benefits from foreign direct investment in China, *International Business Review*, 16, 142-158.

Buckley, P. J., Clegg, J., Wang, C., and Wang, Y.E. (2009), "FDI Spillovers and the Entry Speed of Foreign Firms: the Case of China", In *2009 Proceedings of EIBA International Conference*, December 13-15, Valencia.

Cantwell, J. (1989), *Technological Innovation and Multinational Corporations*, Basil Blackwell, Oxford.

Cantwell, J. (1999), *Foreign Direct Investment and Technological Change, Volume I and II*, Edward Elgar Publishing Limited, USA.

Castellani, D. and Zanfei, A. (2007), Multinational Companies and Productivity Spillovers: is there a specification error, *Applied Economics Letters*, 14, 1047-1051.

Cohen, W. and Levinthal, D. (1989), Innovation and Learning: the Two Faces of R&D, *Economic Journal*, 99, 569-596.

Cohen, W. and Levinthal, D. (1990), Absorptive Capability: a New Perspective on Learning and Innovation, *Administrative Science Quarterly*, Vol. 35, pp 128-152.

Chung, W. (2001), Identifying Technology Transfer in Foreign Direct Investment: Influence of Industry Conditions and Investing firm Motives, *Journal of International Business Studies*, 32, 211-229.

Crevoisier, O. and Roth, M. (2005), FDI, International Ownership Structures and Regional Development in the Finance Driven Economy: Where did the Billions of FDI (1995-2001) go? the Case of Switzerland, Dossier/IRER, No. 54, University of Neuchâtel.

Crespo, N., Proença, I., and Fontoura, M. P. (2008), FD Spillovers at the Regional Level: Evidence From Portugal, *Working Paper*, No. 05/08, Lisbon University Institute.

Dimelis, S. and Louri, H. (2002), Foreign Investment and Efficiency Benefits: A Conditional Quantile Analysis, *Oxford Economic Papers*, 54, 449-469.

Dimelis, S.P. (2005), Spillovers from Foreign Direct Investment and Firm Growth: Technological, Financial and Market Structure Effects", *International Journal of the Economics of Business,* Vol. 12, No. 1, pp. 85-104.

Driffield, N. (2004), "Regional Policy and spillovers from FDI in the UK, *The Annuals of Regional Science,* 38, 579-594.

Dunning, J. H. and Gugler, P. (2008), *Foreign Direct Investment, Location and Competitiveness,* Elsevier, Oxford.

Dunning, J. H. and Rugman, A. M. (1985), The Influence of Hymer's Dissertation on the Theory of Foreign Direct Investment, *The American Economic Review,* 75, 228-232.

Flôres, R.G., Fontoura, M. P. and Santos, R. G. (2002), Foreign Direct Investment Spillovers: Additional Lessons From a Country Study, *Working Paper,* No. 455, Graduate School of Economics, Brazil.

Girma, S., Greenaway, D., and Wakelin, K. (1999), Wages, Productivity and Foreign Ownership in UK Manufacturing, University of Nottingham, *Working Paper,* No. 99/14.

Girma, S. and Görg, H. (2007), The Role of the Efficiency Gap for Spillovers from FDI: Evidence from the UK Electronics and Engineering Sectors, *Open Economies Review,* 18, 215-232.

Girma, S. (2005), Absorptive Capacity and Productivity Spillovers from FDI: A Threshold Regression Analysis, *Oxford Bulletin of Economics and Statistics,* 67, 281-306.

Giroud, A., Tavani,Z. N., and Sinkovics, R. (2009), Reverse Knowledge Transfer within MNCs: The Case of Knowledge-Intensive Services in the U.K, In *Proceedings of EIBA Conference, Reshaping the Boundaries of the Firm in an Era of Global Interdependence,* December 13-15, Valencia.

Gomulka, S. (1990), *The Theory of Technological Change and Economic Growth,* Routledge, London.

Griliches, Z. (1998), The Search for R&D Spillovers, NBER Chapters, In Griliches, Z. (ed.), *R&D and Productivity: The Econometric Evidence,* pp. 251-268, National Bureau of Economic Research, Inc.

Haddad, M. and Harrison, A. (1993), Are there Positive Spillovers from Direct Foreign Investment? Evidence from Panel Data for Morocco, *Journal of development Economics,* 42, 51-74.

Hale, G. and Long, C. (2006), What Determines Technological Spillovers of Foreign Direct Investment: Evidence from China, *Discussion Paper,* No. 934, Yale University.

Haskel, J. E., Pereira, S. C. and Slaughter, M. J. (2007), Does Inward Foreign Investment Boost the Productivity of Domestic Firms?, *the Review of Economics and Statistics,* 89, 482-496.

Halpern, L. and Muraközy, B. (2005), Does distance matter in spillovers?, *CEPR Discussion Paper*, no. 4857, London.

Higón, D. A. and Vasilakos, N. (2011), Foreign Direct Investment Spillovers: Evidence from the British Retail Sector, *The World Economy*, 34, 642-666.

Hymer, S. (1968), La Grande Firme Multinationale, *Revue Economique*, 14, 949-973, Translated in English in M. C. Casson (Ed.), Multinational Corporations, Edward Elgar, Cheltenam.

Hymer, S. H. (1960), The International Operations of National Firms: A Study of Direct Foreign Investment, Ph.D. Thesis, Published by MIT Press, Cambridge, (also published under same title in 1976).

Karpaty, P. and Lundberg, L. (2004), Foreign Direct Investment and Productivity Spillovers in Swedish Manufacturing, *Working Paper*, No. 2, Orebro University, Sweden.

Kokko, A. (1996), Productivity Spillovers from Competition between Local Firms and Foreign Affiliates, *Journal of International Development*, 8, 517-530.

Kokko, A. (1994) Technology, Market Characteristics, and Spillovers, *Journal of Development Economics*, 43, 279-293.

Kokko, A., Tansini, R., and Zejan, M. C. (1996), Local Technological Capability and Productivity Spillovers from FDI in the Uruguayan Manufacturing Sector, *Journal of Development Studies*, 32, 602-611.

Konings, J. (1999), The Effects of Foreign Direct Investment on Domestic Firms: Evidence from Firm Level Panel Data in Emerging Economics, *LICOS Discussion Paper* DP 8699.

Liu, X. and Wei, Y. (2006), Productivity Spillovers from R&D, Exports and FDI in China's Manufacturing Sector, *Journal of International Business Studies*, 37, 544-557.

Liu, X., Siler, P., Wang, C. and Wei, Y. (2000), Productivity Spillovers from Foreign Direct Investment: Evidence From UK Industry Level Panel Data, *Journal of International Business Studies*, 31/3, 407-425.

Meyer, K. and Sinani, E. (2002), Identifying Spillovers of Technology Transfer from FDI: the Case of Estonia, Working Paper, No. 2002-047, Copenhagen Business School (Also Published in 2004, Spillovers of Technology Transfer from FDI: the Case of Estonia, *Journal of Comparative Economics*, 32, 445-466).

Mody, A. (1989), "Strategies for Developing Information Industries", In Cooper, C. and Kaplinsky, R. (eds.), *Technology and Development in the Third Industrial Revolution*, Frank Cass, London.

Narula, R. and Marin, A. (2003), "FDI Spillovers, Absorptive Capacities and Human Capital Development: Evidence from Argentina", *Working Paper*, No. 2003-016, Maastricht Economic Research Institute on Innovation and Technology, The Netherlands.

Narula, R. (2010), Much Ado about Nothing, or Sirens of a Brave New World? MNE Activity from Developing Countries and its Significance for Development, *Working Paper*, No. 2010-021, UNU-MERIT.

Nelson, R. R. (1982): "The Role of Knowledge in R&D Efficiency", *The Quarterly Journal of Economics*, Vol. 97, pp 453-470

Perez, T. (1998), *Foreign Investment and Spillovers*, Harwood Academic Publishers, the Netherlands.

Robinson, P. and Schweizer, M. (2006), *Swiss Attractiveness Survey: What Foreign Companies Say*, Ernest&Young Ltd., Zurich.

Sermet F. (2003), *Fiscalité Suisse*, Development Economic Western Switzerland.

Silverberg, G. and Verspagen, B. (1994), "Collective Learning, Innovation and Growth in a Boundedly Rational, Evolutionary World", *Journal of Evolutionary Economics*, 4, 207-226.

Sjöholm, F. (1999), Productivity Growth in Indonesia: The Role of Regional Characteristics and Direct Foreign Investment, *Economic Development and Culture change*, 47, 559-584.

Svejnar, J., Gorodnichenko, Y., and Terrell, K. (2007), "When Does FDI Have Positive Spillovers? Evidence from 17 Emerging Market Economies", *IZA Discussion Paper*, No. 3079.

Tian, X. (2007), "Accounting for Sources of FDI Technology Spillovers: Evidence from China", *Journal of International Business Studies*, vol. 38, pp. 147-159.

Wang, J-Y and Blomström, M. (1992), "Foreign Investment and Technology Transfer: A Simple Model", *European Economic Review*, 36, 137-155.

Yeaple, S. R. and Keller, W. (2003), "Multinational Enterprises, International Trade, and Productivity Growth: Firm-Level Evidence from the United States", *IMF Working Paper*, No. 03-248.

Yildizoglu, M. and Jonard, N. (1999), Sources of Technological Diversity, Cahiers de l'Innovation du CNRS, n°99030.

Zhang, Y., Lin, P., and Zhuomin, L.(2009), "Do Chinese Domestic Firms Benefit from FDI Inflow? Evidence of Horizontal and Vertical Spillovers", *China Economic Review*, 20, 677-691.

INDEX

A

abolition, 197, 207
absorptive capacity, viii, ix, xii, 44, 45, 46, 50, 55, 64, 70, 78, 81, 159, 165, 173, 262, 265, 270, 280
access, vii, 1, 5, 8, 10, 11, 12, 14, 16, 18, 26, 28, 34, 35, 36, 37, 54, 86, 158, 169, 177, 179, 196, 207
accounting, 7, 8, 22, 30, 177
accreditation, 169
acquisitions, 5, 40, 156, 176, 177, 184, 186, 237
adaptation, 156, 164
adjustment, 110, 122, 205, 216
administrative support, 169
advancement, 8
advocacy, 160
Africa, v, vii, 1, 2, 4, 6, 7, 10, 11, 12, 13, 15, 16, 35, 37, 38, 39, 40, 41, 163, 210
age, 41, 112, 114, 123, 217, 226
agencies, 157, 160, 170, 171, 173, 177
agglomeration, viii, ix, 44, 45, 46, 51, 52, 55, 56, 57, 65, 66, 67, 68, 69, 70, 71, 179, 230, 231, 232, 234, 235, 236, 238, 276
aggregate demand, 110, 118
aggregate output, 215
aggregation, 74
agriculture, 6, 7, 132
airports, 237
Algeria, 6, 203, 208
amines, 280
analytical framework, 13, 134
Angola, 4
arbitrage, 214, 244, 246
Argentina, 208, 284
Armenia, 171
ARS, 136
Asia, 5, 6, 13, 41, 77, 112, 120, 163, 173, 177, 178, 193
Asian countries, x, 127, 237
assessment, 71, 266, 267

assets, 4, 16, 20, 25, 30, 84, 158, 178, 181, 185, 186, 188, 191, 197, 203, 209, 231
Association of Southeast Asian Nations (ASEAN), vii, x, 76, 79, 100, 127, 128, 129, 130, 131, 134, 135, 136, 140, 142, 146, 150, 151, 196, 202, 203, 206, 208, 263
atmosphere, ix, 73
audit, 21, 23, 29, 36, 41
Austria, 76, 79, 208
aversion, 7, 9

B

backward integration, 23
backwardness, 68
balance sheet, 10
bandwidth, 85
banking, 8, 10, 77, 161, 179, 272
banking sector, 8, 10
banks, 7, 8, 133
bargaining, xi, 164, 213, 214, 215, 216, 217, 218, 219, 220, 221, 222, 223, 224, 225, 226, 227
barriers, 2, 17, 21, 22, 23, 24, 33, 36, 76, 196, 197, 198, 201, 203, 207, 268
base, 17, 83, 86, 109, 162, 169, 173, 232
base year, 83
basic research, 156
behavioral models, 139
behaviors, 112, 271
Beijing, 7, 8, 11, 13, 172, 184
Belgium, 76, 79, 84, 89, 204, 208
beneficial effect, 77, 80
benefits, xii, 26, 38, 68, 69, 76, 157, 158, 159, 165, 166, 169, 170, 171, 196, 197, 199, 208, 238, 265, 267, 268, 269, 271, 272, 280, 282
Bhagwati, 77, 80
bias, 111, 121, 134, 139, 258, 262, 272
bilateral, 140, 227
bilateral trade, x, 76, 79, 127, 150

biotechnology, 157, 161
blueprint, 128
boils, 200
brain, 158, 169
brain drain, 158, 169
brand loyalty, 21, 22
Brazil, 4, 41, 76, 164, 170, 208, 283
breakdown, 24, 75
Britain, 89, 199
bureaucracy, 8, 179
business cycle, 258, 271
business environment, 86, 187, 188
business function, 157
business model, 157, 173
businesses, 12, 17, 104, 111, 169
buyer, vii, 1, 2, 12, 20, 22, 23, 24, 25, 26, 28, 29, 30, 32, 33, 36, 37, 39
buyers, 12, 13, 14, 20, 21, 22, 23, 24, 25, 26, 27, 28, 29, 30, 31, 32, 33, 34, 35, 36, 48

C

Cairo, 210
calibration, 242
candidates, 169
CAP, 136, 140, 141, 143, 144, 145, 147, 148, 149, 189, 190
capacity building, 171
capital accumulation, 75
capital expenditure, 27
capital flows, ix, 73, 163, 167, 196, 197, 207, 252
capital goods, 259, 260
capital inflow, 198
capital markets, vii, 1, 8, 11
capital outflow, 106
capitalism, 86
Caribbean, 163
case studies, 49, 70
case study, vii, 1, 13, 41, 152
catalyst, 157, 201
catching-up, 157
causal relationship, 262
causality, 76, 79, 81, 116, 124, 132
CEE, 206, 210
central bank, 259
Central Europe, 122
certification, 178
Ceuta, 91, 95
challenges, 25, 40, 134, 157, 165, 173, 174
Chamber of Commerce, 30
chemical, 10, 61, 237
chemical industry, 237
CHF, 277

Chiang Mai Initiative, 129
Chicago, 38, 121
Chile, 4, 5, 76, 79, 169, 171
China, v, vi, vii, x, xi, 1, 2, 3, 4, 6, 7, 8, 9, 10, 11, 13, 14, 15, 16, 22, 26, 30, 35, 38, 39, 40, 41, 48, 77, 80, 100, 101, 103, 104, 105, 106, 108, 109, 111, 112, 113, 114, 115, 116, 117, 118, 119, 120, 121, 123, 124, 125, 129, 132, 133, 151, 152, 153, 162, 163, 164, 169, 170, 172, 173, 175, 176, 177, 178, 179, 180, 181, 182, 183, 184, 186, 187, 188, 189, 190, 191, 192, 193, 229, 230, 232, 233, 234, 235, 236, 237, 238, 239, 268, 269, 282, 283, 284, 285
Chinese firms, 6, 7, 42
Chinese government, 187, 230, 232, 236, 237
circulation, 169
cities, 187, 232
civil society, 4, 13
classification, 85, 103, 104, 195, 259
client firms, viii, ix, 44, 47, 48, 58, 59, 60, 61, 62, 63, 65
clients, 10, 61
climate, 160, 167
clustering, 231, 261
clusters, 14, 39, 68, 161, 164, 165, 167, 168, 171, 174, 231
coal, 259
coastal region, 230, 232, 234, 235, 236, 237
Coefficient of Variation, 82
coffee, 166
collaboration, 112, 157, 161, 171
collateral, 28
College Station, 122
colleges, 237
combined effect, 280
commerce, 187
commercial, 36, 167, 197, 204
commercial bank, 36
commodity, vii, 1, 35, 38, 39, 40
common external tariff, 198
Common Market, 210
communication, 150, 201
Communist Party, 8
communities, 22
community, 21, 30, 36, 151
comparative advantage, 9, 109, 118, 119, 174, 196, 200
compensation, 25, 48, 110, 112, 113, 123
competition, x, 12, 17, 23, 25, 33, 42, 47, 70, 71, 76, 78, 86, 120, 134, 151, 155, 157, 158, 159, 168, 177, 179, 196, 198, 218, 242, 253, 256, 262, 268, 270, 271, 276, 277, 278, 280, 281
competitive advantage, 5, 32, 108, 155, 198, 214

competitiveness, 2, 4, 5, 10, 12, 23, 24, 41, 104, 155, 158, 167, 231
competitors, 48, 78, 152, 164, 172, 197
compilation, 20
complement, 158
complexity, 13, 250
composition, 16, 179, 192, 267
computer, 161, 272
concentration ratios, 83
consensus, 2, 78, 219
consent, 219
consolidation, 4, 9
constant prices, 203
construction, vii, xii, 3, 25, 27, 30, 135, 181, 237, 265, 266, 267, 270, 271, 272, 275, 276, 278, 279, 280, 281
consulting, 156
consumer goods, 3, 10, 35
Consumer Price Index (CPI), 242
consumer surplus, 216
consumers, 104
consumption, 3, 4, 134, 187, 191, 243
continuous random variable, 84
contract enforcement, 180
contradiction, 131
controversial, 269
convergence, ix, 37, 50, 53, 55, 67, 74, 75, 78, 81, 86, 87, 88, 89, 90
copper, vii, 1, 2, 3, 4, 5, 13, 14, 15, 16, 17, 18, 19, 20, 26, 35, 36, 37, 39, 40
corporate governance, 8, 10
Corporate Social Responsibility (CSR), 30
corporate tax, vii, xi, 161, 162, 165, 241, 242, 243, 246, 247, 249, 250, 252
corporation tax, 242, 243, 247, 250
correlation, 83, 130, 138, 140, 142, 146, 184, 185, 187, 204, 205
correlation coefficient, 184
corruption, vii, xi, 25, 175, 176, 178, 179, 180, 184, 185, 186, 188, 189, 190, 191, 208, 230
cost, xi, 5, 17, 18, 24, 26, 27, 36, 42, 48, 49, 108, 113, 164, 177, 178, 187, 188, 194, 213, 214, 215, 216, 218, 220, 230, 231, 232, 233, 234, 235, 236, 244, 277
Costa Rica, 165, 166, 167, 173, 174
country of origin, vii, 1, 75, 156
Coup, 193
covering, 65, 76, 230
credit rating, 10
crises, 52
critical value, 226
Cross-national, 67
CSF, 24, 26

currency, xi, 18, 241, 242, 243, 246, 247, 250
current account, 108
current account balance, 108
customer service, 167
customers, 29, 108, 110, 164
cyclical component, 110
Cyprus, 92, 98
Czech Republic, 49, 164, 171

D

data analysis, 76, 101
data availability, 203
data collection, 135
data set, 111, 123, 139, 140, 230, 233, 236, 271, 272
database, x, 18, 74, 75, 83, 127, 162, 163, 181, 184
debts, 36
decentralization, 133
decentralized union, xi, 213, 214, 216, 217, 220, 221, 226
decoding, 281
decomposition, 132, 174
deflation, 247, 250
demand characteristic, 178
Democratic Republic of Congo, 4, 37
Denmark, 76, 79, 83, 90, 208
dependent variable, 59, 60, 62, 75, 110, 114, 115, 116, 125, 136, 137, 152, 186, 188, 189, 190, 202, 233, 234
depreciation, 123, 170
depth, 13, 17, 39, 235
deregulation, 167
deterrence, 179
Deutsche Bundesbank, 107, 120
developed countries, ix, 4, 6, 10, 11, 14, 15, 30, 73, 75, 80, 86, 157, 164, 167, 170, 203, 214, 235
developing countries, x, 4, 6, 9, 11, 12, 40, 41, 52, 74, 75, 76, 77, 78, 79, 80, 81, 100, 132, 155, 157, 158, 162, 164, 165, 168, 170, 172, 173, 174, 199, 200, 201, 207, 229, 235, 238, 262, 266
developing economies, 76, 80, 164, 262
development policy, 201
deviation, 53
diffusion, xii, 54, 68, 70, 75, 158, 159, 200, 203, 231, 255, 268
diminishing returns, 75
direct foreign investment, 67, 68, 69, 71
direct investment, xii, 38, 39, 40, 67, 68, 70, 71, 74, 79, 99, 100, 101, 105, 111, 120, 128, 135, 153, 172, 173, 174, 183, 201, 213, 227, 237, 238, 255, 262
direct investments, xi, 104, 105, 106, 111, 213, 214, 238

discrimination, 170
dislocation, 104
dismantlement, 35
dispersion, 83, 89
disposable income, 188
distortions, 179, 196
distribution, xi, 10, 17, 74, 75, 81, 83, 84, 85, 86, 89, 101, 132, 139, 142, 150, 162, 174, 181, 184, 201, 229, 230, 232, 239, 242, 271
diversification, 41, 166, 172
diversity, 111, 178
domestic credit, 136, 140
domestic currency, xi, 241, 242, 243, 246, 247, 250
domestic economy, 166, 242, 243, 246, 249
domestic industry, 104
domestic investment, 17, 104, 108, 119, 179, 202, 262
domestic labor, 106, 109, 119
domestic markets, 9, 177
dominance, 7
Dominican Republic, 174
donors, 15
draft, 99, 120
duopoly, xi, 213
dynamism, 159, 167, 199

E

earnings, x, 16, 103, 106, 117, 208, 231
East Asia, 77, 81, 100, 101, 109, 120, 178, 193
Eastern Europe, 68, 108, 122, 181
economic activity, viii, 38, 43, 44, 45, 51, 56, 64, 65, 66, 76, 80, 181, 198, 230, 235, 238
economic cooperation, 201
economic crisis, 11, 13, 20, 23, 26, 28, 30, 36, 40, 75
economic development, x, xi, 3, 14, 40, 76, 80, 86, 128, 132, 134, 167, 229, 230, 232, 236, 237, 262
economic downturn, 3, 40
economic efficiency, 13
economic growth, vii, ix, x, 45, 73, 74, 75, 76, 77, 78, 79, 80, 81, 86, 87, 88, 89, 90, 99, 100, 101, 127, 128, 129, 131, 132, 133, 134, 151, 152, 163, 166, 176, 196, 203, 205, 206, 207, 208, 229, 232, 237, 238, 242, 262, 282
economic growth rate, 203, 229
economic integration, x, xi, 127, 128, 130, 131, 132, 134, 135, 136, 138, 140, 142, 145, 146, 150, 195, 196, 197, 198, 200, 201, 205, 207, 208, 210
economic liberalization, 52, 53, 177
economic performance, 100, 262
economic policy, 242
economic reform, 9, 232
economic regionalism, 199

economic relations, xi, 195, 196
economic rent, 5
economic transformation, 37
economics, 51, 68, 71, 133, 180, 213
economies of scale, 34, 166, 198
education, 32, 132, 133, 159, 160, 161, 166, 168, 169, 178, 235, 236, 237
Egypt, 208, 210
elaboration, 81, 82, 84, 88, 93, 98
election, vii, 1
electricity, 21, 187, 191, 259, 260
emerging markets, 173
empirical studies, 12, 75, 76, 78, 79, 128, 132, 199, 207, 256, 262, 266, 267, 269
employees, 8, 21, 22, 59, 108, 111, 118, 159, 167, 185, 186, 215, 216, 268, 269, 270, 271, 276, 277
employment, 16, 78, 83, 86, 88, 90, 105, 108, 111, 112, 120, 123, 152, 159, 161, 166, 214, 215, 217, 219, 220, 228, 255, 269, 278
EMU, 151
endogeneity, 110, 116, 262
endowments, 7
energy, 10, 11, 237, 257, 259, 260
energy input, 257
engineering, 17, 22, 25, 31, 32, 33, 161, 163, 167, 169, 173
England, 238
enrollment, 204, 209
entrepreneurship, 171
environment, ix, 24, 73, 119, 177, 184, 186, 188, 197, 237
environmental regulations, 258
environmental standards, 30
environments, 178
EPR, 284
equality, 129, 142, 146, 278
equilibrium, xi, 110, 176, 213, 215, 218, 219, 220, 221, 245, 247
equipment, 3, 7, 10, 13, 20, 21, 22, 23, 24, 25, 27, 28, 31, 32, 33, 166, 168, 169, 270, 277, 278
equity, xi, xii, 36, 41, 170, 175, 176, 177, 178, 179, 180, 184, 185, 186, 187, 190, 191, 255, 257, 258, 259, 261, 262, 269
EST, 278, 279
Estonia, 89, 91, 98, 284
EU candidate countries, 206
euphoria, 182
Europe, 4, 21, 32, 68, 74, 151, 152, 157, 161, 162, 163, 173, 174, 199, 203, 207
European Commission, 252
European Investment Bank, 172
European regions, ix, 73, 74, 75, 77, 80, 86, 87, 88, 89, 90, 99

European Union (EU), v, vii, ix, 4, 51, 73, 74, 75, 76, 79, 81, 83, 84, 89, 99, 101, 111, 156, 161, 196, 200, 202, 206, 208
EUROSTAT, 74
evidence, vii, viii, ix, x, xi, 11, 43, 44, 45, 46, 47, 48, 49, 50, 51, 53, 54, 55, 56, 57, 59, 60, 63, 64, 65, 66, 67, 69, 70, 77, 78, 89, 99, 100, 116, 118, 128, 129, 132, 134, 139, 142, 144, 150, 152, 155, 166, 175, 176, 177, 179, 188, 191, 235, 238, 256, 262, 266, 268, 269
evolution, 39, 80, 156, 172
exchange rate, vii, xi, 5, 202, 204, 207, 241, 242, 244, 246, 247, 250, 253
exclusion, 28, 33, 34
exercise, 12, 23, 160, 161, 201, 236
expenditures, xi, 42, 83, 90, 121, 123, 162, 175, 176, 277
expertise, 10, 30, 33, 86, 197
exploitation, 177
explosives, 22
export market, 4, 196, 215
export promotion, 11
export-led growth, 237
exports, xi, 2, 11, 16, 56, 70, 76, 79, 83, 101, 107, 110, 123, 166, 196, 197, 198, 203, 213, 214, 215, 216, 218, 219, 220, 221, 222, 244, 259
externalities, viii, 43, 45, 47, 48, 50, 52, 54, 64, 65, 66, 69, 76, 159, 231, 256
extraction, 4, 6, 24
extractive industries, vii, 1, 2, 4, 8, 11, 13, 35, 37, 41

F

facilitators, 165
factor endowments, 76, 79
factories, 7
FDI inflow, ix, xi, 56, 73, 74, 76, 80, 100, 128, 129, 130, 178, 179, 187, 203, 205, 206, 208, 229, 231, 232, 234, 235, 236, 241, 242, 246, 250, 262, 271
FEM, 138, 139, 141, 142, 143, 144, 145, 146, 147, 148, 149, 150
financial, ix, x, xi, 4, 5, 10, 11, 12, 14, 16, 21, 23, 31, 49, 73, 77, 80, 86, 99, 104, 108, 111, 112, 127, 128, 129, 133, 134, 135, 136, 138, 140, 142, 145, 146, 150, 160, 161, 162, 170, 171, 175, 181, 182, 187, 188, 195, 196, 199, 201, 202, 203, 204, 206, 209
financial capital, 86
financial crisis, ix, 73, 104, 128, 161, 181, 182
financial data, 31, 175
financial development, x, 127, 133, 134, 135, 136, 138, 140, 142, 145, 146, 150
financial firms, 181

financial globalization, 133
financial incentives, 160, 161, 170, 171
financial institutions, 133
financial markets, 77, 80, 99
financial records, 21
financial reports, 14, 111
financial sector, 11
financial stability, 199
financial support, 49, 175
financial system, 77
Finland, 39, 41, 76, 79, 208
firm size, 9, 106, 108, 109, 111, 112, 118
first dimension, 256
fixed effect model, x, 127, 138, 139
flexibility, 108
flooding, 24
flotation, 5
fluctuations, 123
food, 13
force, x, 103, 199, 204, 230, 237, 269
Ford, 10
forecasting, 196
foreign companies, 119, 166, 167, 183, 207
foreign direct investment, x, xi, 38, 39, 40, 41, 67, 68, 69, 70, 71, 74, 99, 100, 101, 104, 106, 127, 128, 132, 134, 136, 150, 151, 173, 175, 176, 193, 195, 196, 202, 204, 206, 209, 210, 213, 214, 229, 237, 238, 239, 241, 242, 252, 282
Foreign Direct Investment (FDI), 1, iii, vii, ix, 2, 45, 73, 74, 265
foreign exchange, 16, 17
foreign firms, 74, 169, 196, 198, 207, 256, 257, 260, 261, 269, 270, 272, 273, 274, 275, 276, 277, 278, 280
foreign investment, ix, 52, 67, 70, 71, 73, 77, 100, 104, 108, 131, 164, 177, 179, 186, 196, 200, 201, 237, 261, 268, 271
formation, ix, 73, 78, 123, 140, 168, 170, 171, 196, 209, 231
formula, 113, 123, 253
forward integration, 11
foundations, 68
framing, 162
France, 40, 50, 76, 79, 82, 83, 84, 89, 91, 95, 208, 246
free trade, 119, 166, 187, 196, 198
free trade area, 119, 196
freedom, 78, 178, 205
funding, 5, 16, 159, 161, 168, 170
funds, 7, 8, 11

G

G7 countries, 80
Gabon, 40
GDP, 2, 16, 18, 53, 76, 79, 80, 83, 84, 86, 87, 88, 89, 90, 104, 117, 130, 132, 133, 136, 140, 142, 150, 161, 176, 178, 179, 185, 187, 189, 190, 199, 202, 203, 204, 205, 206, 209, 233
GDP deflator, 202
GDP per capita, 133, 140, 150, 179, 187
geography, x, 51, 127, 129, 133, 155, 158, 164
Georgia, 255
Germany, 40, 41, 76, 79, 84, 89, 169, 208
ginseng, 174
global competition, x, 155
global economy, 41, 68, 74, 155, 253
global markets, 177
global scale, 14
globalization, ix, x, xii, 40, 41, 73, 75, 76, 80, 86, 89, 103, 132, 133, 157, 162, 173, 174, 175, 241, 251
goods and services, 6, 21, 22, 23, 36, 201
governance, vii, 1, 2, 8, 12, 20, 21, 23, 30, 37, 39, 170, 178, 180
government budget, 243
government intervention, 9, 78, 157
government policy, 6, 233
governments, 2, 66, 86, 119, 159, 164, 165, 167, 168, 170, 203, 236, 237, 242
grades, 5
grants, 162, 169, 170
Greece, 48, 51, 70, 76, 79, 81, 99, 208, 213
Gross Domestic Product, 121, 202
growth, ix, 2, 4, 6, 10, 11, 12, 31, 33, 37, 45, 56, 70, 71, 73, 74, 75, 76, 77, 78, 79, 80, 81, 82, 83, 87, 89, 90, 98, 99, 100, 104, 105, 107, 108, 109, 110, 112, 113, 114, 115, 116, 117, 118, 119, 123, 125, 128, 129, 132, 133, 134, 151, 152, 158, 161, 165, 177, 185, 186, 188, 202, 204, 206, 207, 230, 231, 232, 236, 237, 238, 239, 242, 262, 266, 269
growth models, 75
growth rate, 4, 80, 82, 83, 87, 89, 98, 110, 112, 114, 115, 116, 117, 118, 123, 125, 185, 186, 202, 204
growth theory, 75, 231
Guangdong, 7, 152, 184
guidelines, 11, 16

H

heterogeneity, viii, 43, 45, 48, 55, 64, 66, 70, 78, 137, 139, 205, 266, 270, 276
heteroskedasticity, 138, 139, 144, 261, 278
higher education, 199, 233
highlands, 85, 93, 98, 232
highways, 233
hiring, 47
homogeneity, 236
Hong Kong, 6, 11, 16, 111, 184, 232, 236, 242, 249
host, viii, ix, xii, 4, 7, 9, 11, 40, 43, 44, 45, 46, 47, 48, 49, 51, 52, 64, 65, 66, 70, 73, 76, 77, 78, 79, 80, 86, 100, 109, 118, 156, 157, 158, 159, 165, 170, 176, 179, 180, 184, 196, 198, 199, 200, 207, 214, 215, 216, 217, 219, 220, 221, 222, 231, 255, 257, 261, 262, 265, 266
hot spots, 163
housing, 3
hub, 22, 36
human, ix, x, 4, 73, 77, 78, 80, 88, 90, 103, 105, 106, 107, 110, 112, 113, 114, 115, 116, 117, 123, 125, 132, 134, 143, 157, 158, 159, 160, 164, 165, 169, 178, 187, 200, 202, 204, 207, 230, 232, 234, 235, 236, 237, 269, 270, 275, 276, 278, 280, 281
human capital, ix, x, 73, 77, 78, 80, 88, 89, 90, 103, 105, 106, 107, 110, 112, 113, 114, 115, 116, 117, 123, 125, 132, 157, 158, 159, 160, 164, 165, 169, 178, 187, 202, 204, 207, 230, 232, 234, 235, 236, 237, 269, 270, 275, 276, 278, 280, 281
human development, 143
human resources, 200, 237
human rights, 4
Hungary, 52, 164, 238, 268

I

images, 151, 160
immigrants, 169
immigration, 161, 169, 214, 237
import penetration, x, 103
import prices, 247
import restrictions, 52
import substitution, 17, 52
imports, 4, 17, 22, 70, 76, 83, 104, 107, 110, 196, 203, 259
improvements, 12, 55, 59, 62, 64, 86, 108, 158, 164
in transition, 182, 194
income, vii, x, xi, 18, 76, 78, 80, 87, 100, 101, 104, 108, 114, 117, 123, 127, 128, 129, 130, 131, 132, 133, 134, 135, 136, 140, 141, 142, 144, 145, 146, 150, 151, 152, 153, 162, 164, 169, 173, 232, 241, 242, 243, 246, 247, 248, 249, 250, 252, 277
income inequality, vii, x, 77, 80, 101, 127, 128, 129, 130, 131, 132, 133, 134, 136, 140, 141, 142, 144, 145, 146, 150, 151, 152, 153
income tax, 114, 123, 169, 242, 246, 252
increased competition, 207, 266, 269, 277
independence, 205

independent variable, 60, 75, 77, 85, 87, 89, 136, 137, 138, 179, 186
India, vii, 1, 2, 3, 4, 6, 9, 10, 11, 13, 15, 16, 23, 35, 38, 39, 40, 41, 163, 164, 169, 170, 172, 239
Indians, 21
indirect effect, 47, 158
individuals, 183
Indonesia, x, 4, 48, 50, 51, 71, 76, 79, 127, 130, 131, 140, 203, 208, 256, 259, 262, 263, 264, 285
Indonesian manufacturing, xii, 255, 258
induction, 218
industrial development, vii, 1, 162
industrial organization, 86, 177, 214
industrial policies, 18, 166, 171
industrialisation, vii, 1, 2, 8, 11, 12, 17, 34, 35, 40
industrialization, 2, 71, 75
industrialized countries, 238
industries, vii, viii, xii, 1, 2, 4, 5, 7, 8, 9, 11, 13, 35, 36, 37, 40, 41, 43, 45, 47, 48, 49, 50, 51, 52, 54, 55, 56, 61, 64, 68, 69, 70, 78, 81, 104, 109, 119, 156, 161, 165, 167, 168, 169, 173, 177, 231, 237, 255, 256, 259, 262, 265, 266, 268
industry, vii, viii, ix, x, xii, 2, 4, 5, 13, 17, 26, 31, 35, 38, 43, 44, 45, 46, 47, 48, 50, 51, 53, 54, 55, 56, 61, 64, 65, 67, 68, 69, 70, 77, 78, 81, 88, 89, 90, 100, 103, 104, 105, 108, 109, 112, 117, 119, 120, 122, 161, 162, 164, 165, 166, 172, 175, 176, 177, 178, 180, 181, 191, 208, 231, 232, 249, 255, 256, 257, 258, 259, 260, 261, 265, 266, 267, 268, 269, 270, 271, 273, 275, 276, 277, 278, 279, 280, 281, 282
inequality, x, 77, 127, 128, 129, 130, 131, 132, 133, 134, 138, 141, 142, 144, 145, 146, 150, 151, 152, 232
INF, 202, 204, 205, 206
inflation, 33, 76, 138, 139, 181, 202, 204, 207, 209, 211, 236, 242, 247, 250
information exchange, 28
information sharing, 12
information technology, 10
infrastructure, 3, 4, 8, 56, 77, 134, 143, 157, 159, 160, 161, 162, 164, 167, 168, 169, 178, 180, 187, 201, 230, 231, 232, 234, 235, 236, 237, 258
ingredients, 281
initiation, 130, 207
insertion, 39
institutions, 10, 14, 17, 20, 74, 77, 161, 164, 167, 168, 169, 171, 179, 222, 231, 266, 272, 273, 274
integration, ix, x, xi, 67, 70, 73, 76, 79, 127, 128, 129, 130, 131, 134, 135, 142, 146, 150, 171, 195, 196, 197, 198, 199, 200, 201, 202, 203, 204, 206, 207, 208, 209, 210, 211
intellectual property, 77, 170, 173, 201

intelligence, 7, 160
intelligence gathering, 160
interaction effect, 51, 280, 281
interaction effects, 51, 281
Inter-American Development Bank, 174, 211
interdependence, 201
interest rates, 10, 18, 35
inter-firm linkages, viii, 40, 43, 44, 45, 46, 48, 49, 51, 64, 65, 66
internal barriers, 197
internalised, 32
internalization, 178, 214, 270
international competition, 119, 242
international competitiveness, 8
international investment, 52, 103, 163, 171, 173
International Monetary Fund (IMF), 3, 18, 41, 100, 151, 161, 192, 210, 285
international standards, 8, 10, 17, 242
international trade, ix, xi, 73, 133, 157, 196, 215, 220, 241, 250
internationalization, 40, 71, 155, 156, 172, 197
intervention, 157, 159, 168, 208, 216
intra-regional trade, 200
investment, vii, ix, x, 2, 4, 5, 6, 7, 8, 9, 10, 11, 12, 13, 14, 15, 16, 18, 20, 22, 24, 26, 27, 28, 29, 30, 35, 36, 37, 38, 40, 41, 52, 67, 69, 71, 73, 78, 83, 88, 89, 90, 101, 103, 104, 106, 112, 117, 119, 127, 128, 129, 130, 131, 132, 134, 143, 150, 156, 160, 162, 163, 165, 167, 168, 169, 170, 171, 173, 176, 177, 178, 179, 183, 186, 187, 188, 189, 191, 197, 198, 199, 200, 230, 231, 237, 252, 267, 268, 270, 271, 277, 278, 280, 281
investment capital, 7, 16
investments, xi, 2, 4, 5, 6, 7, 9, 10, 11, 13, 16, 69, 86, 99, 108, 109, 112, 119, 156, 160, 161, 162, 175, 176, 177, 178, 181, 183, 186, 187, 188, 191, 199, 201, 231, 236, 238
investors, vii, x, 1, 4, 7, 8, 9, 10, 11, 13, 15, 20, 69, 119, 127, 129, 160, 161, 164, 165, 169, 170, 177, 197, 199, 231, 232, 236, 256, 266
involution, 210
Ireland, 51, 76, 78, 79, 81, 99, 156, 161, 162, 170, 171, 172, 174, 203, 208, 238, 249
Italy, 50, 51, 74, 76, 79, 84, 208, 269

J

Japan, 109, 120, 129, 156, 162, 208, 230, 241, 242, 246
joint ventures, 156, 177, 178, 183, 186
Jordan, 175

K

Kazakhstan, 4
knowledge capital, 108
knowledge economy, 174
Korea, 129, 166, 208

L

labor force, 108, 112, 122, 166, 167
labor market, 51
labour force, 237
labour market, xi, 166, 213, 214, 215, 216, 217, 219, 220, 221, 222
landscape, 191
language barrier, 22, 25
Latin America, 5, 77, 81, 101, 163, 207, 209
Latvia, 89, 92, 98
laws, 52
LDCs, 40
lead, 12, 13, 23, 24, 26, 28, 30, 31, 36, 80, 90, 128, 130, 131, 133, 137, 138, 139, 196, 199, 242, 256, 269
leadership, 105
leakage, x, 48, 103, 106
lean production, 13
learning, 24, 26, 36, 39, 68, 157, 164, 168, 169, 172, 207, 266, 267, 268, 269, 270, 272, 276, 280, 281
learning process, 24, 168, 272
LED, 121
legislation, 169, 215, 216, 220
lending, 8, 40, 181
level of education, 77, 88
liberalisation, 9, 151
liberalization, x, 71, 119, 127, 129, 131, 134, 150, 167, 168, 197, 208
light, 5, 14, 16, 69, 136, 176, 177
Likert scale, 60
linear model, 233
liquidity, 17, 23
Lithuania, 89, 92, 98
living environment, 169
loans, 7, 8, 9, 58, 170
local government, 236
logistics, 27, 155, 166
long-term debt, 185, 186
low labor-cost, 108
lower prices, 23, 104
lubricants, 22, 259, 260
Luo, 152

M

machinery, 4, 7, 13, 109, 259
macro-regions, xi, 229, 230, 235, 236, 237
magnitude, 176, 179, 247, 251
majority, 10, 14, 16, 21, 46, 48, 53, 54, 55, 60, 89, 259, 271
Malaysia, x, 76, 79, 80, 100, 127, 130, 140, 161, 164, 170, 174, 208
management, 4, 5, 8, 17, 28, 30, 31, 33, 36, 37, 158, 196, 207
manipulation, 214
manpower, 27
manufacturing, xii, 4, 6, 7, 10, 11, 16, 17, 31, 33, 34, 35, 37, 41, 50, 53, 54, 56, 57, 67, 68, 69, 70, 71, 76, 78, 81, 104, 111, 129, 133, 151, 152, 155, 156, 157, 161, 163, 164, 166, 167, 181, 184, 187, 192, 231, 238, 249, 255, 258, 259, 262, 265, 266, 267, 268, 270, 271, 275, 280, 281
market access, 8, 21, 36, 54
market capitalization, 136, 140
market failure, 32, 157, 159
market penetration, 198
market position, 21
market share, 34, 47, 176, 177, 191, 218, 266, 270
market structure, 214
marketing, 9, 10, 86, 157, 160, 168, 171, 207, 265
market-seeking, 9, 164, 167, 179, 187, 230, 234, 235
Markov chain, 81, 99
mass, 201
materials, 26, 237, 258, 259, 260
matrix, 84, 136, 137, 138
matter, 60, 62, 69, 128, 142, 284
measurement, 138, 270
measurements, 180, 276
media, 162
median, 123
medical, 161, 166
Mediterranean, 202, 203, 207, 210
membership, 202, 215
MERCOSUR, 198, 200, 202, 203, 206, 208, 210
mergers, 40, 156, 197, 237
meta-analysis, 173
metals, 166
methodology, 78, 114, 135, 201, 207, 208, 222, 230, 234, 257
Mexican producer, viii, ix, 44, 46, 58, 63, 65
Mexico, v, vii, viii, ix, 4, 43, 44, 46, 52, 53, 54, 55, 56, 57, 60, 65, 66, 67, 68, 69, 70, 71, 76, 79, 170, 174, 208, 256, 263
Microsoft, 167, 177
middle class, 164
Middle East, 163

migrants, 17
mineral resources, 7, 16, 40
model specification, x, 127, 136, 137
models, 56, 76, 106, 120, 121, 141, 142, 144, 145, 152, 186, 188, 189, 190, 191, 199, 202, 213, 233, 234
modernization, 196
monetary policy, 251, 253
monopolistic competition, 244
monopoly, 216
Morocco, 50, 69, 208, 256, 263, 283
motivation, 164, 218, 220, 230
Multilateral, 174
multinational companies, x, 15, 155, 161, 162, 166
multinational corporations, 86, 161, 164, 196
multinational enterprises, xii, 238, 241, 242, 250, 255, 261
multinational firms, 103, 173, 175, 177
multiple regression, 139
multivariate analysis, viii, ix, 44, 57, 65

N

nanotechnology, 157
national income, xi, 241, 244, 245, 247, 250
national mandate, 166
national policy, 158, 236
nationality, 32
natural gas, 237
natural resources, 6, 7, 8, 119, 177, 237
negative consequences, ix, 24, 73
negative effects, 106, 109, 117, 118, 214, 268
negative relation, 78, 129, 133, 150, 207
negotiating, 166
negotiation, 12
Netherlands, 15, 43, 76, 79, 84, 89, 152, 208, 284, 285
networking, 169
neutral, 214, 215
Nigeria, 4, 6
non-OECD, 6, 77, 80
non-price competition, 13
nontariff barriers, 197, 208
normal distribution, 139
North America, 4, 16, 20, 21, 52, 163, 173
North American Free Trade Agreement (NAFTA), 52, 56, 68, 71, 196, 198, 200, 201, 202, 203, 206, 208, 210
Northern Ireland, 49, 93, 98
Nuevo León, 57, 65
null hypothesis, 116, 138, 139, 140, 260

O

offshoring, 170, 173
oil, 5, 10, 11, 22, 41, 237
omission, 276
openness, xi, 77, 90, 110, 130, 133, 136, 140, 142, 152, 178, 180, 187, 203, 207, 208, 229, 242, 243
operations, 17, 24, 25, 35, 45, 47, 49, 57, 65, 109, 112, 159, 164, 167, 176, 177, 178, 180, 181, 184, 187, 191
opportunities, vii, x, 1, 2, 6, 10, 12, 13, 21, 22, 29, 32, 35, 36, 155, 158, 162, 164, 165, 167, 171, 173, 177, 181, 184, 198, 231
ores, 270, 283
Organization for Economic Cooperation and Development (OECD), 6, 7, 39, 40, 52, 70, 77, 80, 108, 156, 157, 158, 161, 166, 170, 173, 174, 199, 207, 211, 246, 247, 249, 282
outsourcing, vii, 1, 21, 22, 28, 67, 123, 157, 163
outsourcing strategies, vii, 1
overhead costs, 18
overseas investment, 104, 107, 108, 109, 119
ownership, vii, xii, 1, 7, 8, 10, 13, 15, 17, 20, 21, 24, 27, 32, 35, 38, 41, 42, 46, 52, 60, 61, 62, 63, 65, 67, 68, 70, 74, 156, 158, 167, 178, 197, 255, 256, 257, 258, 260, 261, 262, 282
ownership structure, 8, 13, 15, 74

P

Pacific, 38, 41, 120, 163, 173, 178, 193
paints, 33
Pakistan, 132, 152
Paraguay, 208
parallel, 14, 162
parameter estimates, 139, 142
participants, 11, 12, 23, 28, 120
per capita income, 78, 86, 87, 89, 90, 151, 199
percentile, 270
performers, 84, 85, 89
permission, iv
petroleum, 40
pharmaceutical, 33, 173
pharmaceuticals, 10, 157, 161
Philippines, x, 76, 79, 127, 130, 140
Phillips curve, 211
plants, xii, 7, 16, 17, 20, 54, 68, 78, 81, 104, 166, 176, 186, 231, 255, 256, 257, 258, 260, 261, 262
plastic products, 10
plastics, 166
platform, 161, 172, 201
Poland, 4, 50, 71, 238

policy, vii, x, xi, xii, 2, 6, 7, 8, 9, 10, 11, 13, 14, 16, 30, 36, 37, 40, 41, 52, 66, 68, 71, 74, 75, 90, 103, 106, 118, 119, 128, 129, 134, 150, 155, 156, 157, 158, 159, 160, 161, 164, 168, 169, 170, 171, 172, 173, 174, 177, 197, 201, 213, 215, 216, 218, 221, 222, 229, 230, 232, 233, 234, 235, 241, 242, 243, 246, 247, 248, 249, 250, 251, 255, 262, 271, 281
policy instruments, 157, 160
policy makers, 119, 128, 159, 271
policy making, 66, 118
policy options, x, 155, 158, 174
policy reform, 160
policymakers, x, 127, 160, 181
political instability, 5, 181
political leaders, 8
political problems, 236
politics, 180
pollution, 230
pools, 163
population, 14, 83, 84, 136, 140, 163, 199, 201, 230, 232, 233, 237, 272
portfolio, 133
portfolio investment, 133
Portugal, 67, 76, 79, 208, 238, 282
positive correlation, 78, 179, 187
positive externalities, ix, 45, 47, 50, 51, 65, 73, 78, 81, 159
positive influences, 236
positive relationship, x, 78, 87, 108, 127, 128, 132, 133, 146, 150, 187, 191
potential benefits, 158
poverty, 128, 134, 151, 152, 230, 237
poverty reduction, 152
PRC, 136, 140, 141, 143, 144, 145, 147, 148, 149
preparation, iv
price deflator, 259
price index, 123, 243, 244, 247, 251
primary data, vii, 1, 14
primary products, 166
primary sector, 11
private enterprises, 9, 10
private firms, 160
private investment, 168
private sector, 6, 8, 10, 14, 17, 18, 37, 136, 140, 160, 167
privatization, 39, 167
probability, 59, 60, 61, 62, 84, 139, 187
probability distribution, 84
problem solving, 26
process innovation, 262, 277
procurement, 12, 14, 17, 20, 21, 22, 25, 28, 36, 42, 164

procurement systems, 20
producers, 2, 104, 108, 109, 110, 112, 196, 204
product design, 37, 57, 109
product life cycle, 177
product market, 217, 218
product performance, 24
production costs, 26, 177, 188, 197, 198
production function, 106, 107, 215, 256, 257
production networks, 5, 12, 34, 38, 39
production technology, 265
productivity growth, 50, 53, 55, 68, 77, 80, 110, 231, 238, 276, 277, 278
profit, 7, 10, 11, 13, 26, 28, 29, 30, 33, 217, 218, 224, 225, 243, 244, 246
profit margin, 26, 28, 33
profitability, 8, 177
project, 4, 7, 16, 25, 39, 41, 162, 200, 201
proliferation, vii, 199
property rights, 160, 208
proposition, 12, 249, 250
prosperity, 150, 236
protection, 77, 81, 100, 199, 200, 201
public interest, 175
public policy, 39
public sector, vii, 1
public service, 166
public-private partnerships, 161
pumps, 23
purchasing power, 244
purchasing power parity, 244
P-value, 115, 124, 125

Q

qualifications, 169
qualitative research, viii, 43, 49
quality assurance, 28, 29, 31, 32, 34, 168
quality control, 49, 57, 58, 166
quality improvement, 28, 29, 32, 34
quality of life, 165
quantitative research, 66
Queensland, 101

R

race, 177
radar, 168
ratification, 200
raw materials, 5, 29, 237, 259
real estate, 129
real national income, xi, 241, 244, 245
real terms, 18, 33, 83, 105, 233

recession, 161, 242
recommendations, iv, 29, 197, 208, 262
recovery, 16
recruiting, 168, 270
reform, 6, 7, 8, 40, 41, 152, 170
reforms, 6, 8, 9, 10, 177, 179, 196, 198, 206, 208, 216, 237
regional integration, xi, 157, 195, 196, 197, 198, 199, 200, 201, 202, 204, 206, 207, 208
regional manufacturing, 56
regional spillovers, xii, 56, 265, 266, 267, 268, 270, 271, 273, 278, 279, 281
regression, 46, 56, 59, 60, 68, 79, 80, 81, 109, 110, 114, 117, 132, 137, 139, 146, 180, 185, 186, 188, 189, 207, 267, 270, 272, 278, 281
regression analysis, 46, 68, 272
regression model, 56, 59, 60, 109, 146
regulations, 10, 77, 81, 99
regulatory framework, 201
rehabilitation, 16, 41
rejection, 55
relative size, 106
relevance, 155, 162, 269
reliability, 11, 23, 26, 28, 29, 31, 32, 34, 36, 165, 172, 231
REM, 138, 139, 141, 142, 143, 144, 145, 146, 147, 148, 149, 150
repair, 17, 24
reputation, 25, 231, 265
requirements, vii, 1, 2, 9, 13, 17, 21, 23, 24, 26, 36, 160, 165, 167, 168, 170, 171
research institutions, 165, 167
researchers, 4, 21, 132, 162, 169, 214
reserves, 7
residuals, 138, 139, 146
resources, ix, 9, 10, 11, 16, 22, 24, 30, 32, 34, 35, 36, 59, 60, 73, 109, 151, 155, 161, 200, 237, 262
resource-seeking, 167, 231, 235, 236, 237
response, viii, 2, 3, 9, 11, 12, 26, 27, 28, 35, 43, 45, 52, 64, 176, 247, 250, 272
restrictions, 9, 52, 129, 179, 219, 224, 225
restructuring, 157, 159, 168
retail, 12, 268, 272
retained earnings, 5, 11
returns to scale, 215
revenue, 107, 109, 110, 112, 114, 118
rights, 179, 201
risk, 8, 22, 23, 24, 158, 159, 164, 170, 178, 180, 188, 201, 205, 215, 235, 236
risk profile, 8
risks, 5, 7, 9, 13, 23, 36, 200
Romania, 48, 89
root, 81, 149, 150
roots, 146, 225
rubber, 10, 22
rubber products, 22
rules, 198, 199, 201
rules of origin, 198
rural areas, 187
Russia, 4, 41, 164, 168, 237

S

safety, 13, 30
sample mean, 113, 278, 279
scale economies, 47
scaling, 83
scarcity, 23, 32
school, 30, 198, 202, 204, 206
school enrollment, 202, 204, 206
schooling, 56
science, 161, 164, 168, 169, 173, 174
scope, ix, 9, 44, 46, 48, 50, 51, 55, 61, 62, 64, 76, 77, 156, 167, 168, 175, 222
secondary schools, 187, 237
security, 8, 129, 150, 166, 201
seed, 164
seller, 177
sellers, 48
semiconductors, 104, 167
seminars, 170
sensitivity, 107, 146
service provider, 17, 24, 35
services, xii, 6, 9, 10, 12, 16, 17, 22, 23, 24, 25, 27, 29, 31, 32, 34, 37, 104, 109, 111, 128, 156, 160, 161, 162, 165, 166, 169, 171, 181, 201, 265, 266, 267, 269, 270, 271, 272, 273, 274, 275, 276, 278, 279, 280, 281
SFI, 161
SFT, 193
shape, 39, 55, 84, 89, 132, 270
shareholder value, 26
shortage, 166
showing, 49, 90, 104, 262, 278
Siberia, 11
signals, 109, 112
significance level, 58, 61, 141, 143, 144, 145, 147, 148, 149, 150, 260
signs, 145, 146, 147, 156, 166, 178, 186, 187, 188, 190, 191, 232, 234, 250, 278
silk, 38
simulation, 111, 152
Singapore, x, 11, 76, 79, 127, 130, 140, 170, 208, 242, 249, 252
single market, 74, 128
skeleton, 107

skill acquisition, 78
skilled workers, 78, 166, 169, 231, 236
Slovakia, 89, 156
small firms, 8, 112
smoothing, 85
social conflicts, 236
social network, 18
social responsibility, 36
social welfare, xi, 213, 215, 216, 218, 219, 220, 221, 226
society, 4, 222
software, 9, 10, 157, 166, 172
South Africa, vii, 1, 2, 4, 6, 11, 13, 14, 15, 16, 17, 20, 21, 22, 28, 30, 32, 35, 36, 37, 39, 41, 170, 210
South Korea, 109
sovereignty, 86
Soviet Union, 181, 232
Spain, 50, 73, 76, 78, 79, 81, 84, 99, 155, 169, 208
specialization, 60, 163, 200
specific knowledge, 277
specifications, 25, 57, 58, 59, 186, 191, 257, 261
spillover effects, ix, xii, 49, 65, 69, 73, 100, 207, 255, 256, 257, 258, 261, 262, 265, 266, 267, 268, 269, 270, 280
spillovers, vii, viii, ix, xii, 43, 44, 45, 46, 47, 48, 49, 50, 51, 52, 53, 54, 55, 56, 57, 59, 60, 63, 64, 65, 66, 67, 68, 69, 70, 71, 76, 77, 78, 81, 99, 107, 120, 134, 158, 159, 165, 166, 170, 173, 231, 255, 256, 257, 258, 259, 261, 262, 265, 266, 267, 268, 269, 270, 271, 273, 275, 276, 277, 278, 279, 280, 281, 283, 284
SSA, 18
stability, 77, 150, 165, 168, 189, 191, 208, 236
stabilization, 71
staff members, 252
standard error, 111, 138, 139, 260, 261, 279
state, vii, 1, 4, 5, 6, 8, 9, 10, 11, 13, 16, 17, 36, 40, 56, 57, 65, 75, 76, 77, 79, 86, 87, 88, 132, 160, 167, 178, 179, 215, 219, 237, 261
state-owned banks, 5
state-owned enterprises, 16, 40, 167, 179, 237
states, 54, 55, 56, 76, 78, 80, 81, 87, 99, 107, 215, 231, 269
statistics, xi, 101, 105, 116, 140, 185, 204, 205, 206, 229
steel, 9, 22, 33, 237
stock, 4, 6, 7, 8, 10, 15, 16, 28, 53, 83, 108, 132, 133, 171, 178, 201, 215, 229, 231, 251, 260, 266
stock exchange, 8, 10
stockholders, 104
stress, 89, 161
structural adjustment, 4
structural adjustment programmes, 4

structural changes, 105, 167
structural funds, 133
structure, vii, xi, 19, 107, 122, 168, 196, 213, 214, 215, 216, 217, 218, 219, 220, 221, 222, 226, 267, 272
subgame, 218
sub-Saharan Africa, 39, 40
subsidy, 194
substitution, x, 9, 34, 103, 107
succession, 167
Sudan, 6, 10
Sun, 11, 41, 134, 151, 178, 193, 235, 256, 259, 262, 264
supervision, 16
suppliers, vii, viii, ix, x, 1, 2, 12, 13, 14, 17, 20, 21, 22, 23, 24, 25, 26, 27, 28, 29, 30, 31, 32, 33, 34, 35, 36, 38, 43, 44, 45, 46, 48, 49, 51, 54, 55, 56, 57, 58, 59, 61, 62, 63, 64, 65, 66, 67, 68, 69, 70, 103, 104, 119, 158, 165, 166, 167, 171, 178, 231
supply chain, 5, 16, 17, 20, 21, 22, 23, 24, 25, 26, 27, 28, 29, 30, 31, 33, 35, 36, 68, 156
support services, 162, 171
sustainability, 4
sustainable development, 151, 239
Sweden, 76, 79, 84, 89, 100, 120, 208, 269, 284
Switzerland, xii, 15, 20, 41, 265, 266, 271, 272, 273, 274, 275, 281, 282, 285
synthesis, 252

T

Taiwan, x, 76, 79, 100, 103, 104, 105, 106, 107, 108, 109, 111, 112, 114, 115, 117, 118, 119, 120, 121, 122, 123, 125, 166, 232, 236
takeover, 261
talent, 160, 169
target, 108, 242, 246
tariff, 136, 140, 170, 197, 198, 199, 201, 208
tariff rates, 136, 140
tax credits, 170
tax deduction, 162
tax incentive, 7, 119
tax rates, 242, 249
taxation, 208, 215, 252
taxes, 8, 242
technical assistance, 157
technical efficiency, 68
technical support, 167
techniques, 5, 17, 31, 59, 76, 78, 79, 132, 150, 199, 204, 207, 269
technological capacities, xii, 265, 266, 267, 270, 271, 278, 279, 281
technological change, 101, 107

technological progress, 159
technologies, viii, xii, 9, 12, 44, 45, 47, 48, 49, 50, 51, 55, 58, 61, 62, 64, 65, 66, 78, 86, 104, 106, 107, 109, 110, 118, 161, 207, 265, 266, 272
technology, viii, ix, x, xii, 8, 32, 34, 37, 44, 45, 46, 47, 48, 49, 50, 54, 55, 56, 57, 58, 59, 60, 61, 62, 63, 64, 65, 66, 67, 68, 69, 70, 73, 75, 76, 78, 79, 83, 90, 103, 110, 118, 134, 156, 157, 158, 160, 161, 164, 165, 166, 168, 169, 170, 171, 172, 173, 196, 200, 203, 207, 215, 237, 255, 256, 258, 259, 262, 265, 266, 270, 271, 276, 278, 279, 280, 281
technology flows, 47
technology gap, viii, ix, 44, 45, 46, 49, 50, 54, 55, 56, 57, 59, 60, 61, 62, 63, 64, 65, 66, 70, 256, 270, 279
technology transfer, viii, ix, x, 44, 46, 49, 57, 58, 59, 61, 63, 64, 65, 66, 67, 68, 70, 78, 103, 110, 170, 171, 173, 256, 265, 280
telecommunications, 9, 104, 157
tensions, 86
territory, 207
tertiary education, 88
test statistic, 142, 144
testing, 139, 152, 165, 167, 186, 187, 205, 260, 266, 268
textiles, 166
Thailand, x, 76, 79, 127, 130, 140, 164, 208
theft, 170
threshold level, 157, 159, 165, 168
time periods, 53, 137, 140, 230, 233, 235
time series, 53, 100, 101, 111, 132
total factor productivity, 76, 256
tourism, 17, 237, 266
trade, vii, x, xi, 2, 9, 10, 28, 38, 39, 52, 53, 70, 71, 76, 77, 79, 86, 90, 104, 109, 110, 119, 127, 128, 129, 130, 132, 133, 134, 135, 136, 138, 140, 142, 143, 145, 146, 150, 158, 174, 178, 195, 196, 197, 198, 199, 200, 201, 202, 203, 206, 207, 208, 209, 215, 232, 241, 242, 246, 247, 251, 266, 272, 273, 274, 275
trade agreement, 52
trade costs, 133
trade creation, 196
trade deficit, 104, 109
trade diversion, 196
trade liberalization, 70, 71, 133, 134, 199, 208
trade policy, 77, 119, 199
trade-off, 28, 158
training, 12, 17, 28, 29, 31, 32, 34, 49, 57, 76, 119, 159, 161, 162, 166, 262, 266, 267, 269, 270, 276, 277, 278, 281
training programs, 49, 57
trajectory, 2, 13, 31, 32, 33, 34, 35, 267

transaction costs, 21, 177, 231
transactions, 11, 12, 18, 29, 60, 61, 201
transformations, 40, 167
transmission, 60, 158, 267
transparency, 4, 8, 26
transport, 10, 17, 28, 31, 34, 35, 133, 196, 198, 203, 215, 232, 244, 266, 272
transport costs, 28, 133, 196, 198, 203
transportation, 3, 10, 150, 232, 235, 237
transportation infrastructure, 235
treaties, 200
treatment, 8, 170, 222
Turkey, 208
turnover, 47, 48, 111

U

UNDP, 6, 41
UNESCO, 209
unions, 196, 214, 215, 218, 219, 220, 221, 222, 226, 228
unit cost, xi, 213, 214, 215, 218, 220
United Kingdom (UK), 11, 15, 38, 39, 40, 41, 48, 49, 50, 51, 52, 68, 70, 71, 76, 78, 79, 81, 84, 89, 98, 100, 104, 122, 152, 169, 208, 210, 211, 213, 214, 229, 246, 256, 263, 268, 269, 270, 283, 284
United Nations, 41, 71, 101, 174, 176, 194, 264
United States (USA), 39, 67, 69, 74, 104, 120, 193, 208, 230, 231, 238, 282, 285
universities, 159, 160, 161, 162, 165, 168, 169, 170, 237
urban, 68, 71, 77, 80
Uruguay, 208

V

Valencia, 282, 283
variables, xi, 7, 56, 60, 62, 76, 83, 87, 88, 90, 107, 110, 111, 112, 114, 115, 116, 124, 125, 130, 131, 133, 136, 137, 139, 140, 141, 142, 146, 178, 185, 186, 187, 188, 189, 190, 191, 195, 196, 199, 200, 202, 204, 205, 206, 207, 208, 209, 224, 232, 233, 234, 235, 242, 245, 247, 259, 260, 261, 272, 274, 275, 276, 278, 279, 280
vector, 88, 107, 137, 138
vehicles, 259, 272
vein, 77, 89, 198
Venezuela, 67, 208, 256, 263, 281
venue, 191
Vietnam, x, 127, 130, 131, 140
voting, 8

W

wage bargaining, xi, 213, 214, 216, 217, 218, 219, 220, 221, 222, 223, 224, 226, 227
wage level, 56, 179, 235
wage rate, 244
wages, 20, 53, 88, 89, 90, 105, 178, 179, 187, 199, 214, 215, 217, 218, 220, 222, 235, 246, 256
Wales, 93, 98
Washington, 38, 39, 40, 41, 69, 70, 174, 177, 193
waste, 200
waterways, 233, 237
welfare, xi, 213, 215, 216, 218, 219, 220, 221, 226, 241, 242, 243, 246, 247, 248, 249, 250, 253
Western countries, 20
Western Europe, 163
wholesale, 123, 259, 266, 272
wholesale price index, 123, 259
work ethic, 215
workers, 26, 27, 31, 34, 47, 110, 113, 118, 173, 216, 217, 219, 233, 259
workforce, 32, 33, 161, 207
working conditions, 161
World Bank, x, xi, 4, 17, 38, 39, 40, 41, 68, 69, 127, 128, 130, 131, 140, 153, 164, 171, 172, 173, 174, 175, 180, 184, 185, 186, 189, 190, 191, 210, 263
World Trade Organization (WTO), 171, 179, 181, 193

Y

Yale University, 227, 283